ON THE WORD OF COMMAND

A Pictorial History of the
**REGIMENTAL
SERGEANT MAJOR**

ON THE WORD OF COMMAND

A Pictorial History of the
REGIMENTAL
SERGEANT MAJOR

Richard Alford

Foreword by

GENERAL
SIR GEOFFREY HOWLETT KBE MC

SPELLMOUNT LTD
Tunbridge Wells, Kent

In the Spellmount Nutshell Military list:

The Territorial Battalions – A pictorial history
The Yeomanry Regiments – A pictorial history
Over the Rhine – The Last Days of War in Europe
History of the Cambridge University OTC
Yeoman Service
The Fighting Troops of the Austro-Hungarian Army
Intelligence Officer in the Peninsula
The Scottish Regiments – A pictorial history
The Royal Marines – A pictorial history
The Royal Tank Regiment – A pictorial history
The Irish Regiments – A pictorial history
British Sieges of the Peninsular War
Victoria's Victories
Heaven and Hell – German paratroop war diary
Rorke's Drift
Came the Dawn – Fifty years an Army Officer
Marlborough – as Military Commander
A Medal for Life – Capt Leefe Robinson VC
The Fall of France
Scandinavian Misadventure
Kitchener's Army – A pictorial history

In the Military Machine list:

Napoleon's Military Machine
Falklands' Military Machine
Wellington's Military Machine

In the Nautical list:

Sea of Memories
Evolution of Engineering in the Royal Navy Vol I 1827-1939
In Perilous Seas

In the Aviation list:

Diary of a Bomb Aimer
Operation 'Bograt' – from France to Burma

Half title page:
RSM J. C. Lord, MBE at The Parachute Regiment ITC Aldershot 1946/7 giving his famous 'Eyes — Front'.
Frontispiece:
RSM P. A. Lewis, MBE, RSM of the 1st Bn, Grenadier Guards, 1967-69.   Major P. A. Lewis

Dedication

Dedicated to the memory of John Maskell, a very young barefooted boy who followed a battalion of Coldstream Guardsmen on a route march in the early 1890s, was helped by the Sergeant Major into a Gordon Boys Home, and a few years later became a smart Drummer Boy in the 1st Battalion, Coldstream Guards . . .

The circumstances of many contributors to this book will have changed during the course of research and publication, and apologies are extended for any out of date information given in relation to rank and appointment.

First published in the UK in 1990 by
Spellmount Ltd, Publishers
12 Dene Way, Speldhurst
Tunbridge Wells, Kent TN3 0NX
ISBN 0-946771-65-0

© Richard Alford 1990

British Library Cataloguing in Publication Data
Alford, Richard
  On the word of command: pictorial history of RSM
  1. Great Britain. Army regiments. Sergeant majors, history
  I. Title II. Series
  355.3'32'0941

ISBN 0-946771-65-0

Design by Words & Images, Speldhurst, Kent
Typesetting by Vitaset, Paddock Wood, Kent
Printed and bound in Great Britain by
Biddles Ltd, Guildford and King's Lynn

Contents

Foreword

**By General
Sir Geoffrey Howlett
KBE, MC
Colonel Commandant,
The Parachute Regiment,
and former
Commander-in-Chief,
Allied Forces Northern
Europe**

What an immense privilege it is for me to be associated, even briefly, with this story, and it is extraordinary that no one before has tried to put together the incredibly influential part that the Regimental Sergeant Major has played in Army and Royal Marine life.

As the senior Warrant Officer or Non Commissioned rank in a Regiment, Battalion, School or Depot, the RSM is the key link between the Commanding Officer and his officers, and the men or soldiers of that unit. If he is good the unit will nearly always prosper, and if he is bad everyone will suffer.

The RSM has achieved his position by experience and has risen from the lowest rank to reach this pinnacle (for this is what it is) by hard work, example and personality. I would suggest that no commissioned rank holds such authority nor is held in such awe. Why are the RSMs, fellow Warrant Officers and Sergeants, held in such affectionate esteem by the Commissioned Officers of the British Army, than are those of the Continental armies or United States Army? I believe that it stems from the fact that Warrant Officers and Sergeants play such a prominent part in the early training of Officer Cadets, teaching and influencing them in a way largely unknown in other armies, though the Commonwealth Countries have wisely followed our example.

The pages of this book contain not only the stories of RSMs, but of history. The men written about were, from the very earliest days, characters whose courage, kindness and loyalty up and down the ranks – comes bounding through. Of course the barrack square plays a large part and so it should, but so too does battle, from Waterloo and just before, through to the Falklands, and including the two World Wars. Inevitably there are gaps for RSMs are not normally known, as are Generals, for writing their memoirs!

The influence of RSMs upon my own service was strong, not only in my own regiment where their help to me as a young officer, Adjutant, Company Commander, and Commanding Officer was vital, but also as an instructor at Eaton Hall and Mons Officer Cadet Schools, and as an Officer Cadet and Commandant of the Royal Military Academy, Sandhurst.

I believe as did so many of my generation in the Army, that the example of RSM (later Academy Sergeant Major) John Lord was to affect me more than any other soldier in my life. As a Brigadier I was one of many openly weeping at his Memorial Service at Sandhurst in February 1968.

Behind the parade ground stiffness and formality, the courage and military skill on the battlefield, there is always a kindly side, and humour too. I remember an occasion in 1958 at Mons Officer Cadet School when Desmond Lynch was RSM (later Capt Desmond Lynch MBE DCM). The dress rehearsal for a Passing Out Parade was going on accompanied by a band from the Parachute Regiment. As the young Parachute Regiment Captain at Mons I thought that I should drop in to see all was well – and it wasn't. The band was in the RSM's view obviously useless and appeared to keep coming in at the wrong time.

Finally it was more than the RSM could take, and after another 'mistake' Desmond Lynch in his famous Irish brogue shouted 'As you were . . . we will now go on again if this 'ere skiffle group will let us'. This was too much for the equally Irish bandmaster even from an RSM of Desmond Lynch's standing. He marched his band off the square and back towards their barracks in Aldershot. Here I thought Howlett, is where you earn your pay – for otherwise there would be no Passing Out Parade later in the week. I ran after the band, extracted the bandmaster and asked him to join me. By now RSM Lynch was dismissing the Parade. I rather nervously approached the RSM and as it was almost lunch time asked if he would invite the bandmaster and I to the Warrant Officers and Sergeants Mess. It was a difficult first half hour but Irish good sense and a liberal supply of a very dark brown liquid eventually won. I left them after two hours still hard at it, and the parade went splendidly a day or two later.

I believe that this work has lessons in it for all, be they young or old, particularly for those who have taken, or are about to take the Queen's Shilling. I know too that if ever I was asked on that Radio Programme *Desert Island Discs* who I would like as a companion (for the sake of tact wives excluded) I would choose a particular old RSM from the Parachute Regiment. I won't say who he is – but I'd never be bored.

PART ONE

On Campaign through the Ranks with the RSM

*Only time separates us from the following events, for soldiering changes but little –
and the field of battle cannot change . . .
Come soldiering – on campaign through the ranks, with the Regimental Sergeant Major.*

Third assault of Badajos. The 88th Regiment pouring into the Castle during the Peninsular War.

CHAPTER 1

The rank of Sergeant Major before 1800

The Regimental Sergeant Major commands such charisma and mystique, that it is surprising to find the rank dating back for only a relatively short time in the British Army. There is little written material available about the rank, and those in appointment tend to pass their knowledge from one to another, rarely if ever recording their experience of campaign or ceremonial service.

A notable booklet entitled *The Sergeant Major – the origin and history of his rank*, was produced not by a Sergeant Major, but by Lt Francis J. Davies, of the Grenadier Guards. He researched and wrote in 1886 a splendid authority on the subject, and the following pages have been based largely upon his studies. In the very early days of our army, the commander of the infantry was named the Captain-General of the Footmen, and within his command was a Serjeant Major who was later referred to as the Serjeant Major General. He was clearly a high ranking officer as evidenced by the pay documents of the time, and the importance of his duties, which are described in the *Order of a Campe or Army Royal* in 1518.

The office of Serjeant-Major in the fields and campe with the duties thereunto belonging: Ffirst, the Serjeant-Major of the campe is to receive at the handes of the High Marshall the whole numbers of footmen that be in the Army; and beinge so received he must divide the weapons severallye that he may knowe what number he hathe of everye kind of weapon, and so to set the order of the battaills accordinglie.

Furthermore, it is the duty of the said Serjeant-Major, that yf the enemie drawe so near unto yower army, that the battle is appointed, then it is most mete and convenient that the said Serjeant-Major repaire to the High Marshall to attend him when he goeth to viewe the field, where he intendeth the battle to be pitched, he is to take viewe of the ground and then return, and make report to the Lord Leyvetenent-General howe he hath surveyed the ground, and the most advantage thereof, and make declaration what order he thinketh is most mete and convenient to set the battaille in.

Having taken the orders of the said Leyvetenent-General, he is to repaire to the field and set in order the battaile to the most advantage according to the ground.

He is also to se that the King's standard be placed in the middest of the mayne battaille.

Item, the said Serjeant-Major must also se that the shotte be placed within the wings of every battaille, for the impalement and garde of the aforesaid battailles. He is also to appoint a forlorn hope in his order before the front of the battaille. It is also the office of the said Serjeant-Major to serve with his owne person in the forefront of the battail, and to lead the battail.

70 years later the *Rates for the Entertainment of the Officers of the Companies appointed for Service in the year 1588* reveal that the Serjeant-Major was the third ranking officer, following the Colonel-General of the Footmen and the Lieutenant of the Army.

The records of pay of the army in Ireland under the Earl of Essex, signed by Queen Elizabeth on 24 March 1598, place the Serjeant-Major fifth in order of command, to the Lord Lieutenant-General, the Lieutenant of the Army, the General of the Horse and the Marshall of the Camp. Many modern sounding commissioned ranks follow, such as Colonels, Captains of both Horse and Foot, Lieutenants, Cornets of Horse, and Ensigns of Foot. The highest non-commissioned officer at that time was the Serjeant.

By 1598, a regimental officer bearing the rank of Serjeant-Major was introduced, following the Lieutenant-Colonel in rank, and seeming to perform many of the duties of the modern Adjutant. The pay documents suggest that the original rank also continued, and so it would seem that two commissioned officers bore the same title for a time, although at very different levels of command.

In 1639 *A list of the Several Entertainments of the Officers General of the Field, Lord General's Train, Officers of Foot etc* sets out the ranks, and under the heading *Officers General of the Field* includes, The Lord General, The Lieutenant General, and the Serjeant Major General. In the *Lord General's Train* is also listed amongst others, Colonels of the four regiments of foot, four Lieutenant Colonels, and four Serjeant Majors.

Warde's *Animadversions on Warre* 1639, describes very fully the duties of the latter regimental officer, as indicated by the following short extracts:

. . . his place and office doth somewhat correspond with that of the Serjeant Major General's, onely his duty is tending to officiate between the Colonel and the officers of the regiment; hee is to be learned of all the liberal sciences, hee ought to have both speculative and prackticke knowledge in all things belonging to his profession; hee must be very civil, wise and discreet in his carriage and actions, in rearde he is to manage a world of affaires of high consequence, which may serve to the conserving or ruining of the Army.

. . . hee is not onely to be a good scholler, and witty, but he must be of quick apprehension, and be furnished with an able memory, hee must have a paper book, pen and incke, to set down all the orders and commands, that he may not erre or vary one tittle from what is delivered unto him in charge . . .

. . . hee ought to have able officers to his own company, because hee cannot tend unto them, his duties are so great; hee ought to have a swift nagge to carry him about the quarters, and to visit his guards, for his duties lie confudedly in the Army . . .

This Serjeant-Major, who subsequently became the Major – seems to have had everything to do and little wonder that he required the help of able officers with which to run the affairs of his own company. For example, the lengthy measures necessary to safeguard the security of each night's password were alone very detailed and time consuming.

The rank is further mentioned in the *Army Lists of the Roundheads and Cavaliers 1642* edited by William Peacock FSA, when every regiment includes a Serjeant Major, ranking between Lieutenant Colonel and Senior Captain. In 1685 an extract from Grose provides final confirmation of the ranks:

In the time of James II the Serjeant-Major General – sometimes called the Serjeant-Major of the Camp – was what is now called the Major General, as Serjeant-Major of a regiment formerly signified the officer now called Major.

In the documentation of following years the term 'Serjeant' was gradually dropped from ranks, one result being the illogical precedence of the modern Lieutenant General and the Major General. Eventually there were no commissioned officers in the British Army bearing the rank of Serjeant-Major.

In 1724 comes the important introduction of a *non* commissioned Sergeant Major, and one of the first references is contained in an order dated January 18 1724, issued to the Brigade of Guards:

The three Regiments of Foot Guards are to furnish a detachment of 100 men as often as due notice is given, under command of a Lieutenant Colonel, a Captain, an Ensign, an Adjutant, and a Sergeant Major, as Guards for the balls and operas at the King's Theatre in the Haymarket, and to be aiding and assisting in the preservation of the peace, and preventing all manner of profanity, rudeness, drunkenness, or indecencies, and not to permit any person whatever to enter the said theatre in habits worn by the clergy.

Obviously by the size of the detachment a necessary duty, but one at least which the Major did not have to perform. A direct requirement of the Sergeant Major was also contained in a similar order of 15 February 1725:

A detachment of 100 men from the three Regiments of Guards to attend at the King's Theatre Haymarket, as often as a ballet is held there, and upon all such occasions to direct the Sergeant Major to oblige the musicians and butlers to retire in good time.

The documentation of the next 25 years does not reveal any more positive development of the role of Sergeant Major, indeed, he is missing altogether from such sources as *Exercise of Horse, Foot and Dragoons* of 1728, the official drill book of 1739, and Bland's *Military Discipline* of 1743 – except for a brief mention in the latter work, that the men would probably not parade so carefully before the Sergeant Major as they would before the Adjutant – things were to change. At last in *A Military Course* by Thomas Simes in 1777, there appears the following important passage:

Of the choice and duty of the Sergeant Major. He should be a man of real merit, a complete Sergeant and a good scholar, sensible and agreeable in conversation, in order to attract the eye of the non commissioned officers; he should be a person who has discovered an early genius of discipline, and that had been taken notice of, for neglecting every other study but that; he must be ready at his pen, and expert in making out details and rosters etc.

With the emphasis now on discipline and a knowledge of the standing orders, the rank was already taking form, and a small role on parade was added in a further passage from the same work, on the method of forming the battalion:

The Adjutant and Sergeant Major are then to spring from the right and left of the battalion, dressing most exactly every rank, and seeing that the officers and non commissioned officers are always in a line.

Furthermore in some of the plates illustrating battalion drill, a location was given for the first time to the Sergeant Major. He was now classed as a Staff Sergeant, but there was no distinctive badge for many years, until he was said to wear epaulettes – or a single silver epaulette.

The rank of Sergeant Major, almost as we would recognise it, became established in the British Army from 1797, and in 1800 Grose was to write: 'As the Adjutant is an assistant to the Major, so in like manner he is assisted by the Chief Sergeant, stiled Sergeant Major.'

The rank therefore originated in the high command of the (Serjeant) Major General, where the whole panoply of war awaited his placing of the King's Standard in the centre of the army before battle was joined. Then entering also at regimental level, where the (Serjeant) Major fulfilled his many responsibilities – sufficiently urgent in nature – to ensure the 'conserving or ruining of the Army'. Finally to find identity as the Sergeant Major – the Senior Sergeant, at a crucial point of the regiment, where word of command translates into trained and disciplined action.

The men who were promoted to the new rank had served a full apprenticeship in the army, and brought with them a lifetime of regimental campaign experience. They knew the structure of their regiment and how to gain the best in appearance and performance from the men. Above all they knew the regulations of the time, how to abide by them, and how to gain the compliance of the NCOs and men.

Soldiering had always reflected the attitudes of society, and the formative years of the rank belonged to a hard and spartan society. Life was harsh and disciplined for the civilian population, and for the soldier in the ranks it was particularly so.

From this short general history, the following chapters trace the development of the rank in detail through the stories of individual Sergeant Majors.

CHAPTER 2

Sergeant Major M. MacIntosh, 79th Regiment, Cameron Highlanders

The battle of Toulouse on Easter Sunday 10 April 1814, was the first action fought by Masterton MacIntosh as Sergeant Major of the 79th Regiment, Cameron Highlanders. Promoted from Colour Sergeant on January 6 that year, he had taken the place of James Robertson who had been commissioned as Ensign.

The strength of the regiment was below 500 men even before the battle, but the Cameron Highlanders performed magnificently as part of Pack's Brigade of the Sixth Division, earning with three other regiments, the commendation of Lord Wellington for their bravery and conduct. At the end of the day the strength of the regiment was reduced to 264 men. Wellington's army decisively won the battle and the abdication of Napoleon on the following day ended almost 11 years of conflict with France. The Peninsular Campaign lasted for six long years, during which the army had endured terrible hardships, but the last year had been one of almost continuous success and at last victory had been gained.

Masterton MacIntosh had enlisted into the service of King George III in 1794, and apart from a brief period of peace in 1802, had fought the French throughout that time. He then experienced peace-time soldiering for the first time in 12 years, and as Sergeant Major, would, under the command of Lt-Col Neil Douglas, feature strongly in the rebuilding and training of the regiment from its present weak state. With his tenth battle behind him, he might well have fought his last battle.

It had been 20 years since Masterton MacIntosh studied the recruiting notices so prominently displayed in Scotland following the declaration of war by France. Britain had allowed her army to decline badly during the brief period of peace, and so had been obliged to raise many new regiments to meet the fifth period of war with France within a century. At the time invasion appeared imminent, and the notices stated that six fencible regiments were to be raised in Scotland. As a stocky confident Highlander of 20 years, with fresh complexion, brown hair and black eyes, Masterton MacIntosh had decided to enlist in the Loyal Inverness Fencible Regiment.

With rebellion threatening in Ireland, the Scottish fencible regiments were soon required to replace line regiments on garrison duty there, in order to free them for war service. The Loyal Inverness Fencibles were posted initially to Kilkenny, then later to Dublin. Enlisting as a private soldier, Masterton MacIntosh soon revealed soldierly qualities, and before the end of two years' service was promoted to Sergeant.

In June 1800, when the regiment was stationed at Baltinglass, notices had been posted within the fencible regiments, inviting men to volunteer for permanent service in one of five line regiments requiring recruits – the 21st, 71st, 72nd, 79th and 92nd Regiments of Foot. A bounty of ten guineas had been offered, and the Loyal Inverness Fencibles made it known that they would allow 150 men to volunteer. Sgt MacIntosh had given his name for the 79th Cameron Highlanders, knowing that by so doing he would revert to the rank of private soldier. The volunteers from the various fencible regiments for the 79th Regiment assembled at Fermoy, where on 8 July 1800 they signed and were accepted into regular service.

Malta was retaken from the French in September 1800, and it was whilst Sir Ralph Abercromby's expeditionary force to Egypt called there, that the 79th Regt had received the large draft of 279 volunteers from the fencible regiments.

The CO, Lt-Col Alan Cameron, founder of the regiment, must have been well pleased when he viewed the draft, for they were obviously good quality recruits. All were trained men and some had additional experience as NCOs, so they could soon be expected to attain the standard of the 79th Regt given the attention of Sgt-Maj Muir and his NCOs.

The draft received training in field and musketry drills, particularly with the firing of the smooth bored muzzle loading musket, with its methodical procedure. The drill for priming and loading had shortened over the years, but still required precise movements to ensure that the weapon would discharge with full force. In the hands of good infantry the 'Brown Bess' could be primed, loaded, and discharged four times per minute, a sufficient rate of fire to drive off ordinary infantry. The need for long and hard drills had been appreciated when volleys were fired, for clouds of dense smoke obscured everything and only well drilled movements could be maintained.

Before the expeditionary force was ready to depart from Malta, the 79th Regt paraded before its commanding officer in full strength and readiness, with red coated Highlanders standing immaculately in the kilts of 79th tartan, hackled feathered bonnets, and white buff leather crossbelts, with shoulder belt plates proudly bearing the number 79 and the words Cameronian Volunteers.

In February 1801, the expeditionary force made successful landings at Aboukir Bay in Egypt, on beaches contested by the French, and Masterton MacIntosh – who had two months earlier been promoted Corporal – received his baptism of fire in actions prior to and during the battle of Alexandria. With the French garrisons in Cairo and Alexandria capitulating, Cpl MacIntosh had completed his first operational campaign, and after only seven months was promoted to Sergeant, a rank which he was to hold with distinction for many years. A brief period of peace with France followed, during which Sgt MacIntosh spent considerable time recruiting men for the regiment at Stirling.

At this time the chevron badge of rank was adopted throughout the British Army, a Corporal wearing two white lace chevrons upon his right arm, a Sergeant three chevrons, and a Sergeant Major four chevrons of silver lace edged with blue cloth.

The precarious peace came to an end in May 1803, when Britain declared war upon France following Napoleon's continued conquests. Soon the threat of invasion upon this country loomed large again. The home army had been enlarged and a Second Battalion of the Cameron Highlanders formed, but only at that time to train and provide replacements for the 79th Regiment.

The British Navy prevented Napoleon from mounting an invasion across the Channel, but when Spain entered the conflict in support of France, their combined fleets greatly increased the danger. Lord Nelson ended the threat at Trafalgar, when he finally caught the enemy out of harbour, but at the sad cost of his life.

Sgt MacIntosh rejoined the regiment from Stirling soon after the outbreak of war, and went with the unit to perform garrison duties in Ireland for almost three years. On 9 January 1806 however, in company with many other regiments which had fought in Egypt, the 79th were selected to form part of the huge cortege on Horse Guards Parade in London, for the state funeral of Lord Nelson. As the nation mourned, the victory that had saved Britain from invasion seemed to have been gained at too tragic a cost.

Masterton MacIntosh served for 13 years in the rank of Sergeant, taking part in the expedition to Copenhagen to intern the ships of the Danish fleet, in order to prevent their use by Napoleon to mount a fresh invasion threat. The 79th Regt was then included in the abortive expedition to Sweden, and without disembarking from the transports, was transferred to a force leaving England for service in Portugal. This resulted in a period at sea of over 50 days.

Spain, no longer an ally of France, had by now been invaded by Napoleon's forces, and a British army commanded by Sir John Moore, was sent to support the Spanish armies in their resistance against the French. The 79th Regt joined this force in August 1808. The CO Lt-Col

General Sir John Moore is carried from the field before Corunna during the evacuating of the British army during the Peninsular War early 1809.

Badajos – the third assault. Wellington stands in the S. Trinidad breach.

Alan Cameron, had received promotion as Brigadier General, and was succeeded by his eldest son Lt-Col Philips Cameron, who at the age of 26 had already held the command of the Second Battalion for four years.

In the army of Sir John Moore, Sgt MacIntosh had taken part in the terrible 200 miles retreat to Corunna, during which the bearing and discipline of the regiment had held firm in the hands of Lt-Col Philips Cameron, his officers, Sgt-Maj John Sinclair and his NCOs. When the returning transports docked at ports along the south coast of England, the condition of the troops appalled and shocked the populace. The ragged soldiers even on disembarking looked as if they had come straight from the battlefield. The 79th landed at Portsmouth and marched to Weeley Barracks, where typhus fever struck down almost every man.

By July 1809, the Corunna regiments had recovered sufficiently to take part in a further disastrous expedition which crossed the Scheldt to attack dockyards and shipping in order to avert the fresh threat of an invasion. Within

months the regiments returned home, leaving a force to garrison Walcheren, defeated more by fever than the actions of the enemy. The 79th had lost only one officer from disease, but was hit by fever after returning home and lost several men.

Sir Arthur Wellesley returned to Portugal with a small army in early 1809, and capturing Oporto, went on to fight a successful battle at Talavera. In recognition of this he was made a peer with the title of Lord Wellington. The 79th was one of the first regiments to recover from the effects of the Walcheren expedition, and was sent to reinforce the army in Portugal. On arrival at Lisbon, the regiment had been transported on to Cadiz where in February 1810 it landed to support the besieged garrison. Here the Cameron Highlanders had been delighted to find themselves posted to a brigade which was commanded by their former founder and commanding officer, Maj-Gen Alan Cameron.

In August, the regiment left the well defended isthmus to join Wellington's 1st Division, and Sgt MacIntosh took part in the battle of Busaco, and in the following withdrawal to the lines of Torres Vedras. This magnificent line of fortifications had been prepared in secret by Wellington, and brought the long French advance to an abrupt halt. It had then been the French army's turn to withdraw or starve, and during the following months Wellington's army slowly pursued the retreating French. At Salamanca, stores and reinforcements were awaiting Messina's forces, and again the advantage passed to the French.

In early May 1811, the 79th featured prominently in the defence of Fuentes de Onoro against the strengthened and again advancing French, when Lt-Col Philips Cameron was placed in command of several regiments defending the village. In a desperate two day battle the Highlanders and Irish Infantrymen had stood off a huge French attacking force, which included the Imperial Guard. The village changed hands throughout the fiercely fought battle, but eventually the British regiments charged in anger after learning that Lt-Col Cameron had been shot and severely wounded, and the French were finally driven out of the village. Sadly Philips Cameron died a few days later, and Wellington and his staff joined the distressed Cameron Highlanders when their commanding officer was buried with full military honours.

Sgt MacIntosh had experienced the vicious close quarter bayonet fighting in the streets of the village, and suffered a serious wound to his right leg. Later as the wounded recovered in winter cantonments, an attack of fever and dysentery swept through the 79th Regt, bringing down almost all of the men. Lt-Col Robert Fulton took command of the regiment, and although in April and July 1812, Wellington's army had successfully fought the battles of Badojoz and Salamanca, the 79th was not heavily involved. A triumphant entry had then been made into Madrid by Wellington's forces.

September 1812 found the army assembled before the castle of Burgos, and this proved to be a most costly endeavour. The Light Companies of several regiments, including the 79th, had been formed into a Light Regiment, commanded by Maj The Hon Charles Cocks, and as part of an extensive assault plan, had mounted an attack upon a horn-work, a strong section of an outer defence system of the castle. Sgt MacIntosh volunteered to join the storming party commanded by Maj Cocks which began the assault on September 19. Intense musketry fire from loopholes in palisading met the advance of the storming party and immediate casualties were caused. The foremost men were hoisted bodily over the palisades, a Sgt MacKenzie being lifted by Sgt MacIntosh, who had then followed with Maj Cocks and other members of the party close behind. Very bitter close quarter fighting ensued within the horn-work, before it had become clear that the general assault plan had failed, and the storming party had been withdrawn. Many members of the party had been killed or wounded, and Sgt MacIntosh received his second wound in action, a severe injury to his left knee. He and another Sergeant of the Light Company had been brought to the notice of Lord Wellington for their gallantry, and were recommended for commissions. In the Light Regiment Orders for 20 September had appeared:

Maj Cocks cannot pass over the events of yesterday and last night without returning his most hearty thanks to the officers, non-commissioned officers, and privates of Col Stirling's brigade.

To praise valour which was so conspicuous is as unnecessary as to distinguish merit which was so universally displayed – is impossible; but Maj Cocks must say, it never was his lot to see, much less his good fortune to command, troops who displayed more zeal, more discipline, or more steady intrepidity.

Maj Charles Cocks was greatly respected and was destined for high command. He had been about to take the place of Lt-Col Robert Fulton, who was retiring from the army, as CO of the 79th Regiment, when during the continued assault upon Burgos, he was killed in action. His loss was strongly felt and he received a burial with full military honours, with the attendance of Lord Wellington and his Staff, in recognition of his distinguished service.

The siege of Burgos continued in constant rain and without siege artillery until late October, when Wellington

Major The Hon Charles Somers-Cocks (in the uniform of the 16th Light Dragoons). Killed at the assault upon Burgos.

abandoned the attempt and withdrew his army back into Portugal. In the retreat both Madrid and Salamanca had been given up, and it was a weary and dispirited force that entered winter quarters. Lt-Col Fulton then left the regiment for home and a new Sergeant Major was appointed named James Robertson.

New Year 1813 brought the encouraging news that Napoleon's Grande Armee in Russia had suffered a disastrous retreat from Moscow, with only a small portion having survived. With the wounded of Burgos recovering, and strong reinforcements and supplies having been received, Wellington's army faced the new year with optimism. On 20 February 1813, Lt-Col Neil Douglas arrived from Britain to take command of the 79th Regiment. He had, before being wounded at Busaco, served as a commissioned officer with the regiment throughout its campaigns. Lord Wellington's army now entered Spain and continued its advance towards France with a magnificent success at Vittoria, including the capture of a vast amount of artillery and stores.

Sgt MacIntosh fought with the 79th in the series of actions forming the Battle of the Pyrenees, and then in September 1813 was transferred from the Light Company to Number 4 Company. This probably marked the month in which he became the regiment's first Colour Sergeant. Colour Sergeants from each company were appointed to form an escort to the Colours, which were carried into battle by Ensigns. At the centre point of the regiment, the Ensigns and Colour Party were inevitably always to attract heavy losses.

The French continued to withdraw slowly and by defending every possible position stubbornly, caused Wellington's forces heavy casualties. St Sebastien and Pampeluna fell, and then on November 10, Wellington's army crossed the frontier into France. A series of actions forming the battle of Nivelle ended with the French being driven from a strong line of entrenchments. One month later the Cameron Highlanders took part in Wellington's successful assault upon strong defensive positions on each side of the flooded River Nive.

On 6 January 1814, came one of Masterton MacIntosh's proudest moments, when upon the promotion of James Robertson to Ensign, he was appointed Sergeant Major of the 79th Regiment.

The regiment marched to the port of St Jean de Luz to

The siege on Burgos.

collect much needed clothing, and so missed the battle of Orthes, but was back with the 6th Div in time to join the assault on the fortifications and redoubts of Toulouse. Much of the fighting centred around two strong redoubts, La Colombette and Le Tour Des Augustin and at a late stage of the hard fought battle, when Pack's Brigade had been forced to retire, Lt-Col Neil Douglas rallied the 79th and led them in a charge which succeeded in driving the French from both positions. Four of the regiments of the 6th Div were commended by Wellington, for their conduct during the battle, the 30th, 42nd, 61st and 79th Regiments. When the French again retired from the field, this marked not only the end of the battle, but also the campaign and the end of the war. With Napoleon at last defeated, Europe could contemplate a long and welcome period of peace.

At little more than quarter strength, the regiment went into cantonments in the south of France, and whilst there received a small draft of replacements. Within three months the Cameron Highlanders embarked for Britain, and July 1814 found them stationed in barracks at Cork.

On 25 December welcome reinforcements arrived with Capt Sinclair from the 2nd Battalion with a draft of 261 men. Sgt-Maj MacIntosh and his NCOs, many newly promoted, represented a most experienced and battle hardened group, and they soon gained the standard required from the recruits.

On 24 January 1815, the regiment was ordered to join a force intended to reinforce the army in North America, where many of the former Peninsula regiments were already serving. After two unsuccessful attempts to sail against contrary winds, the expedition was postponed and the 79th was instead sent to the north of Ireland eventually arriving at Belfast. It appeared that the Cameron Highlanders were destined for garrison duty, when the startling news broke that Napoleon had escaped from Elba! He was already re-establishing himself in France, where his old armies were flocking to his banner.

In May 1815, the regiment was ordered to join the Duke of Wellington's Army in Flanders, and within a short time marched from Belfast to Dublin. Transports then conveyed them to Ostend, where there was great activity with the arrival of other regiments. The 79th continued its journey by canal boats to Ghent, where the men were delighted to find themselves in company with the 1st, 42nd and 92nd Regiments. A reunion was held between men who had previously fought together in Egypt, Denmark, Spain and France, and the skirl of the pipes filled the air.

On 28 May the regiments marched to Brussels, where they joined Wellington's Army of the Low Countries. The Cameron Highlanders with the 28th, 32nd and 95th Regiments, were formed into the 8th Brigade, commanded by Lt-Gen Sir James Kempt. Their comrades of the 1st, 42nd and 92nd Regiments joined the 44th Regiment, to form the 9th Brigade, commanded by Maj-Gen Sir Denis Pack. The two brigades formed the 5th Division, which was to be commanded by Lt-Gen Sir Thomas Picton, whom the regiments remembered from the Peninsula as a tough and tenacious general, with a lifetime of service in the army behind him.

The Duke of Wellington's army had been assembling in Flanders since April and already included English, Scottish, Irish, German, Dutch and Belgian troops. 18 of the British regiments had served in the Peninsula and others were on the way from North America. It was anticipated that upon their arrival the army would move forward into France, to remove Napoleon from power.

A period of great activity developed in Brussels, with brigade parades and inspections by Sir James Kempt and Sir Denis Pack, and then on 3 June, the 5th Divison was assembled and inspected by Field Marshal the Duke of Wellington, accompanied by Field Marshal The Prince Blucher, Commander of the Prussian Forces. The Duke was known for his austere manner and critical eye, but he expressed his pleasure at the appearance of the division, remarking that he was happy again to see some regiments which had served with great distinction in the Peninsula.

Although Wellington had many second and third battalion units in the British section of his army as well as many weaker foreign units, he had every reason to be satisfied with the 8th Brigade, as it was composed wholly of battle hardened first battalions. There were many brigade and regimental duties to perform in Brussels, with guards and town patrols, but in the evenings Sgt-Maj MacIntosh was able to relax with the Colour Sergeants, many of whom he had known for years. Col-Sgt Samuel Owens had enlisted on the same day from the Loyal Inverness Fencibles and Col-Sgt George Manuel had joined from the Caithness Fencibles. They had shared campaigns together since Egypt, but now faced further action with almost half of the regiment never having fired a musket in anger. However, they were better prepared than many other regiments, as these were largely made up of untrained recruits and former militiamen.

The waiting time was unsettling, especially with the persistent rumours circulating of Napoleon's approaching army. Whilst orders were given not to heed such talk, it was not easy when such obvious preparations were being made to town defences. On 15 June following a day in which messengers had been seen to be so active, Brussels remained tense with speculation, and even though Wellington and many of his officers were seen to be socialising at the Duchess of Richmond's ball, the streets remained thronging with people watching the activity in the warmth of the summer evening.

At 10pm all regiments were alerted and ordered to be prepared to march at a moment's notice, and NCOs were seen to be checking ration and ammunition wagons. Just before midnight the drums sounded the call to arms and throughout Brussels the streets filled with excited and anxious people, as word circulated that Napoleon's army was close. The Cameron Highlanders assembled upon the Place Royale, where rations were placed in canvas haversacks and water canteens filled. Col Douglas and his field officers mounted their horses and the order was given to march off towards the divisional rendezvous.

At 2am Sir Thomas Picton led the 5th Div south out of Brussels in the bright moonlight and as the 79th Regt marched through the Namur Gate with pipes playing, the crowds waved and cheered walking along with them. Sir James Kempt's 8th Brigade led the division out towards the forest of Soignes.

Sgt-Maj MacIntosh marched with the Colour party in the centre of the regiment close behind the Colonel, and as the sun slowly rose the forest roads became warmer. After six hours the sound of horses came from the rear and orders followed to march to attention. The Duke of Wellington with his large group of Staff officers then gently rode past, the Duke wearing blue riding coat with breeches, small hat, and Hussar style boots. Any cheering by the new men was quickly stifled as it was well known that the Duke found such outward show distasteful.

At Soignes a halt was called under the shade of trees and the men began to cook food, but before this could be taken the order came to resume the march. The heat and rising dust caused thirst and a shortage of water, but local people lining the roads handed out drinks of water and milk.

1st Bn Queen's Own Cameron Highlanders 1912. The Senior NCOs. 2nd left seated, C/Sgt J. Tomney; 3rd left seated, RSM A. J. MacDonald; centre, possibly Lt-Col J. D. McLachlan DSO; 2nd right seated, RSM G. P. Burt DCM.

Col A. A. Fairrie, Curator, Museum of Queen's Own Highlanders (Seaforth and Camerons)

CHAPTER 3

Sergeant Major M. MacIntosh with the 79th Regiment at Waterloo

The 5th Division marched on through the heat, and as they neared Genappe the distant sounds of gunfire could be heard. The divisional wagons were left behind as the roads were by now being kept clear for cavalry and artillery; soon wounded Dutch and Belgian soldiers appeared, assisting each other past the column.

The 5th Division had covered 22 miles when the crossroads at Quatre Bras came into view and a brief halt was called. Now the men had their first sight of the French infantry advancing with skirmishers out in front, down a slope only a few hundred yards away, where a Belgian regiment was retiring in good order. The 5th Div assembled and by regiment moved off into the rye fields to form divisional lines. Hardly had they taken position when the French opened a heavy cannonade. Their skirmishers concentrated their fire upon the divisional officers on horseback and the few artillerymen working the only allied guns yet to have arrived.

Casualties mounted as the Light Companies of the 8th Brigade engaged battle. Eventually the French infantry were forced to retreat by the closely pursuing Highlanders. In turn the 79th were halted, although they still fired volleys into the French until their ammunition ran low and they were ordered to withdraw. The French fire increased in intensity for a time, then ceased as the mass of their cavalry approached through the dense rye, and the order to form square sounded within each regiment of the 5th. Waves of cuirassiers burst forth through the high growing crops and the first volleys crashed from the waiting squares.

Clouds of smoke obscured each regiment – providing immediate justification for the hours of musketry drill – and the well regulated volleys continued to meet the onrushing horsemen as they veered to surround the squares of steady bayonets. The French cavalry charged and withdrew repeatedly and the centre of the divisional line suffered particularly heavily. Between rushes the French artillery fired upon the squares and their sharpshooters moved forwards to fire into the closed ranks. As the day wore on and the regiments of the 5th became thinned by casualties, orders came to form combined squares.

During the day of battle, Col Douglas and both of his field officers – Maj Brown and Maj Cameron – had been severely wounded, as also had many of the captains in command of companies. Sgt-Maj MacIntosh was repeatedly needed to seek out the next senior officer in succession to take command of the regiment; by now many of the companies were commanded by junior officers or NCOs, and there was an acute shortage of ammunition.

During the day Wellington's forces had been arriving at Quatre Bras and it was at last possible for two fresh brigades to reinforce the weakened 5th. With evening came the stifling atmosphere of an electrical storm and, as the clouds built up, peals of thunder mingled with artillery fire. At last the sound of gunfire ceased, but then for the first time the harrowing cries of the wounded could be heard.

The regiments of the 5th were ordered to bivouac in position and large fires were lit and food consumed. Sgt-Maj MacIntosh now consulted with his Colour Sergeants to prepare lists of casualties for the CO. These revealed that over 300 officers and men had been killed or wounded – a number exceeding the whole of the last draft – and heightened by the severe loss of officers. Many of the nearby wounded were helped to the hospitals set up in local farm buildings. Whilst most of the exhausted men of the 79th settled down to rest, the CO ordered Sgt-Maj MacIntosh to find men for piquet duty.

Assembly sounded at sunrise on 17 June, and the regiments cleaned weapons and reformed lines. However orders came to clear the remainder of the wounded from the field and withdraw back towards Brussels.

The infantry was the first to depart, and having been in the lead upon arrival, the 79th was one of the last to leave. As they returned along the road through the divisional positions, the dead remained where they had fallen in lines and squares, with men of the 28th and 32nd and Highlanders of the 79th, 42nd and 92nd Regiments lying intermingled with French infantrymen, cuirassiers and their horses. As the 5th Division marched a violent storm broke over their heads with torrential rain quickly turning the roadway into a muddy stream.

Sounds of gunfire occasionally broke through the storm as the rearguard of the cavalry and the horse artillery fought to delay the mounting French pursuit. Sgt-Maj MacIntosh however, would have been more concerned with considering and recommending promotions in order to replace lost senior and junior NCOs. He would also have been considerably relieved that the army was withdrawing towards their badly needed ammunition and stores left at Soignes.

Near Mont St Jean the division took up positions along a

The charge of the Scots Greys and 92nd Gordon Highlanders at the battle of Waterloo. Oil painting by Stanley Berkeley

roadway which crossed fields of standing corn. Still the rain poured down, but before long Sgt-Maj MacIntosh was making his way round seeking out men for picquet duty. The regiment stood in column as darkness fell and the thunder rolled overhead. Other soaking regiments arrived throughout the night and in the early hours the sound of hooves and jingling equipment announced the arrival of cavalry. Some of the men sat on knapsacks as the rainwater fell off them, but most stood shifting from foot to foot waiting for the morning to come.

Sunday 18 June dawned grey and misty with a soft drizzle falling. To the right of the Highlanders stood the bedraggled ranks of the 32nd Regiment with the Brussels road beyond them, whilst on the opposite flank stood the 28th Regiment. Visibility increased as the rain eased and other regiments appeared out of the gloom. Mist slowly lifted across undulating slopes to their front and a further ridge of ground came into view almost a mile ahead. There, positioned in three great lines, stood the ranks of the French army. They had arrived during the night, and as the Highlanders watched, still more approached from the rear. Assembly sounded as a weak sun appeared. Sgt-Maj MacIntosh and his NCOs busily moved amongst the ranks, as the crack of musket fire all along the ridge indicated the drying out of muskets.

Large formations of cavalry were massed behind the division and for the first time the size of the Duke of Wellington's army could be seen stretching out as far as the eye could see in either direction.

Staff officers directed the allied regiments into position and as they marched with bands playing and colours flying, the mens spirits began to lift. Wellington himself could be seen on horseback conferring with his aides; as he began his slow inspection of the lines, word arrived that Marshal Blucher was on his way to support them. As time passed the expected attack did not develop, instead a lengthy review began in the French lines, accompanied by the sounds of cheering and chanting, drumming and the music of bands.

Suddenly at mid-morning an extremely loud and heavy French cannonade began, to be immediately returned by Wellington's artillery. The thunderous noise of gunfire quickly dispelled the atmosphere of ceremonial and thick banks of smoke rolled over the field to obscure both armies from sight.

In the early afternoon large divisional formations of French infantry with a wide screen of skirmishers spread out in front, slowly advanced through the smoke. These deep columns of infantry, thousands strong and supported by cavalry, made their way across the centre ground. Showers of artillery grapeshot fell amongst them slowing their progress as did the thick mud – but they were heading straight for the 5th Division.

The massed ranks closed, and hard and desperate close quarter bayonet fighting took place. The thinly spread 5th was in danger of being overwhelmed by the depth of the huge French force and their situation had become critical by the time the thunder of hooves pronounced the advance of Wellington's cavalry. With the Royals on the left and Life Guards on the right, the horsemen surged into the French infantry and using their sabres to deadly effect they scattered them widely. The 5th moved forward again with bayonets fixed and more allied cavalry charging from the ranks forced the French to break into retreat. The cavalry swept on, forcing the withdrawal into a rout and inflicting fearful casualties amongst the massed running men.

Recall sounded along the line and the 5th slowly retraced their steps back into position. Word now passed that their commander, Sir Thomas Picton had been killed during the first charge. Sir James Kempt was now in command of the 5th and Col Belson of the 28th Regiment had taken command of the 8th Brigade.

The allied cavalry had advanced a long way towards the French lines, but now units of enemy cavalry were moving across the centre ground to support their retiring infantry. As they swept towards the ridge the 5th Division formed squares to present ranks bristling with bayonets and the sound of pipes encouraged them with the stirring *Cogadh no Sith*, an ancient Highland gathering tune. Although the French cavalry moved forward with great verve, they could make little impression against the bayonets and after a time the horsemen drew off and the bombardment recommenced. The regiments of the 8th were by now low in ammunition and were temporarily pulled back as the French infantry gathered for a second attack.

Soon came the warning 'Prepare to repel cavalry' and along the ridge the regiments again formed squares. The ground began to tremble with the thunder of the approaching force – but great banks of artillery smoke hid them from sight. With a surge of sound they swept into view further along to the right, and for what seemed an age, the sound of clashing steel sounded where the French cavalry fought in vain to gain a decisive breakthrough. Further great formations of cavalry joined the attack, but the field was too congested and obstructed by fallen men and horses for the allied squares to be broken. The French cavalry surged forward and receded many times, but eventually they turned and made their way back down the slope leaving heaps of riders and horses sprawled around the squares.

The Prussian forces were now entering the field on the far left flank, but in front of the 5th the French infantry had gained the great tactical advantage of a nearby farm and they brought artillery pieces forward to fire grapeshot into Wellington's lines at almost point blank range. Every shot caused several men to fall and soon a serious gap formed on the right flank of the 5th. There were no reserves left to close the gaps and with the centre of his army now in great danger, the Duke himself directed and led units of Brunswickers and two brigades of cavalry into the gap to ease the situation.

It is only possible to assume that the duties of Sgt-Maj MacIntosh included the ordering of the constant closing up of ranks to avoid gaps within the regiment and that in the absence of killed or wounded officers, NCOs had to be directed to take command of companies. During the day command of the regiment had passed through the hands of several officers and now rested with Lt Alexander Cameron of the Grenadier Company. The regiment was by now however a little more than one third of its original strength.

The conflict continued with the men of the 5th covered in black deposit from hours of musketry, which – added to dried mud and blood – made it difficult to recognise the few officers and NCOs still standing, but they methodically went on with their loading and priming drill.

Now over the clamour of battle came the steady drum beat and chanting which heralded the arrival of the French Imperial Guard. The 79th were too heavily committed with enemy infantry to worry about them, but the crescendo of sound from further along the line highlighted one of the crucial encounters of the day's battle.

The 5th continued to hold its ground, but was fast weakening and both Gen Kempt and Maj-Gen Pack were injured. As the evening wore on cheering was heard and there was a perceptible lessening of fire from the enemy – word was passing along the lines that the Imperial Guard had broken – and was in retreat!

The French line wavered and then moved back off the ridge. The allied regiments streamed forwards and within moments were pouring down the slope firing into the mass of withdrawing French. The tattered Colours were held aloft as the remnants of the 5th advanced over the French dead and wounded. The enemy streamed back in utter confusion discarding weapons and equipment in their haste to escape. The ground over which the 79th advanced was littered with every kind of debris, smashed guns, drums and equipment as well as the bodies of French infantry and cavalry and a great many horses. All around Waterloo the French troops were fleeing from the entire battle area, with units of Prussian cavalry sweeping after them in hot pursuit.

Now Prussians, British and Allied forces met in the centre of the former French positions. The last sounds of battle were coming from the actions around the solitary squares of the French Imperial Guard, who fought bravely on rather than surrender.

As darkness approached reaction set in and Wellington's exhausted regiments began to bivouac where they were, stretching out amongst the litter and debris. The actual fighting was virtually over – but the suffering was not, and for the wounded the ordeal was just beginning.

Next morning, 19 June, the regiments began to stir in search of water and food and congregating groups attempted to discover who had survived. Sgt-Maj MacIntosh found on summoning his Colour Sergeants that only three responded, one had been killed and four wounded, three very severely. Most of the companies were down to between one quarter and one half strength.

Lt Alexander Cameron was wounded but able to retain temporary command of the 79th Regiment. Only three other Lieutenants and one Ensign remained unscathed. In No 8 Company Sgt-Maj MacIntosh found that only 14 men answered their names out of an original 69. The Grenadier Company was commanded by a wounded Sergeant and numbered 23 of an original 92 men. No 5 Company was also commanded by a Sergeant.

The regiment had marched from Brussels with a strength of over 700 men, but now mustered under 300. Nevertheless, later in the day the depleted 79th marched off the battlefield with the Duke of Wellington's army in pursuit of the French. 18 days later the regiment was bivouacing close to Paris when Napoleon surrendered and the conflict with France was finally ended.

The army was reviewed on 24 July 1815 by the Emperors of Austria and Russia, the King of Prussia, and many distinguished allied Commanders. Thoughts that the 79th Regiment might now return home were dismissed however, as they went on to garrison towns in France.

On 25 December, the 2nd Battalion was stood down, and a system of depots and depot companies replaced it.

Wellington and his staff in the gathering dusk at Waterloo.
R. Bowyer, 1816

On 7 January 1816 the last draft from the former 2nd Bn arrived, and as the wounded men of the Waterloo campaign gradually recovered and rejoined, the strength of the regiment built up. The 79th then became part of the Army of Occupation, and was to remain in France for the next three years.

The victory at Waterloo was to provide one of the longest periods of peace and stability in Europe's history. A grateful nation rewarded its soldiers firstly financially according to rank, then by awarding an additional two years service for every man at Waterloo, and finally by awarding the Waterloo Silver Medal to every soldier who took part in the battle.

Sgt-Maj Masterton MacIntosh served on in the 79th until 30 June 1819, when at the age of 44, he was discharged to pension, and his place was taken by Col-Sgt William Dewar. A testimonial written and signed by Lt-Col Neil Douglas on 14 May 1819 states:

Masterton MacIntosh's conduct as a soldier has been very good. He was present with the regiment in all the campaigns and actions from 1800 to 1814, and was also present in the actions of the 16th and 18th June 1815 at Quatre Bras and Waterloo. At the storming of the horn-work of Burgos Castle on 19 September 1812, when he particularly distinguished himself, he was the first man who entered the work, for which he was recommended for an Ensigncy. He was also recommended for an Ensigncy after the battle of Waterloo, and promised one, but in consequence of the reduction of the veteran battalions, he was disappointed.

From my knowledge of his character the last 15 years that I have been in the regiment, I recommend him for a faithful, steady and brave soldier. Wounded severely through the right leg on 5 May 1811 at Fuentes de Onor, and at Burgos in the left knee on 19 September 1812.

Alexander Cruikshank, Fort Major of Edinburgh Castle in 1852, who as a private soldier served under Sergeant Major Masterton MacIntosh in the Light Company of the 79th Regt at Waterloo. Portrait from a painting by the artist R. R. McIan.

Col A. A. Fairrie, Curator, Museum of Queen's Own Highlanders (Seaforth and Camerons)

79th Cameron Highlanders Depot at Aberdeen in May 1855. L to R. C/Sgt in Review Order. Orderly Room Clerk Henry MacKay. Depot Sgt-Maj John Notman. Drummer R. White. Sgt Donald Robertson and QMS Donald Gow.

Col A. A. Fairrie, Curator, Museum of Queen's Own Highlanders (Seaforth and Camerons)

The certificate of service shows a total of 28 years 108 days, which counting the Waterloo award of two years, would suggest that he served in a volunteer company before joining the Loyal Inverness Fencibles.

Masterton MacIntosh returned to his native Scotland and in 1820 married Mary Stewart. They lived in Waterloo Place in Inverness and had four children.

Three of the subsequent Sergeant Majors of the 79th Regiment fought at Waterloo, William Dewar of course holding the rank of Colour Sergeant in the Light Company.

Colin MacDonald was twice wounded as a Sergeant in the Grenadier Company at Waterloo. He had previously been wounded at the Battle of the Pyrenees and also at Toulouse. He became Sergeant Major of the 79th in 1824, and later served in Canada with the regiment, becoming town major of Montreal in 1835.

Angus Ross was slightly wounded as a Corporal in Number 2 Company at Waterloo. He went on to become Sergeant Major of the 79th in 1836, and held the rank until 1837.

In the Light Company at Waterloo was a Pte Alexander Cruikshank, who had served through the campaigns of the 79th since 1805. He had been captured at Fuentes de Onoro when his company was surrounded by the French, but had later escaped. He was wounded at Toulouse, but went through the battles of Quatre Bras and Waterloo unscathed.

Alexander Cruikshank went on through the ranks to become RQMS in 1833, Quartermaster in 1838, and he was finally appointed Fort Major of Edinburgh Castle in 1851. He died at the castle at the age of 70, on 22 August 1857, and interestingly – his broadsword, dirk, pipe, and belt buckle were presented to the regimental museum at Fort George, as recently as 1984, by one of his descendants.

The 79th Cameron Highlanders, in which MacIntosh proudly served from 1800-10 remained a single battalion regiment until 1907, 16 years longer than any other regiment. As a small regiment it nevertheless had a very strong tradition of family service, and many generations of men served. At Parkhurst Barracks, Isle of Wight, on 17 April 1873, HM Queen Victoria presented new Colours, and soon afterwards honoured the regiment with the title 79th Queen's Own Cameron Highlanders. 20 years later the Queen was to intervene to prevent the regiment from becoming the 3rd Battalion of the Scots Guards.

The Colours and Colour Party of the 79th Queen's Own Highlanders Dublin, 1907. A photograph which contains a great deal of Regimental history.

C/Sgt Hugh Smellie (rear rank 1st left) became CSM 6th Bn. Killed in action, France 26 Sept 1915.

C/Sgt Peter Bannerman Anderson (rear 2nd left) became RSM 8th Bn 1915, and Major 2 i/c. Died 25 June 1952.

C/Sgt George Burt, DCM (rear 3rd left) became RSM 1st Bn 1912. Killed in action, France 25 Sept 1914.

C/Sgt Donald Dixon Farmer, VC (rear 4th left) first Cameron Highlander to be awarded VC in 1901. Became RSM Liv Scottish Regt 1914. Retired 1921 as Lt-Col. Died 23 Dec 1956.

C/Sgt Alexander McKinnon, DCM (centre 1st left) became RSM 5th Bn. Awarded bar to DCM 1915. Died 12 April 1946.

C/Sgt David Cameron (centre 2nd left) holding the King's Colour. Became RSM 3rd Bn 1911. Commissioned 1917. Died in India 1920, when with the 1st Bn.

C/Sgt Sidney Axten, DCM (centre 3rd left) holding the Regimental Colour. Became RSM 1st Bn 1914, and awarded

MC. Served in the Local Defence Home Guard during WW2. Died 3 Oct 1959, aged 85.

C/Sgt Charles Boate (centre 4th left) became RSM in the Lincolnshire Regt.

RSM Arthur James Macdonald (front left). RSM 1st Bn 1901 and then 6th Bn. Commissioned 1914 in 8th Bn, then 5th Bn. Died on 19 Nov 1936.

Capt John Arthur, ORR (front centre) made Adjutant of the 1st Bn 5 Dec 1904 to 4 Dec 1907. Attended Staff College in 1914, but killed in action, France 22 Oct 1914.

C/Sgt Inst of Musketry, James Tomney (front right) became RQMS of the 8th Bn and was a noted marksman. Died on 20 Dec 1950.

Col A. A. Fairrie, Curator, Museum of Queen's Own Highlanders (Seaforth and Camerons)

Right: *Presentation of New Colours to the 1st Bn The Queen's Own Cameron Highlanders, by HM the Queen at Balmoral on 30 May 1955. The Queen inspects the Bn attended by Col N. D. Leslie OBE.*

Col A. A. Fairrie, Curator, Museum of Queen's Own Highlanders (Seaforth and Camerons)

In the Great War of 1914-18, 12 battalions of the Queen's Own Cameron Highlanders were raised. In the Second World War seven battalions were raised, one of which, the Seventh Battalion, became the Fifth Scottish Battalion of the Parachute Regiment in 1942.

On 7 February 1961, as part of the reorganisation of the British Army, two distinguished Highland regiments, The Seaforth Highlanders, and the The Queen's Own Cameron Highlanders, were amalgamated to form The Queen's Own Highlanders (Seaforth and Cameron).

With the kind permission of Lt-Col R. C. V. Hunt, I went to Fort George Barracks in 1986, to visit RSM William Kintrea, of the 1st Battalion, Queen's Own Highlanders (Seaforth and Cameron) who hails from Forres, and whom has since been commissioned. I was most interested to meet the present day equivalent of Sgt-Maj Masterton MacIntosh, whose task in the old days was almost wholly drill orientated. I was shown to RSM Kintrea's large office, where I met an extremely busy executive whose telephone hardly ceased to ring. The variety of matters dealt with surprised me and the large amount of detailed work for action by the RSM. Although the basic discipline and authority is clearly visible, the extra knowledge and awareness of public relations and administrational efficiency calls for a highly trained and experienced Warrant Officer, with a combination of management skills. RSM Kintrea reflected, as do so many of the present day RSMs, the excellent background training of the Oswestry Junior Leaders Regiment of the 1960s, and

he conceded the preparation afforded there had been 'simply brilliant'.

Since joining the regiment in February 1969, he has moved through the ranks quickly, reaching Sergeant by 1976. There followed a very enjoyable and successful tour at the RMAS as a Colour Sergeant Instructor, under the able direction of AcSM Denis Cleary, Irish Guards. RSM Kintrea had been influenced in training by such men as RSM J. Bing, Grenadier Guards, RSM G. Hooper, Coldstream Guards, and of course AcSM D. Cleary. He also remembered particularly well RSM C. Kiel, Queen's Own Highlanders, who although strict, had a marvellous attitude towards the young NCOs.

Although parade ground work now falls much more upon the CSMs, RSM Kintrea is still involved in the public duties of the battalion, and at the time of my visit, was working on the arms drill for the new SA 80. In relation to past parades, he expressed fond memories of the presentation of the new Colours at Tidworth in 1983, when he had the honour of being the CSM for the New Colours.

It was a most enjoyable experience to talk with the RSM of the regiment, which has such strong links with the old 79th Regiment. Also to meet him in the historic surroundings of Fort George, which although remaining an operational barracks able to accommodate a full infantry battalion, reveals so clearly the kind of massive fortifications built at the time of the formation of so many of the great Scottish Highland Regiments.

CHAPTER 4

Sergeant Majors commissioned without sanction. First Sikh War

When reading *The Life and Campaigns of Hugh 1st Viscount Gough* by Robert S. Rait, published in 1903 by Archibald Constable & Co. I was most intrigued to learn that Lt-Gen Sir Hugh Gough had during the First Sikh War in 1845-46, gazetted a number of Sergeant Majors of Line Regiments as Ensigns, without having first gained the sanction of the commander in chief. Such had been his loss in officers in the battles of Moodkee (or Mudki) and Ferozeshah on 18, 21 and 22 December 1845, that – as he explained in a letter to his son:

I scarcely had an alternative: my loss in officers was so great that it was absolutely necessary: and I must say that I felt the policy of giving every stimulus to induce to future acts of daring. I felt the struggle was but begun, and that it would be one of life and death, firm possession or shameful abandonment of our Indian Empire. I did then what I should do again even with the ban of His Grace's displeasure.

His C in C at Horse Guards, London, was the Duke of Wellington, who had throughout his career, been required to seek sanction for commissions in the field, from his superiors. I have been unable to discover how displeased the Duke of Wellington was, but the author Robert Rait made separate comment that:

This departure from military rules involved an encroachment not only upon the powers of the Duke of Wellington as head of the British Army, but even on the royal prerogative itself, and considerable comment was made upon it in England.

It seems to me both interesting and important to attempt to discover both the identities of the Sergeant Majors, and any available information about their subsequent careers. Little did I realise that the necessary research would continue through several years, and that a doubt would still remain as to the identity of the men actually commissioned without sanction.

Firstly, I should state that an important variation occurs in the book about Sir Hugh Gough, regarding the descriptions of the promotions. Sir Hugh states in his letter to his son that he had gazetted the Sergeant Majors of every Queen's Regiment, whilst Robert Rait states: 'In view of the loss of British Officers at Moodkee and Ferozeshah, Sir Hugh Gough had taken the serious responsibility of conferring commissions upon five non commissioned officers, who had distinguished themselves in the battles.'

Should I therefore search for five NCOs who had earned commissions in the field, or for details of the Sergeant Majors of every Queen's Regiment present?

Five British regiments fought in the first battle of the First Sikh War, at Moodkee, The 3rd Light Dragoons and the 9th, 31st, 50th and 80th Foot. The promotions related also to the second battle, at Ferozeshah, however, and in addition to those regiments mentioned, the 29th Foot and the 62nd Foot, also fought.

Clearly it would be necessary to seek the identities of all seven Sergeant Majors, and those of any NCO commissioned in the field at that time. In that respect enquiries were commenced with the curators of the regimental museums concerned. Many hours of research were also spent at three marvellous establishments, the regimental museum of the Border Regiment, at Carlisle, where Col R. K. May so kindly allowed my wife Eileen and myself to search through *Hart's Army Lists*, the Guildhall Library in London, where a search was made through the copies of the *Gazette*, and at the Public Record Office in London, where searches were carried out through numerous records and returns.

As a result of all of these enquiries, it was eventually possible to verify that the seven soldiers commissioned in the field by Sir Hugh Gough were:

Sgt-Maj George E. F. Kountze, 3rd Light Dragoons
Sgt-Maj John Whiteside, 9th Foot

The fierce battle of Ferozeshah during the 1st Sikh War. Commander, Gen Sir Hugh Gough.

Sgt-Maj George Mitchell, 29th Foot
QMS William Jones, 31st Foot
Sgt-Maj Richard Heaton, 50th Foot
Sgt-Maj William Rudman, 62nd Foot
Col-Sgt Matthew Kirkland, 80th Foot

Had Sir Hugh Gough commissioned *every* Sergeant Major, the list would include Sgt-Maj William Byrne of the 31st Foot, who replaced Sgt Maj Mulligan, killed at Moodkee, and Sgt-Maj John Brown of the 80th Foot, but these NCOs were not promoted at that time. If only five of those listed were commissioned without sanction, it has not proved possible to establish the identity of the five, and it would seem more likely that all seven were similarly commissioned.

Before giving details of each man's service history, that of Sir Hugh Gough should be mentioned as there are many indications in his biography of a great soldier, who led and directed his army from the front on horseback, and indeed wore a white battle coat so that he could be easily seen in action. It was said that when he came off the battlefields it was his habit to remove and shake his coat – when all manner of debris fell out! Although wounded in action on occasion, he must have led a charmed life, as he would deliberately draw fire upon himself in order to save his troops.

Hugh Gough was born at Woodstown, Co Limerick, on 3 November 1779, and first served in his father's Militia Corps at the age of 13. Responsibility came quickly when he was promoted as Ensign at 14, and soon afterwards as Lieutenant in the 119th Regiment. He was by his 15th year serving as Adjutant. One year later he was transferred to the 78th Regiment, and experienced his first close quarter fighting. 1796 found him in the 87th Regiment, with which he was to remain closely linked.

Appointed Major in August 1805, he sailed with the regiment three years later for service in the Peninsula. During the Talavera campaign of July 1809, Maj Gough was severely wounded in his right side. Promoted as Brevet Lieutenant Colonel, he commanded the 87th throughout an epic defence of a breach in the walling of Tarifa in 1812, when his garrison of less than 1,000 men held off with musket and bayonet a French force of many times its size. Lt-Col Gough wrote very highly of the 87th Regiment.

Fellows like these, fighting as they have done, and feeling as they do, what is there not to be expected from them? I may abolish a guard room, and talk of the cat-o-nine-tails as an obsolete term.

And then in October 1812, when the regiment was marching to join Gen Sir Roland Hill's army:

My men have astonished the division in marching. I never saw such a set of fellows. I came yesterday seven and 20 miles, over a most wretched road, and it rained all the time, in eight hours and a half, without having one man out of his section an inch. The Guards saw us come in to their astonishment. Skerrett . . who was present, cried out, 'God damn me my brigade, let them look at

Gen Sir Hugh Gough, Commander of Forces in India during the First and Second Sikh Wars, wearing his famous white 'Battle Coat'. The 5th Viscount Gough

that regiment, and be ashamed of themselves.' I trust the fellows will continue, if they do there will be nothing but comfort.

Harder times were to follow, but there were always warm feelings between Hugh Gough and the men of the 87th.

Lt-Col Gough and the 87th fought at Vittoria, and then in the Nivelle actions, during which Hugh Gough received a serious wound to his hip, which kept him from the remainder of the Peninsular War. The 87th went on to fight at Orthes where heavy losses were suffered, and then shared the victory at Toulouse.

In 1815 The Prince Regent conferred a knighthood upon Hugh Gough, and having held the Brevet rank of Lieutenant Colonel for six years, he was gazetted in that rank on 25 May. Following a two year period upon half-pay, Lt-Col Gough was given command of the 22nd Regiment, which after service in Ireland was ordered to the West Indies, but as Col Gough did not wish to accompany the regiment, he instead entered a long period of

The British Cavalry, largely comprised of Indian irregular units. Assembly before the battle of Gujerat 21 Feb 1849.

unattached half-pay and had no military involvement until 1837.

On 22 July 1830, he was gazetted Major General, but it was a further seven years before his military career recommenced, when he was unexpectedly offered the command of the Mysore Division of the Madras Army. Following three years of service at Bangalore, Gen Gough accepted the command of an expedition to China, and after two years was promoted to Lieutenant General, and was offered the command of all forces in India.

The first Sikh War was fought in the same massed field formations as the Waterloo campaign had been fought 30 years before, and with the same Brown Bess musket and bayonet. The losses of the regiments were extremely high as the Sikh army – the Khalsa – was very well trained on European lines and was equipped with heavy modern artillery which was well served.

Many Indian cavalry and infantry regiments fought under Gough's command, probably double the number of British units, and their loss was almost equally high. There were also European units of the Honourable East India Company, such as the 1st Bengal European Light Infantry, which fought at Ferozeshah.

There were four main battles during the first war, Moodkee on 18 December 1845, Ferozeshah on 21 and 22 December, Aliwal on 28 January 1846, and Sobraon on 10 February.

The Sergeant Major of the 3rd King's Own Light Dragoons

was George E. F. Kountze, who had previously served with the regiment through the Afghanistan campaign and the Khytul expedition. The regiment was stationed at Umballa when hostilities broke out with the Sikhs, and in the first battle of Moodkee the regiment charged the length of the Sikh lines, causing great slaughter and fear. Their own losses were severe, and following the killing of their wounded by the Sikhs, the regiment gave no quarter in future actions, and charged with the cry 'Remember Moodkee!'

On the day following Moodkee, Sgt-Maj Kountze was promoted as Cornet to replace Cornet J. D. White. The next day the regiment fought in the battle of Ferozeshah where again charges were made against the formidable Sikh artillery batteries, and where they were said to have advanced in perfect line as if on parade. At Sobraon, Cornet Kountze was badly wounded in the severe fighting which formed the last battle of the campaign.

In 1848-49, the second Sikh War took place, and the 3rd King's Own Light Dragoons fought at Ramnugger, Sadoolapore, Chillianwallah and Gujerat, before the Sikh army was finally defeated. George Kountze was promoted as Lieutenant in the beginning of the second war, and was appointed Adjutant in late 1848. He survived the second war, and later transferred to the 42nd Regiment, Black Watch, on being promoted Captain. At about that time, he wrote a book on *The historical records of the 3rd King's Own Regt of Light Dragoons, 1685-1857*. He then further transferred as Captain to the 7th Princess Royal's Dragoon Guards, and was made Major on the 10 May 1864. He retired as a Major at the latter end of 1867.

Sgt-Maj John Whiteside first enlisted in the 9th Foot (later the Royal Norfolk Regiment) in January 1831, and served throughout the Afghanistan campaign of 1842. He was appointed Sergeant Major on 1 March 1843, and had therefore been in post for two years nine months when the first Sikh War commenced.

The day following the battle of Moodkee, he was commissioned as Ensign without purchase to replace Henry Thomas, who had been made Lieutenant. Col-Sgt George Corsons was promoted to Sergeant Major to replace John Whiteside. Having suffered only light losses at Moodkee, the regiment fought at Ferozeshah losing over 270 in killed and wounded, and then at Sobraon had further losses of over 30 casualties.

Ensign Whiteside returned to England in August 1847, and did not take part in the second Sikh War. He was promoted Lieutenant in November, and early in 1848 transferred to the 22nd Foot, then six months later exchanged to the 96th Foot. After eight years service with

British field artillery brought into line to shell the Sikh positions at Gujerat.

that regiment, he was promoted as Captain and on 3 March 1857, exchanged into the 8th Foot where he fought in India during the Mutiny. Capt John Whiteside is mentioned in the historical record of the 8th Foot (King's Liverpool Regiment).

The regiment arrived at Mynpooree on 27 January 1858, and in that station was joined a few days later by a draft from England consisting of Capt Whiteside, Lt Corfield, Ensigns Whelan and Moynihan and 135 other ranks. The march was resumed and Agra was reached on 9 February. In October 1858, the commander in chief organised and set in motion several moveable columns for the subjugation of Oude, where after the capture of Lucknow, the main force of the rebels were concentrated. The King's Regiment was directed to form part of one of these columns, which was commanded by Brig-Gen Hale CB. On 18 October, the regiment – at a strength of about 550 other ranks – under the command of Capt Whiteside, left its cantonments, crossed the Ganges, and joined this column.

Early in the morning of 24 October, Brig-Gen Hale reached Sandee, a fort strongly situated on the river Ghurra, and held by a numerous body of rebels. In order to enable the infantry and guns to cross the river, it was necessary to construct a bridge. This work owing to a hot fire from the fort, was attended with considerable difficulty. Three companies of the King's were sent across to clear the walls, and for several hours the fort was shelled by a battery of eight-inch mortars. The enemy then evacuated the place and succeeded in effecting their escape. The column having marched into and taken possession of the fort, its defences were blown up and effectively destroyed.

Capt Whiteside later commanded the right wing of the regiment (three companies) to join another column, which destroyed several strong forts, made forced marches, and

was much involved in action.

On 13 February 1866, Capt Whiteside was promoted as Major, and transferred to the 11th Foot, until he retired on full pay with the honorary rank of Lieutenant Colonel on 11 November 1866. He lived to enjoy a long retirement in Folkestone, and was over 80 when he died on 10 January 1895. He had served through the ranks from Private to Major, in five regiments, and was able to take full advantage of his commission in the field.

Everard, in his history of the 29th Foot (later the Worcestershire Regiment) records, 'For the distinguished part taken by the regiment at Ferozeshah, Sir Hugh Gough was pleased to appoint Sgt-Maj George Mitchell to a vacant Ensigncy in the regiment.' The 29th Regiment did not take part in the battle of Moodkee, but at Ferozeshah suffered 250 casualties.

George Mitchell enlisted in the regiment at Glasgow on 23 July 1826, was promoted Corporal in 1831, Sergeant in 1833, and Colour Sergeant in 1835. He was appointed Sergeant Major of the regiment on 14 November 1844. Then on 19 December he was commissioned as Ensign to replace Ensign White, and Col-Sgt Edward Carter was made Sergeant Major. At Sobraon the regiment lost 173 men killed and wounded, and one of those severely wounded, whilst carrying the Regimental Colour, was Ensign George Mitchell. He was struck either by a grape or gingall shot which pounded the shin bone, close to the ankle joint of his right leg, into fragments. It is stated that 'amputation was performed at the calf of the leg, and never was an operation borne with more firmness – nay with positive indifference – the patient himself assisting.' Sadly, it is added that irritative fever set in, and George Mitchell died on 18 February 1846 at Ferozepore.

QMS William Jones of the 31st Foot (later the East Surrey Regiment), was granted a field commission for his actions at Moodkee. The regiment fought in all four of the major battles, suffering severe losses of over 150 casualties at each. The total loss of the regiment was close to 500 officers and men killed or wounded, which represented over half of the original strength at the start of the war.

At Moodkee, the CO Lt-Col John Byrne, was severely wounded and the two officers carrying the Colours were killed, together with the Colour Party. QMS William Jones immediately raised the Colour and carried it throughout the rest of the battle. The Sergeant Major of the 31st Foot, Sgt-Maj Mulligan, was also killed and William Byrne who replaced him, was killed in a later action.

Ensign William Jones carried the Colour at Ferozeshah, Aliwal, and at Sobraon, but in the latter battle he was dangerously wounded and it is presumed that he died of his wound as his name does not appear in any subsequent roll or army list.

Sgt-Maj Richard Heaton of the 50th Foot (later the Queen's Own Royal West Kent Regiment), fought in all four major battles of the war, and the regiment suffered the highest loss of any infantry unit, with the loss of almost 550 casualties, again representing over half of the original strength. To compound these losses, the regiment was also hit by a terrible storm which destroyed part of their barracks and killed and injured a further 200 men, women and children.

Richard Heaton was promoted to Ensign, and he was replaced by Col-Sgt John Cantwell. Ensign Heaton fought at and survived all four battles, and in June 1846 was posted to the regimental depot. He was still serving in the 50th Foot as Ensign at Fort William in Calcutta, when on 28 September 1847, he died 'of an affection of the heart'.

Sgt-Maj William Rudman of the 62nd Foot (later the Wiltshire Regiment Duke of Edinburgh's), fought at Ferozeshah, where the regiment suffered almost 300 casualties, from an original strength of about 800. 17 of the 23 officers were killed or wounded, and many of the companies were commanded by Sergeants in the latter part of the battle. Extracts from the historical records of the Wiltshire Regiment state:

Next day, 23 December, the regiment buried its dead in a communal grave. Three-quarters of the officers were casualties and over half the men. The Colours were brought out of action by two Sergeants, four officers having been killed or wounded while carrying them during the first attack. The centre-Sergeant of the Colour Party, Sgt Dring, was shot through both knees with grape shot, and lay on the field all night. He survived to become a Colonel and Chief Paymaster at Aldershot. Of the non-commissioned officers who commanded companies, Col-Sgt Joseph Sanderson later became a Colonel and a Military Knight of Windsor. Col-Sgt Gamble was hit by a bullet which entered his thigh and came out of his back. He not only continued commanding his company, but did not go into hospital afterwards, being attended by that versatile soldier L-Cpl W. Morris. Both men came from Bath and were great friends. Gamble recovered to fight at Sobraon six weeks later. Afterwards as Sergeant Major, he fought with the regiment in the Crimea, returning to England in 1872 to become a Captain. Another Acting CO was Col-Sgt Harvey, and all these men brought their companies out of action on 21 December, continuing to lead them till returning to Ferozepore. The Sergeant-Major at Ferozeshah was Rudman, who was made and Ensign after the battle.

Sgt-Maj William Rudman replaced Ensign Charles Roberts, who had been promoted Lieutenant to replace Lt Scott who had been killed in action. Col-Sgt Thomas Boyd took over as Sergeant Major. Ensign Rudman was made acting unconfirmed Adjutant, and with others was 'mentioned in terms of admiration' at the battle of Sobraon. From that time there are but occasional mentions of him in the regimental records, as being at the depot at Ferozepore in September 1846, on board the *Adelaide* in March 1847, and as being on garrison duty in September of that year.

On 11 February 1848, he was made Lieutenant in the 32nd Foot, then promoted as Captain on 15 May 1857. The

final comment about him is that he was made Brevet Major on 24 March 1858, and presumably he retired from the army whilst holding that rank.

Almost all of the available information on William Rudman came as a result of the researches carried out by Maj (Retd) John Peters MBE, Curator of the regimental museum, The Duke of Edinburgh's Royal Regiment (Berkshire and Wiltshire), at Salisbury.

Major J. H. Peters was formerly RSM of the Depot Wessex Brigade in 1970-71, and he well remembers taking part in the annual Ferozeshah Parade held on each 21 December. The Regimental Colours are ceremonially handed into the safe keeping of the Warrant Officers and Sergeants for 24 hours, to commemorate the day when the Colour Sergeants were virtually in command of the regiment. The only problem in relation to the anniversary of the battle is that the parade often has to be held in extremely cold weather. When talking with Maj John Peters, he paid tribute to his own training RSM, Harry (Shiner) Green DCM of the Royal Berkshire Regiment, who went on to become Quartermaster.

The 80th Foot (later the 2nd Bn South Staffordshire Regt) fought at Moodkee, Ferozeshah and Sobraon, whilst a detachment also fought at Aliwal.

Col-Sgt Matthew Kirkland of the Grenadier Company was promoted Ensign in the field, for gallantry, by Sir Hugh Gough in general orders on 22 December 1845. He replaced Ensign Robertson. The Sergeant-Major of the Regiment was John Brown, who was not at that time promoted.

The Ferozeshah Parade held annually on 21 December. Here shown in the early 1970s when RSM J. H. Peters and the Escorts present arms as the Colours are given into the safe custody of the Sergeants for 24 hours. Major J. H. Peters

Matthew Kirkland was born in Kilbride, Glasgow, and enlisted on 20 March 1833 at the age of 19 years seven months, 5ft 9in in height, and was previously a shopkeeper. His part in the battle of Ferozeshah is dealt with in the regimental journal *The Stafford Knot.*

The anniversary of the battle of Ferozeshah, fought on 21 and 22 December 1845, is one of our two main regimental days. Each year the Colours are handed over to the Sergeants from mid-day to midnight: this very unusual custom being taken to commemorate in particular the capture of the Black Flag, now in Lichfield Cathedral, by Col-Sgt Matthew Kirkland, who was commissioned in the field for his gallantry.

The Black Flag story is taken from an account written by an officer of the 80th named Cumming, who describes how Capts Best and Scheberas and Sgt Browne were killed in trying to seize the Standard, and how Col-Sgt Matthew Kirkland eventually succeeded, being severely wounded in the process.

Cumming's account was actually part of a very long letter written to his family about six months afterwards describing the whole campaign, the relevant extract being published later under the title *The Night of Ferozeshah.* It contains various apparent inaccuracies and it is probably safe to say that after six months he got the sequence of events mixed up in his mind.

It seems fair to assume that the Black Flag was captured by Kirkland in the afternoon fighting, after Cpl Browne and probably either Best or Scheberas, or possibly both of them, had been killed in the attempt. Kirkland was afterwards severely wounded in the night attack. There is good evidence that the two other Sikh Colours which are with the Black Flag in the cathedral, were captured at Sobraon.

Below the captured Colours and Standard in Lichfield Cathedral is a large monument, which commemorates the officers and men of the 80th Regiment of Foot who fell in the First Sikh War. At the side of the monument is a memorial tablet upon which are recorded the names of those who died while the regiment was on active service in Burma between 1 March 1852 and 30 November 1853. The tenth name on the roll is that of Lt Matthew Kirkland.

As there is no record in the regimental museum of Lt Kirkland having been killed or wounded, it is assumed that he died of disease, and from another officer's diary, this appears to have been in 1853. A terrible reminder of the ravages from disease suffered by the British Army in many of its campaigns is that only one NCO and nine men out of the 352 soldiers commemorated on the tablet were actually killed in action.

It should be stressed that it was quite common for NCOs to be commissioned in the field as Ensigns for bravery, and many more were promoted during the First Sikh War as additional regiments joined the army to fight at Aliwal and Sobraon, but not without the sanction of higher authority. It was said to be difficult for former NCOs to progress further than Ensign unless they were able to purchase a higher rank. The extremely heavy casualties of the time – suffered as a result of both warfare and disease – must have increased opportunities, however, and a willingness to transfer frequently between regiments may also have facilitated promotion.

Of the seven soldiers mentioned, Sgt-Maj Mitchell and QMS Jones did not survive the First Sikh War. Richard Heaton died in 1847, Matthew Kirkland died in 1853, and the remaining three, George Kountze, John Whiteside, and William Rudman, retired as Majors.

A Second Sikh War was fought by Sir Hugh Gough in 1848-49 with equally heavy fighting, and many British regiments bear the battle honours of Sadoolpore, Chillianwallah, and Gujerat. The commander of the army in India, Sir Hugh Gough, died in 1869, and his white battle coat can be seen in the National Army Museum.

Within only a few years many Sikhs were to fight for the British in the Indian Mutiny.

The Regiments of Foot mentioned in the story of Sgt-Maj Masterton MacIntosh, and the Sergeant Majors commissioned in the field during the First Sikh War, are listed below with their modern titles.

Regiment of Foot	1881 Title	Present Title
1st	The Royal Scots (Lothian Regt)	The Royal Scots (Royal Regt)
8th	The King's Regt (Liverpool)	The King's Regt
11th	The Devonshire Regt	Devonshire and Dorset Regt
22nd	The Cheshire Regt	Unchanged
28th	The Gloucestershire Regt	Unchanged
30th	The East Lancashire Regt	The Queen's Lancashire Regt (Loyals and Lancashire)
32nd	The Duke of Cornwall's LI	The Light Infantry
42nd	The Black Watch (Royal Highland Regt)	Unchanged
44th	The Essex Regt	The Royal Anglian Regt
61st	The Gloucestershire Regt	Unchanged
71st	The Highland LI	The Royal Highland Fusiliers (Princess Margaret's Own Glasgow & Ayrshire Regt)
72nd and 78th	The Seaforth Highlanders	The Queen's Own Highlanders (Seaforth and Camerons)
79th	The Queen's Own Cameron Highlanders	As above
87th	Princess Victoria's (The Royal Irish Fus)	The Royal Irish Rangers
92nd	The Gordon Highlanders	Unchanged
95th	Rifle Regt – later The Rifle Brigade	The Royal Green Jackets
96th	2nd Battalion, The Manchester Regt	The King's Regt

CHAPTER 5

Through the ranks with T. Gowing at Alma, Inkerman, and Sebastopol

Although Tim Gowing of the 7th Royal Fusiliers produced in 1885 one of the few books to be written by a Sergeant Major, giving a graphic and moving account of his experiences in the Crimean War, the Indian Mutiny, and in Afghanistan, he unfortunately dealt little with his service or duties as a Sergeant Major.

His narrative of the Crimean campaign however, describes much about his time as an NCO, and in the following abridged extracts from his book, provides a vividly clear picture of the conditions there. Entitled *A Soldier's Experience – or a Voice from the Ranks* the book is an enlarged edition of an earlier account, and includes much extra information relating to other campaigns of the British Army.

Tim Gowing confirms that the bayonet was considered to be the 'Queen of battle' in 1855, and the actual field of battle had changed little from the time of Waterloo. Disease – or as he refers to it, the enemy within – was exacting a heavier price in lives than was the fighting in action. He also reflects critically upon the fact that many of the British regiments were still equipped with the obsolete Brown Bess musket, which placed them at a severe disadvantage.

There are many similarities with the campaigns of Wellington's forces over 40 years before, but also many grim portents of the future, such as the developing power of artillery and the increasing use of trenches. Tim Gowing writes:

I first saw the light of day in the quiet little town of Halesworth, in Suffolk, on 5 April 1834. My parents were good Christian people, and I remained with them in Halesworth until I was about five years old, when I moved with them to Norwich. Like many more I was forever getting out of one scrape into another. I had my own way to a dangerous length through having a fond mother.

As a youth I admired much the appearance of a soldier, little thinking of all that lay behind the scenes. I had read of Nelson's exploits from boyhood, studied all of his principal battles, and also read with eagerness of Wellington's brilliant career through life. In 1853 and the early part of 1854, the Turks were trying to defend themselves against their ancient foes the Russians. The fighting had been raging for upwards of 12 long months, and although the Turks fought desperately, numbers began to prevail. Russia was finally requested to withdraw her vast armies from Turkish soil, which she refused to do, and in March 1854 the Western Powers, England and France, declared war upon her.

In the early part of January 1854, I enlisted into one of the smartest regiments of our army – the Royal Fusiliers. On joining I was about six feet in height, very active and steady, and was soon brought to the notice of my officers, going up the ladder of promotion quickly. Soon after I joined – war was declared, and all regiments were at once put upon a war footing, and thousands who had an appetite for excitement rushed to the standards. We were about to face in deadly conflict the strongest nation of the civilised world, that could bring into the field one million bayonets.

The Fusiliers were quickly made up to about 1,000 strong, and on 5 April 1854 embarked at Southampton for the East, under the command of Col Lacy Walter Yea, a soldier in every sense of the word. As the regiment left I had to remain behind to have a little more knocked into my head in the way of marching and counter marching! The depot was soon removed from Manchester to Winchester, where I completed my drill, and with steadiness went up to the rank of Corporal.

On about 15 June 1854, a strong draft was selected to join the service companies then in Turkey, and after having passed a close medical inspection, I was told off for the draft. I pictured myself coming home much higher in rank, and with my breast covered with honours, but I little dreamed of the hardships that were before me.

We marched out of Winchester about 1,200 strong, detachments of various regiments, with a light heart. Conveyed to Portsmouth, we sailed with cheers ringing in our ears. On 14 September 1854 we landed in the Crimea at Old Fort, and were not opposed, although a few Cossacks were looking on at a respectful distance. No attempt was made to molest us, but a company of ours – and one or two of the Rifles – were at once sent forward to be on the look out.

We made fires the best way we could with broken bits of boats and rafts – it was a fearful night. When morning broke we presented a woeful appearance, but we soon collected ourselves and assembled on the common. Next day we managed to get hold of a few country carts or wagons full of forage, drawn by oxen and camels. We were then a force of some 26,000 British, with 54 field guns. The French had about 24,000 men, with 70 guns, the Turks about 4,500 men, no guns or cavalry, but they had managed to bring tents with them. The army consisted of 54,000 men with 124 guns.

That first night in the Crimea was long to be remembered by those who were there. It came on to rain in torrents while the wind blew a perfect hurricane, and all from the commander down to the drummer boys had to stand and take it as it came – whilst the rain fell only as it does in the tropics. In the morning we looked like a lot of drowned rats, and had the enemy come on in strength, nothing could have saved us. We were now in an enemy's country, and they were known to be in force not far from us, yet we were absolutely unprovided for with camp equipment or stores. They say that fortune favours the brave, and happily the Russians let the opportunity slip.

On 16 September we still gathered stores on shore in readiness to meet the enemy, but the 18th saw us on our legs advancing up the country. We then suffered from the want of water, and what we did get was quite brackish. On the morning of the 19th we marched on, the Light Division in front – with the French on our

right. We continued to suffer, a number of men falling out for the want of a few drops of water, but it could not be got, and we continued to march all day without sighting the enemy.

It began to get exciting in the afternoon. In front of us was a handful of cavalry – a part of the 11th Hussars, and presently a battery of Horse Artillery dashed off at a break-neck pace, and began pounding away at a target we could not see. We passed that day the first wounded man on our side – a Corporal of the 11th Hussars – with his leg nearly off, but we were soon to get accustomed to such sights.

As we topped the rising ground we could see the enemy retiring. Our cavalry still in front feeling the way as the Cossacks slowly gave way before it. We advanced until it began to get dark, when strong picquets were thrown out. I shall ever remember that night as long as I live, as we sat talking for some time of our homes and firesides far away. My comrade had just had a short sleep when on waking he told me that he had suffered a presentiment that he would fall in the first action.

The morning of the 20th found us once more on our legs, and as Marshal St Arnaud rode along our line we cheered him. On passing the 88th Regt the Marshal of France called out in English, 'I hope you will fight well today!'

We marched at a steady pace until about midday – the Light and Second Divisions leading in columns of brigades. As we approached the village of Burlark, which was on our side of the River Alma, the Russians set fire to it, but still we pressed on – we on the right – the Second Division on the left. We now advanced in line into the valley beneath, sometimes taking ground to the right, then to the left. As we kept advancing we had to move our pins to get out of the way of their roundshot, and presently they began to pitch their shot and shell right amongst us and our men began to fall. I know that I felt horribly sick – a cold shivering running through my veins – and I must acknowledge that I felt very uncomfortable. I am happy to say that feeling passed off soon as I began to get warm to it. We were now fairly under the enemy's fire and our poor fellows began to fall fast all around me.

We had deployed into line, and now lay down in order to avoid the hurricane of shot and shell that was being poured into us. We kept advancing and then lying down again, then we made a rush up to the river and in we went. Our men's feelings were now

Crimea on 14 September, all units put ashore with no opposition from over-confident Russians.

wrought up to such a state that it was not easy to stop them. Pulling off their knapsacks and camp kettles they dashed into the river, nearly up to their armpits, with ammunition and rifles held on top of their heads to keep them dry. A number of our fellows were drowned or shot down with grape and canister.

We scrambled out the best way we could and commenced to ascend the hill, our artillery playing about our heads, and we firing and advancing all the time. The smoke was now so great that we could hardly see what we were doing, and our fellows were falling all around. It was a dirty rugged hill. We were only about 600 yards from the mouths of the guns – the thunderbolts of war were not far apart – and death loves a crowd.

We got mixed up with the 95th and someone called out, 'Come on young 95th! – the old 7th are in front!' There were 14 guns of heavy calibre just in front of us, and others on our flanks, in all some 42 guns were raining death and destruction upon us. Up we went step by step, but with horrid carnage. I was not 21 years old – and it set me thinking of the comfortable home in Norwich that I had left.

I could see that we were leading, and that the French were on our right, and the 23rd Fusiliers on our left. The fighting was now desperate, and my comrade said to me, 'We shall have to shift those fellows with the bayonet . . .' pointing forwards. We still kept moving on at the encouragement of all of our mounted officers, and at last Gen Sir George Brown, Brig Codrington, and our Colonel, called upon us for one more grand push, and a charge brought us to the top of the hill.

Into the enemy battery we jumped – spiking the guns and bayoneting or shooting the gunners. Here we lost a great number of men, and by overwhelming numbers – we, the 23rd, 33rd, 95th were mobbed out of the battery and part of the way down the hill again. The 7th halted, fronted, and lay down, keeping up a withering fire upon the enemy at point blank range which told heavily upon their crowded ranks. We blazed into their huge columns as hard as we could load and fire. After about 20 minutes, help came close to hand as up came the Guards and the

Highlanders, with HRH the Duke of Cambridge leading them. They got a warm reception, but still pressed on up that fatal hill.

Up we went – Guards, Highlanders, and a number of other regiments of the 2nd Division, and with deafening shouts – the heights of Alma were soon ours. We now had time to count our loss, and had paid the penalty for leading the way, as we had left more than half our number dead or wounded upon the field. One of our Colours was gone, but the enemy had not got it as it was found upon the field, cut into pieces with a heap of dead and wounded all around it. At one stage the 7th Royal Fusiliers had confronted a whole Russian brigade, and kept them at bay until assistance came up.

The assembly was sounded, and our old Colonel exclaimed 'A Colour gone . . . where's my poor old Fusiliers . . .' and he cried like a child.

I then obtained leave to go down the hill. I had lost my comrade and was determined to find him if possible. I had no difficulty in tracing the way we had advanced, for the ground was covered with our poor fellows – in some places sixes and sevens, at others tens and twelves, and at others whole ranks were lying.

My comrade was dead close to the river. He had been shot in the mouth and left breast, and death must have been instantaneous. He could not have gone 100 yards from the spot where he had spoken to me. I sat down beside him and thought my heart would break as I recalled some of the things he had said to me. I buried him with the assistance of some of our men. We laid him in his grave, with nothing but an overcoat wrapped around him, and I left him with a heavy heart.

On returning up the hill, I provided myself with all the water bottles I could from the dead, in order to help revive the wounded as much as possible, and the sights all the way were sickening. The sailors were taking off the wounded as fast as possible, but many lay there all night just as they had fallen. I rejoined my regiment on the top of the hill, and was made Sergeant that night.

A Russian wounded General, in giving up his sword as a prisoner of war, stated that they had been confident of holding their positions for some days, no matter what force the Allies could bring against them, but added that they had come to fight men – and not devils!

On the morning of 5 November 1854, the enemy attacked us in our trenches in broad daylight. Our heavy guns gave it them and mowed down their dense columns by wholesale. Then after some stiff fighting, which lasted for more than an hour, they were compelled to beat a hasty retreat, our heavy guns sweeping lanes through them, and we plying them with musketry, both in front and flank. A sortie has no chance of success unless the besieging army can be taken by surprise, but no doubt this attack was made in order to distract our commander's attention from the vital point.

A memorable battle was then raging on our right rear, and by

At Alma, the Black Watch added yet another honour to their unrivelled history.

the shouts of the combatants and the tremendous firing, we knew that something very serious was going on, so as many of us as the General could spare were ordered to march as fast as our legs could carry us to the assistance of our comrades, then at the dreadful fight raging at Inkerman.

As we had just drubbed the enemy, our blood was up, but we were hungry, many of us having had nothing to eat for 24 hours, and were wet through to the skin. The fog was so dense that at times we could not see 20 yards. Our men were falling very fast, for the enemy were in overwhelming strength, particularly in guns. The Allies had been taken completely by surprise in the fog, and only the intrepidity of the picquets of the Light and Second Divisions had saved the entire Allied armies from an overwhelming disaster. The Russian rushes were hurled back time after time.

Our Fourth Division composed of the 20th, 21st, 57th, 63rd, 68th Regiments, and the 1st Bn Rifle Brigade, fought at a disadvantage, having been armed with the old Brown Bess musket, against the Needle Rifle, with which the enemy was armed. Our weapons were almost as much use as broom sticks.

Our loss was heavy – three Generals – and every mounted officer falling, but our men fought to the bitter end on the rocky ridge. At the fight that was now raging, a mere handful of Britons were contending. The yells of the massive Russian columns were answered by volley after volley – at point blank range, and then we closed upon them with the bayonet. We had no supports or reserves, but every man as fast as he could reach the field went straight at them, and so the fight went on hour after hour.

Our Guards were the admiration of the whole army, their deeds at Inkerman will never fade. Led by HRH the Duke of Cambridge, they repeatedly buried themselves in the Russian columns. They set a glorious example, and their daring, courage and obstinacy was grand. The terrible odds that they faced in this field justified their high prestige in the army. The 7th Royal Fusiliers however, were not behind when hard fighting had to be done.

It was here that I received two bayonet wounds, one in each

21st Royal North British Fusiliers hold the Barrier at the battle of Inkerman, Nov 1854.   Oil painting by Marjory Wetherstone

thigh, and would most likely have been despatched, but that help was close at hand, and the fellows who wounded me fell at once by the same weapon. Revolvers and bayonets told heavily that foggy morn, and our men were so short of ammunition that they pitched stones at the enemy. My legs were quickly bandaged, and after giving them a few parting shots at close quarters, I managed to hobble off the field, using my rifle – and another I picked up – as crutches.

As soon as it came my turn, I was attended to and my wounds dressed and bandaged. I remained for two days, and then a number of us were sent to Scutari. We were taken down to Balaclava on mules and received a good shaking, but eventually found ourselves on board an old steamer. It was a horrible scene, poor fellows having every description of wound, and many died before we left the harbour. We were packed on board and away we went. I was not very comfortable with poor fellows dying fast all round me. There were not sufficient medical officers to look after 50 men, much less three or four hundred.

After some four or five days we reached Scutari to find it so full of sick and wounded, that we were not allowed to land, and on we had to go to Malta . . . Describe the scene between decks I could not . . . In one month I was on my feet again, convalescent, and with plenty of good nourishment, I soon began to gather strength, and in January 1855 wanted to be off again, but I had to remain another month.

We reached the snug little harbour of Balaclava on the morning of 8 March 1855, and as usual found it crammed with shipping. We had to remain outside until our Captain obtained permission to enter, then we went in and landed. At once we marched to the front to the Light Division, and I again found myself in the midst of old chums, but what a difference! Poor half starved miserable looking men, mere wrecks of humanity – but with that unconquerable look about them.

The army was on half rations, half a pound of mouldy biscuit, and half a pound of salt junk (beef or pork). Coffee was issued, but in its raw green state, with no means of roasting it. No wood was to be had for fires, except a few roots that were dug up. Men would return to camp from the trenches soaked to the skin and ravenously hungry, when a half pound of mouldy biscuit would be issued, with salt junk so hard that one almost wanted a good hatchet to break it. The whole camp was one vast sheet of mud, the trenches in many places being knee deep. Men died at their posts from sheer exhaustion or starvation rather than complain, for if they reported themselves sick – the medical chests were empty. Amidst all these privations the enemy kept firing at them.

During the worst of the winter no two men were dressed alike, yet there was but little murmuring so long as the men could get sufficient to eat, and in the midst of all their troubles they were loyal to the backbone, and would sing aloud *God save the Queen*. I soon found my way into the trenches again, and had a very narrow escape from being taken in and done for. In the dark after posting some sentries, I took a wrong turn and went almost into the midst of the enemy.

We had now some hard hitting almost every day or night. We commenced gradually to creep up on to the doomed city of Sebastopol – here a bit and there a bit, shots being continually exchanged. All of the enemy's outworks had to be seized, and the taking of their rifle pits was fearful work, as it was all done with the bayonet in the darkness of night.

On the morning of Easter Monday the camp was shaken by the commencement of the second bombardment of Sebastopol, the French opening fire with some 350 heavy guns, and our people with about 220 guns and mortars. The enemy returned the fire with spirit, with some 600 of the heaviest guns and mortars – exclusive of their shipping. It was grand but awful, and the ground seemed to tremble beneath the terrible fire. I was in camp but felt compelled to go to the Victoria Redoubt to have a look.

The Russians frequently fired in salvoes against both us and our Allies, and this duel of artillery went on day after day, but it all ended in nothing – the enemy's works appearing to be as strong as before. As Sir George Brown once said – the longer we looked at the place – the uglier it got, and it would have to be taken in the old way – let the consequences be what they might – the bayonet must do what shot and shell could not . . . We mustered strongly in our old advanced works. The French went at the Mamelon in a masterly style, column after column, and as fast as one column melted away – another took its place.

Our turn came next at about 5.30pm, and away we went to attack the quarries with a dash, the 7th and 88th Regiment leading the way. It was England and Ireland side by side. The enemy might well look astonished, for our bayonets were soon in the midst of them – and they were routed out of the quarries – as our people set to work with pick and shovel as hard as men could work. The enemy came back repeatedly and tried to retake the position, but the Fusiliers and Connaught Rangers – assisted by detachments of various regiments of the Second and Light Divisions – on each occasion sent them reeling back. At times with no ammunition left, we had to do as we had done at Inkerman – pitch stones at them. I am not altogether certain that some of the 88th did not use their teeth!

On Sunday 17 June 1855 the third bombardment of Sebastopol opened with a tremendous crash, and from morning until night they kept it up as hard as they could load and fire. The very earth seemed to shake beneath the crash of guns. We all marched into the trenches full of hope that the grand and final struggle was about to commence. We were to lead the way, but it was not the first time we had done it, and from the Colonel downwards – all were in good spirits.

At 2am on 18 June – the 40th anniversary of Waterloo – the French went off for the Malakoff, which looked like a vast volcano, with a continual stream of men going at it. We then went off at a rapid pace, with our Colonel in front, sword in hand and revolver in the other. The enemy let us get well out into the open so that we had no cover, and then such a fire met us that the whole column seemed to melt away. Still on we went staggering beneath the terrible hail.

The Colonel advanced shouting 'Fusiliers – follow me. Prove yourselves worthy of your title!' I was close to him as he had ordered a number of active NCOs to keep up with him, and as we ran forward he shouted and waved his sword, then stopping he looked around at the truly awful scene – and fell dead. The Adjutant also fell, and almost every officer we had with us, but we pressed on until we were stopped by the chevaux-de-frise, and in front of that our poor fellows lay in piles. We were there met with a perfect hell of fire at about 150 yards from us, of grapeshot – shell – canister – and musketry, and could not return a shot: Our men could not advance – and would not retire, but were trying to pull down the barrier or chevaux-de-frise. The retire was sounding all over the field, but the men stood sullen and would not heed it. Our men and those of other regiments were fast dropping, and at last the remnant of the attacking column retired to the trenches amidst a storm of grape which nearly swept away whole companies at a time.

It must be confessed that we had received a good sound drubbing . . . We had been beaten – both French and English combined – and our men could hardly believe it. In returning to camp that morning, one could not get a civil answer from any of them. Out of my company which went into action with our Captain, two Lieutenants, four Sergeants, four Corporals, two Drummers, and 90 men – all that came out of it with a whole skin were 13 men besides myself . . . Number 3 Company returned to camp with nine men out of 96! My clothing was cut to pieces and I had no fewer than nine shot holes through my cap coat and trousers.

British troops in action against the Russian defenders of Sebastapol during the Crimean War.   Musée de l'Armee, Paris

On the morning of 5 September 1855, the last bombardment opened with a terrific shock, close upon 1,500 guns and mortars were now blazing away at each other, the earth trembling the while. We remained under awful fire all day, and just as we were looking out for our relief, an officer belonging to the Staff came up and asked me our strength. I was directed to furnish 100 men to repair the quarry battery. I was left in temporary charge as my officers had gone off on some duty. Shortly after I was directed to take the remainder of my party to the leading trench and remain there for further orders.

Something was in the wind – although everything was kept very quiet. To the front trench I went with my men, where we were about 200 yards from the Redan, and I had not been there long when an officer came up and wanted one officer – one Sergeant, and 30 men to go forward as scouts or sentries. I told him my strength and that I had no officer, and he at once went and obtained sufficient men from the 31st Regiment, then came back and talked to me until it got quite dark, which is what we were waiting for. He found that I well knew the ground, and was no stranger to the works. I requested that the men we were to take should be all picked men and not lads. We were to creep nearly up to the Redan – and it required men with all their wits about them – so a number were changed.

We crept over the top of the trench in the dark, and cautiously advanced about 80 yards, then commenced planting sentinals at about six yard intervals. We had done the job and the officer lay down beside me and gave me further orders, and then he crept back to the trench leaving me in command. My orders were not to attempt to hold my ground should the enemy attack, but to retire and give the alarm. After lying for some time we were attacked by an overwhelming force – and retired. They tried to cut us off and take us prisoners, but found us no easy matter. During our absence from the trench however, it had been filled with men of various regiments – and not knowing that we were out in front – they opened fire and we were caught between two fires. Some of our poor fellows were shot dead close to the trench by our own people. We called as loudly as possible but with the noise they could not hear us.

On collecting my party afterwards in the trench, I had to take all their names as most of them were strangers to me, and found that we had lost 19 men and two Corporals – out of 30 – yet it lasted only two or three minutes. The general officer inquired what regiment I belonged to and when I told him he expressed surprise, telling me that I had no business there, but ought to be in camp

resting – as there was some sharp work cut out for the Fusiliers in the morning! That was the first hint I got of the storming of the town, but the officer then directed me to go with an officer and another party – as I knew the ground – to show the officer where to place his men. I went out again, posted all the sentries, and then returned to the trench, in doing which I stumbled across a poor fellow lying wounded and brought him in the best way I could.

I reported myself to the General commanding, and he directed me to take my party home to camp at once. I reached the camp at about 1.30am and found that true enough – there was a warm job cut out for us – as we were to support the stormers moving immediately behind them. A still small voice told me that I should fall . . . I know that I tried to pray – begging the Lord to forgive my sins, and asked for His protecting arm around me . . . I then retired for a little rest until about 5am, when our men were up and there was no more sleep. I wrote a number of letters that morning for poor fellows – some of whom were laid low by mid-day.

We fell in at 9am, and a dram of rum was issued to each man as he stood in the ranks, all hands having previously been served with two days rations. There were a great number of very young men who had not much idea of the terrible work that lay before them, but there were others who knew only too well. The Redan and Malakoff appeared to be much stronger than when we first looked at them, although no fewer than 1,600,000 shot and shell had been hurled at them.

After remaining for a short time under arms, we marched off at about 9.30am. There was no pomp or martial music and the older soldiers were very quiet, but they had that set look of determination about them that speaks volumes. The bombardment was still raging on that terrible 8 September 1855. The stormers had all got into their places – they consisted of about 1,000 men of the Light and Second Divisions, and supports were formed up as closely as possible to them, and all appeared in readiness. The storming of a fortress is an awful task. There we stood and not a word was spoken, everyone seeming to be full of thoughts.

Sgt-Maj T. Gowing, 7th Royal Fusiliers, who fought at Alma, Inkerman, and at the siege of Sebastopol.

It was about 11.15am and our heavy guns were firing in such a way as I had never heard before. The batteries fired in volleys or salvoes as hard as they could load and fire, the balls passing a few feet above our heads, while the air seemed full of shell. The enemy was not idle for round shot, shells, grape, and musket-balls, were bounding and whizzing about us, and earth and stones were rattling about our heads like hail. We knew well that this could not last long before we advanced to the attack.

A number of the older hands – both officers and men – were smoking, and taking not the slightest notice as men were carried past dead, and others limping to the rear. We lost a number of men before it was time to go forward. We looked at each other in amazement for we were now – at about 11.30am – under such a fire as was without parallel. It was a warm reception for a number of lads that had just joined us, and it really seemed a pity to send them out to meet such a fire.

As the hour of 12 drew near, all hands were on the alert, and several who had gone through the whole campaign shook hands. At about 15 minutes before noon, our guns were brought to bear upon the chevaux-de-frise, and sent it into a thousand pieces, so that it should not stop us, as it had done on 18 June. Our numbers looked very small to attack such a place as the Redan, and the greater portion of the attacking and supporting columns – too young and inexperienced for such a fiery ordeal.

I was close to one of our Generals, who stood watch in hand, when at 12 midday the French drums and bugles sounded the charge – and they sprang forward – headed by the Zouaves, at the Malakoff. We in our advanced works had a splendid view, and the deafening shouts told that they were carrying all before them. They were now completely enveloped in smoke, but column after column kept advancing, and then at about 12.15 up went the proud flag of France – and now it was our turn.

We had waited for months, and as soon as the French flag was seen upon the Malakoff, our stormers sprang forward led by Col Windham, the Light Division leading – consisting of 300 men of the 90th, 300 of the 97th, and 400 of the 2Bn Rifle Brigade, along with detachments of the 2nd and Light Divisions, with a number of Blue Jackets carrying scaling ladders.

We the supports – moved forward to back the storming party, but anyone could see that we had not the same cool resolute men as at Alma and Inkerman, though the older men were determined to make the best of a bad job. Some of us old hands lit our pipes, and a brave young officer told me he would give all he was worth to be able to take it as comfortably as some of our people did – it was his first time under fire – he was as pale as death and shaking from head to foot – yet he bravely faced the foe. The poor boy . . . for he was not much more – requested me not to leave him, and he fell dead by my side just outside the Redan.

We advanced as quickly as we could, until we came to the foremost trench, when we leaped the parapet, then made a rush at the walls of the Redan. We had a clear run of over 200 yards under a murderous fire, and however anyone lived to pass seemed a miracle, for our poor fellows fell one upon the other. We had a front and two cross fires to meet and it seemed to me that we were rushing into the very jaws of death, but I for one reached the Redan without a scratch.

While standing on the brink of the ditch, I pondered for a moment how best to get into it, for it appeared to be about 20 feet deep, with many of our fellows at the bottom – dead and dying – with their bayonets sticking up. It was solved for me as our men came rushing on with a cheer, and in we all went – neck or nothing – scrambling up the other side the best way we could, and into the redoubt we charged. The fighting inside was all butt and bayonet – foot and fist. The enemy's guns were at once spiked. Some of the older hands did their best to gather sufficient men for one charge, but our fellows melted away almost as fast as they scaled those bloody parapets, from a cross fire the enemy brought to bear upon us from the rear of that work.

The struggle at the Redan lasted about an hour and a half, and we lost in all ranks some 2,472 men. Insufficient men had been sent – for 20,000 men should have been let loose. We should not have lost so many but many officers and men were killed when retiring, and we were but a handful when compared with the vast hordes of the enemy.

I was totally unconscious when taken from the Redan, and for some hours afterwards. At about 6pm I found myself in our front trench with a dead 33rd Regt man lying across me. I got him off the best way I could, and then tried to get up, but found that I could not stand, for I had almost bled to death. I had received five wounds in different parts of the body, my left hand being shattered, and two nasty wounds in the head.

Dr Hale VC did all he could for me, and I then had to remain

and take my chance of being carried to camp, where I arrived at about 7.30pm. My wounds were dressed and a cup of beef tea revived me. An Irishman named Welsh had saved my life . . . It turned out that he had noticed me fall, and when he found that he had to retire from the Redan, he carried me up to the ditch and let me slip in, and then with assistance got me out of it. He carried me back across that terrible 200 yards – being shot through both legs in doing so. Before he reached our leading trench, some other good Samaritan brought me in. He was a rough diamond – but every inch a soldier, and a good loyal subject.

Men were continually being brought back to camp with every description of wounds. The night of 8 September was long remembered as our camp was startled by a series of terrible explosions, and at length we discovered that the enemy was retiring under cover of the blowing up of the vast forts and magazines. The Redan was blown up – and a number of our men went up with it – but Sebastopol had fallen . . .

With Sgt Tim Gowing taken to hospital, the giving up of the Redan by the Russians and their loss of Sebastopol marked virtually the end of the campaign. A further winter was to be spent in the field before peace was declared in the spring of 1856. Sgt Gowing's recovery was understandably slow; in a letter to his parents dated 26 December 1855, he mentions that he is recovering but still convalescent. His arm was still in a sling and his hand still painful. The wounds to his head were rapidly healing.

The casualty figures quoted by him reveal that the 7th Royal Fusiliers lost over 600 men killed, wounded and missing during the campaign, but in the same period 600 men died of disease. As so often with soldiers – the bitterness of the fighting was soon forgotten, and Sgt Gowing records:

The Russians came into our camp in droves and we entertained them as friends, regaling them with the best that our stores could produce. An exchange of prisoners took place, some of our men having been held for upwards of 12 months.

The Russians made themselves at home – walking about with us arm in arm! We were repeatedly invited over to their camp to spend the day with them, and our NCOs and men went in numbers and were hospitably entertained.

Ceremonial and drill made a prompt reappearance, and a great review was organised by the English, French, Sardinians and Turks, in which a total of almost 300,000 troops took part. Most of the wounded were sufficiently recovered to take their places in the ranks, and the parade was of such length that it was said to have taken from morning until late night for the regiments to march past the saluting base. Preparations were then made for the army to return home, and Tim Gowing describes the moment:

We at last broke up camp and embarked for England, leaving those cold bleak inhospitable regions behind. The first night on board ship – homeward bound – what a night for reflection . . . I thought of the battles – of my comrade who lay buried beside the river Alma.

We arrived in Portsmouth Harbour on 26 July 1856 to a great welcome – and the dear children did not in many cases recognise their long bearded fathers.

Sgt Gowing soon went to India with his Regiment, continuing to serve there for over 18 years, and his book reveals in very sad detail the terrible circumstances of the Indian Mutiny.

He was made Colour Sergeant in April 1861, and became Acting Sergeant Major in 1863. On 26 July 1866 Tim Gowing was promoted to Sergeant Major, and in that happy position one would have wished to take our leave of him. Unfortunately whilst serving with the 5th Northumberland Fusiliers in Central India in 1869, the regiment was struck by cholera, and during a period of only two weeks – 149 men, 11 women, and 27 children died of the dreaded disease, amongst whom tragically – were six children of Sgt Gowing and his wife. Mrs Gowing was given up for dead at one stage, but slowly recovered.

In April 1872 Tim Gowing was appointed Garrison Sergeant Major of Allahabad, and he remained there until February 1876. At the age of 41 and after 22 years of service, Sgt-Maj Gowing was discharged from the army, and it is to be hoped that his busy research and writing reflected a long and happy retirement. Of his total service of 21 years 260 days, Tim Gowing's overseas service represented no less than 20½ years.

Copies of his book containing such stirring and moving memories, are still to be found on the shelves of good military book dealers.

Sgt-Maj Edwards, Scots Fusilier Guards, 1856. From Crown and Camera *by Roger Taylor and Frances Dimond, 1987:*
'Sergeant Major Edwards had acted since March 1852 as Drilling Sergeant to the Prince of Wales and Prince Alfred. After distinguished service in the Crimean War, Sergeant Major Edwards returned home and took part in the triumphant march of the Guards Regiments to Buckingham Palace, which was watched by the Queen and Royal Family on 9th July 1856.' Four wide chevrons with the Royal Coat of Arms superimposed – surely one of the most impressive arm badges of rank ever worn.

CHAPTER 6

Sergeant Major Stephen Wright, Coldstream Guards. The Boer War

The glorious reign of Queen Victoria began before the first Sikh War and saw the development of the greatest empire the world had known. British troops fought and were garrisoned in many countries of the world. The Crimean War had been fought and had revealed many terrible truths about the conditions of service, and about leadership.

Reforms were slowly being introduced, but the lash remained the common penalty for most offences. Flogging parades were held regularly for regiments to witness the punishment of offenders, and whilst the Sergeant Major did not actually mete out the strokes, he was responsible for the correctness of the arrangements and for the parading of the men.

The regimental system had long depended upon such punishments and it was widely held that discipline would fail without it. Commission after review commission recommended not only its continuation, but expressed the view that punishment should remain in full view of the regiment, to provide an example. Public opinion would eventually force change upon parliament, and whilst the branding of deserters was abolished in the early 1870s, and flogging in 1881, these penalties were replaced by long periods of imprisonment with hard labour.

Many changes occurred in style of uniform and insignia, and the arm badge of rank of the Sergeant Major was particularly subject to alteration. By 1859 the Queen's Regulations stipulated that a crown badge be worn above the four chevrons. This brought uniformity within most cavalry and infantry regiments, but did not include the Guards. The Sergeant Major of the Guards had in the past been employed as extra staff for the marshalling of carriages, reception of guests, and general security duties associated with royal events, and were given the title Marshals of the Court. They were allowed the distinction of wearing the Royal Coat of Arms as their badge of rank, and this resulted in a period of some 20 years during which the Sergeant Majors of the Guards wore their four wide chevrons with the Royal Coat of Arms superimposed. As shown by the photograph of Sgt-Maj Edwards of the Scots Fusilier Guards, this badge of rank was one of the most impressive, especially as during that period the insignia was worn on each arm. Possibly in those days of close encounter in the field such badges would prove to be too distinctive.

In 1869 the chevrons were moved to the cuff below the elbow, and were worn point upwards with the crown mounted above, as shown in the photograph of Sgt-Maj T. Gowing of the 7th Royal Fusiliers. During the 1870s the impressive chevrons were discarded from the badges of rank of the infantry Sergeant Majors and only the crown remained. In the Guards regiments the Royal Coat of Arms alone was worn on the right upper arm.

In 1881 the Secretary of State for War granted Warrant rank to certain Staff Sergeants, including Regimental Sergeant Majors, Bandmasters, Master Gunners, and others, when previously only the Conductors of Supplies and Stores had been termed Warrant Officers.

In 1881 young Stephen Wright enlisted in the Coldstream Guards from the 1st Volunteer Battalion, South Staffordshire Regiment, in which he had spent one year. The stories of the Army's campaigns in Ashanti, of the last of the Kaffir wars, and more recently the defence of Rorke's Drift by the detachment of the 2nd Warwickshire Regiment, against the Zulus (after the regiment had fought almost to extinction at Isandlhwana) had much influenced his childhood and early manhood.

Before enlistment Stephen Wright worked as a sawyer, then in a local Birmingham office, where he had shown much promise. He desired an army career however, and following his year as a volunteer, was attested for the Coldstream Guards on his nineteenth birthday – the 26 September 1881. He reported to the Guards Depot at Caterham a few days later, where RSM S. White, Coldstream Guards, was very much in charge.

Of medium height and build, with brown eyes and dark complexion, Wright's confident manner and superior voice initially attracted the attention of the rougher element of the recruits, but he quickly proved that he was more than capable of looking after himself, and was soon accepted as a leader. After training he was posted to the 2nd Bn, Coldstream Guards, and within months went on active service with the battalion in Egypt, taking part in the highly successful battle of Tel-el-Kebir. It was during this campaign that field punishments were introduced to replace flogging or imprisonment for some less serious offences, the offender being chained or roped to the wheel of a gun limber for prescribed periods.

Four months later the 2nd Battalion returned home, and Stephen Wright was promoted to Lance Corporal, and then in May to Corporal. Three years later the British Empire

RSM Stephen Wright during service in the Boer War 1899-1902.
Coldstream Guards HQ.

celebrated Queen Victoria's Golden Jubilee amidst great royal pageantry.

Life settled down into barrack and ceremonial routine for the battalion, and Cpl Wright soon became Lance Sergeant, and then in 1888 Sergeant. During this period he gained a Sergeant Instructors certificate at the Hythe School of Musketry, and later qualified in riding and field works. He also completed two tours as a Drill Instructor at the Guards Depot. From January 1889 to April 1890 he was made Acting Sergeant Major of the School of Instruction for Officers of the Militia and Voluntary Forces, at Wellington Barracks.

Following this prestigious appointment he was promoted to Drill and Colour Sergeant. His improved circumstances enabled him to marry Harriett Greening on 1 July 1891, and they were placed on the married establishment. On 3 April 1895 the great day came when Stephen Wright was promoted as Sergeant Major of the 2nd Bn Coldstream Guards. On his first parade however, a senior officer – perhaps unaware of his promotion – addressed him as 'Sergeant' Wright, and with great dignity Stephen Wright corrected him. 'Sergeant Major Sir . . .' The officer promptly apologised, and later admitted that it

was the first time he had made such a mistake and the first time he had ever needed to apologise to a subordinate.

Two months after becoming Sergeant Major, Stephen Wright and his wife were blessed with a baby son, Warren Stephen, and for the next four years the family continued their regimental life and routine. In 1897 the British Empire celebrated the Queen's Diamond Jubilee with thousands of troops from the Colonies attending the huge procession.

During 1899 Britain built up its forces in Natal, South Africa, in preparation for further operations in Matabeleland, but President Paul Kruger of the Boer republics of Transvaal and Orange Free State issued an ultimatum that the forces be dispersed under threat of war, and when this was refused the Boers declared war upon Britain. They had a small but highly trained army of particularly good shots, well equipped with artillery of German origin. Upon declaration of war the Boers moved into Natal; soon British troops were under siege in the towns of Ladysmith, Kimberley and Mafeking.

Sgt-Maj and Mrs Wright were expecting their second child when orders came for the 2nd Bn Coldstream Guards, with many other regiments, to prepare for war service in South Africa. The necessary kit was issued and the battalion marched through the streets of London amidst great excitement to entrain for Southampton. Only nine days had passed since declaration of war when the battalion embarked for Cape Town. The 1st Bn Coldstream Guards was stationed at Gibraltar, and also left within days for South Africa.

The 2nd Bn arrived at Cape Town on 12 November 1899, and within a short period was advancing as part of the Guards Brigade – consisting of Grenadier, Coldstream and Scots Guards – towards the beseiged town of Kimberley. 11 days later both battalions of the Coldstream Guards were engaged in the battle of Belmont, where they suffered light casualties.

On 28 November, the battalions were roused at 4am, and marched towards the Modder River Station where they would halt for breakfast. Three hours later the Guards – in advance of the force – were within sight of the station, when a sudden blast of rifle and artillery fire hit them. The Guardsmen flung themselves down and were forced by the accuracy of the Boer fire to remain where they were for many hours in the heat of the sun. Casualties began to mount. British artillery came in to action and efforts were made to outflank the Boer position. At one stage of the battle, a charge of ammunition carts was carried out, and the service record of Sgt-Maj Wright reveals that he 'showed great coolness and was of great value at a critical time.' At last as night approached a force successfully crossed the river to threaten the Boer flank, but when an attack was made upon their main position at dawn it was discovered that the Boers had withdrawn under cover of darkness.

Lord Methuen mentioned the following men of the 2nd

Bn in his dispatches. Capt-Adj J. McL. Steele, Sgt-Maj S. Wright, Drill Sgts J. Plackett and G. Price, L-Cpl A. Webb, and Ammunition Cart driver Matthew Thomas. Sadly the commanding officer of the 2nd Bn, Lt-Col H. R. Stopford was killed, with another officer and 10 other ranks. One officer and 58 other ranks were wounded.

Lord Methuen advanced against Magersfontein, but during the worst week in the campaign – from 10-16 December – not only was his force defeated, but Gen Gatacre's force at Stormberg was similarly driven back, and Gen Sir Redvers Buller's main army was defeated at Colenso. The Guards Brigade returned to the Modder River area until mid February 1900, when FM Viscount Roberts took command of the army, and with reinforcements began to advance on all fronts. Gen Buller relieved Ladysmith on 28 February, and in mid May came the famous headlines *Mafeking relieved!* Col Baden-Powell

Stephen Wright when Quartermaster c1905.   R. G. Harris

had conducted a brilliant seven month defence of the town which gained him great fame.

The 2nd Battalion with the Guards Brigade took part in the actions leading to the capture of Paadeburg, Poplar Grove, Dresfontein, Bloemfontein, Johannesburg, Diamond Hill and Belfast. At one stage of the advance the 2nd Bn made a forced march of 43 miles in 27¼ hours, a tremendous performance, especially because they were on half rations for the latter part of the march. At about the time that Sgt-Maj Wright received word from his wife that a baby daughter had been born, the 2nd Bn led the advance of Lord Robert's army into Pretoria.

With the Transvaal capital of Pretoria occupied, the Boers were driven into Portuguese territory and Kruger went into exile. The campaign changed character and the Boer forces conducted a long guerrilla war which lasted a further two years. In late September 1900 when the 1st and 2nd Bn Coldstream Guards, were returning to Pretoria from operations by rail, the train was derailed and attacked by a Boer force, and in the ensuing action seven men of the 2nd Bn were killed and 12 wounded. Lord Roberts

RSM Stephen Wright, Coldstream Guards, 1903.   Guards Magazine

returned home to Britain in December, and his Chief of Staff FM Earl Kitchener took command, slowly but ruthlessly bringing the guerrilla war to an end.

Queen Victoria was not to see the return of her troops from South Africa, as she died on 22 January 1901. When the army came home in October 1902 it was to an Edwardian Britain where technological advances had continued at great pace, and automobiles were beginning to share the roads with horsedrawn vehicles, with obvious implications for the army.

Sgt-Maj Wright saw his two and a half year old daughter for the first time, and as she had been born only five months after the Modder River action, she had been named Gladys Modder Wright. His son, Warren, had grown from a toddler to an active seven year old who had been eagerly awaiting the return of his soldier father.

For three years RSM Wright returned to the regimental life of the barracks, and then he was commissioned as Lieutenant Quartermaster, when his duties significantly included the catering arrangements for the battalion. He developed particularly strong views in relation to both cooking and catering and dealt strictly with any slackness on the part of the cooks, or with any attempt by the suppliers to deliver inferior foodstuffs. For 12 years his reputation increased as the battalion enjoyed the benefits of his meticulous standards. He was one of the Quartermasters to remain clear of the scandals before the First World War, relating to illicit dealings with army contractors.

Only days after the First World War commenced, the British Expeditionary Force embarked for France, and the Guards Brigade was soon in action. Lt-QM Wright served through the early battles of Mons, the Marne, the Aisne and Ypres, but then in November 1914, he received a surprising posting home which reflected the high reputation he had gained for his sound knowledge of catering. He was recalled to help with the organising of the training of many thousands of cooks enlisting to feed the huge Volunteer Army of men forming in response to Kitchener's appeals.

During the following four years Stephen Wright worked non-stop to prepare the hundreds of field kitchens required, never taking leave or any time for sickness. He was given honorary rank of Major, and was largely responsible for the wholesome food available to the millions of serving soldiers.

In 1917, when food supplies became critical, he devised many dishes in which potato was used in place of flour. In recognition of his efforts Stephen Wright was promoted Major in January 1918, and then Temporary Lieutenant Colonel three months later. He was classed as Inspector of Catering, and continued happily in this capacity after the war ended.

At the age of 58 he retired from the regular army, but almost immediately was employed by the War Office as Civilian Inspector of Army Catering, and he continued with his task of regulating the soldiers diets as before. His

Lt-Col Retired Stephen Wright when Mayor of Windsor, 1929 and 1931.   Coldstream Guards HQ

diet sheets were in use throughout the British Army for many years.

Lt-Col Wright, or Old Steve as he was affectionately known, held his important role until 1927, bringing about many reforms in army catering, but at the age of 65 he decided to concentrate upon other things. He became Mayor of Windsor in 1929 and 1931, and was also a Councillor in the Berkshire County Council. His local service in the community included work in the Courts as a Magistrate, and one can well imagine his great care with deserving cases and stern attitude with the hardened offender.

After a lifetime of service to his country and local community, Col Stephen Wright CBE DCM CC JP died in the King Edward VII Hospital in Windsor on 24 February 1936, at the age of 73.

CHAPTER 7

RSM Harold Scott trains the Second Bradford Pals

Harold Scott, like many men of firm character, gave a lifetime of service to his local community and country, firstly through the ranks as a soldier and then as a policeman. He retired at the end of 1934 as a police inspector. During the First World War he was the RSM of the Second Bradford Pals, the 18th Service Battalion, The Prince of Wales's Own West Yorkshire Regiment. They were formed in February 1915 as part of Lord Kitchener's New Army, the largest force of volunteers ever raised in this country, and destined to go to the Western Front to take part in the Big Push.

Harold Scott was born in 1884 and was brought up in Morley, just south of Leeds. He worked for a time as a mechanic's labourer, but when old enough to join the army, decided to enlist in the King's Own Yorkshire Light Infantry. A pleasant looking young man of 5ft 9in, with grey eyes and fair brown hair, he had a steady and serious personality. In August 1901, he transferred to the Coldstream Guards, and signed on for seven years with the Colours and five on the reserve.

His training at the Guards Depot, Caterham, was under RSM J. Boyd, Coldstream Guards, and this four month period took him beyond the time for campaigning in South Africa. He was posted to the 1st Bn Coldstream Guards, on 2 December 1901, and was promoted to Lance Corporal within six months. His postings took him back to the Guards Depot for a time, but the remainder of his Colour service was spent with the 1st Bn.

Four magnificent RSMs of the 1890s

Top left: Sgt-Maj W. G. A. Garton, Grenadier Guards, enlisted at the age of twelve years, and became RSM of the 3rd Bn on 9 Jan 1890.

Top right: Sgt-Maj A. Best, Coldstream Guards, enlisted 1883 and made RSM in 1894.

Far left: Sgt-Maj F. Walker, Scots Guards, enlisted 1883 and made RSM in 1892.

Left: Sgt-Maj J. Fowles, enlisted in 1879 in the Grenadier Guards, and was made RSM in 1890. As RSM of the 1st Bn he once marched the battalion on to the frozen Serpentine only to hear ominous cracking sounds! There followed two quick orders 'Break step' and 'Scatter!' and an embarrassing spectacle was averted. Upon the formation of the Irish Guards he transferred as Quartermaster, and on commencement of WW1 went on to serve as Lt-Col in the 21st London Regt. Guards Magazine

Harold Scott completed his service with the Colours as a Sergeant, having remained in this country throughout. On release he almost immediately joined the Bradford City Police Force, and served as a constable within that area for over six years until the First World War brought a halt to his police career. He married his wife Jane in December 1910, and completed his period as a reservist in 1913.

He was now aged 30 and employed in a reserved occupation so consequently his call up was deferred for a time, but he accompanied Capt A. W. Brown who drilled the first volunteers for the army, in the Peel Park Drill Hall in Bradford. Within five days of the declaration of war, Britain's small regular army mobilised its reservists and embarked for France.

Germany's massive invasion found the British Expeditionary Force in position at Mons, where its first shots of the war were fired – rapid well aimed shots, which caused the German massed infantry enormous losses. During the following year the regular army expended almost the whole of its strength at Le Cateau, and in the battles of the Marne and the Aisne. Transferred to positions in Flanders, it continued to hold the attacks of the Germans in the first battle of Ypres, but by spring 1915 the trained battalions of the Territorial Army were becoming absorbed into the line. By the end of that year it would be the turn of Kitchener's New Volunteer Army to be introduced to the Western Front.

From the beginning of the war men flocked to the recruiting depots in such vast numbers that the regimental system could not absorb them. Men with any previous experience of military training were at a premium and were immediately made into instructors. Later these men would become part of the main structure of the new battalions, serving as Officers, Warrant Officers and NCOs.

A particularly attractive feature of the recruiting drive, was for men from towns or organisations to enlist together to form 'Pals Battalions' and many towns were quick to seek War Office approval for the forming of Citizens Army Leagues so that they could raise local battalions. Each league would then bear the cost of clothing, feeding and training, its own volunteers until they were ready as a unit to be accepted into the army.

A Bradford Citizen Army League was formed on 20 September 1914, with the Lord Mayor as chairman. Men who had worked, camped and attended organisations together, hurried to enlist in the First Bradford Pals

Harold Scott when a young Coldstream Guardsman c1901.

Mrs Margaret Mawby

Battalion. A number of youngsters of 16 and 17 enlisted by falsifying their ages for fear of being left behind, and soon these young men were training seriously, in company with older family men.

At first the volunteers paraded twice each day in civilian clothing, to be drilled in the local parks, or on any space available. Platoons and companies were formed and the battalion was then designated – the 16th Bn, Prince of Wales's Own West Yorkshire Regiment. Soon the men were issued with Melton blue uniforms, and although they remained living at home, the unit of approximately 1,000 men began to take on the appearance of an army battalion

Many local policemen had earlier served in the army and they helped in their spare time to drill the volunteers until they were themselves released from the force to join the ranks of the battalion as NCOs and instructors. As a former Coldstream Guardsman NCO, Harold Scott was often to be seen drilling the larger formations, and it was quite an experience for those on parade for the first time. A friend of Albert Jowett (former Bradford Pal) was to admit to him after being drilled that he was – 'frightened to death of Mr Scott' adding 'Oh – he had a word of command . . you could hear him from here to Wigan!'

For quiet unsophisticated family men these were

Capt G. S. Blagborough and Lt Robinson drill volunteers in Manningham Park in 1914. Major Blagborough, when serving as Second in Command of 16th Bn 'First Bradford Pals' was killed in action in France, 23 Dec 1916.

George Martin, and Stephen Kerry of Bradford Art Galleries and Museums

Sgt Harold Scott, Coldstream Guards c1904. Mrs Margaret Mawby

extraordinary times – with smart blue uniforms, marching men with drums beating, and the high pitched orders of officers and NCOs ringing out in the local parks. Many people crowded to watch, relatives and friends proudly pointing out their men. These enthusiastic people cheering and patting the men on their backs, were a major factor in encouraging others to join. Most of the men of military age and many under, wanted to enlist, and their only fear was that the war might end before they could get into uniform.

After three months of training, the First Bradford Pals Battalion was marched to the Town Hall square in January 1915, and following inspection by the Lord Mayor, departed to Skipton, where the battalion was to be accommodated in a purpose built camp. For many men this was their first real departure from home. Hardly had they marched off when plans were laid for the forming of a Second Bradford Pals, and eager volunteers were ready to fill the ranks. In February 1915, the 18th Battalion, Prince of Wales's Own West Yorkshire Regiment was raised, and instead of remaining at home, the men were housed in a tented camp in Bowling Park.

Harold Scott continued to help with the training of the volunteers, and on 18 February received a warrant signed by the Secretary of State for War, confirming his entry into the army as WO1. In 1915 the rank of Warrant Officer had been divided into two classes by army order, the Warrant Officer Class One being authorised to wear a new small badge of the Royal Arms on the right arm cuff, and the Warrant Officer Class Two, a Crown in the same position.

The Regimental Sergeant Majors of the Brigade of Guards in fact decided to retain their large Royal Arms badge of rank, which had strong links with their earlier duties as Marshals of the Court. The War Office refused to allow the cost and so the Brigade of Guards arranged for the large badge to be made and paid for privately.

As RSM of the 18th Bn, Harold Scott was to receive a commendation for the speed of his preparation of the battalion, and its smartness on parade. Crowds of relatives continued to visit the area of the tented camp, but after three months of training the volunteers marched off to a camp near Ripon. As great crowds watched their departure the reality dawned that serious soldiering was about to begin.

One of the first things to be arranged by RSM Scott was for his younger brother Alfred to be claimed from the 16th Bn, so that they could serve together, and for much of the war Alfred was to serve in the 18th Bn as a CQMS. A former Bradford Pal, Tony Miller, remembers those early days:

Well, it was pretty rough! Left right, left right, and all that carry on . . . Mr Scott was our RSM and when you were on parade – you were *on parade* with him. Off parade he was a gentleman and never swore at us or anything like that. He used to wear a Sam Browne belt and we would think that he was an officer, so we would start to salute him. He'd say 'Use your eyesight . . . watch what you're doing!'

In September 1915, the 16th and 18th Bns joined the 15th POW Own West Yorkshire Regiment (Leeds Pals) and the 18th Durham Light Infantry (Durham Pals) to form the 93rd Brigade. After eight months of preparation, the men were now march trained, could shoot straight, were smart and soldierly, and were keen to show their worth. They anticipated a swift introduction to trench warfare on the Western Front, where losses remained heavy – but the brigade was surprisingly issued with tropical kit, and in December the men were placed into trains for Liverpool where the brigade was embarked on the troopship *Empress of Britain*. The forces in Egypt were at this time being strengthened to meet a possible threat from the Turks, once the Allied forces in Gallipoli had been evacuated.

The journey of the convoy through the Mediterranean was not without incident, as the *Empress of Britain* collided with and sank a French steamer off Malta. All but two of the crew and passengers were rescued from the steamer, but it was necessary for the battalions aboard the troopship to go to boat stations. The GOC later commended the troops for their calm and orderly conduct. Then off Cyprus a surfaced U boat was sighted and the ship went to action stations. Two shots were fired from the troopship's gun, and the U boat dived. Another U boat was later seen, but this also dived.

The brigade disembarked at Port Said and for several weeks the troops were used inland to maintain and extend defensive positions, but in early 1916 the Turkish threat ceased, and the men of the 93rd Brigade learned that they were to go to the Western Front to join the preparations for the long awaited Big Push. The Allied offensive which was confidently expected to push the Germans back out of France and win the war.

Much of the brigade sailed from Port Said on 29 February 1916, but the main party of the 18th Bn, in which Headquarter Company was included, left in early March. Arriving at Marsailles on 15 March, the party began a long journey by troop train which gradually became colder as they travelled northwards. At one stage they passed trainloads of wounded French soldiers travelling south to recuperate from the terrible fighting at Verdun.

After some 500 miles of slow and cramped travel, the men began to look out upon country in which there were more frequent signs of war, with tented camps, parks of stores, and transport moving along the roads, but above all, the constantly audible grumbling and rumbling of gunfire. At last the tedious journey ended at Pont Remy, a railhead near Abbeyville. With relief the party left the train and were marched off through the cold and snow to Citerne, where welcome billets awaited them. Here the party was reunited with the rest of the battalion, and order was quickly regained.

The 31st Division was composed wholly of volunteers enlisted from the northern counties, as follows:

92nd Brigade
10th Bn East Yorkshire Regiment (Hull
  Commercials)

The tented camp of the 18th Bn in Mitchell Fields near Bowling Park Bradford. Stephen Kerry of the Bradford Art Galleries and Museums

11th Bn East Yorkshire Regiment (Hull
  Tradesmen)
12th Bn East Yorkshire Regiment (Hull
  Sportsmen)
13th Bn East Yorkshire Regiment (Hull T'others)
93rd Brigade
15th Bn West Yorkshire Regiment (Leeds Pals)
16th Bn West Yorkshire Regiment (First Bradford
  Pals)
18th Bn West Yorkshire Regiment (Second
  Bradford Pals)
18th Bn Durham Light Infantry (Durham Pals)

94th Brigade
11th Bn East Lancs Regiment (Accrington Pals)
12th Bn York and Lancs Regiment (Sheffield City
  Bn)
13th Bn York and Lancs Regiment (First Barnsley
  Pals)
14th Bn York and Lancs Regiment (Second
  Barnsley Pals)

The Divisional Pioneer Battalion was the 12th Bn KOYLI (Halifax Pals). The Division had a strength of over 12,000 men, all of excellent spirit and education, and now physically fit.

RSM Harold Scott was ordered to arrange parties of half company strength to be conveyed to the front line 25 miles away, in order to provide a short period of experience. The parties approached with the rumble of gunfire sounding ever closer until the sharp crack of individual batteries became clear. On through the artillery belt, along the assembly and reserve lines until they came forward to the front line trenches. Here for a very brief time they experienced the stark contrasts, of relative quietness – during which all kinds of domestic chores could be undertaken – and the sharp moments of reality when enemy shells whined and exploded their way into the trenches.

On 25 March, both 16th and 18th Battalions set off for the Beaumont Hamel sector, marching roughly 10 miles each day, and resting in villages along the way. Six days later the 18th Bn arrived at Beaussart where A Company entered the front line for 24 hours further experience. During the following days all of the companies received similar spells of activity.

On 18 April the CO, Lt-Col E. C. H. Kennard, left the battalion for England, to be replaced by Acting Lt-Col M. N. Kennard, whilst Acting Maj H. F. G. Carter became Second in Command. On the following day the battalion took over a sub-sector of trenches south of the Serre Road, facing the Redan Ridge and the Quadrilateral Redoubt. This was their first front line responsibility and the take over from the 18th Bn Durham Pals was completed without

The 16th Bn 'First Bradford Pals' leaving Bradford for further training, 15 Jan 1915. Many appear to be still wearing civilian clothing, whilst others are dressed in Melton Blue uniforms.
Stephen Kerry of the Bradford Art Galleries and Museums

difficulty. The activity must have been noticed because flares were soon fired overhead by the enemy, and when mortar and artillery fire followed, the battalion lost the first two of its volunteers killed.

Next day the officers and NCOs went through their particular duties and RSM Scott could test out the organisation of the ammunition and food supplies. The battalion busied itself with repairs to the trenches, whilst patrols went forward and returned to report that some of the wire in front was in need of repair. The following day, as shelling continued from both sides, work went on with the draining of trenches. Later that night as it fell quiet, the men listened to the sounds of enemy transport moving behind the German lines. During the next three days shelling continued and as a number of rifle grenades were fired upon them, patrols were sent forward to make sure that nearby shell craters were not being occupied by the enemy.

Two tours of duty were spent in the front line, with the loss of two men killed and 17 wounded, before preparations began for the huge Allied offensive. Orders were received for parties of men to attend lectures and periods of special instruction, and then amidst great activity and movement, the battalion was marched to Gezaincourt on 20 June, along roads packed with transport, troops and guns. On the following day most of the officers and NCOs were taken over a large area of ground which had been fortified to represent the German front line, and here the timings and

Bradford Recruiting HQ Feb 1915.   Stephen Kerry of Bradford Art Galleries and Museums

formations of the coming attack were explained.

The 18th Bn was paraded in full on 22 June, then marched to the training ground where instructors guided the men over the ground. No running forward or cheering was allowed, but a slow methodical advance intended to 'occupy the German trenches'. No grouping or going to ground was required, but a steady line with spaces maintained. Full equipment would be worn and certain men were detailed to carry extra items, such as wire cutters, spare belts of barbed wire, extra ammunition, spades, picks and so on. Officers and WOs were to wear the same uniforms as the troops, with badges of rank worn only at the shoulders.

Next day the battalion was paraded in full equipment, and on this occasion the whole brigade advanced slowly across the training area in steady lines with dressing maintained. Maj-Gen G. Wanless O'Gowan later addressed the brigade, probably to explain that the enemy lines would be pulverized by artillery bombardment prior to the offensive.

At about this time, two men of the battalion deserted, and Herbert Bradley of the 18th Bn explained (in an interview with Stephen Kerry of the Bradford Art Galleries and Museums in 1981):

They knew what was coming. They were caught at Boulogne, but they got a chance to go over the top on their own, you know. Alf Scott's brother was the RSM. He gave these two fellows chance to go over the top and give themselves up, be killed or taken prisoner you see . . . but they wouldn't go, so they were shot.

The RSM would not of course have authority to make such a bargain with the men, but he would carry out the orders of his CO in this respect. The sad outcome suggests not only that the ultimate penalty applied just as strongly to volunteer units, but that RSM Scott was required to detail the firing party.

On 25 June a massive bombardment of the German trench system began, which represented at that time the most intense barrage ever used. Every gun available fired a non-stop stream of shells and the German line disappeared beneath great clouds of smoke and exploding shells. The incessant crack and bark of gunfire could be heard all over the Western Front and far back behind the lines, the rumble of the barrage was even heard in some parts of England.

Working parties urgently pumped and drained water from the network of assembly trenches and patrols edged forward into no-mans-land each night when the artillery barrage was lifted, in order to assess the damage to the German wire and trenches. Reports would differ, with some sectors smashed beyond recognition, others reporting wire intact and trenches relatively undamaged. The following day's bombardment would concentrate upon areas requiring saturation, and as gas attacks were added, it was difficult to imagine anyone being able to survive in the enemy lines. The troops were then notified that zero hour for the advance was to be 7.30am on 29 June 1916.

The huge plan of attack called for tremendous organisation in order that waves of advancing infantry arrived against specific areas, and follow up troops exploited the gains. Nothing less than a complete breakthrough would end the deadlock of trench warfare and create opportunities for the enemy to be pushed back out of France.

The task of the 31st Div was to take and fortify the village of Serre, and to incline left to protect the advance of the 4th and 29th Divisions. The brigade and battalion objectives were clearly detailed, and the first battalion of the brigade to advance would be the 15th West Yorkshire Regiment (Leeds Pals).

As the bombardment continued to pound the German line, word came at 2pm on 28 June, that zero hour had been put back for 48 hours to 1 July. With only 31 hours remaining before zero hour, Lt M. Clough was detailed to lead a fighting patrol from the 18th Bn in order to inspect the German wire and trenches for damage. The following report describes what he found:

Party left our front line trenches as scheduled at 12.28am. Advance was slow owing to numerous shell holes and flares. Apparently our party was seen almost as soon as we had left our own trenches, for they seemed prepared for us, and we were met by bombs when between 25 and 30 yards from their trenches.

They sent up a single green rocket and formed a barrage of hand grenades in front of us and trench mortars and artillery behind us. The trenches seemed fairly knocked about and the wire was cut where we were in sufficient quantity to allow of the passage of troops. Their trenches seemed very full of men and apparently very deep.

Finding we could not get forward, I brought my party back as well and as soon as I could. This took some two hours. As far as I can judge at present my casualties are about 10 killed and 12 wounded. At present two officers, Lt F. Watson and 2nd Lt Worsnip, are missing. I have been slightly wounded myself in two places. Our HE shells were all dropping a little over half-way between our line and the German line, and quite 20 yards short of their wire, and this was taking place during our scheduled hour for the raid. My watch was synchronised with an Artillery officer.

In addition to those killed and wounded (two of whom died of their wounds) nine were missing, and only nine men of the patrol returned unscathed. The Germans were obviously watchful and alert, and the report of only slight damage must have given Lt-Col M. N. Kennard a fearful period of anxiety. Reveille was early the following morning and all officers, the RSM and NCOs were busily supervising the donning of equipment and the mass of extra items to be carried. Iron rations and water were distributed, and the 18th Bn set off for the front line.

The approach through the village of Colincamps was slow due to congestion on the roads and the constant enemy shelling. The hours passed as the 93rd Brigade worked its way forwards through the communication trenches, and it was 4.30am, only three hours off zero hour, before the 18th Bn was finally positioned in the forward trenches. Some anger was raised when a warning was circulated that 'battle police' had been ordered to shoot anyone who refused to go over the top at zero hour. The men of the 31st Volunteer Division considered such measures to be unnecessary on for them.

With the sky already light, the bombardment reached a crescendo as shells rained down upon the German positions, but still the enemy returned fire which crashed into trenches packed with waiting men. A and D Companies were ready in Dunmow trench, whilst C and B waited in Languard trench, and now a welcome issue of rum was distributed which helped to settle mounting nerves. As zero hour approached, the bombardment changed in sound from artillery fire to that of trench mortars, and the long planned and carefully rehearsed Big Push was about to begin.

CHAPTER 8

The Bradford Pals on 1 July 1916

7.21am and the first two companies of men from the 15th Bn Leeds Pals rose from their trenches and began to form line as if on parade, and then slowly advanced but men already began to fall. The sound of enemy machine-guns could be heard and more men in the line crumpled and fell, until the line took on the appearance more of groups. Within moments of zero hour, and with only 100 yards covered, many of the Leeds Pals were already strewn dead across the ground.

Without hesitation the second wave arose from Leeds trench, and attempted to form line as they had previously rehearsed. Machine-guns had not been chattering then however. Now the fire transferred from the front groups to the second wave and these men too began to fall. The line started forward but was almost immediately decimated, and with gaps forming, groups came together for support. Officers and NCOs in the lead fell but the volunteers crouched and still continued forwards.

Minutes later at 7.30am, shrill whistles sounded along the north and south Monk trenches situated behind the Leeds trench, and with officers leading, the men of A and C Companies of the First Bradford Pals and D Company of the Durham Pals, clambered out and began to form line in a hail of shell and machine-gun fire. B and D Companies rose from the Bradford trench into the same inferno of fire. Sgt-Maj G. Cussins, who went out with B Company HQ, is recorded as saying:

A lot of men never got off the ladder, but fell back from the parapet. On getting out of the trenches to take up our positions in front, we lost heavily through the line to shrapnel – machine-gun – and rapid rifle fire. By the time we attained our position in front of Bradford trench most of the officers and NCOs and many men had been knocked out. We advanced and continued to advance until the Company Headquarters with which I was, found ourselves in front of the battalion – all in front having been hit. We found ourselves then halfway between Leeds trench and the front line. In our advance we passed the majority of A Company laying killed or wounded. I found in the front line a good many men of the 15th Bn West Yorks Regiment, and what was left of the DLI Company who were attached to us. Also a few of the KOYLI. I found no officers or NCOs of these regiments, or of my own regiment.

D Company of the 16th Bn fared a little better initially, and reached the front line trenches without heavy casualties, but on venturing across no-mans-land, the machine-guns found them and many men and all four officers were lost. Very little communication was possible because every man in Battalion Headquarters had become a casualty.

In Dunmow and Languard trenches, the 18th Bn, Second Bradford Pals waited for their scheduled time of advance, and as enemy shell fire raked the area, the order rang out from trench to trench 'Battalion to fix bayonets.' At Bn HQ a message was received at 8.20am from brigade to the effect that the 16th Bn had been held up, and ordering the CO to go forward to Sap A to investigate. This was situated in the front line and a considerable distance away, and was a strange request at a time only minutes before the battalion was due to attack. The War Diary confirms that Lt-Col Kennard set off for Sap A, but was killed by artillery fire at about 8.30am, whilst on the way. Ralph Hudson's excellent book *The Bradford Pals* from which much information has been gained, differs from the War Diary in describing Lt-Col Kennard as being killed whilst leading his battalion forward.

At 8.40am it was time for the 18th Bn to advance, and it is doubtful whether the company commanders knew of the death of Lt-Col Kennard. The RSM often accompanied the CO in his movements, but there is no indication that RSM Scott moved forward, and so it is to be assumed that he remained with Battalion HQ, or went with the Second in Command.

The order came for the battalion to advance, and A and D Companies from Dunmow and C and B Companies from Languard trenches climbed over the parapets – straight into the heavy artillery fire which had been directed at their trenches for some 15 minutes. Many of the officers including the Adjutant, were killed almost immediately, and men fell before they had opportunity to take position in line. The line moved slowly forward but within a few yards machine-guns opened fire on them from the Quadrilateral Redoubt area. As they struggled forward, rapid rifle fire hit them from the front and although the companies went on they were already badly thinned by casualties.

Some platoon groups finding themselves fairly free from fire, moved forward as far as they could and eventually joined the survivors from earlier waves of attackers in the forward trenches and in no-mans-land. Some isolated groups achieved the seemingly impossible – as Lt Akam of B Company did with his platoon, and Sgt Bullock (the Bn Signals Sgt) did with one of his men and a party of men from

*18th Bn, PWO West Yorkshire Regt. 'Second Bradford Pals'
Orderly Room Staff. (L to R standing) Pte H. Rawson,
L-Cpl J. E. Squires, Pte S. Tweedale, and L-Cpl C. P.
Burgoyne. (Sitting) O-Rm Sgt C. F. Mallet, Capt-Adj F. T.
Williams, RSM H. Scott and Sgt W. Pitchers.*

Brigadier (Retd) J. M. Cubiss, CBE MC, PWO Regt of Yorkshire.

another division – and reached the German front line.
Much of the battalion however was spread out over a wide
area, either as casualties on the ground or as groups of men
in advanced shell holes or trenches. Charles Heseltine
described (in interview with Stephen Kerry in 1981):

I couldn't get over that battle of the Somme. I thought everything
went wrong, everything . . . we never got near the front line. But
we got in a dug out, and it was 'that' thick with water at the
bottom. Sgt-Maj Pass and three more of us. Sgt-Maj Pass said
'We'd better entrench ourselves in here.' There were a lot of sand-
bags knocking about you know, and we collected them. They put
me on guard while they filled the sand-bags. We hadn't been in
long when we started sniping and looking through. Then he (the
enemy) sent one over and scattered the lot. Sgt-Maj Pass was
killed, and I don't know how the others went . . . We were laid out
there for two days.

There is no mention in the records of the men of
Battalion HQ, and it is only possible to assume that they
either remained in their original position under fire, or
moved forward with or behind the companies. Such was the
chaos that once the battalion had moved forward, contact
was lost and the further forward some groups went, the
more the companies, the battalions and even the divisions,
became mixed. A great many men disappeared for ever and
it was months before others were found dead, some in the
German lines. We will never know how brave and
determined some of those men were, and the greatest
stories of all are unknown.

For hours the battlefield reflected the disaster that had
befallen it, and the 31st Division area devastation was
mirrored many times up and down the Allied line, although
where opposition had not been so strong, there had been
some small success. A vast number of men were on the
ground in varying conditions, many were dead, some
terribly wounded, many less so, but a few were so far
unscathed. All of those alive were trying to remain so, but
the shell fire and machine-guns continued to rake the
ground and casualties went on mounting. Some men were
still working their way forward, returning the enemy fire
from where they were. Others managed to return to the
relative safety of their own forward trenches, but by far the
greater number were forced to await nightfall – many hours
away – before they could hope for help, or contemplate
moving back.

Everywhere was the shock and confusion that
accompanies a disaster, yet some HQs were still receiving
orders detailing further attacks. Few realised that the
attacking battalions had virtually disappeared and that only
survivors and reserve troops were holding much of the front
line from German counter-attacks.

RSM Scott's movements are not known, but he probably
accompanied Maj Carter, and both of them may have
advanced with one of the companies of the battalion, or
with Bn HQ. Wherever they were situated, it would soon
have become clear that instead of planning for the
battalion's further advance and the associated supply

RSM Harold Scott when serving in the 18th Bn, PWO West Yorkshire Regt. The 'Second Bradford Pals'. Mrs Margaret Mawby

requirements, a major rescue operation was going to be necessary if the battalion was to remain in existence. Those small groups still working their way forward would need urgent support, or careful withdrawal back to the British lines, and there was no contact with them.

The great numbers of wounded spread everywhere needed an army of stretcher bearers to bring them back to the field hospitals, but many were too far forward to reach, with the whole area under heavy artillery and sniper fire. To send men out to collect them would simply cause more casualties.

The unwounded men were largely pinned down in shell holes in open ground, where movement back or forwards was impossible. Others were crowded into the forward trenches without leadership. All of these dreadful problems faced the new CO – compounded by a total lack of communication and the complete mixing of many units on the ground. Priorities were impossible to fix as every aspect demanded immediate action. Little wonder that as the hours passed many groups of men began to work out their own hopes of salvation. Gradually some of those who

had been wounded while still close to the trenches managed to inch their way back, while unwounded men set off to try and find their own battalions.

Sgt-Maj Cussins of the 16th Bn, now in the front line, had collected together a number of men with the intention of continuing forwards, as he could see groups of the earlier waves still moving closer to the German lines, but as fast as he gathered men they became casualties. He was ordered by a wounded officer to return to Bn HQ to report that there were no men left with which to advance. Sgt-Maj Cussins set off through the trenches crowded with wounded.

I made my way to what I took to be Brigade HQ . . . but it turned out to be the 94th Brigade. They telephoned my information to division, and also gave me orders to proceed to 93rd Bde HQ. This took me some time, and on getting to Sackville Street (a main arterial trench situated a little way back from the front line) I was ordered with others to line that trench to quell a German counter-attack which had just started. This report proved to be false, and as soon as the necessity for this was over, I reported myself to Brigade HQ. I was told that what remained of the 16th Battalion were being collected in Sackville Street and that I was to return there and look after them.

Later in the afternoon Sgt-Maj Cussins was ordered to move the remnants of the battalion to Brigade HQ, then at about 5pm, to take them into position in Dunmow trench. He had in the meantime listed the names of the 50 survivors who were with him, and found that the highest ranked NCO was a Lance Corporal. On the way to Dunmow trench he met the first reinforcements, and handed over his 'battalion' to a commissioned officer. During the morning, the Brigadier General visited the trenches and decided that due to the heavy casualties and lack of officers and NCOs, no further attempts should be made to advance.

For a time the front line was held in the 93rd Brigade sector by three Lieutenants of the 18th Bn, with a mixed force of about 200 men, but then three companies of the 18th Durham Light Infantry were found to take over the front trenches. Maj Carter was ordered to take command of the 18th Bn at 4pm, and some 60 survivors of the Second Bradford Pals assembled in Dunmow trench represented his command. He made a search of all nearby trenches, but found only a few more wounded men.

12 hours after zero hour, he received orders for his battalion party to hold Monk trench, and during that period his command increased to six officers and 120 men, as small groups found their way back to the battalion. At 9pm he was asked to send guides back to meet reinforcements, who were bringing extra stretcher-bearers with them and quantities of rations. The enemy artillery was now making the front line untenable, and during the early hours of 2 July, arrangements had to be made for the remnants of the Second Bradford Pals to vacate Monk so that the 18th Durham Light Infantry could withdraw back into it. The Second Bradford Pals fell back to Languard, and Battalion HQ was placed in a dug out in Grey Street which was

probably where Maj Carter and RSM Scott were located.

Brigade was notified at 5am that the battalion strength had with reinforcements increased to seven officers and 170 other ranks, and during the remainder of the day more rejoined to raise the strength slightly. At 10.30pm brigade advised that the Germans had been seen carrying gas cylinders into their front line and ordered gas helmets be inspected.

On 3 July, Maj Carter was notified that his battalion was to be prepared to take over the front line sector, but after he and company officers had toured the line and detailed men ready to move forward, the plan was cancelled. The welcome news came instead that 48th Div would be taking over the area during the morning of 4 July.

At 4am that morning, a major stand-to was ordered as a heavy artillery and machine-gun attack fell on the 94th Brigade on the right flank, and this developed into a gas attack. All troops in the front line area were ordered to don gas helmets and the trenches were fully manned. At last at 10.30am relief came, and Languard trench was taken over by the 8th Worcester Bn. The withdrawal from the line by the 93rd Brigade took a very long time, as a heavy storm filled the trenches with water to a depth of four feet in

Major H. F. C. Carter with WOs and Senior NCOs of the 'Second Bradford Pals'. RSM Harold Scott is on the Major's right George Martin, and Stephen Kerry of Bradford Art Galleries and Museums

places and stretcher bearers had great difficulty in removing the wounded. 3am found the exhausted Second Bradford Pals at Bertrancourt, where hot tea laced with rum was served. A further one hour's weary march brought them to Louvencourt where a hot meal awaited them.

12 hours later and a little more rested, the battalion was assembled by RSM Scott for Maj Carter to address them. The Corps Commander also visited the battalion and congratulated all ranks on the discipline, courage, and determination shown during the attack, and saluted the 31st Division as heroes of whom he was proud to be a comrade.

Before zero hour the two battalions had mustered a combined strength of over 1,350 men, but they were now so weak that one complete battalion could not be formed. The 16th Bn was reduced to below 250, having lost two out of every three men, and the 18th Bn numbered only 177, having lost almost five out of every seven men. A large number were missing and although a few would later rejoin and some of the less seriously wounded would return after treatment, a large number of the volunteers, who had so eagerly trained in the parks of Bradford 16 months before, would never return home.

The offensive launched on 1 July had failed in many sectors within two hours and the hundreds of battalions of volunteers were counting the cost. It was because they had tried so courageously to fulfil all that was expected of them,

and that their casualties were so heavy, that they constitute the highest loss ever suffered by the British Army in a single action. Lord Kitchener, the founder of the two million strong volunteer army, had drowned and lost his life before the battle, when the ship in which he was being conveyed to Russia struck a mine off the Orkneys.

A most poignant testimony to the bravery and determination of the volunteer battalions, comes from an extract of a report compiled by Capt A. D. Stephenson, who commanded C Company of the Second Bradford Pals:

. . . the enemy artillery was a great surprise to our troops, who had expected to find most of the enemy guns put out of action. The enemy infantry, standing on their parapet firing at our advancing troops, seemed to consider themselves quite safe from our guns. Could our advancing troops not have laid down while our guns shelled the enemy down with shrapnel . . .?

This moving question not only strikes at the very heart of the planning of the operation, but underlines the steadfast bravery of the men who walked on right through a hail of fire.

By early 1916 the number of men volunteering for service had greatly decreased so conscription was brought into force. This introduced the final category of soldier to the fighting front. The Regular, Territorial and Volunteer soldiers had gone because they wished to serve, but from now on men would serve compulsorily.

The appalling hardships of the front line had necessitated a rigid structure of discipline to prevent men from deserting or from failing to carry out their duties. Where regular soldiers and volunteers had been known to fail, the conscript – with his inexperience and probable lack of commitment – might especially be expected to do so, and therefore the structure had to be even more rigidly applied. Men failing to carry out their orders – or deemed to be malingering – faced harsh field punishments, or lengthy periods of imprisonment with hard labour. For desertion, the soldier could expect to receive the ultimate penalty of the firing squad.

That such a large majority of the men in the line, whether regular soldiers, volunteers, or conscripted men, performed their tasks so courageously, speaks volumes for their indomitable spirit and character.

The Regimental Sergeant Major was firmly positioned within the structure and many of the detailed arrangements for the wide range of punishments fell upon him. He was usually required to be present to ensure that everything was carried out correctly, and one would like to believe that he could bring an element of humanity into even the setting up of a firing party by selecting men who were good steady marksmen, and getting the task over with as quickly as possible.

It has to be remembered however that in a society that favoured corporal and capital punishment the bulk of the high command of the Army, and probably the Regimental officers, Warrant officers and NCOs, considered such

measures to be both justified and necessary. If so many men who were trying to be good soldiers, were being killed doing their duty, why shouldn't a man who left his post or deserted, lose his life.

The Somme offensive continued for a further four months, with fearful loss and marginal gain, but what was left of the 31st Division was marched away on 6 July to rest and to be brought up to strength. Three weeks later the 93rd Brigade re-entered the line, to man a sector of former German trenches at Neuve Chapelle. The country differed greatly from the Somme area, being flat and enclosed, and few would ever forget the place, for the British had earlier assaulted and taken the trenches but with heavy loss, and the dead lay everywhere. The flat terrain prevented their removal as the Germans fired on any movement and so the rotting bodies remained; even the parapets of the trenches were built up with the remains of them. The sights, smells and the atmosphere would always remain in the minds of the unfortunate men who served there.

In August, RSM G Cussins of the 16th Bn was awarded the Distinguished Conduct Medal, for his bravery and devotion to duty on 1 July. For three months the two battalions served for periods in the front line at Festuburt, Neuve Chapelle and Givinchy before moving in October 1916, to the Hebuterne sector.

The British offensive on the banks of the River Ancre commenced in November and both battalions took their place in the line, where they suffered over 50 casualties from enemy shelling. There followed further spells of line duty, with the occasional provision of working parties, which proved equally dangerous. A month of training then came during which the RSM and NCOs were able to carry out their more traditional roles.

Maj Guyon and Lt-Col M. N. Kennard, the COs of the 16th and 18th Bns, had both been killed on 1 July, and whilst Lt-Col H. F. G. Carter had been given command of the 18th, Maj H. H. Kennedy had been appointed to command the 16th. On being promoted as Acting Lt-Col, he departed from the 16th to take command of the 6th Bn Scottish Rifles, and his place was taken by Lt Col A C Croydon, an officer who had risen through the ranks and had previously served as RSM in the Lincoln Regiment. He was a strict disciplinarian of gruff manner, but was to prove a most able soldier and commanding officer.

In early 1917 orders had been received that soldiers under the age of 19 would no longer be permitted to serve in the front line. This resulted from public concern over the loss of so many young men of 18 and under at the Somme. Some 20 young soldiers of the two battalions were withdrawn from action and posted to the Etaples Training Centre as instructors, until they reached the age of 19.

At this stage the Germans began their withdrawal to the well fortified Hindenburg Line, which effectively straightened out a salient. Patrols soon discovered this, but the occupation of the German first, second and third lines of trenches proved a costly operation as the Germans

Royal Scots Greys during the Somme offensive, 1916. RHQ

brought heavy fire to bear upon the British troops from Rossignol Wood. The 16th Bn assaulted and made an entry into the wood but at a cost of 222 casualties. The 18th Bn relieved the 16th on 28 February, and then in a combined attack with the 18th DLI on 3 March the wood was taken.

The brigade moved back to the Bethune area at the end of March, where the 18th were fortunate to be housed in barracks. There they were allowed a welcome clean up and order was restored with parades and route marches. After four weeks the division moved to the Arras front, where the Allied spring offensive had gained some success and the enemy had been driven from the Vimy Ridge. The 31st Div now joined in the offensive towards Fresnoy and entered what had previously been the German line.

An attack was prepared to be made by the 15th, 16th and 18th Bns upon Oppy Wood and zero hour was fixed for 3.45am on 3 May. The Allied artillery had now developed the creeping barrage behind which the infantry was to advance. As at the Somme, the enemy artillery laid an intensive barrage down on the assembly trenches just before the attack was due to begin, and the 18th Bn suffered particularly badly from this tactic.

At zero hour all three battalions rose from their trenches and advanced thorugh heavy fire with men falling as thickly as they had on 1 July. The moon was still shining in the early morning effectively silhouetting the advancing infantrymen. First objectives were taken and some went on to the second objective, but resistance increased and the

advance was gradually forced to a halt. As daylight came the enemy made strong attempts to cut off and isolate the attacking force. Fierce fighting continued all that day and into the night. Each of the battalion headquarters became involved in battle and Lt-Col A. C. Croydon MC formed his 16th HQ into bombing parties, whilst Lt-Col H. Carter formed a defence line with his 18th HQ. The assaulting battalions were eventually forced to retire, and further heavy casualties were suffered in doing so. The battalions had for the second time advanced into extremely heavy fire and each had lost approximately 325 men.

RSM Harold Scott received a Certificate of Merit signed by the CO which stated:

For conspicuous gallantry and devotion to duty during the attack on the Oppy-Gavrelle Line on 3 May 1917. By his coolness and courageous behaviour under very heavy shell fire he did a great deal to sustain the confidence of the men, and he also organised all ammunition, water supplies etc, excellently, under very trying circumstances.

During the night of 4 May, both battalions were relieved and marched back to a camp near Arras, where they were re-organised temporarily into two-company battalions. The men were rested and given opportunity to clean up without any parades being held. Within four days the battalions were back in the Gavrelle sector acting as brigade reserve, and were heavily shelled in their trenches, losing 26 more men.

A period of duty supplying working and carrying parties followed, and then back to the Gavrelle line on 9 June where a period of rain and storm left the trenches flooded and thick with mud. Nevertheless a great deal of patrol activity took place. On 18 June whilst the 18 Bn were resting in bivouacs behind Railway Cutting, a long range shell fell on the orderly room tent killing three clerks and wounding Lt-Col H. Carter.

The 93rd Brig continued with patrol activity until 20 July 1917, when a move came to Neuville St Vaast, and back into the front line. Whilst on the march a shell landed directly in front of D Company of the 16th Bn, killing two officers and four other ranks, but also wounding 41 others, one of whom later died.

On 30 August 1917 there occurred an action which clearly reveals how experienced Lt-Col H. F. G. Carter and his battalion had become. A heavy period of shelling by the Germans suggested to Col Carter that a raid was being planned upon his lines, and by careful study of the trench system he anticipated a likely point of attack. He gave his orders accordingly, and when at 3am on 31 August two strong German raiding parties approached the sector they were intercepted and driven off with heavy loss. Both Col Carter and his battalion were congratulated by the Corps Commander, for the accurate appreciation of the enemy's intentions and the effective steps taken to frustrate them.

For the remainder of the year the battalions continued to spend regular periods in the front line. On 7 November 1917 FM Sir Douglas Haig mentioned RSM Harold Scott in a despatch, for gallant and distinguished services in the field. The Secretary of State for War subsequently advised that he had it in command from HM The King to record his appreciation of the services rendered.

The winter of 1917-18 was extremely severe, with frozen iron-hard ground making trench work very difficult and snow covering the approaches added great danger to the task of patrolling. In December heavy rain brought a temporary thaw and the trenches were transformed into vast muddy pools which prevented thoroughfare. Movement could only be made on the surface at night, leaving advanced posts isolated during daylight hours. Visibility was very poor and consequently there was little activity other than in patrolling, and this became particularly deadly.

On 19 December 1917, the 18th Bn was relieved from the front line and marched to Ecurie Wood where they were to clean up and re-organise before being occupied on trench works. At the end of January 1918, came the shock news that the 18th Bn was to be disbanded. On 1 February Lt-Col H. F. G. Carter MC addressed the battalion at Bray Camp to confirm the news and to express his great appreciation of the way the men had served.

The 16th Bn was relieved from the line on 11 February and was then also disbanded. Men from both battalions were then formed into drafts to be sent to other battalions of the Prince of Wales's Own West Yorkshire Regiment. On 13 February, RSM G. Cussins DCM was posted to the 15th Bn, with many other men of the 16th Bn. RSM Harold Scott and a few remaining men of the 18th Bn were transferred to the 31st Machine-Gun Battalion on 15 February. As RSM he was again to be commended upon the speed of setting up the new battalion and upon its smartness on parade. His younger brother Alfred survived the battles as a CQMS, and was transferred to the 6th Bn West Yorkshire Regt.

In March and April 1918 came the tremendous German offensive which almost broke through the Allied lines, and many of the long and terribly costly gains of 1916-17 were lost. This was probably the worst test yet for what remained of the volunteer army, and for the soldiers of the conscripted army. This was the final act however, and when the offensive gradually broke down and fresh Allied divisions from the United States of America poured into the field the German forces reached breaking point and began to retreat in August 1918. Germany could not continue the terrible struggle, and after four years of conflict in Europe an armistice was reached in November.

A large military cemetery was formed upon the old area of no-mans-land over which the men of the 31st Division advanced on 1 July 1916. One of hundreds of such cemeteries, this was marked as Serre Road Number One and this contains the graves of many of the men belonging to the Pals battalions. Many of the volunteers were never found however and their names are to be seen commemorated on the Thiepval Memorial.

A memorial to the Sheffield City Battalion stands in the village of Serre to mark the bravery of the small group of men who survived the artillery and machine-gun fire to fight their way into the village only to end their lives there.

Maj L. C. Drouet MBE Grenadier Guards, and Maj A. P. Joyce MBE MM BEM Welsh Guards, served throughout the Second World War, and they visited many of the First World War battlefields in 1978. They wrote of their journey and experiences in the *Guards Magazine* in a paper entitled *Lest we Forget* and the following short extracts may best pay tribute to those soldiers of 1916.

The area of the Somme today is of great beauty . . . the orchards and peacefulness disguise what was probably the greatest battlefield of all time; when the British Army went over the top on 1 July 1916, and attacked the German trenches, they suffered nearly 60,000 casualties. That is two men for every yard of the front! This is the combined battle casualties of the Crimea, Boer and Korean wars. This is 50 times the daily losses of El Alamein, and 15 times the British casualties on D Day! This was the blackest day in the history of the British Army. By the time the battle of the Somme was finally won, British casualties were 600,000 and the Germans had lost 700,000, not to mention the losses of the French and other armies.

. . . The Thiepval Memorial to the missing of the Somme,

designed by Sir Edwin Lutyens, is most impressive. It is larger than the Arc de Triomphe in Paris and has to be seen to be believed. It commemorates a total of 73,000 men who have no known graves, including many from the Brigade of Guards. Not to have a feeling of deep sorrow when viewing this monument, one would be devoid of all feeling towards those who mourn for someone who 'Sleeps in some corner of a foreign field' . . .

. . . It might be asked, what appeal do these things have for soldiers today or anyone else? The battlefields of the First World War should be seen by all recruits coming into our army. It would instil pride into them to know of the discipline of the soldier of those days to his unit and country. It makes us feel very inadequate in comparison to those great First World War soldiers. The more one reads of those battles of two generations ago does not diminish but adds lustre to their fame. We who fought in the Second World War can be thankful that at least some of our Generals knew how to prepare a battle based on their Great War experiences. Montgomery, Alexander and Slim had learned not to budge in their campaigns unless the preparations for battle were correct. The great loyalties of these soldiers towards each other were spelt out in hardships, and their comradeship bought by blood. What greater lesson is there than this?

We would recommend a tour of some of the First World War battlefields to anyone who considers they have anything to complain about. They will come away feeling as we do, very chastened and humbled by these soldiers who were the flower of the British Empire . . .

We should all be grateful for the silent dignity, the taste and the character achieved by the devotion of all members of the Commonwealth War Graves Commission in their task to ensure that . . .

THEIR NAME LIVETH FOR EVERMORE

The King's Colours of the 16th and 18th Battalions of the Bradford Pals hang in Bradford Cathedral for all to see and remember. There were very many battalions of the Prince of Wales's Own West Yorkshire Regiment fighting in the First World War, and the total number of men killed would almost equal a modern division.

RSM Harold Scott was demobilized in December 1918, and after home leave rejoined the Bradford City Police Force. RSM G. Cussins DCM also joined the police force in Bingley. Not surprisingly, Harold Scott was made Drill Instructor for the force within months of rejoining, and he was to be complimented on many occasions by visiting government inspectors upon the high standard of drill and smartness achieved in the annual police parades.

Two years after the war, in July 1920, he was promoted to Police Sergeant, and seven years later became an Inspector in charge of the great Horton, Low Moor and Wyke areas of Bradford. Insp Scott retired on 31 December 1934, at the age of almost 51, and he was complimented upon his record of service by the Bradford Watch Committee. Harold Scott had a long and happy retirement and was very active in the Bradford Pals Old

Superintendent of Police, Harold Scott, 1927-34, Bradford City Police Force. Mrs Margaret Mawby

Comrades Association, formed soon after the end of the war. He was chairman for many years and was very popular with the old volunteers of the 18th. When he died on 16 April 1960 aged 75, a few of the gallant surviving Pals stood to attention at the gates of Schoolmore Cemetery to pay tribute to their old RSM.

The Bradford Pals OC Association remained until the end of February 1979, having met together for over 60 years, but the Association came to an end when too few Pals remained to continue the meetings. When Ralph Hudson talked to many of the old vounteers of the 16th and 18th Battalions, in order to research his book *The Bradford Pals*, he was amazed to learn that these marvellous old soldiers would have gone to do it all again if they had been required to.

Alfred Scott suffered from asthma for the rest of his life from the effects of gas, but he lived until the age of 89 and always attended the meetings of the Bradford Pals OC Association until it ended.

CHAPTER 9

Service as RSMs between the Wars

With the kind permission of Col G. A. Allan OBE (Retd) Adjutant of the Royal Hospital Chelsea, I was in 1982 privileged to be able to visit three Chelsea Pensioners who had during their service between the two World Wars served as RSMs. AssSM Thomas Cook BEM, formerly of the Coldstream Guards, helped with the practical arrangements, and I recognised him as occasionally assisting at the Festival of Remembrance at the Albert Hall when the Chelsea Pensioners march so impressively.

I was also helped a great deal during the day by Pensioner George Barber, a former Eighth Army Sergeant of the King's Royal Rifle Corps, who had fought through the Second World War from the regiment's rearguard action in Calais, to North Africa, Italy and Greece. A fine soldier whose story and wit could form a book of its own.

The Royal Chelsea Hospital has been blessed with some fine RSMs, such as RSM Jimmy Ives BEM, who served there for almost 20 years, and who had when with the East Surrey Regiment been captured by the Japanese at Singapore. Both he and RSM L. J. Lamb BEM, who has recently retired from the appointment, will be well remembered for their bearing in leading the Pensioners into the Albert Hall each year. The new Sergeant Major is RSM C. C. Matthews, formerly of the Somerset and Cornwall Light Infantry.

The Armistice on 11 November 1918 ended a fearful war in which ordinary places like Mons, Ypres, Verdun, Beaumont Hamel and Passchendaele, gained a terrible prominence, representing not single battles but whole campaigns which caused huge losses to both sides. The vast relief and celebrations of peace came from soldiers and civilians alike and at last a young man of 18 could contemplate a life offering more than the probability of service in the trenches. The huge armies of men could return home and thoughts turn towards family and employment.

Demobilization, however, was not as prompt as the conscripted army had been led to believe, and demonstrations soon broke out by men who had reverted to civilian thinking as soon as hostilities ended. Later would come the bitterness of returning home to unemployment and long hardships in a land most definitely not fit for heroes.

Twice through the ranks

Charles Estall MC had enlisted in the 8th Bn East Surrey

Regiment in 1914 at the age of 18. He had proudly stood on parade with the battalion to be inspected by HM King George V before embarking to join the BEF in France, and had progressed through the ranks to acting RSM. He was known in the regiment as 'Hindenburg' partly as a result of his stature, but also by his 'gentle methods' of dealing with 'scrimshankers'.

Disillusioned by civilian life after only a short time, Charles Estall re-enlisted in the regiment as a private soldier, and on joining the 1st Bn East Surrey Regiment was soon on his way to serve in north Russia. With his previous experience he was soon promoted to Sergeant, and was to remain in that rank for several years. The 1st Bn moved to Dublin in 1920 on return from Russia, and Sgt Estall was to remember that a new RSM came to the battalion from the Grenadier Guards, RSM Maynard. The battalion then went abroad to Hong Kong for three years, and during that period the RSM became W. G. Gingell MBE MM who came from the Coldstream Guards (and whose son Laurie Gingell later became a Major General).

Charles Estall was promoted to CSM in 1926, nine years after first holding that rank in 1917. Then in 1931 he was appointed RSM of the 2nd Bn, following RSM S. G. Thompson MBE. He was on parade at the state funeral of HM King George V in 1935 and also at the coronation of HM King George VI. In December 1937, he was appointed Garrison Sergeant Major in Hong Kong, and 300 guests attended his 2nd Bn Sergeants Mess farewell.

For almost four years GSM Estell remained in Hong Kong, leaving in March 1941 nine months before the Japanese invasion and occupation. Three months after returning home he was commissioned as Lieutenant Quartermaster with the Durham Light Infantry, and he ended the Second World War as a combatant Staff Captain.

During his 35 years service Charles Estall MC took part in many well remembered parades, such as the Northern Command Tattoo in 1931, the Aldershot Command Tattoo in 1935, and many ceremonies of Trooping the Colour in Egypt, Hong Kong, India and at Shorncliffe and Colchester in this country. His last parades were the state funeral of HM King George VI and the coronation of HM Queen Elizabeth II. For many years he has attended state ceremonial occasions as a member of the Yeomen of the Guard. I received a marvellous letter from him in May 1985 in which although he claimed 'My memory – unlike good wine – does not improve with age' was a creditable

RSM Charles Estall, MC, RSM of the 2nd East Surrey Regt 1932-7. Dan James and the East Surrey Regimental Journal

achievement of memory for a grand former Regimental Sergeant Major of 89.

From horses to motor transport

Former acting RSM John Cameron McClellan of the Royal Military Police enlisted in the 2/5th Bn King's Own Scottish Borderers in 1914 at the tender age of 15 years five months. When the battalion departed for action however he was sent to a Holding Battalion in Catterick Camp as he was too young, and ruefully states that he was kept there until March 1918 when as a trained Lewis gunner he was posted to the 6th BN KOSBs. The battalion fought in the line mainly in the Armentières sector, and was involved in the final advance in 1918. John McClellan described to me . . .

The battalion was resting outside Cortrai in November 1918 preparing to return into the line. We were occupying a large factory building and were settling down to sleep at about 10pm when I heard the sound of bagpipes. This was unusual at that late hour, and blowing out the candles I opened a fanlight to peer out. The building was bright with lights and the street below was packed with people. The Pipe Major was marching up and down playing the regimental march and there was great excitement. We dressed and joined the throng, and I soon picked up the shouts that the war was finished. Moving along the street I was handed a bottle of wine and with the Pipe Major leading we all congregated in the courtyard in front of the battalion headquarters. The CO came out onto a balcony and held up his arm for silence. 'Well,' he began, 'I have some news for you. The Germans have agreed to sign an armistice tomorrow morning at 11am, so that means that the war is finished.' His last words were drowned by cheers and after that it was just celebrations.

Instead of returning to the front line we began to prepare for the march into Germany, and fresh equipment and uniforms were issued. I was sent back to the band as a Drummer as they wanted a full band to lead the battalion, and on 8 December we crossed the frontier marching in echelon with the Americans. We went to the steel works area and my first billet was in part of an orphanage. The local population was practically starving when we marched in and I was giving the children anything I could get hold of. I would cut a slice of bread into fingers and pass them around. I had learnt a little German at school and this soon blossomed into conversation so that I could speak to anyone.

In May 1919 I was ordered to pack my kit and report to the orderly room. There I was given an envelope and travel warrant and sent to Brigade HQ and from there on to Army HQ. At Cologne railway station transport awaited a group of us and we were taken to a large school where HQ was situated, and were given a meal. Next morning we were paraded in the main hall and then individual tests were carried out into our ability to speak German. I was graded 'A' and at the end of the tests the smartest RSM of the Military Police I have ever seen told me that I was to be transferred to the Mounted Military Police! I pointed out that I had never sat on a horse in my life, but he replied 'I know that you speak German well, and I will soon teach you to ride a horse, much quicker than I could teach you to speak German!' and he did so. In no time at all I was taking my horse out alone for two hours at a time.

Soon we were going out on patrol accompanied by German Mounted Police. The Deputy Provost Marshal of the division would go to the German Police Chief's office and arrange to have our Mounted Military Police at certain points. And German counterparts would be there to meet us. We would then patrol areas in pairs. These duties continued until late 1919 when the division broke up and we were transferred to Squadron HQ in Cologne. We had quite a time with the horses at first in the city as they had been used to rural areas. I took a short local leave in October 1920 and learned when I returned that I had been discharged from the mounted branch! Then I found that I had become a regular soldier (instead of a conscript for the duration of war service) and also that I was to be transferred to work in the SIB, and that this could only be from the Foot Military Police. This was in plain clothing and I finished with parades and uniforms for some years. I worked in liaison with the French and American authorities and was given passes to allow me into their sectors.

In 1926 we evacuated Cologne and moved to Weisbaden, and I realized that as I would be considered for promotion to Sergeant it could be said that I had little actual uniformed police experience behind me, so I discussed this with my CO. Soon afterwards I was returned to the uniformed branch and found my experience in the SIB to my distinct advantage. As a Corporal I would tour an area and check that everybody was correctly on duty, and one place I visited was the main railway station at Weisbaden. I would not enter by the main entrance as I knew of a quiet way via a tunnel under the tracks! I knew of places on the station quite unknown to the uniformed men and would turn up out of the blue to catch them on the hop or taking a jug of beer, instead of patrolling the platform.

Chelsea Pensioner former RSM John C. McClellan, Corps of Royal Military Police.   Photo by the author

I was soon returned to England and in 1927 was promoted to Sergeant in charge of a detachment of Military Police at Devonport, and I remained there for three years until being made CQMS. At that time orders came for the Military Police to mechanise, and I had the task of preparing the men for motorcycles, and disposing of many of the horses. I worked on this major change until I was transferred to Aldershot Command where I remained from 1930-32. I was then sent to Egypt where we had our largest unit of Military Police, and again organised the changeover from horses to motorcycles and lorries.

In 1936 I was promoted to CSM in charge of MPs in Egypt, which tallied with Acting Regimental Sergeant Major. I was informed that I would return to London District in March 1939 as RSM, and that I would serve there until 1941 when I was due to retire from the army. At the end of October 1938 however, I was offered a position with a firm of Scottish brewers and decided to take the opportunity of such security. In early 1939 I resigned from the army and started work with the brewery and remained with them for the next 38 years.

I was later to work within Aldershot Command as area manager until 1967 when the depot in the area closed down. During that time I was able to get to know many of the great RSMs including AcSM John Lord and RSM Ronald Brittain when he was at the Mons OCS. I also saw many of the famous old barracks pulled down, such as the Waterloo Lines and the Wellington Lines. My particular memory of a fine RSM is of a very gentlemanly depot RSM Preston, whom I would go to for advice when a Sergeant in charge of a detachment. Every RSM has to work by the regulations but each one is a distinct individual and always leaves his mark upon the Unit and its soldiers.

John McClellan has been at the Royal Hospital Chelsea for 17 years, and at the age of 92 remains a very smart soldier, and a great credit to the Corps of Royal Military Police.

To Form a Battalion From Scratch

In September 1982 I talked with Frank Hoyle, former RSM of the King's Own Yorkshire Light Infantry, at the Royal Hospital Chelsea. Although he described himself as having been a strict RSM, a great deal of gentleness and care came through his conversation, and I am certain that he was well respected and liked by his men. He joined the army in March 1922 and described how his first difficulty came from his army number!

Before going to the KOYLI depot in Pontefract, I had belonged to a cadet unit of the West Yorkshire Regiment in my home town of Bradford, and this caused confusion over my army number. I was given a KOYLI number commencing with the serial 468, but later it was found that I had earlier been allocated a West Yorkshire Regimental number commencing with 452 and so reverted to my original number. An unusual start I thought.

At the depot our senior CSM was Bob Grant and as he was a 6ft 6in former Guardsman, he made a strong impression upon us. I always found that the influence of a good RSM came down right through the ranks, and this was especially so when we were posted to a battalion after training. I went to the 2nd Bn KOYLI in India where the RSM was W. H. Ledger DCM, a war veteran and great disciplinarian.

Our journey out was unusual in that we went through the Suez Canal three times! On our first passage the troop ship was turned back because of trouble near Alexandria from the Turks. We saw the smoke of fires but were kept aboard ship. We set off through the canal a second time but again returned because of disturbances. Finally on the third passage we travelled on to India where at first we remained in the south, but later marched up country to the Punjab. As we marched into camp we could see eight sets of football goalposts, one set of rugby posts and a good athletics field. We were to get plenty of opportunity for such sport as there was little else to do in our spare time. I played many sports including tennis and hockey which the Sikhs played extremely well barefooted.

During our years in India I was promoted to unpaid Lance Corporal, then to Corporal and to Sergeant. We moved to the North West Frontier and traversed the Khyber Pass several times. We guarded communications there and unfortunately left some men in the cemetery situated at the foot of the Pass. After nine years abroad I rejoined the 1st Bn in Tidworth and well remember that HM Duchess of York presented us with our medals. She spoke to me – as she was to do again 50 years later when as Queen Mother she visited us at the Royal Hospital Chelsea.

As a Sergeant Instructor in musketry I was given the training of our shooting teams for the King's Trophy, and our regimental team was placed second in the British Army. I also ran a six week cadre for junior NCOs. When the battalion went to Gibraltar I remained behind for a time to take weapon training, but rejoined later. This was at about the time of the Spanish Civil War, and whilst we had no trouble with that, we did see some activities at sea from a distance. We could not of course visit Spain but were able to spend a little time at Tangiers, where our families were allowed to accompany us.

When a vacancy came I was appointed Colour Sergeant, and then later became Company Sergeant Major of HQ Company. At that stage I volunteered to return to the 2nd Bn which was serving in Burma and in 1938 travelled out to join it. The climate there was terrible compared with India, but the time went quickly as we trained and prepared defences. War came in September 1939 and the War Office circulated a paper requesting men of long experience to return home as instructors to prepare the thousands of men called up for service. After confirming that families would accompany us a number of us were brought home, and it was at that time I was appointed Regimental Sergeant Major.

At Port Said our young band boys were sent home on a vessel sailing ahead of ours, and we were very sad to hear later that their ship had been torpedoed in the English Channel with the loss of a number of them. We disembarked at Marseille and then travelled by train to Cherbourg where we went into hutments. Later we were taken by sea to Portsmouth without incident, other than stopping mid-channel to pick up a parachutist whose plane had crashed.

At the depot Col H. Redman advised us that we were to move to Glasgow to train and form a new battalion of conscript soldiers. This was designated the 7th Bn King's Own Yorkshire Light Infantry. We worked extremely hard and it became a very good battalion. Once trained we were moved to the south coast to join the army guarding against invasion. Our CO then moved on with promotion and the battalion moved first to Cheltenham racecourse and then abroad to Burma. I remained in this country as I had to enter hospital, but later went to France after D Day and continued work as an RSM.

From France I went to Belgium, and was on the German frontier when the war in Europe ended. I was in number 11 release group, but was interviewed by my CO with the question 'Mr Hoyle, would you like to stay on for a further three years?' I respectfully declined and he asked 'How about two years?' 'No thank you Sir' I replied. 'Well just one year then?' I declined and explained 'I've been serving continuously since 1922 and with a wife and family it is time that I tried civilian life.' Before final release I applied for work with the barracks department and was fortunate to be accepted. Following six weeks leave I became a barrack inventory accountant with some 21 establishments on my books. One of them was a German POW camp on the racecourse at Doncaster, and it was not long before the race track was required for a return to racing and the camp was closed. As the army was wound down the barracks gradually closed and eventually my job also ceased.

I thoroughly enjoyed my service and look back with pleasure on my days as an instructor in weapon and drill training. Our drill was of course at light infantry pace, and I remember preparing companies for a brigade drill competition. I used all of the little points remembered over the years, and with the Provost Staff available to give that final polish to boots etc just before the march on, the companies did well in the results taking all of the leading positions except third place. Although counting myself as having been strict I can only remember once ever having to place a man in the guard room. It was a great regiment and I always counted myself fortunate to have been able to help form the 7th Battalion from scratch. I remain in touch with my former CO who went on to become Maj-Gen Sir Harold Redman.

Promoted Straight from Staff Sergeant to Regimental Sergeant Major

Albert Bennel RA, a very smart old gentleman of over 75 talked with me at the Royal Hospital Chelsea about his days as RSM in the Royal Artillery. I was to learn with surprise that he had not been an in pensioner for more than six months, as he retained such a military appearance. He remembered his first RSM.

I had joined the East Lancashire Regiment in 1922 and our RSM was a former Guardsman named Black Jack Hawkins, as the name implies an impressive man of very dark complexion. He was at least 6ft 3in and had a huge voice to match. He would shout at us from hundreds of yards distance. Later on when training us as junior NCOs he would take us on 'voice training' when against the

wind I had difficulty in projecting my orders more than 60 yards! I certainly did not think at that time that I would ever become an RSM myself. I was a keen swimmer and athlete and later when I was transferred to the Royal Regiment of Artillery this was a factor behind my promotion to Sergeant in 1934.

When war was declared in September 1939 our unit left for France within three days, and we began a routine of digging out forward, main, and rear gunpits for our converted 25 pounders, but when fighting started we were driven out before we could use them. When we did fire it was over open sights, with the enemy often only 80 yards away. Driven back towards Dunkirk most of our officers were lost and we eventually had to destroy our own guns. I spent only one night on the Dunkirk beaches and made it out to the ferry which was one of the hundreds of small civilian craft picking up the exhausted troops.

In England we were sent first to Woolwich and then to the Ross on Wye area, where we received fresh kit and started training again. There were few weapons and our drill periods were with broom handles for rifles! In late 1941 we formed part of the newly established 6th Armourd Div, and I was promoted to Staff Sergeant. Gradually we went through more extensive training until the division prepared in the mountains of Ayrshire for battle. We took part in the landings at Algiers in November 1942, assembling on the racecourse there for two days, and then pursuing the Germans inland over the mountains. There followed the Tunisian campaign in which all units had a hard time. Eventually we joined up near Tunis with the 7th Armoured Div which had advanced from El Alamein. I was mentioned in despatches just before Tunis when removing some wounded under fire.

During spare periods sports activities were held when I boxed as a welter weight, I was called Biff for a time until another boxer turned up with the same nickname so I became Ben. The invasion of Sicily and Italy followed and I received a sudden posting to HQ 1st Army Group RA where the RSM was being sent home wounded. Maybe I was the nearest senior Sergeant available but I was fortunate to be made straight up to RSM. I arrived at the unit on the Adriatic coast and was offered a room for my billet. I wished to meet the staff however and preferred to join them in their billets in the stables. I did so and saved my own life as the room offered was hit by a shell.

We were switched from area to area, at one time being based near Monte Casino which was becoming a terrible nut to crack. We moved again and it became too cold to fight, and I was asked to act as bookmaker at a military sponsored horse race meeting to keep the troops occupied. A percentage of the proceeds went to the Red Cross. The final race of the day was a mule race with 31 runners, and this was the only race to lose money. I offered 4 to 1 the field and thought that I was on to a good thing until a young officer placed a £100 bet on one mule and it lead throughout! I asked the officer how he could make such a confident bet. He replied 'I look after all of the mules!'

The Italian campaign slowly progressed as the Germans withdrew through northern Italy and we were at a village named Picola Grande when the war in Europe came to an end. Our Brigadier asked me to use my ability to speak Italian to arrange a party in the village to which all of the villagers, partisans and troops were invited.

We advanced into Austria and followed Tito's partisan army out of the area, and then followed the Russian army into arranged lines of demarcation. Instead of fighting we were now administering whole areas – a totally new experience for me. We organised the vital civilian services such as hospitals, telephone system, courts and prisons and a host of other tasks, and were more or less acting policemen. During the hard winter of 1945-46 we converted some tanks into snowploughs in order to keep the roads open. A task we did not care for was to repatriate many thousands of White Russians who had earlier fled from Russia during the Revolution.

In 1946 we were moved to Udine in Italy for a few months until being brought home to the UK in late 1946, and I was posted to the Depot at Woolwich. Then I was sent to HQRA Western Command at Chester and as I went on to represent Chester and Cheshire in the water polo team, I believe that the Brigadier who was Secretary of the Army Swimming Union arranged my posting there! I finally moved to Eastern Command at Hounslow in 1949 where I looked after administration and a little ceremonial working for a time with Lt-Col Ted Heath, Honourable Artillery Company, until I was discharged from the regular army in 1952. As I was completing my army service my son was going through his training as an officer cadet at Mons OCS under RSM Ronald Brittain. My service had spanned the years from just after the end of the First War until the end of the Second War and I counted myself fortunate on so many occasions.

Every Rank from Boy Soldier to RSM

Former RSM L. Roy Tankard served at the Royal Military Academy Sandhurst from 1941-50, for the last four years as RSM of Old College, and for the last two years under the great RSM J. C. Lord. He remembers many of the RSMs of that time.

I enlisted as a boy soldier of just over 14 years in 1923 and held every rank up to RSM, including that of Drum Major. This represented quite a grind in peace time when promotion was slow and by no means automatic.

My first RSM was RSM Speller in 1923. I served in the 2nd and 3rd Bns Grenadier Guards but never the 1st Battalion. The next was RSM R. R. Beard DCM or Tabby as we named him because of a wound in the foot sustained during the First World War. He had special boots made for him. He served with the 2nd Bn in Turkey during 1922-3 and was later made Quartermaster. I also knew RSM Dobson who was awarded the Military Cross during the 1914-18 war. Everyone called him Harry. There was RSM Tommy Garnett who entered the regiment as a boy soldier. He served in the Machine Gun Battalion as Drum Major, then in the 2nd Bn in 1919-20 as a Platoon Sergeant. He also went on up the ladder to become Quartermaster. I knew RSM Patterson, a Scot. He instigated and standardised all of the drill movements, firstly in the Guards Brigade, and then in the British Army.

After serving with the 2nd Bn in France and Belgium, I came out through the Dunkirk evacuation, and then was posted to the RMA Sandhurst to train officer cadets. I served under RSM Arthur Brand until 1948, and then under RSM J. C. Lord. Other RSMs I have served with were Bernard Pratt, who was wounded in the BEF before Dunkirk, Harry Randall who joined the 2nd Bn as RSM at Parkstone after the evacuation and RSM Clements who was RSM of the Honourable Artillery Company OCTU in 1941. I was selected to come to Canada to serve as RSM of the Seaforth Highlanders of Canada, and was with that regiment for 10 years.

Former RSM Roy Tankard settled and remained in Canada.

The standard required to win the Pace Stick Competition. RMAS winning team in 1962. Team Capt in rear CSM Bostock, Coldstream Gds. L to R Sgt Mack, Scots Gds; Sgt F. P. Horstall, Coldstream Gds; Sgt Sims, Coldstream Gds and Sgt W. R. Clarke, Grenadier Gds. Photo Peter Horsfall collection

CHAPTER 10

Through the ranks to Arnhem with Fred Grimshaw, Border Regiment

Former RSM Fred Grimshaw and I worked in the same building for a time when he was a court official, but it was when he talked with me about his service in the army that I really came to know him. He proved to be a warm, fun loving man who delighted in describing events against himself. Throughout the hours he allowed his comments to be recorded, there was a constant respect for the men with whom he had served, for his regiment and for the rank of Regimental Sergeant Major.

I shall always remember his cheerful optimism and wit, which reflected through all of his story. Sadly, Fred Grimshaw died not long after making his recordings and he was not to see the results of his kind help. His full story would support a separate book, but the following extracts provide a fascinating glimpse of service through the ranks between the wars, and during the Second World War, by one of those unbeatable infantrymen.

Fred Grimshaw was born in Manchester, and after working as a fitter/turner for a time, decided with a friend to apply for the Royal Navy. During the preliminary attestation, he decided not to follow his skill as an artificer, preferring to travel and see the world as an able seaman. Unfortunately the RN did not agree and gave him a travel warrant back home. Not wishing to return to his former employers admitting that he had not gained entry, Fred visited the Army Recruiting Office. His father was serving in the Royal Veterinary Corps at the time so he was confident of acceptance. The problem was that he would not be 18 years old for a further two months . . . Fred explained his efforts:

'What do you want?' asked the recruiting sergeant.
'I want to join the army' I said.
'How old are you?' he asked.
'Eighteen in March' I replied.
'Come back in March!' he retorted simply.

Not to be defeated so easily Fred went to another recruiting office and claimed to be already 18 years old and was accepted. (He had to keep his incorrect date of birth throughout his service.) Fred was attested for the Manchester Regiment, but realising that the barracks was 'just up the road' he objected and the Sergeant thought again. The only other regiment recruiting in that area was the Border Regiment, and Fred after further questions enlisted in that regiment.

I arrived at Carlisle on a very wet day, and eventually found the castle. The large gates were shut and the place looked deserted. I had just decided that this place was not for me – when a khaki clad soldier appeared and propelled me into what I thought was a prison. This turned out to be a Sgt Robinson, and he gave me a sharp lecture on what happened to deserters, plus a long list of do's and don'ts – mainly don'ts.

We did six months at the depot in Carlisle before being sent to the 1st Battalion in Hollywood, Northern Ireland, which for me was like going abroad. They had said 'When you get to the battalion, watch out for the RSM!' Peters was his name, an Irish Guardsman and a towering figure of a man. 'What's he like?' I had asked, and they had described a man mountain with a big moustache.

During the first week we formed up for the RSM's parade, and then RSM Peters came on. He *was* big and he wore riding breeches and puttees, and had the largest boots I had ever seen! When he came on parade there was a deathly hush amongst the 1,000 men. He had a voice like a bull – I've since heard Tibby Brittain give orders but I would bet that Peters was louder. He put the fear of God into us.

At that time we wore collars with two clips at the top, and a little while later as a Lance Corporal I came out of the Company HQ and was going round the edge of the square, when I heard this very loud voice, 'CORPORAL!' I stopped and stood to attention facing the voice – and there was RSM Peters at the other side of the square, over 100 yards away, and he roared 'DO YOUR COLLAR UP!' My top clip was undone. I did so in quick time, and as I hurried away from this first encounter with him I was dumbfounded . . . how could he have possibly seen? Well – he couldn't of course, but he knew that men invariably undid their top hooks when not on parade, but I thought he was a genius at the time.

There were two battalions then, and the 2nd Bn was in India on the North West Frontier. The 1st Bn fed the 2nd Bn with draft twice yearly, and I would have liked to go, but I was posted to a signals section. I went to see my CSM – who was almost as big as RSM Peters – we in fact called him Chainbreaker as he was reputed to have wrapped a chain around his chest and snapped it by breathing in! A huge big barrel-chested man, he had an unfortunate habit of gripping hold of your arm as you passed. With his fingers under the muscle he would almost paralyse you! We were terrified of him but he had a heart of gold really and was a great man.

I went to see him to volunteer for the India draft, and he pointed out '*You* are not going to India – *You* have just been made a Lance Corporal!' as if this were royalty – I wasn't even getting paid for the rank – just acting unpaid L-Cpl. He added '*You* are going to be a great signaller one day.' It was a load of flannel really, but I thought that maybe he was right. All my friends went on the draft however, and when the next trooping season came I went to see him again, and this time he said 'If you ever come to see me again about India, I'll drive you into the ground like a tent peg!' I didn't bother again.

RSM F. Grimshaw at the Border Regt Depot, Carlisle Castle, 1959. Cumberland News, Carlisle

Regimental life was very strict in those times, you never seemed to be off the square. Always someone barking orders at you and instilling discipline into you. I often thought it was a bit hard at the beginning. I've thought about it a lot since because the modern army doesn't bear any comparison. Different kind of discipline I think, but all of our discipline came from the RSM. It was he who held the standard to be maintained. We obeyed orders instinctively. If he had said 'Grimshaw – climb that wall' Grimshaw would have climbed that wall or died in the attempt. In my day when you were on parade you were *there*. Men might write to their MP in my day – but the MP knew better than to take it up.

Our Colonel was a marvellous man – a true old campaigner. He would punish according to the Bible . . . I was never on a charge before him but brought men before him and his Bible would be by his side. He would listen to the facts of the charge and ask the man if he had anything to say. Whilst the man talked he would be turning the pages . . . and would then announce 'For an offence like this – in Jesus Christ's time – you would have received 40 lashes! – but I am not going to give you 40 lashes – but 14 days confined to barracks . . . If you come before me again' he would add – fingering a large bull whip kept on his desk. Few came before him twice.

Discipline was hard and it depended upon the Provost Sergeant as to how hard CB would be. I have known some very hard Provost Sergeants – defaulter parades would be called frequently to make sure that the man was in barracks. The first call was 15 minutes after reveille, then at various times during the day, and in

the evening every half hour from 6 to 10pm. I have known the Provost Sergeant to make defaulters parade showing clean all of their bedding – and on their next call – the bed! Then their kit box etc.

RSM Peters was probably the best RSM I ever came across. He became GSM in Belfast at a later stage before the war. He would take NCO drill instruction by lining us up on opposite sides of the barrack square, and conduct the giving of orders. He had a terrific voice himself. He also used to take the subalterns on drill, and I remember that one of his things was that one should never move when giving drill. I think he was right too. It helps one to be more concerned with voice control if you remain in one place. He would bring out each subaltern to take the drill – and we had many more drill movements then than we have now.

I watched one subaltern taking the drill on our large square which had buildings all around it. Certain commands have of course to be given on the correct foot, and he was trying to wait for the right foot – and the squad was getting further and further away and in danger of going out of sight altogether. RSM Peters' voice suddenly thundered out 'Say *something* – Mr B . . ., even if it's only Goodbye!'

We left N Ireland soon after to go to Catterick, and I shall never forget RSM Peters standing on a quayside shouting 'Good old Borders!' as we went across Hollywood Loch. Across the water a long way away we could still hear him . . . just the right pitch. At that time he had been father, mother and uncle to all of us.

In May 1936 the 1st Battalion was sent out to Palestine to quell the troubles there. We went on the *SS California* and battled through the Bay of Biscay with rough seas, where some 75 per cent of the men were sick. We called at Gibraltar, Malta and Haifa, then to Tel Aviv where we went on company detachments doing rail patrols on the track from Tel Aviv to Haifa.

We remained in Palestine until July 1939 by which time I had been made up to Sergeant in the Signal Section. We then set off for home to be based at Aldershot after leave. Our CO was to leave us on promotion to Brigadier in India, but he advised us that there was to be another war with Germany. We were surprised having heard little about it all whilst abroad. In the Signal Section we still had little radio although it was just starting up. We relied upon morse, heliograph and semaphore with lamps.

The 1st Battalion Border Regiment was shipped to France on 3 September 1939, and as part of the BEF moved to the Belgian frontier and then in the winter we moved to a position in front of the Maginot Line. Here the ground was too frozen to dig so there were no trenches. We took over a sandbagged raised position with a covered top, but it was so cold that we were advised to make ourselves sandbag boots stuffed with straw. We had open brazier fires which could be seen at night. The Maginot Line from above was just mounds of grass with gun slits showing and was very strong . . . but when the Germans attacked they by-passed the Line with its fortifications.

Retreat inevitably followed and as communication was so sketchy, we knew little of what was happening. We retreated from place to place leaving positions as soon as they were prepared, as they were by-passed. At one stage we were digging in on the side of the Albert Canal and were watching others do the same on the other side. A burst of gunfire soon revealed that they were Germans and we were off again.

We kept together as a unit but lost a lot of men from stuka bombing. As we retreated we joined civilian refugees and it was only when they scattered to avoid the stukas that we could press on. Orders then came for us to make a stand and form a line so that the army would have time to reach the coast, but it was difficult to get to where the line was to be formed, because of the packed roads and our lack of transport. We eventually stopped close to a four-storey deserted convent.

The German armour started to penetrate the area and there was little we could do to stop them. The Major kept us well forward retiring only slowly from map reference to reference, from village to village. Gradually we fell back towards the coast, and eventually joined in the defence ring around Dunkirk. Later when much of the BEF had gone we were told that some of the beaches were cleared of troops, and now we should take our chance on finding a boat. Once we reached the beaches we in fact found plenty of troops still there. We tried for a time to reach a boat moored to a landing stage, but both jetty and boat were hit by bombing so we headed for the safety of the open beaches again. Although many of the battalion were missing, there were still a fair number of us, and we still maintained order – and still carried our rifles.

Some of us got onto a RN motor boat and we slowly chugged out with the shelling and bombing still going on. Adversity brings the best out of most soldiers and I remember the lads being in high spirits and everyone was optimistic. The call soon came 'Anyone for cocoa?'

I don't think that either the Germans or ourselves realised how weak our we were after Dunkirk. I was walking with others when we were challenged by the local Home Guards. They did a proper job – 'Halt!' then 'Advance and be recognised.' We did so and identified ourselves, and as we walked on I commented to them, 'You'd do better with rifles wouldn't you'. 'Yes', conceded one of

them 'and we get them tomorrow!' They were brave lads and would no doubt have gone for any Germans with broom handles.

We were later being trained for the Far East, when we were suddenly told that we were to be trained as Air Landing Troops and soon after received red berets! This was I think because our battalion was at full strength, and being fit was ready to undertake the training. In addition to our 1st Battalion of the Border Regiment, the South Staffs and the Kings Own Scottish Borderers were also selected. No choice was given but we received an extra 1/- per day for being Airborne, and rations were increased.

We moved to Andover where we started special training, and it was a remarkable change in our role. As we were to be landed ahead of the army it was decided that we must be able to drive any vehicle found or requisitioned, and also be able to handle the weapons and grenades of other units as well as those belonging to the enemy. Some very intensive training followed with use of German weapons. We learned to ride cycles and tiny airborne motorcycles – great little machines! I remember going to collect all of these from Lincoln. There must have been 40 motorcycles grouped together, with an NCO leading – and me at the back. We sounded like an angry swarm of bees as we were held up at a level crossing.

We then learned all about gliders . . . and I went on a parachute course at Hardwick Hall, receiving my wings after about 12 jumps. On initiative tests we were dropped 30 miles from camp and told to get ourselves back. On one such test our lads broke into a transport park and stole a number of bren gun carriers. They didn't share – but took one each! There was hell . . . but our Major didn't care at all and he simply parked all the carriers for collection and pointed out that it had been a grave breach of security that our men had been able to take them so easily. He congratulated our men – but I'll bet some heads rolled somewhere.

Every company had to qualify their men on all sorts of vehicles, and at week-ends it was marvellous to see a line of mixed lorries – cars and motorcycles moving along, then the column would stop – and all the drivers would change vehicle!

We moved to a camp near Kidlington where there were eight seater Hotspur gliders – indestructable! We were given a flight in the tug aircraft to make sure that we were air-climatized, and then went on to train with the Hotspur, landing – making a fast exit and taking up defensive positions.

Our RSM at Barton Stacey had been George Gardner, a Midlander who was killed at Sicily. Apart from RSM Peters, all of our RSMs were promoted from the regiment. Notices had appeared whilst we were there, for volunteers to join the Parachute Regiment, and I put my name forward – I fancied parachuting more than I did gliding! I was interviewed by the company commander who agreed to pass my name on, but told me that he was certain I would not get there. I had been through Dunkirk with the Major who was now Colonel in command, and when I made my application before him to go parachuting he simply said 'Out. Get out!' I asked the RSM if I should go in again, and he replied 'Of course not . . . he's likely to shoot you!'

Two weeks later the notice appeared again. This time he replied 'Look – you are not going to be a parachutist!' I pointed out that the notice had said that anyone could apply. 'No. You are not going!' he repeated. 'I have to think of this unit . . . but I'll tell you what I will do, I will send you on a parachute course, but you will remain in this battalion.' 'Yes Sir.' I again said, 'I just want to jump'. Next day he had me sign a paper to that effect.

Four senior NCOs from the Border Regiment reported to Chesterfield for the next parachute course. I believe that our course was shorter than the full jumping course, so we did not receive the parachute 'wings' or receive para pay.

Our First Airborne Division now went to North Africa, some going by air, but we went by sea. There our unit joined up with the

American 1st Army, through to Sousse. Compared with the Parachute battalions, we did not have too bad a time in Tunisia. We had trained on the Horsa glider by now, and when one came down in the sea we found that being made of wood, it did not sink. We also used the American Waco glider, and we were not impressed with it on looking it over, as one of the men put his foot through the canvas cover (spread over tubular steel rods). The Waco held about 12 men, whilst the Horsa could take more, or a jeep and gun.

We were now briefed for the invasion of Sicily, and this was very thorough – to the nearest tree! The photographs were good, and tasks were allocated at section level, let alone company. The drill was that we would be towed within one mile of the coast, then released to glide the rest.

Our battalion of about 1000 men was allocated to some 100 Waco's and these were to be towed by Dakotas. The fleet of aircraft took off, but something was wrong with our tug as it could not get us off the ground. The Company Commander was in our glider and as soon as it came to a halt he demanded a fresh plane quickly. The next tug got us off, and we started the operation behind the rest of the force. We flew alone for a time, and being in full kit I did not bother to blow up my Mae West. It was dark and as we gradually caught up the main glider force we passed over the invasion ships making for Sicily. We eventually felt the glider being released from the tug, and said to ourselves 'This is it'.

The two pilots were British – and no sooner had we been detached than the pilot was saying urgently 'Prepare to ditch!' – and we were down in the sea. As we had approached the coast, sat facing each other, lots of tracer shots had come up – one shot went right through the glider with a blue flash. This flak I think caused us to be released too soon.

As we ditched a rush of water came in and I pushed men out as fast as I could, and then followed. Before taking off we had been issued with the usual ammunition, but not to be caught short – I had taken extra. In the water I tried to get some air into my Mae West, but the weight of my equipment dragged me down. I kicked my way up but could not climb over the depth of the glider wing. I went under again, and it's true that your life flashes before you when you are drowning. I struggled gulping air, and I remember being determined to make it. As I surfaced briefly I felt my hair being grabbed and I heard my saviour say 'Bloody 'ell, it's the Sergeant Major!' I was pulled onto the wing and I saw that it was by a man whom I had always had to chase. A good man in action, but a terrible solder in peacetime.

When I had recovered a little, I insisted that each man remove his boots, tie the laces together and loop them around his neck. It was dark and there was little we could do. I held a roll call and found that two medics were missing, but as we heard splashing nearby one of them was pulled onto the wing. We talked of making for the shore, but some of the men could not swim, and even by holding all together it was too far off shore to hope of making it. We spent some ten hours on that wing, then as dawn approached we spread out a Union Jack for attention. A launch eventually came towards us but his wash almost swamped the glider, and as it nudged the wing the glider started to go under. We hastily scrambled aboard the launch, and that was the second time in my life I heard the call 'Anyone for cocoa?'.

So in the invasion we got within a mile of Sicily, but no closer.

Our battalion took a long time to re-gather as the men were all over the place, but eventually we rejoined the 1st Airborne Division in Italy and were taken to Taranto Harbour by RN cruiser. We went ashore and moved forward as far as Fogia where we kept up with the German rearguard. Soon after this our unit returned and was shipped back to Sousse. Here the joyous news awaited us that we were to return home for further training, in readiness for the Second Front as the coming invasion of Europe was known.

When we arrived home at Barton Stacey near Andover, we found ourselves in an 'Airborne area' with Parachute battalions at Bulford and American Airborne Divisions nearby. We trained very hard, but rumours slowly circulated that we would not be required for D Day, instead we would be held in reserve. Whilst we were abroad the 6th Airborne Division had been formed and D Day was to be their show. There seemed little doubt that we should be needed however, as soon as the army was held up. Our Colonel reminded us how good the Germans were defensively and we were to go on training and be prepared to go into action at short notice.

Soon after D Day the bridgehead was established in Normandy, and it was not long before the Allied army broke out and swept across France towards Belgium and Holland. We were briefed fully for several operations which were cancelled at the last moment; it was very nerve racking as we were fully prepared to take off the following morning and carry out special tasks.

As events seemed to be passing us by, we became depressed and it looked as if the war could even end without us.

We were then briefed for a large operation in which we would be dropped well ahead of the main army to take and hold three bridges. The 1st Airborne Division would do all three bridges in one aircraft lift. The enormity of the task was then realised and American Airborne Divisions were added, requiring a vast number of aircraft. At Barton Stacey we were briefed with excellent maps and photographs, and battalions were given specific tasks. We were told that only German administration troops were in the Arnhem area, so we need not expect too bad a reception. We were not to know that two Panzer divisions, battered in the earlier fighting, were resting there.

On 17 September 1944 the operation commenced and the air was black with aircraft. The flight was good and we were very well escorted, and in the sunny bright day the journey was quite uneventful. When we arrived there was obviously going to be difficulty in getting so many gliders down in a zone surrounded by woods, but fortunately it was a young plantation and many gliders survived landing amongst the trees. As CSM I went with A Company, and our Coy Commander was a Maj Montgomery, a cousin of Monty but unlike him in being 6ft 4in tall.

After we landed we took up defensive positions, digging in and remaining around the dropping zone to safeguard the arrival of the second lift of troops the following day. Our job was to await the arrival of the rest of the 1st A/B Division, then move off to form an outer perimeter of defence outside Arnhem. We dug slit trenches in the sandy surface and awaited the arrival of the second lift. When they came in they received a great deal more opposition than we had earlier. Eventually we moved off and with heavy fighting going on all around, made our way to the planned position. By now it was clear that the opposition was far heavier than expected, and with the Second Army unable to break through to the division, a defensive position was taken up by the remnants of the division at Oosterbeek, and we were ordered to join its perimeter. Our RSM had been distributing ammunition by jeep and trailer to the various companies, when he was killed by a direct hit.

We took up our positions on a section of the perimeter with Arnhem to our right front. We had a good field of fire, but our bren guns were so accurate that we would sometimes have preferred a wider cone of fire. Our sten guns were makeshift and cheap compared with the German schmeiser or the very fast and accurate spandau.

As the time went on the opposition increased, and the German 88mms outgunned us. Their tanks would come towards us head on – where their armour was at its thickest and we had only PIATs to meet them with. We had been told supplies of ammunition, food and clothing, would be dropped by air in that order, but despite the very brave attempts by the pilots of the transport planes, very few supply canisters reached us and we became short of everything.

Many of our men were in action for the first time and some tended to open fire at targets with maximum firepower, so I was constantly going around our section of perimeter in company with the Major, urging men to conserve ammunition. We spent much time trying to pinpoint German machine-guns in the woods. A burst of fire would send us to ground, but I would see the Major standing up – and he would explain that the falling leaves from the trees indicated that the fire was high! He was absolutely calm in action and encouraged his company to be the same.

I spent about five days on the perimeter, and we had such good positions in the woods that we were not pushed back, although the German attacks became more frequent. Our battalion cooks fought as infantry and were placed near to me so that I could watch over them. One lad had remarkably good hearing, and could detect mortar shells coming down before anyone else. The Germans were only 150 yards away, but could not close in because as soon as we saw movement, we fired tracers and our airborne artillery opened up on them.

When there was a lull in the firing and mortaring, I would nip around to see if we had any wounded and to hand out more ammunition. During a further spell of mortaring however, I was wounded in the shoulder, and one of our stretcher bearers gave me first aid. I was told by an RAMC man that he could only cover it up with a field dressing and that I should go to the Regimental Aid Post. There the doctor probed around but could not feel anything and directed me to a hospital which was run by a Dutch woman. I went there and found that everyone had to leave their weapons outside. Every room and passage was full of wounded men, but the hole in my shoulder was examined and redressed as nothing could be found in it.

It was 22 September when I was hit and that night, in a small room, we heard tanks approaching, and we said 'Thank goodness – at last 30 Corps has arrived!' The armour went on rumbling past, then a soldier appeared in the doorway. He looked about seven feet tall – was dressed in black – and was a German officer.

Every man who could walk was assembled and taken into Arnhem, where the Queen Elizabeth Hospital was in their hands. A team of doctors, both Dutch and German, examined everyone. Wounds were redressed with paper bandages and after giving us some soup, many of us were moved by truck to Apeldoorn. There we were searched and things like watches were taken off us and our airborne smocks were removed.

Two days later we were taken to Stalag 11b.

I remember RSM J. C Lord at Stalag 11b. He was already there when we arrived, and took control of the prisoners with the help of a Staff Sergeant, an older man with first war medal ribbons, who was in charge of the rations.

Most of the NCOs were marched to Fallingbostel station where a train of cattle trucks was waiting, and we were allocated about 20 men to each truck. There was a ledge in each truck for sleeping, and our boots were removed to be kept separately, so that we would find it difficult to escape. We were handed half a loaf each so did not expect to be going very far on this train. We travelled for four days however, and some of the men who had consumed their bread quickly were literally starving. Those with some left had to guard it carefully. The train halted during air raids but we remained locked in for hours. Nor were we allowed out for toilets, but had to use the ash trays of the combustion stoves.

Eventually we arrived at an area in Silesia close to the Polish border, where there seemed to be many POW camps. We were starving and in a filthy state as we marched to our fresh camp, but soon after arrival a party brought in cans of macaroni stew. We learned that this had been donated by officers of Stalag Luft 3 because we were Airborne – kindred spirits as it were . . . A totally unexpected gesture.

One day three lorry loads of guards came in to the compound, and screamed at us to stand by our beds. We were told that because some German POWs in North Africa had lost their sheets from their beds, they proposed to remove our mattresses as a reprisal. We were ordered to place them in one of the trucks in the compound. The men in our hut began to do so, but as the mattresses went out of the door and were checked out, the lads passed them in again through a window further round the hut. The German officer then realised what was happening and sending for more guards – the whole things was repeated. Out of the door where they were checked out – in through another window. It all took three hours – and we still had our mattresses when they left!

A German Captain often called in to our hut to learn the news from the front, as our wireless was reliable, made of course by our boffins out of two bean tins still innocently labelled. Every night somebody took down the news and we passed the truth around – and claimed that we did it by mental telepathy! There were loud speakers always blaring out propaganda, and whilst some early prisoners believed it, we being captured later, knew that many of the places mentioned had long been in Allied hands. The German Captain had at first been friendly, asking us where we were captured, so we told him – at Arnhem, adding to his discomfort that soon the war would be over – and then he would be our prisoner.

We knew from our news broadcasts that the Rusians had been making great advances towards Germany and whereas before, escape was pointless, now it was becoming feasible. Escape committees were formed and maps prepared. Our German Captain became very uneasy and he was joined by a friendly Sergeant Major who had served on the Russian front. They called often to talk and ask if there was anything they could do for us, and to please remember that they had been helpful – when the time came.

We were paraded one morning to be told that we would be moving, as the Russians were getting close. Eventually about 25,000 prisoners were assembled and we set off. We travelled about 30km each day and blisters soon formed on our feet. For two days we headed west and our group of 150 men became separated in the charge of the German Sergeant Major. He was remarkable because whenever we stopped, a stock of boiled potatoes was produced. He was a kindly man and clearly had his fill of fighting on the Russian front. We went on marching into Germany and were not bothered by anyone, although by now some of the lads were suffering from dysentery. Once we stopped in a town which had just been attacked by the RAF with incendiaries, and we were farmed out to help with the damage and look in wrecked houses for food.

Eventually we struggled into Hanover, where there was gunfire and an air raid taking place. The column scattered, guards and all, into a nearby quarry. We foraged around for food, and after a few days were wandering about when we heard a vehicle which sounded like a jeep. We jumped out and were very nearly shot. It was an American unit on patrol, and there was I darting about in a very long greatcoat shouting 'British!' We must have looked most doubtful and were treated at first with suspicion.

We explained that we had been POWs and they relaxed giving us cigarettes in 100 boxes! 'Stay here – and transport will be sent for you' they promised. We were eventually flown home by the RAF. I travelled in a Lancaster bomber with five others, we landed somewhere near Herne and were soon sent home on leave. First however we went to a reception unit for ex POWs where we were documented and de-loused! We were interviewed by specialists, and the final question was 'Do you wish to stay on in the army?' I was a regular soldier with half my service completed, so I said 'Yes'.

I joined the battalion at Alford, Lincolnshire, and later, in 1946, we went to Germany, close to Hanover, so I had travelled in a circle. The battalion continued to travel, first to Palestine in 1948, then to Egypt and on to East Africa.

I was then posted home to attend a drill course at the All Arms Drill Wing at Pirbright, where the Sergeant Major in charge was D-Sgt Desmond Lynch, Irish Guards. I attended with RSM Chips Chandler, and by then we had lost our airborne status and had returned to being normal infantry. At one stage Chips Chandler and I were the only two who had not been checked on parade for equipment to be shown on 'show clean parade'. One day, however, D-Sgt Lynch checked me saying – 'Your bayonet's filthy Grimshaw!' and moving on to Chips added 'and your bayonet's filthy too Sergeant Major!' and as he walked on he ordered 'Show parade tomorrow morning'. After parade Chips and I compared our bayonets which were gleaming and sparkling, and going to the Sergeant in charge asked, 'What's wrong with these bayonets?' 'Have you been checked?', he asked. 'Yes', we replied. 'Well they're filthy then!' he decided. On the following day we had not touched our shining bayonets, but on 'Show clean' D-Sgt Lynch came around, looked at them happily and said, 'Remarkable improvement!'.

I later went out by sea to take part in the Suez Campaign, and then in 1954 completed a tour as permanent instructor with the Territorial Army. I then met Col Haddon, whom I had known since 1934, and he invited me to go to Germany with the 1st Bn, and going out as a CSM, I eventually became RQMS. I enjoyed that for about one year, but when the King's Own Regiment amalgamated with the Border Regiment, I was told that there would not be a vacancy for RQMS in the combined regiment. I

was getting close to the end of my service after 25 years, but the CO talked with me about the appointment of Depot Regimental Sergeant Major. I had actually declined the rank of RSM in the Territorial Army, but this was different. Quite a challenge.

The depot was at one stage going to be moved to Preston, but it remained at Carlisle Castle, and I became RSM there in 1959. This was great as I had first joined the regiment there. I took all of the depot parades starting each morning with a muster parade. I had previous experience as when we were stationed at Barnard Castle in the 1950s, we had no permanent RSM for a time, and I had, as Senior CSM, taken all of the battalion parades.

I do not think that I was a particularly hard RSM, but my philosophy was always simple – do it *now*. I had been brought up in an army where the discipline was always to do exactly as you were told. It needed a good RSM to have a good Sergeants Mess and if you had a good mess – you had a good battalion. Apart from parades and the enforcing of discipline, it is one of the most important things to have a good Sergeants Mess. To show a good example and fairness in the mess setting. Some of the Sergeants Mess' I have been in over the years were very strict, and there was silence when the RSM came in. Certainly things should be organised in a disciplined way in order to maintain standards, but the routine should not stop because the RSM comes in. He should not rule by fear, but by example.

I shall always remember, as a Regimental Sergeant Major, what a lovely feeling it was to have a lot of men on parade. I have always liked instructing, and have spent most of my life giving instruction. I loved drill . . . and a vital thing it proved to be.

Former Corporal Ray Sheriff wounded and blinded at Arnhem, visits his old RSM at The Parachute Regiment ITC at Aldershot in 1946/7. On the left is D-Sgt John Alcock. On the right RSM John Lord.

CHAPTER 11

RSMs of the Royal Marine Commando

It is the highest tribute to Sir Winston Churchill, that when France had fallen and the BEF had escaped so narrowly from Dunkirk without its equipment and transport, and when a German invasion of this country seemed so imminent, he urged that commando and parachute forces should be formed with offensive action against the enemy in mind. The stories of the formation and development of the Army and Royal Marine Commando Forces, the Parachute Regiment, Glider Pilot Regiment, the Special Air and Boat Services, and other special units have all been told.

Two complete divisions of Parachute and Air Landing Troops, the 1st Airborne and 6th Airborne, were eventually formed, with separate brigades of Army and Royal Marine Commandoes. 40 RM Commando went into action in August 1942 at Dieppe alongside army commando units and a strong force of Canadian troops. The operation proved to be a costly failure but through no lack of courage or determination on the part of any of the services involved.

Eight further RM Commando units of battalion strength were formed 41, 42, 43, 44, 45, 46, 47 and 48 Commando, and whilst it is not possible to follow the course of each unit in this book, all performed magnificently during the war, as did all of the Special Forces.

It would be difficult to find a better example of superb combined planning, or a more courageously and professionally carried out operation, than the D Day landings in France on 6 June 1944, when Army and Royal Marine Commandos and similar allied units, combined with special forces, assaulted the might of Hitler's Atlantic Wall. They fought their way inland to link up with the airborne forces, who had landed by parachute and glider to safeguard the flanks of the invasion area and to secure selected targets.

The Allies had learned well that when there are special tasks to perform, there is a need for special men in special units. It will always be so and if such units are not maintained in the future, they would have to be freshly formed if there was sufficient time. Many if not most of the units were disbanded at the end of the war, although one or two were reactivated for short periods. A Brigade of RM Commando units has remained, 40 RM Commando, 42 RM Commando, and 45 RM Commando, and a Brigade of the Parachute Regiment, 1 Para, 2 Para and 3 Para.

If one had attempted in 1982 to estimate where the main risks of armed conflict existed, the Falkland Islands would not have featured on any list. The prospect of this country having to assemble the largest task force of ships since the end of the 1939-1945 war, to convey two full brigades of selected troops a distance of 8,000 miles to fight the Argentinian forces was equally remote. That this country did so, was to show not only that it retained the capacity to mount such an operation, but as illustrated so often in past campaigns across the world, that the quality of its troops could outweigh the numerical superiority of the opposition.

The Falkland Islands lie in the South Atlantic some 300 miles from the South American mainland and have been British since 1833. The population of British origin has for many years fluctuated between 1,800 and 2,300 people. During the mid 1800s a small garrison of Royal Marines was stationed there, and the islands featured in WW1 when in a naval battle Admiral Sturdee's force gained a clear victory over that of Admiral Graf Von Spee. During the Second World War a large garrison was maintained on the island until 1945, and a number of local men and women served in the Forces. The British cruisers *HMS Exeter*, *HMS Ajax*, and *HMS Achilles*, docked at Stanley when returning from the battle of the River Plate in December 1939, for their wounded to be nursed in the local hospital.

When Argentina invaded the Falkland Islands on 2 April, and South Georgia 800 miles away on 3 April 1982, many of the men in the British Forces had just departed on Easter leave.

The Task Force consisted of more than 100 ships and almost 30,000 men and women, including 3 Commando Brigade – which was reinforced by two parachute battalions, and 5 Infantry Brigade. The story of the Falklands Campaign is told by three Regimental Sergeant Majors of the Royal Marine Commando.

40 Commando RMs was commanded by Lt-Col Malcolm Hunt. The RSM was G. A. Pearson, who had joined the Royal Marines in September 1960 and had progressed through the ranks to become SNCO at the age of 22. He was appointed RSM of 40 Commando RMs in June 1981. He had served operationally in Aden, Singapore and the Persian Gulf. When I met him in Plymouth he talked of his earlier training RSMs.

When I was a young marine of 17 years, our RSM was the kind of man one always remembers. His name was RSM J 'Sticky' Baines BEM MM. He was a strict disciplinarian but not at all the bawling and shouting type and would come up quietly and speak into one's ear. I remember him visiting our troop location on my first commando exercise at Sennybridge. It was a particularly rough day and he remarked that he had served in Korea where it had been tough, but he thought it was even more so at Sennybridge! Another highly respected RSM was RSM Roger Tyack. He taught me my earlier trade of drill instructor. Few could emulate him at pace stick drill.

In the early days there was a lot of drill on the training progamme, and there was nothing more satisfying for me than to take my own drill squad to pass out at Deal. In later years however there was to be a great decrease in drill but I always considered that it had a place in instilling discipline, building character, and improving bodily posture.

Whilst I remember no particular parade amongst the many, I do recall that we once went as representative ship to Bordeaux at the European Trade Fair. We trained 12 men for the Quarter Guard, and one day were receiving VIPs on to the ship. The quarter deck was small and the guard had to work in very close order. The VIP on this day was an Admiral of the Port. He was piped aboard, met the Captain, who introduced him to the First Lieutenant. At this point the CO brought the guard to attention, then to the shoulder arms, and gave the present arms. As the officer came to the salute with his sword, the tip of the blade caught the glove of the Admiral, and with the second movement the sword was held aloft with the glove flying like a pennant.

42 RM Commando was commanded by Lt-Col Nick Vaux. The RSM was D. A. Chisnall BEM who had joined the RM in 1964 at Deal, and progressed through the ranks to be appointed RSM in November 1981. He had served operationally in Borneo, Aden, and Northern Ireland. A Mountain Leader by trade, he also qualified as a parachutist in Abingdon in 1968 and has since exceeded 1,000 parachute drops. In 1980 he had been awarded the British Empire Medal in Northern Ireland. In conversation in Plymouth he told me of his earlier training RSMs.

I remember that my first RSM, who trained us at Deal, was RSM J. E. Pollitt BEM and many of our present day standards come from his time. He was later to become Mayor of Exeter. Also from the 1960s I remember RSM Maurice Rough.

RSM W. H. G. Carroll well fitted the image of the RSM, and we were terrified when we met him coming round a corner. He was also a standards man, and was RSM of the Commando Training Centre in 1968. He was always known as Double R and Double L.

I remember several RSMs of 40 RM Commando in which I served for two tours of duty. RSM Jack French who in the late 1970s was responsible for training most of the senior officers within the Royal Marines. More recently Gus Pearson was my RSM, and he was followed by RSM Graham George who was RSM of logistics at the Falklands. I remember taking part in many parades, such as the withdrawal from Singapore in 1972, the Cenotaph Parade on Armistice Day 1980 when I was CSM. Also at the Albert Hall Anniversary Parade when GSM Alex Dumon was such a great help to us all. I shall always remember the departure of 42 RM Commando from Bickleigh Barracks for the Falklands, when our Commanding Officer gave the order 'To the South Atlantic – Quick March!' My service ambition had always been to become the RSM.

45 RM Commando was commanded by Lt-Col A.

Whitehead. The RSM was P. R. Chapman who had joined the Royal Marines as a boy soldier, a junior marine in September 1959. A close friend and colleague of David Chisnall, they had shadowed each other through their service. Pat Chapman rose through the ranks to become RSM of 41 RM Commando in January 1981 until its disbandment six months later, when he was appointed RSM of 45 RM Commando. He had served in Aden, Borneo and Northern Ireland. In 1966 he qualified as a parachutist, then completed a course to become an Assistant Parachute Jump Instructor. He has not maintained a record of jumps since made. I went to talk with him in Scotland about his service.

The RSMs I particularly remember were RSMs MacDonnell and W. Chisholm. Both were serving in the 1960s and although I did not get an opportunity to learn much about them, they were very impressive Marines. The 1st RM Commando RSM I came into contact with was RSM J. Baines BEM MM, who was RSM of 43 RM Commando when it was reformed for a period in Plymouth. Two parades will always remain in my memory. The first was with 41 RM Commando. It was the first time that the Trooping of the Colour was held at Deal since 1951. I had the privilege of drawing my sword on parade, and of receiving the Colour as an RSM. That was quite an honour. The second parade came after the Falklands.

Prior to the Falklands, I had served on the islands on two occasions, firstly in 1962 on ice patrol vessel *Protector*. There was no garrison on the islands at that time. We were there as a boarding party and also worked aboard ship. We stayed for about one month at Moody Brook whilst the ship sailed on scientific tasks to the South Antarctic. We learned quite a lot about the Falklands at that time. I later served as detachment SM in 1972 when the ice patrol vessel *Endurance* went to the Falklands to replace the *Protector*. This knowledge was all to come in useful.

Many of the present and former Regimental Sergeant Majors whom I have been fortunate enough to meet, have impressed as having all of the soldierly qualities which would enable them to cope with virtually any situation on the parade ground or on active service. This is not surprising as such men have been selected and promoted through the ranks for their ability to calmly take charge of and control situations which would baffle and defeat most individuals.

With their quiet calm manner of trained efficiency, Gus Pearson, David Chisnall and Pat Chapman impressed me enormously and the extremely difficult tasks which await such forces as the RM Commando and the Parachute Regiment, are in the safest possible hands – as they so clearly illustrated at the Falklands. I wondered who could have so well trained and influenced such men! Both Gus Pearson and Pat Chapman paid tribute to RSM J. 'Sticky' Baines BEM MM who was clearly an RSM of high quality, and he is well remembered for his personal attributes.

RSM Roger Tyack was also remembered, and the following details of his service also shine with quality. He joined the Royal Marines on 1 March 1949, and on completion of his training at the depot RMs, ITC at Lympstone, and Commando School at Bickleigh, he was awarded the Commando Medal as the best all-round recruit during his Commando Course. He remained at the Commando School for a time during which he qualified as a parachutist and as a Cliff Leader. Roger Tyack was then posted to 41 Independent Royal Marine Commando and saw active service in Korea. He was awarded the Korean and United Nations Medal. On his return home he passed both parts of the JNCO's course and was posted to the Depot RMs as a Drill Leader. He was promoted to Corporal in 1952, and to Sergeant in 1955. He was employed as a Recruit Squad Instructor.

In October 1957 he joined the RM barracks at Eastney for pre-embarkation training before joining *HMS St Angelo* based at Malta. During his three years there he was an instructor at the NCO's cadre. On return to this country

RSM R. J. Tyack, Royal Marines, at the Depot, Deal in 1974-75.
Roger Tyack

he was posted back to the depot for some five years during which he completed the RSMs course at CTRRM, was promoted to Colour Sergeant, and gained experience as the depot training coordination senior NCO. In 1965 he went to Aden with 45 RM Commando as CQMS and returned to the depot where in May 1967 he was made QMS. During the next two years he worked as Sergeant Major HQ Company which involved administrational responsibility for over 400 NCOs and men. He also held overall responsibility for parade ground training.

In November 1969 he was appointed RSM, HQ Training Group RMs and then in January 1971 as Fleet RSM. His next posting was as RSM 45 RM Commando Group in Arbroath Scotland, then he completed operational tours in Northern Ireland, and training periods in Norway. In July 1972 he was automatically made Warrant Officer 1st class

when the warrant rank was introduced into the Royal Marines. Returning to the depot in 1974 RSM Tyack remained until August 1976 when he retired from the Royal Marines. In relation to the rank of RSM Roger Tyack wrote to me:

On promotion to RSM I gave considerable thought to how I would approach my new responsibilities, and reflected on the impressions I had gained from the 14 or so RSMs I had served under, or been associated with during my 20 years service. Of course in practice one must be oneself, applying strengths and weaknesses to the best of one's own ability, and adapt to the modern day changes of service life. I did not dismiss the previous experience and knowledge gained from these individuals however.

Two RSMs of whom I would make special mention are firstly RSM J. Baines BEM MM, for his leadership qualities as the RSM of 41 Independent Royal Marine Commando in Korea. Secondly RSM, T. W. P. Franks BEM, who left an everlasting impression on me. A man of great presence, a ready wit, firm, fair and greatly respected by officers, SNCOs and other ranks. He was fondly known to many of us, out of earshot of course, as Uncle Tom.

So far as special parades are concerned, I participated in two Royal Tournaments at Earls Court, in 1950 as a Marine in a cliff climbing display, and in 1956 as a Sergeant Drill Instructor with the King's Squad drill display. In 1961 I was a member of the parade training team for 41 RM Commando when New Colours were presented by HRH the Duke of Edinburgh at Stonehouse Barracks Plymouth. I was also the QMS responsible for the parade training of 45 Royal Marine Commando when New Colours were presented in 1969 by HM The Queen. This parade should have been held on Plymouth Hoe but sadly the wet weather resulted in a shortened ceremony in the Guildhall, much to the disappointment of all the Marines who had worked and trained extremely hard for the occasion. As an RSM I was only involved with Guards of Honour for visiting dignitaries or with normal unit parades. Whilst now employed by the Sergeant At Arms in the House of Commons, I am also a Yeoman of The Queen's Bodyguard of the Yeoman of the Guard.

Among the prominent RSMs mentioned by David Chisnall was RSM J. E. Pollitt BEM and coming from a Royal Marine family he joined the corps at Plymouth during the latter part of the war. Following the award of the naval gunnery medal during his recruit training he was destined for service at sea, serving on *HMS Newcastle*, *Illustrious*, *Vanguard*, *Kenya* and *Mauritius*. In 1946 he was top of his course and gained a distinction when passing for Corporal, and two years later was joint top student on a course, again gaining a distinction when passed for Sergeant.

James Pollit then qualified as a naval gunnery instructor at Whale Island in 1951 obtaining the highest marks on the course. He reverted to shore establishments after leaving *HMS Mauritius* at both Plymouth commando units and commando units abroad, and was confirmed as CSM in 1957 whilst serving with 45 RM Commando in Cyprus. In 1958 he became Troop Sergeant Major at the Specialist Training Troop at Plymouth which included the Cliff Assault and Assault Engineering Group.

He was appointed RSM in 1959 and was one of the youngest in the corps at that time. He became the RSM at

RSM J. E. Pollitt, BEM, Royal Marines. Photographed when Mayor of Exeter 1984-5. Devon and Cornwall Police/Exeter City Council

Poole where the Special Boat Service and Landing Craft Specialists were based. There followed two tours of active service with 45 RM Commando before returning to the Depot Royal Marines at Deal as the senior RSM in the corps. In 1965 he was granted the first Quartermaster commission under the new quartermaster scheme for specially selected RSMs and served with 45 RM Commando on tours in Northern Ireland. Posted to Lympstone in late 1970, he retired from the Royal Marines in 1972. He had been awarded the BEM for service in the Middle East and during his service had an outstanding sporting career.

Since leaving the Corps he has held responsible positions within his city community, and was the Mayor of Exeter in 1984-5. In 1987 Councillor James Pollitt wrote to me that he remembered 24 RSMs, some with deep impressions, other passing by. During his service as senior RSM at Deal, he must have controlled the training of 5,000 men, but he felt that his training of men must have run into many thousands more.

David Chisnall also mentioned RSM W. H. G. Carroll, who had influenced him during his earlier training, and when in 1987 I approached 'Double R Double L' regarding his memories of service, he gave me the following information.

I joined the Royal Marines on 22 October 1946, and retired on 27 November 1983. I was promoted RSM in December 1965 and served in that appointment until July 1973 but remained as a WO I until my retirement. During my active service days I went on operational tours with 45 RM Commando, 42 RM Commando twice, and 40 RM Commando to such places as Palestine, Transjordan, Hong Kong twice, Egypt, Cyprus and Malaysia, but there were other tasks in between such as an earthquake on a Greek island and floods in Bangladesh.

Of all the RSMs I have served under, or with, who have influenced me, three stand out in my memory. RSM Bill Edlin of 45 RM Commando in 1947-48. He formed my first sight of an operational RSM and was quiet and gentlemanly mannered. He did not make a lot of noise but was a wonderful example to all. Big and powerful, a real father figure, he was full of presence. Second only in order of my contact with him was RSM Tom W. P. Franks. An absolute parade man, immaculate in his turn out and bearing. He was fair, firm and consistent. A non-drinker but always ready to join in with the SNCOs and their families socially and always approachable.

The third RSM, again in order of contact, was RSM Jock Bill Chisholm. He was also always immaculate and was the epitome of physical fitness. A fine man, I have known him for over 25 years and we remain close friends. I suppose that I unconsciously took something from each of them in attitude in my task of being an RSM. There were many others, some of whom I did not even like, but on the whole they were all good in their own ways.

As I was never a parade man, such memories do not really remain amongst my treasured thoughts, but I suppose the most spectacular parade was when the 3 RM Commando Brigade (40 RM Commando, 42 RM Commando and 45 RM Commando) was presented with Colours for the first time in 1952. I was Sergeant then and the parade was held on Floriana Parade in Malta. The parades I most enjoyed were corps reunion annual parades when all of the 'old and bold' returned to remember what it was, and is, all about. These parades always give such pride and pleasure to a lot of ex-Royal Marines of all ranks, and it is amazing how the word of command of the RSM affects such men, even though some of them are disabled and handicapped by walking sticks and age. They suddenly grow six inches taller, and whilst I have taken part in many such parades, I always enjoy them.

My final appointment as RSM was at Royal Marine Barracks Eastney, Portsmouth from 1971-73, and then I transferred to the RN RM careers service in which I remained until retirement in 1983.

Both RSMs Tyack and Carroll spoke of the qualities of RSM Tom W. P. Franks, and as a final tribute to the men who so ably influenced many thousands of young Marines including those who themselves progressed to the rank of RSM and served in the Falkland Islands, the story that follows is of a highly respected former Royal Marine RSM. The details have been compiled from letters sent to me by Tom Franks.

I joined the Royal Marines on 24 July 1934 when I was 17. My grandfather, father and three uncles have served in the corps before me, so I was heavily influenced by family tradition.

When I joined the corps there were no RSMs to my knowledge, and all of the senior instructors were Commissioned Warrant Officers. On completion of recruit training in September 1935, I was sent with the RM Mobile Naval Base Defence Organisation to Egypt. Based in the north coastal area we manned AA guns and installed boom defences in Alexandria harbour. We also installed 6in gun pedestals along the north coast. These were put to good

The Duke of Edinburgh visits the ITC Royal Marines, 1967.
(L to R) Major Grant, HRH Duke of Edinburgh, Col J. F.
Parsons, OBE MC and RSM W. H.G. Carroll.
PR RMs, MOD London

use during the Second World War. All this was brought about by the Italian-Abyssinian War which ended in 1936.

I was promoted to Corporal at the age of 19 and served on the first *HMS Sheffield*, a four triple 6in turret cruiser of 9,000 plus tons, her stainless steel bell now hangs in a museum in Sheffield. I was made Sergeant in 1939, and qualified as an instructor of all drills and also all infantry weapons, serving at Chatham and at the Royal Marine Depot at Deal as recruit instructor. In 1944, and only ten years after joining the corps, I was promoted to RSM, and was said to be the youngest RSM (at 29 years) at that time.

I helped to raise and train the 32nd Bn, part of the RM 117 Infantry Brigade in Europe, and served with the unit until the war ended when we had reached Kiel. Returning to the UK after the war, I served for six months at the Commando Training Unit in North Wales and then joined 42 RM Commando in the Far East in 1945. We subsequently moved to Malta, Tripolitania (now Libya) and then to Egypt. I was awarded the BEM on 10 June 1948 for outstanding zeal and devotion to duty.

In 1949 I returned to the UK to become RSM of training at Chatham Barracks until just before its closure in 1950, and then RSM at the depot in Deal until 1953. Back to 42 RM Commando

for approximately 12 months, I was then appointed to the RM NCO's School at Plymouth, where we trained the corps JNCOs, and future RSMs, and also held revision courses for all ranks of SNCOs.

During my service I trained and took part in many parades, tattoos etc, in many parts of the world. Included were the Freedom of the City of Plymouth presented to our corps, the Trooping of the Colour at Lympstone etc. With a Royal Marine Band under Capt Long, I took a contingent of 140 men to the Edinburgh Tattoo, the first Royal Marines ever to give a display there. I also trained men on two occasions for drill and band displays at Earls Court. One of the press reports at Earls Court in 1951, commented upon the clarity of the orders by the Marine RSM compared with the Army. So far as drill movements are concerned, Trooping the Colour at the Sovereign's Birthday Parade takes a lot of beating. I retired from the Corps in July 1957.

Royal Marine Commando Regimental Sergeant Majors Seminar held at the Commando Training Centre, Nov 1981. (back row L to R) RSMs Mick Euridge, Dave Langdon, Dave Chisnall, and Peter Ramft. (centre row) Bill House, Graham George, Mick Jones, Dave Walker, Ray Lewis, and Bill Holden. (front row) Gus Pearson, Jack French, Lt-Gen Sir Steuart Pringle, Nick Merrit, and Malcolm Harris. Nine of the RSMs in this distinguished group have since completed their service.
PR RMs, MOD, London (CTC Photograph)

RSM T. W. P. Franks, Royal Marines. Receiving the LS & GC Medal from Lord Louis Mountbatten in 1950 at the Depot, Deal.
PR RMs MOD London

CHAPTER 12

The Falklands Campaign with RSMs G. A. Pearson, D. A. Chisnall, and P. R. Chapman

In Eastern Scotland many members of 45 Commando RMs had departed on Easter leave, and RSM Pat Chapman was sleeping in his day cabin following a late mess members dinner which had lasted until 4am. He was abruptly awakened by his phone ringing, and a voice exclaimed simply 'There's been a recall – and you are to muster in the Second IC's office!' Realising that it was now 1 April the RSM carefully questioned the caller, but was assured that the order was genuine. Gathering himself together he made his way to the Second IC's office, and was told that 45 Commando would be going to deal with the Argentine invasion of the Falklands.

At Plymouth RSM Gus Pearson of 40 Commando was making his way to breakfast, when the Adjutant stopped him and advised that there had been a change of plan, and that Charlie Company was to be prepared to leave for the Falklands. (Another company had earlier been designated.) Half of the commando was away on a range week near Liverpool so the shooting programme would have to be adjusted. RSM Pearson acknowledged and replied 'OK Sir – leave it with me, and I'll see what we can come up with'.

In the dining hall he approached the CSM and explained 'Bit of a change of plan this morning – something's happening in the South Atlantic and a company is coming out of the training programme – we are going to have to adjust . . .' 'Not interested Sir!' interrupted the CSM. RSM Pearson began to repeat the details, but again came the reply 'Not interested today Sir . . . day off this morning!' The RSM slowly emphasised '*This* is what is *happening* – Today!' 'Sorry Sir,' apologised the CSM. 'I thought you were having me on – this being 1st April!'

RSM David Chisnall of 42 Commando was at his home having just started Easter leave, and on 2 April he and his family were taking an early breakfast before leaving to catch an early morning train from Plymouth to Arbroath, where they would attend the christening of the Chapman's newly born daughter. Dave Chisnall and Pat Chapman had been friends for many years, having virtually grown up together with the Royal Marines.

The phone then rang and it was the CO Lt-Col Nick Vaux saying 'RSM – I think you had better come in.' David Chisnall was sure when he could detect a joke and replied,

'Thank you Colonel! – but it's not April Fools Day now – I know you are leaving for Washington . . . Give my regards to . . .' 'No,' cut in the CO. 'I think you *had* better come in.' Realising the seriousness in his voice, RSM Chisnall quickly acknowledged, left his family and drove to Bickleigh Barracks, pondering over the recent news from the South Atlantic as he went. Lt-Col Vaux was waiting with the Adjutant when he arrived, and very soon the first steps were taken to recall 42 Commando.

The April Fool factor had caused some very minor delay, but soon long standing contingency plans came into effect. At Arbroath RSM Pat Chapman faced an immediate and extensive recall task, as the majority of 45 Commando were on Easter leave. 'All we knew was that the Argentinians had landed on the Falklands and that we were going to be mobilised. That was all we needed to know, and from that initial 5am meeting in the Second IC's office, we subsequently arranged the rest of the day, stores – meetings – and briefings.

'I think that I was one of the few with previous Falkland service and when an O group was scheduled for 9am, I immediately hurried home and found some maps of the islands, came back and photo-copied them, and distributed copies to those about to attend the O group.'

A similar situation was developing in Plymouth, where RSM Gus Pearson recalls:

We did not have to alter our range training programme, as a further signal came in almost immediately, and our Lt-Col Malcolm Hunt departed for a briefing. Transport was then arranged to return the commando to Seaton Barracks, where without the problem of recalling from leave, we were probably the first unit to be ready and prepared. One of the striking features about the Falkland campaign was the lack of paperwork, as there was time only for signals. On exercises there are heaps of papers and instuctions, but this operation came out as a signal, which led to the CO briefing the Company Commanders, who in turn briefed the Troop Commanders and on to the men. That is how things were done.

At the CO's O group however, when the signal circulation list was read out, this was much longer than for any exercise! – Brigade HQ 40 Commando. 42 Commando. 45 Commando. Logistics Regt – a number of HM ships. The 3rd Battalion, The Parachute Regiment; and so the list continued. Plus one or two of the small special units we had hardly ever heard of . . .

RSM David Chisnall also well remembers the initial preparations.

42 Commando had only recently returned from Norway, and our rear party had still been off-loading skis and equipment before going on leave. Recall immediately commenced however, and we brought men back from all over the country, some from as far as the USA, and within two days most of the commando was present.

M Company assembled and was sent off in advance to Ascension, under the command of Maj Guy Sheridan, and we did not see the company again until the end of the campaign following their successful recapture of South Georgia. In 42 Commando Lt-Col Nick Vaux and I had only recently taken over our ranks – I was appointed RSM in November 1981, but we had knitted together a good team. We all knew each other's qualities, and where also things could go wrong, so we were in a fortunate position. Our Major General – Jeremy Moore, Brigade Commander – Julian Thompson, and our Commanding Officer – Lt-Col Nick Vaux, had only just returned from training together in a war simulated exercise in Norway.

As the commando was being recalled, the traditional task of the RSM, that of looking after ammunition, got under way. The Quarter-Master completed the listing and paperwork, and the RSM made the distribution. TA drivers began to deliver truckloads of ammunition from all over the country. The brigade is always prepared for action, but in my earlier experience in Borneo, Aden, Singapore and Northern Ireland, we had known in advance what kind of situation we were going out to. With the invasion of the Falklands by the Argentinians however, we knew little, indeed initially it seemed to be more a question of whether there would be a political solution. Within a week we were moved to Southampton, and instead of the planned journey to Arbroath, my family went off to relatives in Cambridgeshire. Word then came that we were to embark on the *SS Canberra*.

At Arbroath Pat Chapman was also handling large amounts of ammunition.

I was warned to receive 32 truckloads of various kinds of ammunition, and we were not too familiar with some of it in peacetime. It took hours to muster the crates and to account for it, then it was reloaded onto vehicles to be taken on to Portsmouth. Upon being recalled, 45 Commando was transported to Portsmouth, where eventually the unit was distributed amongst seven small vessels. I was with the bulk of the headquarters on the RFA ship *Stromness*, and we also had a rifle company and support company with us.

In the Royal Marines we are accustomed to serving aboard ship, so for the majority it was home from home, but there were restrictions as the ship was basically RFA crewed and even included some Chinese crewmen.

Alpha Company of 40 Commando went to Portsmouth where they completed much of the loading of ammunition for the Task Force. They then embarked on *HMS Hermes* and sailed on 5 April. RSM Gus Pearson with the remainder of 40 Commando moved to Southampton soon after to join the *Canberra*.

We could not believe it at first that we were to travel in such style. We had been told that a civilian ship would be used – indeed, that an advance party would join the ship in the Med to work out some of the problems we would face with training spaces etc. but when we learned that it was the *Canberra*, it was marvellous.

We had said farewell to our families at Seaton Barracks several days before and had left home expecting not to return, and that had been the hard part. Finally as so often happens, when we expected to return home in the evening, we were suddenly on our way to Southampton.

On Good Friday 9 April 1982 the *Canberra* slowly edged out to sea and the scene could have belonged to many occasions in the past when an expeditionary force had been sent off to fight a distant campaign. The band played and great crowds watched, and relatives waved with that mixture of excitement and sadness. RSM David Chisnall however had other preoccupations.

2 Commando lined the decks of the *Canberra* as she moved out and in my opinion Procedure Alpha as this was termed, was a disciplined stand still attention parade. On this occasion because there were many families present waving goodbye, a few of the men were attempting to wave back, and as the Adjutant and I walked around, we reminded them to stand still. Right in front of me then, a marine waved, and holding his arm down, I shouted that the next person waving would go inside! I intended this to mean – would go below deck, and not take part, but this was no doubt interpreted as going inside the cell. The Adjutant commented, 'That's a bit harsh RSM' and I replied that I was getting a bit concerned with the ill discipline, and that if it was like this now, what would things be like later?

Another man then raised his arm to wave and pushing it down ordered, 'Take this man inside'. Again the Adjutant commented 'Be more compassionate RSM – the man's in tears'. I realised then that the sadness of our leaving was lost to me, as I was of course more concerned with the discipline of the parade. My own family was also down there, but the Regimental Sergeant Major does not have such problems, and will never have such problems . . . It goes with the badge of rank.

Also on board the *Canberra* was 3 Para and 40 Commando. RSM Gus Pearson recalls:

I don't think we really expected to get beyond the Isle of Wight before a political compromise was found, but as we steadily progressed across the Bay of Biscay routines were established. The Officers Mess was formed, and we set up our Sergeants Mess. Also the Corporals Club and the NAAFI were organised.

There were three RSMs on board, Dave Chisnall of 42 Commando, Laurie Ashbridge of 3 Para, and myself of 40 Commando. There was also a RN WO1. We formed a mess committee to cater for the 300 senior NCOs, with no formal rules or bylaws. I was made Mess President, as although I was probably junior to Laurie Ashbridge, the Royal Marines were in the majority.

We took an equal share of work, and suggestions were passed through our own units. Each member contributed £1 into the fund, and so we had £300 mess fund to begin with. We soon generated more by organised games nights, entertainment nights, and our own 'sods opera' nights. The money went back into the system and we could pay for the services of HM Commando Forces Band under its Master John Ware, to do a little entertaining. Once the living quarters were sorted out, meetings and conferences were held by the training officers.

Days were split up into periods, and each unit began to undertake intensive training. Organising the daily physical training for 5,000 men required an amount of juggling at times. The promenade deck was a great asset and people were soon pounding around at 6.30am before breakfast, at their allotted time. Next day they would be out at 8am and the next at 9am. There were also flight decks and other spaces around the ship where individuals could complete their press-ups, so we were able to keep fit and agile. We found that running around deck was mentally fatiguing, and although we had normally run further around the roads of Plymouth, we found that three miles – 12 circuits of the deck – was about enough.

We could do a lot of practical training with aircraft recognition and first aid, and instead of practising the broken leg or artificial respiration, each man practised the injecting of morphine – I think we only had one guy who fainted. The food on board was of course marvellous as we had the normal *Canberra* first class cuisine of the tourist, which soon meant that weight had to be watched!

RSM David Chisnall remembers that they somehow managed to convince the men of 3 Para that they would be better off on deck four as this was below the waterline, and where – they were persuaded – they would not get so seasick.

This was probably the worst place for them! – but it was one of those one-upmanship things. They fitted in extremely well however and in fact suffered no more seasickness than did the marines! One could not have asked for better units with which to form the brigade, but then I had served alongside the Parachute Regiment before, and in fact had taken over from them in the New Lodge area of Northern Ireland in 1972. Part of our handing over routine had been for me to accompany them around to get to know the area, and I wore the red beret and smock. I have worn the two most famous berets – the red and the green – and had earlier, in 1967, qualified as a military parachutist.

On board ship the RSMs formed part of the training organisation, and as I was a qualified mountain leader I was fortunate in becoming involved in some of the pre-planning exercises. The staff were considering whether it would be feasible to go for say – Goose Green by one route – or another.

So far as the men were concerned, we were very fortunate with the *Canberra* because of its set distance around number three deck, four times round equalled one mile. We would run clockwise one day, and anti-clockwise the next. The whole embarked force had to co-ordinate the exercising programme. The units soon became close and shared tasks.

Laurie Ashbridge knew exactly what he wanted for his paras, but he had not lived aboard ship and had not required such a routine before, so he learned new terms of reference.

We did a lot of weapon training, firing off the after end, and a great deal revolved around personal skills with weapons. We paraded daily and demanded the necessary smartness and tidiness – turn out and bearing. Cabins were inspected each day and of course weapons particularly so. Men grew accustomed to having their firearms as an extension of their arms once again.

On the Stores Support Ship *Stromness* RSM Pat Chapman settled for the voyage to Ascension.

We were fortunate in some ways, being on an RFA ship, as our provisions were carried with us. Although not as comfortable as the *Canberra* we were quite well off. The CO and I were able to

45 Commando Royal Marines' practise landing at Ascension Island in early May 1982. (far left) Sgt John Barker. (far right) RSM Pat Chapman. Next to the RSM is C/Sgt Bill Eades. At the stern sits Lt-Col Andrew Whitehead, DSO.

Pat Chapman (PR RMs, MOD, London)

visit some of the other craft upon which 45 Commando were carried when a helicopter was available, and we found them living in far more difficult circumstances, with water rationing, unprepared food and so on.

We made maximum use of the space we had and soon formed a routine with physical training, weapon skills and medical lectures. We half expected to hear of a political settlement; we had mixed feelings at that stage, some people in their hearts hoped for action, whilst others were quite prepared to go down to the Falklands and return home. I was not fussed either way personally, we are paid to do a job and rarely get the opportunity to actually do it.

There was relatively little an RSM could do aboard ship to exercise discipline and leadership, with the commando spread out, and the space so limited. We could only run so many times around deck, or do so many press-ups, go through the skills so many times with weapons. We took time to study the Argentinian Forces, with what little information was available.

As we approached Ascension the climate became warmer, and it was hot when we arrived, so we were glad to go ashore for training. I was able to visit the *Canberra* for lunch on one occasion, with Dave Chisnall and Gus Pearson. It cracked me when the hot rolls were brought up by the waiter!

RSM David Chisnall also recalls the hot sunshine.

Having sailed so recently from north Norway in minus temperatures 42 Commando noticed the heat, but we were very fit having been able to train regularly. I think by comparison that we on the *Canberra* were more physically fit than those on military ships, as we had eaten well, trained hard, and showered with unlimited water, whereas on the other ships everything was restricted.

At Ascension we went ashore on a five day training package, whilst the shipping was being re-arranged and the stores reloaded. We completed some more live firing, and speed marches of about ten mile distance. We would practice going ashore by landing craft, followed by a speed march, the firing of new weapons, then be picked up again. The hurriedly prepared range with unconventional templates provided excellent battle noises, as all arms and explosives were fired. To the younger members of the commando it was the first occasion in which they had experienced such firing in a confined space. A useful foretaste of what was to come.

On the late evening of 8 May the Task Force put to sea and the approach south began towards the Falklands. Most of the men now felt certain that they would be required to make a landing on enemy held shores. RSM Pat Chapman aboard the *Stromness* noticed the change in attitude.

As we sailed south there was a change in the response to lectures and instead of gazing out to sea concentration was given in full. We also read the daily news-sheets eagerly and received bits of hot news from the reporters on board. The emotional range was very wide during that journey south, from the anxiety of some at sailing into unknown waters, elation over the good news, such as the sinking of the *General Belgrano* which was a large unit capable of being a high risk to the Task Force, – and sadness when our own shipping losses were announced. Up until the last three days before we went ashore on the Falklands, there remained a large range of options as to where and how we would operate.

On board the *Canberra* David Chisnall also remembers the urgent attention given to the news bulletins received from the BBC World News.

We had closely followed the actions of our M Company, and it had been a great prestige day for 42 Commando when on St George's Day, 23 April, they had recaptured South Georgia. Then had come the details of sea and air actions, and we had experienced both elation and concern for our own ships. It was not easy to muster any particular feelings of emnity towards the Argentinians at that stage and it was more a case off simply having a job to do.

RSM Gus Pearson recalls

As we journeyed further south the warmth disappeared and as the *Canberra* ploughed through heavier seas deck exercising became more difficult. Each evening we listened to Maj Ward, the Ship's Adjutant, broadcasting the good and the less good, news. We grew confident on the recapture of South Georgia and the sinking of the *Belgrano*, but the loss of *HMS Sheffield* caused a stunned silence and the realisation that we were not playing games any more.

I remember some consternation when London disclosed over the air that so many troops were aboard the *Canberra*. That night the whole ship came alive, and efforts were made to have 3 Para and half of 40 Commando removed, so that the force was not so concentrated. During the night there was much movement as men and amounts of ammunition were dispersed around the fleet. We were by now quite close to the Falklands and the threat of submarines was very real.

RSM David Chisnall was still closely involved with planning.

As we drew closer, our thoughts turned more towards what the men would have to carry, and then once they were ashore, how they would be re-supplied. How much *could* we carry and fight with? The men of the Parachute Regiment are possibly launched into more instant battle. They fight it – and get out. Our battles tend to be more prolonged, and we consequently probably carry more. In the planning, all of the units were given contingency tasks, and I believe that our CO was involved in the planning of Goose Green, but in the event 2 Para was to fight so well there, although one of our company's helped afterwards in the cleaning up operation.

The landing at San Carlos now approached and we were disappointed to learn that 42 Commando would remain in reserve for a time. Col Vaux sent me around the men to point out 'don't worry about it – it must mean that we are being held for something else'.

We waited aboard the *Canberra* and were soon receiving strikes from Argentine aircraft. We watched the action in which *HMS Argonaut* and *HMS Ardent* were both hit. We took cover where we could in hastily arranged action stations, expecting the *Canberra* to take hits. Our machine-guns were mounted on the upper deck and I walked around trying to provide a steadying influence upon those who could not move about. That allowed me to forget what was happening around me. Our single thought at that time was to get off the ship as we knew that our fate was not in our own hands there.

I had positioned myself in the stateroom, priming grenades and distributing ammuniton to men blacked up ready to go and fight ashore. I encouraged them and wished them luck, realising inwardly that it would be a pretty terminal situation if we were struck by an exocet missile with all that ammunition about. Before the assault went in we had seen the remains of one of our helicopters which had been trying to land a party of SAS troops. They had come from the South Georgia operation, and most of the party were killed in the crash. I knew three of them and also one of the marine crewmen.

We watched and listened as the assault ships approached the

RSM 'Gus' Pearson, 40 Commando Royal Marines, San Carlos, May 1982. WOII Mawer, 40 CDO

hore and landed without opposition, but then saw two of our light elicopters shot down whilst flying around a headland. There vere obviously Argentinians present nearby, and Col Vaux quickly took the initiative pointing out – 'now is the time to get my nen ashore!' We disembarked into landing craft in daylight and oon approached a quiet shoreline, which was as a result of our planning, familiar to everyone. The Headquarters went in with he first landing craft and I stood close to the CO and Operations Officer. Although the air activity continued, we walked ashore as f on an exercise.

We came ashore prematurely, but were following up the enemy orce which had destroyed our helicopters. Some Argentinians vere on Fannings Head, and others at Cerro Montevideo, so we

moved forward through the 3 Para positions, advancing as far forward as the CO considered necessary. Highly relieved to be ashore with a task to do, we spent the rest of the day digging in, patrolling, and preparing for whatever the next day would bring. In the night we all heard the *Ardent* blow up. She had been hit earlier in the action, but finally blew up some hours later.

On the *Stromness* RSM Pat Chapman was appointed Amphibious Operations Officer, and with only a short time remaining before landing he struck a problem.

To get the people off the ship onto the landing craft a scrambling net had been supplied to us, but it was found that we could not fit our mountain issue boots into the squares – as these were too small! With a host of others I set about making our own scrambling net of about 50 × 30ft, which was used when the time came.

We were supposed to make a silent night landing, but as certain assets were not available, we actually went ashore by landing craft in broad daylight. The Mountain Arctic Warfare Cadre – or the SBS – I am not sure which, went ashore ahead of us to establish that the ground was clear, and then a rifle company moved in to occupy the beach head.

After organising the commando onto landing craft, I had some ammunition problems to deal with before I could go, but then went ashore by helicopter to take my place with the CO and with Headquarters. It was an unopposed landing without a shot fired, but operationally had been the first landing by landing craft by 45 Commando since the landings at Ouistreham, on D Day 6 June 1944.

The home made scrambling net was in fact later used by *Stromness* to take aboard survivors from *HMS Coventry*, and subsequently was used on the way home for exercise races, so it had good use.

40 Commando was probably the first unit to disembark from *Canberra* but their Headquarters remained on board for a time, and so experienced the air attacks. RSM Gus Pearson remembers,

The enemy aircraft were overhead and there was the sound of gunfire from Fannings Head as we approached the shore. The closest bomb to our landing craft was quite a distance away, and the further we went from the *Canberra* the clearer it became that the firing was not being aimed at us. It was the first time for many years however, that I had worn a steel helmet.

On reaching the shore, I saw that the Commando HQ was already being dug in. A small knoll had been selected by the Operations Officer and he now obtained the help of a Royal Engineers tractor and tipper to quickly dig a large hole, which was lined and topped with timber before receiving three feet of packed earth on top to form a bunker. Our radios went in, and that was where I mainly operated from – as one of the watch keepers on the duty officers roster. Whenever the CO went around the companies, however, I went with him.

When RSM, Pat Chapman joined 45 Commando ashore they were well spread out and were digging defensive positions with overhead cover, which with spades and picks was a time-consuming task.

We had plenty of material for camouflage and soon the commando was well dug in. I had taken one of my ammunition storemen with me ashore and he began to dig out our personal slit trenches, whilst I supervised the ammunition being flown ashore and then I helped him to finish off. We were to remain in those positions for some days, and it soon became quite boring – just like an exercise on Salisbury Plain!

Then the Argentinians began bombing again, and we had an unwelcome grandstand view of our ships coming under attack, and saw *HMS Antelope* being hit. At one stage one of our companies received a peppering from shots fired by our shipping at low flying aircraft and whilst to my knowledge it caused no casualties, it did cause people to look more closely at their overhead cover!

We did a lot of moving around, and I vividly remember visiting the Mortar Troop out on a flank, with a V shaped gorge to the side of them leading towards Ajax Bay. I was in company with the Provost Sgt Bill Eades, a first class Provost Sgt and Drill Instructor, when we saw an Argentinian aircraft shot down. The pilot ejected by parachute and we watched him float down to land in the gorge. It was so close that it was just like watching it on TV. When enemy aircraft appeared everyone tended to blaze away with machine-guns, and I saw two or three brought down.

I accompanied the CO on his rounds, when we made sure that everyone was properly dug in, that routines for feeding had been established and so on. We would crack a joke or pull someone for being particularly improperly dressed, just to keep a finger on the pulse and to remind one or two of the job to be done. We awaited fresh orders and I believe that we had spent about two thirds of our time there when we heard of the assault by 2 Para upon Goose Green. It had been tough and people had been killed there. It was a sobering thought to all of us. Much of the information gained was brought to us by our CO from the O groups.

We were then ordered to move to Port San Carlos and so had to move the commando across the water from Ajax Bay. We left our hill positions to assemble close to a factory where our echelon was based. I left a quantity of our ammunition there as we could not possible carry it all. We then embarked on landing craft and were taken to Port San Carlos.

Next morning we started the move inland towards Douglas, and Lt-Col Whitehead advised me that we had lost four people killed, including two senior Sergeants, in an air raid at Ajax Bay. My initial reaction was to reply, 'Well – we will need to have the Sergeants replaced,' which the CO thought at the time was rather a practical attitude to adopt. I was being realistic however, and this was soon accepted.

RSM David Chisnall with 42 Commando had witnessed the wreckage of the two helicopters and knew that a price had already been paid.

It was cold and wet and we were deprived of our kit as our large packs had not yet been brought ashore. Even after 36 hours we were cooking by diddle dee – a very fine bracken – instead of our heximene block cookers. This was a bit of a culture shock to most people, as they had expected to use equipment we had exercised with in the past.

We were then picked up at night by landing craft from below Cerro Montevideo and brought back to San Carlos, where we began to dig in behind the Paras. It was freezing wet and and miserable and HQ was moved into a school, but we all dug slit trenches as air raid shelters. We awaited what we expected to come – the attack upon Goose Green. We felt sure that we had been included in the planning for it and as we were now positioned behind the Paras we fully expected to go. I had met RSM Laurie Ashbridge a couple of times on the ground whilst going the rounds with our respective COs. I rarely left Lt-Col Vaux's side, and it was very important for us to be seen amongst the men and to let them know what was going on.

There then followed quite a saga, as the CSM of K Company came to me and said that we had left one marine behind at Cerro Montevideo when leaving in the dark the previous night. Anxiety was felt for his safety so a rigid raiding craft was sent to look for him, and after a time returned safely with him. Soon afterwards the CSM came back to ask, 'What shall I do with him?' In jest I suggested that he take him out and shoot him, only – as we would have to hold an orderly room first – deal with it in slow time. Almost immediately an air raid attack began and the sheep shed which we were sharing with 3 Para came under attack.

An unfortunate incident then occurred when there was a negligent discharge – someone fired an LMG round through the knee of the marine who had just been brought back. After my comment to take him out and shoot him, this was particularly sad. He did not fare too badly however, as he was evacuated for having been wounded during an air attack upon San Carlos. The Corporal who had accidentally fired the round had been cleaning and oiling his weapon after our wet landings when the air raid came. He closed the weapon quickly which fed a round and discharged it. He could not have been in a worse spot as the RSM and Provost Sergeant were standing nearby and the CO was about to visit. We held our first field orderly room and the matter was quickly cleared up. The Corporal later did well in action at Mount Harriet. Thankfully the knee wound was clean and the marine is still serving.

Our J Company went in fact, to Goose Green as reserve to 2 Para, helping to clear up afterwards. Maj Mike Norman commanded the company, and it was he who had commanded the original RM Garrison Naval Party 8901 when the Argentinians had first attacked the Falklands. The garrison returned of course with the Task Force and they formed the basis of J Company along with cooks and drivers and spare men. This company then replaced the one sent to recover South Georgia within the organisation of the commando. Instead of going to Goose Green 42 Commando was destined for the attack upon Mount Kent – and subsequently Mount Harriet.

As the San Carlos beachhead was consolidated preparations for the offensive towards Port Stanley were finalised, and on 27 May, 45 Commando and 3 Para set out upon their epic marches on parallel routes across East Falkland. The next few days saw tremendous activity at San Carlos as 42 Commando departed by air and by land for Mount Kent – the 5th Brigade arrived by sea from England, the 1/7 Duke of Edinburgh's Own Gurkha Rifles firstly coming ashore, followed by the 1st Bn Welsh Guards and the 2nd Bn Scots Guards.

As an Argentinian counter-attack on San Carlos was expected by some form of air landing, 40 Commando was to its disappointment, ordered to remain in defence of the beachhead, and RSM Gus Pearson concedes –

The men were disappointed not to be moving inland with the offensive and no-one more so than our CO Lt-Col Hunt, as he had seen 45 and 42 Commandos leave, and with his Tac HQ was actually kitted and booted ready to go when orders came for 40 Commando to remain in the beachhead.

When the Welsh Guards landed we expected them to replace us, and they stood to against slit trenches in readiness, but it was not to be. Although on paper 40 Commando were to remain at San Carlos, our companies eventually went out to various locations. I did not need to get involved with the distribution of ammunition as this had been stockpiled after our initial issue aboard ship. We were fortunate in Headquarters that we had a radio security system with us and therefore knew where all of the units were and what was happening.

On 31 May, RSM David Chisnall accompanied Lt-Col Nick Vaux, with K Company commanded by Capt Peter Babbington, when the group were crammed into Sea King helicopters and flown 40 miles foward through atrocious weather conditions, to support the SAS in an attack upon Mount Kent. Before climbing aboard the packed aircraft there had been some difficulty over the number of non-combatant passengers within the press corps being carried, but a solution had been found by which vital equipment was carried by the passengers and so such positions had to be earned. RSM Chisnall admits however,

I was furious at the time as I was wholly pre-occupied with the need for fighting men! Following a dangerous flight in which all credit was due to the pilots for their flying ability, they landed the overloaded helicopters in the dark, in snowy conditions and K Company began to ascend the slopes of Mount Kent.

Our landing had been under fire in what is termed a hot landing site, and the SAS – who were already there – were in the midst of a small fire fight with some Argentinians. A small group of prisoners was passed to me for safe custody and also a number of dead Argentinians. As it was dark we simply turned them over and piled rocks upon them to make a hasty burial. The next morning Josh Shields, the Provost Sergeant, came to me and admitted, 'Sir, if that was me I would not want to be left face down.' I replied that if he felt strongly about it he should take his team and give the dead Argentinians a proper burial. Sgt Shields did so and they were given what we considered to be a decent burial – right way up and with properly marked graves. This surprised our prisoners who, despite our shortage of food, had already received a share of compo rations and now witnessed the care taken with their dead.

Conditions on Mount Kent were very cold and wet with a thin covering of snow, but during the next two days the rest of 42 Commando were brought in by helicopter. They had begun to march but were then flown for much of the way, whereas 45 Commando was in the process of yomping the whole distance from San Carlos, as was of course, 3 Para.

We could now see our next target, and this was to be a night assault upon Mount Harriet. Brig Julian Thompson visited us and valued the fact that he came straight to me to enquire about the men. 'Well RSM, are the men in good form?' he asked. This was good for the men to hear and it also gave opportunity for questions from the ranks, such as – 'Why are we staying here Sir, can't we get on with it?' Knowing that the CO was standing only yards away, it spoke a great deal for the way that the questions could be put through the RSM. I do not think it would happen in other regiments. The Brigadier had replied that the reasons for remaining there was to allow time for ammunition – particularly artillery stocks – to be built up.

My responsibility was to defend the Headquarter area and to maintain order. When it came to the choice of NCOs for specific tasks the CO would ask, 'RSM, do you think that Sgt ..... should take this patrol?' and I would assist his decision. The CO knew his officers and I knew the NCOs. Corporals often in fact, commanded patrols which was a heavy responsibility, but they were very well experienced and well trained, better perhaps than in some other units. I remember recommending one senior NCO for a certain task because of his sniper training, patience and tolerance and he was later awarded the Military Medal for his conduct during selective recce tasks.

We felt some sympathy for 2 Para being brought forward for

further action after its performance at Goose Green, but there was also professional rivalry of course, and we reckoned to have finesse where the Parachute Regiment had dash. In every other respect both units displayed the same controlled aggression.

From Mount Kent we could see Port Stanley in the distance, a good morale factor during the shelling we were now receiving upon our positions. On the first day however, we had been able to fire on the Argentinians near Stanley, and so they knew that we could reach them there – and of course, anywhere in between. The people of Stanley also realised that we were drawing closer, so those first ranging shots were quite decisive.

As RSM Pat Chapman with 45 Commando set forth on the long march to Douglas from San Carlos, 3 Para were marching on a parallel route and he now concedes,

I think we got it wrong, as we tried to carry everything, whereas 3 Para were more selectively equipped. I mean, some of our men were literally carrying 120lbs weight in kit, in those boggy conditions. We covered about 20 miles in an all night and day march and during a halt we decided that we would strip off equipment to something more sensible. We left our heavy packs and these were brought on to us later by all sorts of means.

Our Recce Troop entered Douglas to make sure that it was clear of Argentinians and I also went ahead to check out where the commando could be housed, bearing in mind that it was only a small settlement. I saw the local farm manager and he arranged for us to use some houses.

We spent 36 hours there and then moved off in the direction of Teal Inlet. This time I was able to telephone from Douglas to Teal, and spoke to the RSM of 3 Para asking if they would leave their slit trenches for us and not fill them in. Laurie Ashbridge agreed, and I went ahead again, eventually meeting our commando as they came in, giving them rations, fuel and water and pointing out where they should bivouac. We took over the positions at Teal from 3 Para, who left some 50 men behind, who like ourselves had suffered bad feet and blisters on the march. We later transported them forward to where 3 Para were finally laid up before the battle of Mount Longdon.

Our own echelon now joined us, and for some reason I took on the job of administration for 45 Commando in terms of rations. As our Assistant Quartermaster was still at Ajax Bay, I became responsible for rations, fuel and water. We were expecting to be air lifted from Teal Inlet to Bluff Cove Peak, near Mount Kent, but because of the weather and a shortage of helicopters – which were concentrating upon moving ammunition forward for the guns – we were marching again.

I was one of the last to leave Teal Inlet, the advance companies having left an hour and a half before, and had not taken more than ten paces when the command came 'Commando, stop!' It was time for the first rest for the front people, and this will give some idea of how far we had become spread out.

We now approached the well planned night assault on Mount Two Sisters by 45 Commando. I went forward to our mortar base position to pre-dock the bulk of our ammunition, priming all the grenades and making sure that all would be ready for a re-supply, and concealed it to make sure it was safe, and then returned to the commando. Headquarters moved up that night for the attack and when we reached my concealed ammunition, I loaded it onto our bandwagons (BV 202 caterpillar tracked vehicles). When the attack went in, Headquarters was positioned at Murrell Bridge en-route. The assault was both quick and effective. Early next morning I went up in company with the Second IC to do the re-supply of ammunition and as this was under fire it was quite interesting!

Whilst I was on the way up I saw some men out on a flank. It turned out to be one of the troops of Zulu Company, which had suffered a number of casualties. When I arrived in our positions, I approached a Para Major – Hector Gullen – and pointing out our wounded below, asked if he could help with a helicopter pick up. He replied that he could, but who would mark the landing site? I said that I would, and running down to the flank in the dark – rather foolishly on reflection – I got things organised down there. The helicopter soon came in and removed the wounded, a further illustration of magnificent flying ability.

The Argentinian artillery fire continued, but was curiously ineffective. It transpired that they were using an inferior shell – thank goodness – or some of us might not have been here. There were stacks of powder going up in the air, but unless you were almost directly hit, you were reasonably safe at 30 metres.

Following the re-supply of ammunition, our party came down the next morning bringing all the captured Argentinians with us. That marked the end of the Two Sister attack. We had lost four men killed and eight were wounded. The next morning we re-organised and I was placed in charge of all the captured weapons. I then spent some time testing all sorts of machine-guns to discover whether they were still serviceable.

As 45 Commando attacked Mount Two Sisters on 11 June, 42 Commando assaulted Mount Harriet, only a few miles from Port Stanley. RSM David Chisnall was proud of the planning for the attack.

The finesse mentioned earlier came out I believe, in the attack on Mount Harriet, as we approached by a circular route so as to attack from the rear – at night – and through a minefield! This was where the character, ability and professionalism of our Commanding Officer came out. We had already lost two marines – with legs blown off – during the reconnaissance patrols, but it was a case of 'getting on with it, and all meeting up at the top'. The enemy fortifications on the summit were extensive but our K Company assaulted and won much of the ground, followed up rapidly by two further companies with which the CO and I positioned ourselves.

We were just faces in the dark of night – part of Tactical HQ. There was a sense of urgency to get to the top before daylight and we fully expected to be counter-attacked before long, or attacked from the air, but surprisingly neither move came against us. We collected and looked after our wounded and also the many Argentinian prisoners. In all there were some 300 prisoners and they came in from all sorts of places. 45 Commando had moved on to attack Two Sisters and the Paras were moving forward towards Stanley, so they were overlapping and providing prisoners in addition to our own. It became my task to look after them, with the Provost Section, and to get them back out of the way.

I remember explaining to a group of 30 prisoners that if they *walked* down to the road they would not be shot at, but if they ran or tried to escape they most certainly would be! I obviously failed to get this over to them as they began to weep and pray, crossing themselves. They must have believed that I was going to shoot them. It was a shame, for they were very frightened and clearly expected bad treatment. They had of course thought themselves to be in an impregnable position but had been shelled for days, then attacked from the rear, and over-run. Our own casualties had been light considering the strength of the position.

Next day I went with a Guards Company Commander to show him around our positions, so that he could gain an advantageous view of his next objective, Mount William. The Argentinian artillery was still firing at us from near Stanley. I had got to the stage where I could mentally count the seconds from the guns firing, and predict the fall of the shells, but on this occasion a shell landed within 20 feet and threw us both to the ground. I got up

with ringing in my ears and began to brush off the mud remarking, 'You can actually get used to this when you have been up here for a few days.' Not surprisingly, I received the reply 'Well, I think I have seen enough RSM!' Fortunately, the blast had gone in another direction and many others had similar experiences that day with close misses.

At that stage we held our second orderly room to promote men in the field to replace those section commanders killed or injured. Lt-Col Vaux was in the process of promoting two marines to become Lance Corporals, when both he and I noticed an aircraft approaching to 'toss bomb' near Stanley. We realised that it was not attacking us so took no notice, but someone in the company looked around and seeing the aircraft shouted 'Take cover!' Everyone sought the ground except Col Vaux and myself, and they looked up at us in some embarrassment. We were sure that it was safe, but it enhanced the esteem of the CO and RSM in front of the men. The marines had been selected for promotion by their company commander, and it was a proud moment for them in front of their company and on the field of battle.

Earlier during the action, we had in HQ been observing in the middle of the night. It was very cold with crystal clear conditions. We had the destroyer HMS Glamorgan providing naval gunfire support away out to sea and we were in touch with her by radio. We then noticed a red glow going out towards her from land and realised that it was an exocet missile. There followed a sudden vivid flash of light and some of our people in HQ cheered believing that the ship had destroyed the missile with one of its own. HMS Glamorgan stopped firing however and it became clear that it was she that had been hit.

Although taking only seconds, this was one of those occasions when one felt able to stop time . . . as if one could have reached out and stopped that red light by hand. Earlier, soon after the landing on Mount Kent, I had stood with Lt-Col Vaux and watched the Sir Galahad being bombed. We had witnessed most of the event and felt once again that we could have plucked the attacking aircraft out of the sky by hand.

Things now happened quickly and more fighting took place during the next two days, while we were prepared to be sent forward as follow up. We then heard that white flags were being waved and that the Argentinians were surrendering. Lt-Col Vaux acted quickly in obtaining helicopters and we were flown forward just short of Moody Brook, which was badly damaged, but which had been the former Royal Marines garrison's barracks. Many Argentinians were streaming in to give themselves up. We took the weapons from them and sent them on to Stanley airfield for eventual repatriation, which became the major task of 42 Commando.

3 Para had by now made a night assault upon Mount Longdon, clearing a large force of Argentinians from the summit in heavy fighting, clearly indicated by the loss of 23 men killed and 47 wounded. 2 Para also made a night attack upon Wireless Ridge, with tremendous artillery support which was so successful that it carried them forward towards Moody Brook.

2nd Battalion Scots Guards, assaulted Mount Tumbledown on 13 June and in sharp fighting cleared their area with the loss of nine men killed and 43 wounded. The Welsh Guards and Gurkha Rifles were operating on Sapper Hill close to Stanley. On Mount Two Sisters 45 Commando was now being briefed for their next objective which was to be Sapper Hill and RSM Pat Chapman recalls,

We were preparing to move forward when it came over the radio that the Argentinians were beginning to surrender! This came

C Company of 3 Para after the battle of Mount Longdon,
Falkland Islands. Troops in joyous mood with their company flag
in Stanley on the day of the Argentinian surrender.

mainly from the Parachute battalions who were advancing beyond
Wireless Ridge and were well in sight of Stanley. We were in fact
kept outside on Sapper Hill for a further night, and it was at that
stage that I came into contact with the Gurkha troops. They had
some observation post parties forward with us, and they were
most effective soldiers, very professional and serious about their
tasks.

Once the cease fire was confirmed 45 Commando moved in
towards Stanley. At that stage we were picked up by the BV 202s
and travelled right past Moody Brook through the minefields until
we eventually arrived in Stanley. Next day we went aboard one of
the LSLs which had been brought in to Stanley. We cleaned up
and showered, which in company with 3 Para, we felt we
deserved, having walked all the way!

I actually remained ashore with my Provost Sergeant and a few
others, to organise some housing for the commando when they
came off the ship. Stanley was quickly split into battalion and
commando areas and although some of the buildings were a
shambles, cover was found for all the companies.

At San Carlos, RSM Gus Pearson with 40 Commando
HQ heard of the cease fire.

This was the stage for our third company to depart for West
Falkland, where there were many Argentinians to collect as
prisoners. Our CO took the company by landing craft behind a
frigate at night across the sound between the islands. It became so
rough and wet however, that the landing craft had to put back to
another location, dry out, and go on the following day. Had they
landed on the intended beach there would have been many
casualties as the beach was, unknown to us, heavily mined against
troops and tanks. It would have been a horrific experience. Later
when the assault engineers were clearing the area, one man lost a
leg when a mine was detonated.

As Stanley was being cleared, our A and C Companies
returned, having moved to reinforce the Welsh Guards following
their awful bombing and landing at Fitzroy. Some of HQ
Company were down at the south side of West Falkland, but they
returned. Soon 40 Commando became a complete unit once more
and we awaited the arrival of the *Canberra* for the journey to Port
Stanley – and eventually to take us home.

Quite suddenly the fighting came to an end and thoughts
could channel along more normal lines. RSM David
Chisnall remembers that groups came together for
photographs to be taken.

On the day following the cease fire Lt-Col Vaux wished to be
flown on to the *Uganda* which had been converted into a hospital
ship. This was an extremely moving situation and the
commanding officer readily admitted, 'I don't much like this RSM
. . . so would you come along with me.' From leading the
commando into battle he now entered a situation for which he had
received little opportunity to prepare.

The next few days were spent cleaning up Stanley. The RSMs were given the task of supervising the clearing of weapons and the security of the prisoners. In my personal opinion, battle weary soldiers should not have had to do the cleaning up, but we got stuck into it and were allocated sectors each day, sometimes moving ammunition off a road or grouping prisoners onto the airfield where they were held. We went around talking to them and there really was a lot of compassion felt for them – strange when we had just been fighting them.

45 Commando also featured in the clearing up operation and RSM Pat Chapman confirms,

Major Hector Gullen of the Parachute Regiment held a meeting each day, with all the RSMs present. Actually, I went down with a Stanley bug for 48 hours, so had to send a deputy. Tasks were shared out and it seemed to work well, as everything was done whether it be the clearing up, or the guarding of the 12,000 prisoners. We then began to organise for the return journey home and as our Zulu Company was to go on the *Canberra* 45 Commando was able to spread out a little on the *Stromness*. We had a more comfortable journey back to Ascension, but were not destined to continue by sea, as the commando was flown home straight to RAF Leuchars, quietly and by the back door. Our Commandant General Sir Steuart Pringle was there to meet us,

RSM D. A. Chisnall, BEM, 42 Commando Royal Marines greets HRH Prince Charles on board Canberra *on return from the Falklands. Major J. M. G. Sheridan, OBE, Second-in-Command 42 CDO, stands nearby.*   PR RMs, MOD, London

with a pipe band and we were welcomed home to base well before the *Canberra* docked.

Canberra had sailed into San Carlos Water to take aboard 40 Commando, and then around to Port Stanley where it laid off to embark the troops of the 3rd Commando Brigade and 5th Infantry Brigade. RSM Gus Pearson remembers that one of the earliest receptions occurred whilst the *Canberra* steamed towards home.

A Royal Naval ship – also returning home – came alongside only yards away, and with men lining the port side, gave three long blasts of her siren to the crowded starboard side of the *Canberra*. The salute was returned and there was much cheering and waving. It was an emotional and memorable moment. The ship then pulled away and both headed on towards home.

RSM David Chisnall was to receive an honoured

responsibility when HRH Prince Charles was flown out to board the *Canberra* in welcome.

Major Gullen appointed me to make the necessary arrangements within the military setting, and to look after Prince Charles in what had become the combined SNCOs Mess. I was very proud and honoured to show him around the ship's loaned facilities. As we later came in to Southampton terminal building, I knew that my family would be waiting in the crowds, and would have liked to look for them over the side, but with the privilege of my duties could not do so until the *Canberra* was actually tied up.

RSM Gus Pearson was scanning the crowds, but adds –

It was slightly disappointing for some of our 40 Commando families, as they travelled by coach from Plymouth, and were not able to get into the building. They could see the *Canberra* but could not get close to it for the crowds. We eventually disembarked from the ship that had taken us so far, but were ushered straight out of a back door on to waiting transport. We soon joined up with the families' coaches however, and the procession of vehicles back to Plymouth was marvellous.

Whilst we had been in the Falklands, my wife Eleanor had been invited to read a lesson at Plymouth Church, and on the return of the brigade, she was again invited to read the lesson at another service held at Plymouth Hoe. She was seated on the rostrum, and of course – as her guest – I was also there, with high ranking officers and their ladies. Afterwards the Lord Mayor held a reception to which we were invited, and met Generals and Air Vice Marshals. Inevitably the question came – about my presence there – and I proudly pointed out that my wife had read the lesson and I was there as her guest!

As part of the welcome home the 40 Commando marched through Plymouth, and that was a moving occasion. We then travelled to Manchester to hold a military funeral for one of our young marines who had been killed at San Carlos. A gun carriage was provided and we all sent representatives for the guard and also for the street lining party. I attended and found it a most moving service in church . . . awful for all of us really . . .

At Arbroath, RSM Pat Chapman took part with 45 Commando in a march past through the town followed by a civic reception.

HRH Prince Charles converses with RSM D. A. Chisnall and Lt-Col N. Vaux, DSO, Commanding Officer 42 Commando Royal Marines, on board Canberra. PR RMs, MOD, London

We had lost 13 members of the commando killed, plus quite a number of men wounded, but the majority of those recovered to remain in the Royal Marines.

We have an independent Royal Engineer Unit with 45 Commando; the Troop-Sgt Peter Ellis was with us in the Falklands, and he sadly lost a leg on a mine the day after the hostilities ceased. Now I had the privilege as RSM of the Sergeants Mess, to make a presentation to him as he was leaving the unit to become a diving instructor. He could have just turned to me to accept the gift – but he walked right around the square of tables upon his false leg . . . what a tremendous spirit.

At the beginning I mentioned that there were two parades in which I had taken part that I would never forget. The second was when I was the RSM of the Royal Marine Commando contingent, and then on the day we formed up in the City of London – and with drums beating – marched through the narrow high streets.

When the parade was completed we attended a reception in the Guildhall where the Prime Minister was present and I was one of those selected to speak with her. During the dinner I sat next to the RSM of the Gurkha Regiment at the Falklands – a marvellous occasion. I was also proud to meet a Royal Engineer Officer who as WO1 had lost an arm when working on bomb disposal on the ships in San Carlos Water. WO1 John Phillips and his Staff Sergeant, Jim Prescott, had been flown from ship to ship on this hazardous task, until a bomb had exploded badly wounding him, and sadly killing his colleague.

After the Falklands campaign, I remained as RSM of 45 Commando for a further two and half years, then in November 1983 left to become RSM of the RM Commando Training Centre at Lympstone for a time. I was commissioned in March 1985, and now work as Motor Transport Officer.

RSM Gus Pearson believes that part of the success of the Falklands units was due to their flexibility. He explains –

When we came back from the Falklands 40 Commando was posted to Northern Ireland after home leave and we re-adjusted ourselves quickly. Possibly there was some scepticism from the people of South Armagh regarding a wartime commando unit coming, but Lt-Col Malcolm Hunt made it quite clear that we were there to do policing duties. We then went on a six month United Nations tour in Cyprus, so we had at the end of those duties 20 year old men wearing three campaign medals! The irony was that our young marine would go home on leave, but could not swap stories with his father – who had not done National Service, so had to say 'Come on grandad – let's go down to the pub and tell dad all about it!' . . . That is the time scale.

My last two years as RSM were at Lympstone, where I instructed RSM courses, and special duties officer courses, so I therefore had a good grounding for my officers training. I was commissioned on 28 February 1986, and now work as Motor Transport Officer.

David Chisnall reflects –

The Falklands was thankfully a short sharp campaign by comparison with others I had experienced, and we were well experienced – trained – and well led. The men performed in every way as we would expect professional soldiers so to do. Ironically – whereas in Northern Ireland young men are excluded if under 17 years of age, some served with us in the Falklands – and performed extremely well. It was our place to be there at that time, and as members of Her Majesty's Armed Forces, we believed that we were doing our duty.

We went without hatred for the Argentinians – and still have none for them. One of the greatest things to me that came out of the campaign, was the Royal Marine Commandos compassion for the Argentine prisoner of war. As to the Regimental Sergeant

Major – it is his task to convey the COs orders to the ranks – all the way through. When the two get on well – and the unit is a happy one – that is what makes a unit. If when promoted an RSM is anxious about how he should exercise that appointment, he should not in my view have been promoted in the first place, as previous experience should have prepared him.

I was commissoned on 3 May 1984, and now work as an Administration Officer.

As with a great many campaigns before it, the Falkland Islands operation in 1982 left many personal memories with every serviceman who went there. For some life would never be the same again and the scars can never fade. For others the memories are already obscured by subsequent events and it will soon be difficult to remember the cold chill winds, the lonely waters, and the bleak ranges of wet misty hills across which the infantrymen of several fine regiments and corps made their way from San Carlos to Stanley.

It takes courage and character for a country to send and use such distinguished forces in order to simply regain the status quo by which negotiations may continue, also to maintain forces of such quality able to meet whatever threat may present itself, or to take their place when necessary with the United Nations Forces.

RSM Pat Chapman and RSM Mike Gibson, The Sergeants Mess, Commando Training Centre, Lympstone, June 1984.
PR RMs, MOD, London

RSM G. A. Pearson and men of 40 Commando Royal Marines at the presentation of South Atlantic and Northern Ireland General Service Medals, July 1983.   PR RMs, MOD, London

PART TWO

On Parade
with the RSM

Come now – to places where standards have been set, and well taught . . .
on parade with the Regimental Sergeant Major.

The Sergeant Majors dealt with in part one were predominantly those serving on active campaign service, with – apart from those training RSMs especially mentioned – perhaps only incidental involvement with ceremonial.

The following Sergeant Majors were largely selected to work in some of the finest military training establishments in the world, for their capacity to teach drill and ceremonial. In detailing their stories however, it will become clear that many were also fighting soldiers whose records contain much additional campaign history.

Commissioning Parade, 23 Jan 1958, at Mons OCS inspected by Lt-Gen Sir Gerald Lathbury, KCB DSO MBE, Director General of Military Training (and at one time Commanding Officer of the 3rd Bn Parachute Regt). RSM C. L. Smy, DCM, Coldstream Guards, in attendance.
RMAS Collection

CHAPTER 13

RSMs and AcSMs of the Royal Military College/Academy, Sandhurst to 1955

Charles Thomas Pearson became RSM of the RM College Sandhurst, on 16 March 1917, and so shared with A. Wombwell the responsibility for training the large number of officer cadets to go through the college during the First World War. He had first been posted to the college as a Sergeant in early December 1913, and was made Acting Staff Sergeant one year later. He married on 3 April 1915 at Aldershot, and moved into married quarters three weeks later, when he was also promoted as Colour Sergeant.

Charles Pearson had first joined the Coldstream Guards on 23 January 1902 aged 19 years 5 months, having initially served for a time in the 2nd Bn East Yorkshire Regiment. According to the attestation forms he almost enlisted into the 21st Lancers. He joined up from Hessle in the East Riding of Yorkshire, and was of medium height and build, with fresh complexion, grey eyes and brown hair. He completed his training at the Guards Depot during the time of RSM J. Boyd, Coldstream Guards.

Twenty months after joining the regiment he was promoted to Lance-Corporal and was soon granted extra good conduct pay, and at about this period there was every likelihood that he came into contact with L-Cpl Harold Scott, who later became RSM of the 18th Bn Prince of Wales's West Yorkshire Regiment (Bradford Pals) and perhaps both served under RSM Stephen Wright.

1905 was not a successful year for Charles Pearson, as he – possibly voluntarily – reverted to Private, and then failed a musketry test, for which his pay was reduced. The following year saw him again promoted to Lance-Corporal however, and when his battalion went to Egypt in September 1906, he not only qualified for his second good conduct badge, but was made up to Corporal in April 1909, and decided to extend his service. In January 1910 he was made Lance-Sergeant, and soon after the regiment returned home to England he was promoted as Sergeant. On 6 June 1913 he passed a course on musketry at the Hythe School with distinction.

As Sgt Pearson was posted to the RM College Sandhurst some months before war broke out, it would seem that his value as an instructor had been realised, and once the great mobilization had begun with the urgent need for trained officers, his place in the role of instructor was relatively fixed. His responsibility increased from Colour Sergeant to Regimental Sergeant Major during the war, and to recognise his work in the training of officers, the *Gazette* of

13 August 1918 reveals that he was brought to the notice of the Secretary of State for War in relation to his valuable services rendered.

During the following 12 years his service was extended on four occasions to permit him to remain as RSM of the RMC Sandhurst, and during that period he was granted the Royal Victorian Medal in Silver in 1919, the Long Service and Good Conduct Medal in 1920, and was awarded the MBE in the King's Birthday Honours List in 1926. On 5 July 1930 RSM Charles Pearson retired from the army and the Asst Commandant Col E. H. Tolemache stated in a testimonial that:

Sgt-Maj Pearson has been of exemplary conduct, sober and trustworthy, very reliable, hardworking and capable. His powers of organisation and command are excellent and he is thoroughly recommended for any position of trust and responsibility.

He has served the Army well and faithfully for 28½ years.

RSM C. T. Pearson, MBE, Coldstream Guards. AcSM RMAS

Top left:

RSM Arthur Crook, Grenadier Guards, RSM of the Royal Military College Sandhurst, Nov 1900-5. Flanked on left by his son-in-law, Cpl A. P. Malone; and on right by his nephew, Cpl Alfred Crook.

Major E. C. Weaver, Grenadier Guards, (Brigadier Crook's collection)

Top right:

RSM Arthur Crook, Grenadier Guards. There is little known of his service as the regiment has no papers for him, but Major E. C. Weaver, MBE, Regimental Archivist, has discovered the following information. 'Arthur Crook went to the RMCS as a Colour Sergeant, was promoted to RSM and remained in that capacity until commissioned in 1905, when he was made Fire Master at Aldershot. He retired as a Major having been awarded the OBE. He had a son who was commissioned in the RA, rose to the rank of Brigadier, and in 1964 was a Military Knight of Windsor.' AcSM RMAS

Left:

RSM Joseph Payne, The Devonshire Regt, RSM of the Royal Military College Sandhurst, 11 Oct 1905 to 20 Sept 1912. From his medals a well campaigned soldier, but it has not proved possible to trace details of his service, either during his seven-year period at the College or afterwards, when he was likely to have returned to his regiment to serve in WW1. AcSM RMAS

RSM A. Wombwell, The Rifle Brigade. RSM of the Royal Military College Sandhurst, Sept 1912 to March 1917. Although Sgt-Maj Wombwell served in the Rifle Brigade, his father had been a Sgt Drummer in the Grenadier Guards and had brought him up virtually as a Guardsman. In February 1901 he was posted to the RMCS as a Sgt Instructor, and served first under RSM A. Crook, and then RSM J. Payne. He subsequently became a Staff Sgt until being promoted to College RSM. He conducted the extensive training system during the early years of WW1, and was then commissioned in March 1917 to serve in the Lincolnshire Regt, but was transferred to the Royal Flying Corps. He remained in the RAF after the war, and was seen by thousands of people when he trained and commanded the Drill Display at the Wembley Tattoo, 1926. AcSM RMAS

RSM Walter Harry Dobson became RSM of the RMC Sandhurst on 5 July 1930, upon the retirement of RSM C. T. Pearson RVM MBE. He was born in London on 17 October 1889, and enlisted in the Grenadier Guards on 17 February 1908, going through the Guards Depot during the time of RSM J. Teece, Grenadier Guards.

He made an early impression for smartness and efficiency and was an outstanding shot. Posted to the 1st Bn, Grenadier Guards, he was made Lance-Corporal one year later, Corporal in 1912, Lance-Sergeant in 1913 and Sergeant in 1914, quick promotion at a time when this was not easily attained.

On declaration of war, he went to France with the 1st Bn, and was wounded at the first battle of Ypres. In 1915 he was promoted to CSM with the 4th Bn and Machine Gun Battalion, and was awarded with the Military Medal in 1916 and then the Military Cross in 1917, for his gallant conduct and leadership. Also in 1917 CSM Dobson was mentioned in despatches, and then a year later was made Drill Sergeant. He served in the 3rd Bn for a number of years before becoming RSM of the 2nd Bn in 1927. He also spent a period as RSM of the Cambridge Officer Training Corps.

In July 1930 he became RSM of the RMC Sandhurst and a great many officer cadets were to pass through his hands before he handed over to RSM Arthur Brand MBE in December 1937. He had completed 29 years of service in wartime and peace, but events were to prove that his service to his country was far from completed.

When the Second World War commenced, Walter Dobson was commissioned as Quartermaster of the Honourable Artillery Company and served on through the war in the rank of Captain. In 1946 he was awarded the MBE, and became the Messenger Sergeant Major and Wardrobe Keeper of the Queen's Bodyguard of the Yeoman of the Guard, during which appointment he was awarded the MVO. He was said to have a remarkable grasp of detail and an eye that missed nothing. Capt Walter Harry Dobson MVO MBE MC MM TD died on 31 December 1956 at the age of 67.

Arthur John Brand was born at Paulton, Bristol, on 13 February 1896, and enlisted in the Grenadier Guards at Midsomer Norton on 4 February 1916, going through the Depot during the period of RSM E. Ellis. He served in the 5th Bn during the First World War and was then transferred to the 1st Bn in which he was selected for the King's Company. In 1918 he was made Lance-Corporal and one year later Corporal. During 1920 he served with the battalion, and also at the Guards Depot, being promoted to Sergeant.

In 1924 he was posted to the RMC Sandhurst as CQMS, and shortly afterwards was made CSM. This was at a similar time as Ronald Brittain, and an element of friendly rivalry developed between the two. Upon promotion to Drill

Left:

RSM W. H. Dobson, MC MM, Grenadier Guards.   AcSM RMAS

RSM A. J. Brand, MBE, Grenadier Guards.   AcSM RMAS

Sergeant in 1932, Arthur Brand served with both 3rd and 2nd Bns before being seconded to the South African Forces for 15 months. He married whilst in South Africa, and upon his return home he was appointed RSM of the Guards Depot, where he remained until August 1936.

In December 1937, Arthur Brand became RSM of the RMC Sandhurst, where during the following 11 years he trained a very large number of officer cadets for war service, and saw the establishment develop from an OCTU unit to the Royal Military Academy. Maj F. J. Clutton MBE MM RVM, was a CSM at the time when in 1948 RSM Brand's service was approaching its end, and he comments:

In my opinion Arthur Brand was the greatest of many great RSMs with whom I have served, including Snapper Robinson, Arthur Spratley and John Lord. In 1948, when Arthur Brand was RSM of the Academy, John Lord was RSM of New College, and I was the lowly CSM of Normandy Company, Victory College.

RSM Brand schooled John Lord privately in the evenings in preparing him to take over the academy, and in so doing, taught him the contents of the *Book of Ceremonial*, including sword, colour and company drill. It was my good fortune to be chosen by RSM Brand to be the stooge – in other words – the recruit cadet. By being so, I had the opportunity of learning a great deal from these great men which stood me in good stead in future years, particularly when I became RSM of the Guards Depot, and later, of the 2nd Bn Grenadier Guards.

RSM A. J. Brand on parade behind the Colour Party. A Passing Out Parade at the RMAS. Guards Magazine

Arthur Brand MVO MBE retired from the army in 1948, and with his wife went back to South Africa for a time, but returned to become licensee of a public house in Sandhurst village. On retiring for the second time, he found that he preferred to work on, and became a storeman at the Ladies Staff College in Frimley. On one occasion he discovered an oil stove on fire in the store and on removing it to safety, received severe burns to his hands which took a considerable time to heal.

He remained a very welcome visitor to the Sergeants Mess at Sandhurst for a number of years. He died on 10 January 1975, aged 79, and the funeral service took place at the Academy Chapel.

It can truly be said that AcSM John Clifford Lord, MBE MVO, had a profound influence upon the whole of the British Army, and the armies of other countries over the last 40 years, quite out of proportion to his rank of Warrant Officer Class One. Like many good RSMs, he demanded the highest possible standard at all times from everyone under his command – and some who were not. He was a great drill instructor and his appearance was always ultra-smart. He could motivate and move men and bring out the very best in them.

John Lord combined these qualities – but much more – he possessed a towering personality with which he could stimulate the smartest response from newest recruit to veteran colleague of equal rank. He had the power, charisma and parade ground voice of the very top echelon of RSMs, yet the sensitivity with which to charm a parade of hundreds of officer cadets into listening to the 'sounds of Sandhurst'.

He normally enjoyed a brisk but gentlemanly approach to instruction, laced with humour and interest, but if provoked would shake a whole parade by the sharpness of his wrath. He enforced his standards upon everyone and had a marvellous repertoire of comment with which he held absolute attention. If one was on parade under RSM Lord, one tried harder than ever before, and somehow found extra speed and sharpness.

It was largely by the training and inspiring of young officer cadets at the RMA Sandhurst that John Lord's standards spread through the regiments and corps of the British Army, and those of many other countries. Then as the officer cadets achieved higher rank, the standards were passed on. His influence also spread by way of the RSMs courses and conferences held at Sandhurst, through training cadres and by the completion of tours of duty by the many instructors from all regiments and corps of the army. John Lord also lectured at all levels of command, and

In the early years of the Second World War, the Parachute Regiment owed part of its basic training to a small nucleus of RSMs – mainly from the Guards Brigade – including RSM John Lord from the Grenadier Guards, who initially brought in the discipline and backbone of the Guards, upon which the unique training of the parachutist was grafted.

In 1978 I asked the librarian at Sandhurst if there was a book about RSM Lord, and when Michael Wright advised me that there was no such work, I found myself saying that there should be and that I would research one myself if necessary. During the next two years I was to be in contact with many serving and former soldiers who had been trained by, or had served with, RSM Lord. These included many old soldiers of the 3rd Bn, Grenadier Guards, of the 1930s. I also met two fine former RSMs of my own training days in the Parachute Regiment in 1946-7, John Alcock, who was Drill Sergeant and then RSM of the ITC at Aldershot, and Alan Watson who was RSM of the Airborne Forces Depot.

I met a number of men of the original 3rd Bn of the Parachute Regiment, of which John Lord was the first

Academy Sgt-Maj J. C. Lord, MBE, Grenadier Guards.
AcSM RMAS

RSM, and with whom he fought and was captured at Arnhem. A large number of former officer cadets were contacted who had trained under him during the years 1948-63, and also many officers who had served with, or had commanded him at various stages of his career.

I also had the pleasure and the honour of meeting former Cpl Ray Sheriff, who had served with John Lord since the formation of the 3rd Bn, Parachute Regiment, through North Africa, Sicily, Italy, to Arnhem, where he was badly wounded, blinded and captured. Ray was to help enormously with the tracing of former members of the battalion, who were themselves to contribute to the story of John Lord.

At the ITC in Aldershot, RSM John Lord would often commence his morning muster parade with the words: 'Settle down – settle down. We are now going to *revel* in God's sunshine!' The book on his life was therefore entitled *To revel in God's sunshine* and was published privately in 1981.

John Lord was born in Southport and by the time he attended school, the First World War was into its second year. He was brought up within a disciplined society and this was maintained after the war when he was placed at a boarding school, where he progressed well, both academically and in sport. He may have intended to enter the family business, but the great depression resulted in his deciding upon a career in the police force. To prepare for this he did what many young men considered necessary at the time and enlisted upon a short term engagement in the Grenadier Guards.

Joining on 27 March 1933, the depot RSM was J. D. Hughes of the Welsh Guards, and although 15 years had elapsed since the end of the war, most of the senior NCOs had served during the conflict, and the discipline belonged to that era. A fellow recuit, Alexander Rea, who has lived in Canada for many years, wrote to me to say that he remembered arriving at the Guards Depot in 1933, in company with John Lord, and both of them immediately being given the task of scrubbing the floor of the receiving room!

During the next year John Lord and his fellow Guardsmen assimilated a very high standard of ceremonial drill which would remain with them for life. On completion of training John Lord was posted to the 3rd Bn, Grenadier Guards, which was due to go abroad to Egypt very soon afterwards, and where it remained for three years. During that period he came under the influence of two great Grenadier RSMs – RSM W. E. Chef Hawkins, who had earlier in 1922-5 been RSM of the Guards Depot – and RSM G. F. G. Turner DCM, who had also been depot RSM, but later came to replace RSM Hawkins as RSM of the 3rd Bn.

In 1936 the battalion returned home and John Lord gained promotion to Lance-Sergeant. Later, close to release, L-Sgt Lord was interviewed by his CSM H.

Oulton, and subsequently also by his CO Lt-Col C. R. Britten MC, with a view to him prolonging his period of service, but he was firm in his intention of a career with the police. Col Britten was instrumental in gaining a place for him in the Brighton Police Force and on release from the Colours, John Lord donned a different uniform, and progressed well in the brief period of time available before the commencement of the Second World War.

He was recalled to the regiment on 4 December 1939, and with other reservists was sent straight to a refresher course at Windsor. With the massive expansion of the army, there was an urgent need for good instructors, and John Lord must have revealed obvious qualities, as he was soon posted to the RMC Sandhurst as a Sergeant Instructor. Here he was introduced for the first time to the training of officer cadets, but for both he and fellow Sergeant Instructor – Desmond Lynch, Irish Guards – it was to prove but the starting point in long careers of distinction closely associated with the training of officer cadets.

For a time they concentrated upon their training roles, but it was not long before they each sought ways of getting into more active service. John Lord, nine years older than Desmond Lynch, was promoted CSM and so remained at the RMC Sandhurst until October 1941, but then was successful in gaining an appointment in the newly formed Airborne Forces. He was made RSM of the 3rd Bn, in what was to become the Parachute Regiment. With thousands of volunteers he was to go through the early hard and dangerous training to complete eight parachute drops, in order to qualify for the parachutists wings and to obtain extra pay.

As all men were volunteers, dedicated to do whatever had to be done, there was a great spirit reminiscent of the Pals battalions of the First World War. With the combination of new methods, hard training and enthusiasm – bonded on to the basic discipline of the Guards – the new battalions were extremely fit, smart and determined.

The 1st Airborne Division was prepared for action by mid 1942, and took part in the North African landings, some units going by air and parachuting into action, whilst the main force went by sea to land at Algiers. The division was soon drawn into the bitter fighting in the hills and mountains of Tunisia, against a resolute enemy – often against their own counterpart – the German Parachute Forces.

RSM Lord with the men of the 'Shiny third' – as the 3rd Bn had come to be known because of its high standard – fought through the North African campaign and the invasion of Sicily, suffering heavy casualties. They then took part in the landings in Italy, before being withdrawn to Britain with most of the division, to be reinforced and trained in readiness for the long awaited Second Front . . . the invasion of Europe.

Following a period of build-up and further extensive training, the 3rd Bn again became a crack unit eager to return to action, but it was the 6th Airborne Division that with American Parachute Forces, was to land by parachute and glider on the flanks of the great seaborne invasion of Normandy. After extremely hard and costly fighting the Allies began a massive advance through France towards the German borders, and it appeared that the war could end before the 1st Airborne Division entered into the action again.

Many operations were planned, but became unnecessary as the army over-ran proposed targets. Then came Montgomery's plan to end the war quickly by an offensive into Germany through the Ruhr. This called for a huge airborne attack by combined American, British and Polish units, upon key bridges in the path of the ground forces. Operation Market-Garden commenced on 17 September 1944, with attacks on major bridges over canals and rivers in the areas of Eindhoven, Nijmegen and Arnhem. The American 101st and 82nd Airborne Divisions were to assault the first two areas, whilst the 1st Airborne Division with the 1st Polish Parachute Brigade, were to attack the Arnhem bridge.

The 1st, 2nd and 3rd Battalions of the Parachute Regiment, together with the 1st Airlanding Brigade, landed a few crucial miles away from Arnhem and immediately began to advance along separate routes towards the bridge. In face of increasingly heavy opposition, only the 2nd Bn, commanded by Lt-Col John Frost, was to reach the north end of the bridge, where with the other small units it made its heroic and historic stand for four days and nights until virtually annihilated. The assaults through the streets of Arnhem by the 1st and 3rd Bns had been blocked by the unexpectedly heavy German forces and eventually – despite the subsequent courageous efforts of the 4th Parachute Brigade and the 1st Polish Parachute Brigade, which had landed in the second and third lifts – what remained of the 1st Airborne Division was forced into a tight perimeter in Oosterbeek.

During the first two days the companies of the 3rd Bn had become split-up in their attemps to reach the Arnhem bridge and although C Company was successful in joining the 2nd Bn to fight to the end at the bridge, the other companies were destroyed attempting to fight their way through the streets. One group in which elements of HQ Company were included, battled their way along the side of the River Rhine until they reached the area of a pavilion, less than one mile from the bridge. Here desperate fighting took place, and most of the group were either killed or wounded. The CO Lt-Col John Fitch was killed, and RSM John Lord was wounded in the right upper arm. The surviving pockets of Airborne troops in Arnhem were gradually overcome, and with the later withdrawal of the remnants of the 1st Airborne Div across the Rhine on the night of the 26 September, the operation which had opened so hopefully ten days before, closed with only one fifth of the division returning. The final offensive into Germany had to await the next year.

Her Majesty The Queen inspects the Sovereign's Parade at the Royal Military Academy Sandhurst on the 12 April 1985. The Commandant, Major General R. C. Keightley, and the Academy Sergeant Major D. P. Cleary, Irish Guards, salute the Colours.

The 79th Regiment, Cameron Highlanders, in square at Waterloo.

Left: *The 62nd Regiment at the Battle of Ferozeshah. With many Officers already casualties, the Sergeants take up the Colours.*
Courtesy of the artist Peter Archer, and of Major John Peters of the Duke of Edinburgh's Royal Regt. (Berkshire and Wiltshire)

Below left: *42 Commando, Royal Marines, assault Mount Harriet on 11 June 1982 during the Falklands Campaign.*
Courtesy of the artist Peter Archer, and of Lt-Col D. A. S. Pennefather, 42 CDO RMs.

Right: *RSM J. C. Lord MBE in conversation with Officer Cadets in front of Old Building, Royal Military Academy Sandhurst. c1956.* Courtesy of Jim Cox. (The Cox Collection.)

Below: *AcSM R. P. Huggins, Grenadier Guards, prepares the Colour Party for the Sovereign's Parade on the steps of the Grand Entrance of the Old Building, RMAS. Very wet conditions in 1979.* Photo by the author.

Above: *GSM London District, A. G. 'Perry' Mason, Coldstream Guards, registers a fault to his orderly. With Brigade Major Lt. Colonel D. V. Erskine-Crum, Scots Guards, he observes the Guardmounting and first practice on Horse Guards for the Queen's Birthday Parade May 1988. This was one of the first parades to be held with the SA80 rifle.* Photo by the author

Right: *RSM D. D. Horn, Sgt Major HAC. Presentation of Colours 1980.*

Opposite page:
Top left: *Academy Sgt-Maj Michael Nesbitt, Grenadier Guards, on the magnificent square of Old Building, RMAS. 1988.*
Photo by the author.

Top right: *GSM London District, A. G. 'Perry' Mason, Coldstream Guards, and Drum Major Anthony C. Austin, 1988.*
Courtesy of Borg Photography

Below left: *GSM London District, A. G. 'Perry' Mason, Coldstream Guards, on parade at Horse Guards 11 May 1988.*
Photo by the author.

Below right: *GSM London District, Alex Dumon, (Coldstream Gds) instructs the Massed Bands of the Guards at Chelsea Barracks – mainly Irish Guards Bandsmen featured. The 6 May 1987, and one of Alex Dumon's last parades before retirement from the army.* Photo by the author

Opposite page:

Top: *RSM L. Winter, Coldstream Gds, observes a squad slow marching off their Passing Out Parade at the Guards Depot, holding their smartness to the end. 20 May 1988.*
Photo by the author

Left: *RSM D. A. Gibson, Coldstream Guards, when Guards Depot RSM.* Courtesy of David Gibson

Right: *RSM L. Winter, Coldstream Gds, Depot RSM, observes a Passing Out Parade with Sergeant G. Fallowfield, Coldstream Gds, in May 1988.* Photo by the author

Overleaf:
Top: *The King's Troop, Royal Artillery. The Serre file returning from the Queen's Birthday Parade 1982. Front L to R. The Master Saddler, the Master Farrier, and the RQMS. Rear L to R. RSM W. G. Clarke, the Equitation Instructor, and in the rear – the Troop Captain.*
Courtesy of Public Relations, and of the Adjutant King's Troop, RHA.

Below: *The Number One Guard, 1st Bn, King's Own Royal Border Regt. One can almost hear this immaculate marching as the Battalion show the Colours in Cockermouth in 1980. The Guard Commander was Major R. W. Smith MBE followed by Major J. B. L. Underwood, Captain R. D. Bruce, Colour Sergeant Major R. Hopton. Colour Sergeant Bancroft was proudly marching through his own home town.*
Courtesy of Jeremy Alford

This page:
Above: *RSM W. G. Clarke. RSM of the King's Troop, Royal Horse Artillery from 1981 to 1984.* Courtesy of John Freeman & Co

Top left: *RSM D. L. Allan of the King's Troop, RHA 1989. RSM David Allan enlisted in November 1965, and trained under RSM W. Pearson. He was appointed RSM in March 1988.*
Courtesy of Beryl Allen

On being wounded, RSM Lord had with other walking wounded, made his way to the St Elizabeth Hospital in Arnhem, and it was there when the Germans occupied the hospital, that he and many others were captured. Within a short time large numbers of captured men of the division were to find themselves being transported by rail in cattle trucks, to Stalag XIb at Fallingbostel in Germany. The officers and many of the WOs were removed to other camps, but John Lord and a few selected WOs remained to administer the camp, which housed some 17,000 prisoners of war of many nationalities.

With winter approaching and appalling conditions in the camp, the men did the best they could to survive and recover from their wounds. Many men died however, and it was in his determination to see that these men received a proper funeral and burial that RSM Lord first began to organise matters. He found a 'Guard of Honour' and drilled them as well as possible, and gradually went on to seek ways of overcoming the dreadful hardships. Routines were developed and as the men regained their self discipline, the British sector of the camp began to operate along more military lines – complete with bugle calls to mark the time of day.

On a bitterly cold day in January 1945, John Lord was told that Cpl Ray Sheriff, who had been missing since he was known to have been wounded in Arnhem, had now arrived at the camp. Making his way to the reception hut, RSM Lord sought him out and found him sitting on some straw amongst a number of Polish POW arrivals. On being greeted by the RSM, Cpl Sheriff rose with difficulty, came to attention, and with obvious relief replied that it was good to hear his voice again. John Lord then realised for the first time that Ray had been blinded as well as wounded. He was so moved and impressed by the quiet dignity and bearing of the Corporal, that whilst he took immediate steps to help him to the camp hospital – and provided gentle support and encouragement during the whole of the remaining months in captivity – he was never to forget the qualities displayed by Ray upon his arrival at the camp.

In future lectures to the recruits of the Parachute Regiment, to officer cadets at the RMA Sandhurst, and to high ranking officers of the Imperial Staff College, John Lord would always refer – often with great difficulty – to the example of Cpl Ray Sheriff as portraying everything that RSM Lord held to be so important in the field of soldiering.

As the final months of the war dragged out, RSMs Sam Wickham, Bill Kibble and CSM Alan Watson with others worked tirelessly with John Lord in the camp, to improve conditions and to do all possible to help POWs still being packed into Stalag XIb.

Selected airborne troops acted as camp police to maintain order as the Allied advance slowly came closer, and finally the German Commandant requested the British administration of the camp to take over as the German system began to break down. In April 1945 when British units at last arrived to liberate the camp, they found smart 'sentries' of the 1st Airborne Div on the gates and RSM John Lord immaculate and waiting on parade to hand over the details of all the men held in captivity there. The great day that all of the men had so constantly thought about had finally come, and not only had they survived the German regime, but could now for the first time truly count on being able to return home.

After a journey home by the former POWs and a long period of leave, the future had to be planned, and whilst for the majority it was to be demobilization, the hope of employment and a return to civilian life, for regular soldiers it was to discover what the army had in store for them.

RSM Lord and certain of the NCOs were to be posted to the two Infantry Training Centres of the Parachute Regiment, where their experience and high standards would help to guide the new men volunteering for the regiment. Soon, as the army reduced in size only one ITC would remain to prepare recruits for their service, and RSM Lord MBE took over this place of maximum importance to the regiment. There were still many battalions in the Parachute Regiment and as so many wartime soldiers were opting for release, a large number of volunteers were required to maintain numbers. All had to be physically fit, classified as first class shots, and to be assessed as being likely to complete the parachute course.

Having volunteered for the regiment in 1946, I arrived at the ITC in company with many others from the primary training centres, and it was quite a shock to us to learn for the first time the true power of the RSM. We were transformed instantly into striving – doubling – frantically polishing recruits, and it is fair to say that the regime of the ITC hit us straight between the eyes! The Sergeant Instructors had been selected for their ability to 'move' young men who only six weeks earlier had been happy civilians.

For the first time we were to experience drill commands given in the high pitched whip crack voice of the Guards, followed by an instant barrage of correction. In a very short time the combination of drill, inspections and show clean parades, made us at least look like soldiers, but an awful lot more was to come. Our intake PR 17 eventually completed its training with a very smart Passing Out Parade in early 1947, and we progressed to the Army Parachute Training School at Upper Heyford.

RSM Lord's regime at the ITC had seemed set for many years to come, but in August 1947 he was appointed RSM of New College at the RMA Sandhurst, and then in June 1948 took the place of the great RSM A. J. Brand MBE, as RSM of the Academy. His place at the ITC of the Parachute Regiment was taken by RSM John Alcock, who had closely worked with him, and who then carried on in a similar pattern until July 1948. The ITC was then closed down and RSM Alcock became a commissioned officer.

John Lord's links with the Parachute Regiment were not ended however, as in June 1950 he drilled and prepared the regular battalions for their first Presentation of Colours.

Extensive drills took place for a period of six weeks until on 19 July 1950, HM King George VI presented the three remaining battalions of the 16th Independent Parachute Brigade with their Colours.

A tremendous standard of drill went with John Lord to the RMAS, and I am convinced that one only needed to watch a company being brought to attention to know that it had been 'JC' trained. Since the book on John Lord's career was published, I received the following absorbing letter from Maj (retd) Phillip Vaughan RA, in relation to his period as an officer cadet during the John Lord era.

So many of your contributors to your book seem to have been terrified by RSM Lord. They needn't have been so. It was all a great game, at least it was during my peacetime soldiering. I believe that he really enjoyed a clever riposte provided you looked him in the eye as you said it. At Sandhurst I cannot remember a cadet receiving any significant punishment as a result of an encounter with RSM Lord. One apocryphal story illustrates this. The Academy was being sorted out prior to a Sovereign's Parade rehearsal on Old College square. When the parade had been handed over to RSM Lord he noted a small movement in the ranks and remarked, 'What's going on? Third man from the right, rear rank, Victory College – idle on parade.'

Three Drill Sergeants hovering in rear of Victory sought the miscreant. 'Got him Sir,' cried Sgt Trimmer of Rhine Company, 'Officer Cadet M..... idle on parade.' The cry was taken up by CSM Young, who stomped up to Victory College RSM Wood and reported, 'Officer Cadet M..... idle on parade.' RSM Wood paced over to RSM Lord and passed on the information, 'Officer Cadet M..... idle on parade.' Before RSM Lord could get out the words to have the culprit doubled over to the guardroom, a very dry voice from the back of Victory College said, 'That's right, tell every bugger!' And after that it was alright. When the sniggers had died down Mr M..... received a mild reprimand and the parade went on as normal.

My memories of RSM Lord relate to the time when he accompanied a party of cadets attending the first RMAS parachuting course during the 1950 Easter holiday. His parachuting techniques went back to Arnhem days, and being an older man he had some difficulty in adopting the new methods, and often tended to bounce on his head during ground training.

After completing all of our ground work, we were unable to get on with our first parachute jump because of high winds on three successive days. Morale was low as we were doing the course in our holidays and every lost day meant less time at home. The RAF found old films about parachuting to show us, but we lost interest and went to sleep in the cinema – and during odd lectures. After one depressing session RSM Lord took charge as we piled out of the cinema. 'Right now – I am going to march you over to the NAAFI, and we're going to show this RAF lot what proper marching is like!' It wasn't just straight marching, but everything in the book. Sentry go, left and right inclines on the march, breaking into slow time etc etc, while the RAF looked on amazed! Then after five minutes and still 100 yards from the NAAFI – 'Last man into the NAAFI buys my tea!!' Everything was alright again, morale back at its peak.

He was at his best in the air however. He was in my stick and persisted in conversing with me as we floated down together with remarks such as – 'Come along Mr Vaughan Sir! Kick out of that seat strap . . . Idle while parachuting!'

At the conclusion of the course everyone dispersed to their homes or mistresses, but I wished to return to the RMA Sandhurst to pick up my motorbike, which had been left for repair with a local garage. I was fortunate to scrounge a lift with RSM Lord,

who was then prosperous enough to own a respectable For Prefect. He drove for the entire journey of 100 miles or so, fully a attention and wearing his cap. In every town he slowed to a snail pace so that he could stare out all of the National Servicemen o weekend leave, who committed the cardinal sin of undoing th battledress collar and placing the beret under the epaulette.

We arrived at the Blackwater garage at about 10pm, and m motorcycle had been left in the forecourt as arranged.
'Where are you going on that, Sir?' he asked.
'Home to Shropshire, Sir.'
'What time will you get in?'
'Oh, about 3 or 4am I should think.'
'Well you're not Sir; you're going to spend the night at my house Eventually I persuaded him that my mother was accustomed t my arriving at all hours and was never worried as I was ver thoroughly insured. Reluctantly he agreed to let me go and helpe me strap my gear on to the pillion.

My next encounter with RSM Lord was at the beginning of m next (senior) term on the first Saturday morning Academ parade. After all the divisions had formed up, the parade wa handed over to RSM Lord. He went through the 'Academy – righ dress!' routine, followed by his famous 'Eyes – front!', but the before marching over to the Assistant Adjutant to report th parade present, he made a departure from the usual drill. H moved to the front, about turned to face the 800 or so cadets, an roared – 'I see you got back alright Mr Vaughan!' Receiving n reply he returned to the business at hand.

At the end of June 1950, we of the senior division ha completed all of our exams and just couldn't wait to march up Ol College steps, but passing out was still about 10 days away. It wa a hot summer and there were 300 cadets more or less at a loos end. Inevitably inter-college rags and riots broke out. I remembe walking down from our hutted accommodation on rising groun behind Victory College, after a night of clandestine activity an seeing about 30 rented Academy bicycles all threaded over a 50 lamp post! Also attached to one of the chimneys on Victor College was a large barrel, and underneath someone ha whitewashed on the roof slates the text, 'We want Watney's', in very large letters. Anyway, there was big trouble . . . The senio intake was the worst they had ever had at Sandhurst and som rapid discipline was required. The whole senior intake woul attend a punishment drill parade in best kit on *Saturda afternoon*! – and it would be taken by RSM Lord.

This was the end! The passing out parade was to be held in th following week and the Saturday afternoon was the only free tim we would have had to organise our personal administration Accommodation to be fixed for parents and girl friends attending Arrangements for our guests at the July Ball. Heavy kit to be sen home luggage in advance. (Few personal cars then.) Final fitting for our fancy new uniforms. Consequently, the 300 cadets wh marched on to Old College square that Saturday afternoon wer now confirmed Bolsheviks.

The parade was formed up and handed over to RSM Lord 'Right dress! Eyes – front!' Now RSM Lord got down to i 'Academy will fix bayonets. Academy – fix! Bayonets! . . . Shun Academy will unfix bayonets. Academy – unfix! Bayonets! 'Shun Now gentlemen, that was terrible.' (He never used the wor 'orrible.) 'There are some people over the other side of Europe I'm not allowed to mention their names – but they've got bayonet . . . and they're that long!' (Here RSM Lord held his hands ope like a fisherman describing a three-foot salmon.) 'The Britis Government can only afford little bayonets like these . . . s you've got to get them out much faster.'

Well after that we were all eating out of his hand. We went to with a will. Diagonal marching, left and right form, retire in thre from the right, Old College leading, advance in review order. An we did sentry go too, all 300 of us . . . I am pretty sure it wa

RSM J. C. Lord discusses the daily routine with his College RSMs, T. Taylor, E. J. R. Rose, and D. Randell, Royal Military Academy, Sandhurst, 1960-2. AcSM RMAS

without the band, but we didn't need one as we were all practically singing. We enjoyed it and it didn't matter any more. I think that episode shows what a remarkable hold RSM Lord had over us. He knew what our mood was and he had the personality to bring us out of it.

Tom Taylor MVO MBE, Grenadier Guards, served as Garrison Sergeant Major, London District, from 1965-77, and has his own impressive story to relate in this book, but at two earlier points of his career he completed tours at the RMAS, and he states of those times when he served under John Lord:

When I arrived at the RMAS in 1953 I soon found that RSM Lord was a great instructor, and he never allowed anything to go by without his careful supervision. Every week without fail we had an Instructors hour when he would take every session. He had tremendous control and co-ordination. In an area of some 20 yards square he would take a drill movement, such as saluting on the march, or the about turn, each of which had several individual

movements, and he would demonstrate and break down each movement with a fine art. He would then go through all of the drill to be used during the next five days, so that each of us would know exactly what was expected.

RSM Lord was a great thinker and instructor and he made a great impression upon others. He influenced me in approach tremendously. One learned a whole vocabulary of positive military words – words that gained the very best from men on the drill square. He also featured strongly in the *Drill Manual*, bringing the drill forward from the pre-war days. Officer cadets and instructors had a great admiration for him, and they would always remember his sayings. He would have the whole of the Academy on Saturday morning swank parade, and would get the very best out of everyone with the music of the band playing. During parades even the crows flying overhead became the 'spirits of officer cadets departed' and he would move the cadets along by reciting *If* to them, and on occasion also 'Polonius' speech to Laertaes'. Even during a rest period when the officer cadets were gasping for breath he would still be talking to them and teaching. Never a dull moment.

At Sandhurst the officer cadets had to have three belts, the best of course being for Academy parades. RSM Lord used to tell the story of his going into a cadet's room and finding eight belts hanging up. He asked, 'What on earth are you doing with this lot?' and the cadet explained, 'Well Sir, *that* belt is for moving about on Academy training, *that* one is for breakfast roll call, *that* one is for company drill parade, *that* one for college drill parade, *that* . . . for passing off the square,' etc etc, until only one remained at the end . . . a gleaming, magnificent belt. 'And what's that for?' asked the RSM. The cadet simply shook his head, sucking in his breath, '*that* one . . . is just to look at.'

At the time of the introduction of the FN rifle, John Lord fought a long and hard battle with the Ministry of Defence as he had perfected a drill movement for the slope arms, but the abbreviated movement was adopted.

I remember very well being present at the *This is your life* programme at the RMAS when John Lord was the subject. A mock quiz show was advertised and John and his wife Audrey came in to the Sergeants Mess before going to the show. I had heard comments and confided to Audrey that there was talk that this was not to be a quiz, but a programme of *This is your life* – and I received a sharp kick in the shins. Again when we went to sit in the theatre, Audrey sat down in the second seat making sure that John was on the aisle. I did not know of course – as John did not. I asked Audrey, 'Why are we sat here?' I could not have made things very easy for her, but the moment that Eamonn Andrews introduced his programme and came to John Lord I understood.

John did very well considering the surprise – not to say shock. One guest, Guardsman Entwistle of the 1930s, told the audience that John Lord had, as a guardsman, been turned out for inspection with the guard, and had gone through the inspection with his pipe in his mouth! The following day at Sandhurst we had a Senior Division parade and at the end when John gave the order 'Dismiss', the parade turned to the right and all popped pipes into their mouths! The officer cadets had spent the previous evening going around the Academy to borrow pipes. John Lord was very taken with the joke. He was a magnificent instructor and anyone who could not learn from John Lord, could never learn.

Capt (retd) Alistair MacDonald wrote to me in 1985,

I remember AcSm Lord with great fondness. I entered the RMAS in 1954 through Anzio Company, and was commissioned following our (then) two year course in 1956 at the August Passing Out Parade. My memories are of a man who was strong – yet kindly and gentle, a disciplinarian – yet caring and compassionate. He was truly a benevolent autocrat whose dedication to all soldiers was an example to all of us.

There was an occasion when the Commandant, Maj-Gen Hobbs, was inspecting an Academy parade. This was always a great occasion with many included in the inspection party, the Commandant, Assistant Commandant, at that time Brig Graham of the famous moustache, the Adjutant, the College Commander, the Company Commander, the College RSM, the Company Sergeant Major, the Company Junior Under Officer, a number of Drill Sergeants and of course, the Academy Sergeant Major. All proceeding through the ranks on inspection. One poor cadet was heard to have a 'slack waistbelt' and after an interminable time whilst the rear of the rank was inspected, we heard the cry, 'Officer Cadet ..... Slack waistbelt. Back and front Sir! Name taken Sir.' Not a vestige of a smile from the AcSM, at this heinous double offence.

I remember another famous offence I am sure invented by the AcSM himself, that of having 'Idle fluffs on beret' on breakfast roll call parade. Not just 'fluffs', but 'idle fluffs'.

Lt-Col (QM) Retd W. J. Holbrook MBE, Cold-stream Guards, has a prominent place in this book as he was the RSM of the Guards Depot from 1969-72. John Holbrook served under RSM Lord at the RMAS from 1956-9 and has allowed me the following memories of his service there.

I first met and came to serve under AcSM John Lord when I was selected by my regiment, whilst serving at Krefeld in Germany, for posting to the RMAS as a Drill and Weapon Training Sergeant Instructor. Little did I realise that I was about to enter one of the most enjoyable and character forming periods of my military career.

The first requirement for all instructors joining the RMAS was to attend and pass a Drill and Weapon Training Cadre Course, the drill part of which was taken by John Lord in person, assisted by a supernumerary Sergeant. I had attended drill courses before, both in my battalion and at the Guards Depot, but right from the start it was very apparent that this one was going to be different.

My fellow Sergeant students on the cadre came from a cross section of Regiments of the Line, but John Lord created the feeling that every man was 'an Emperor'. The squad was made to work hard without being chased or ridiculed. Bad language was not tolerated in any shape or form, and the first of many 'JC' quotes was put firmly across.

'Never swear, it's not fair. It only shows you are the one with ruffled hair – not him.'

I also found it most interesting to see subject matter of which I had a reasonable knowledge, presented in such an attractive, interesting and varied way. We were also always given the reason and need for teaching the drill movement in question and made to consider and discuss alternative methods of presenting the subject.

We were also introduced to a method of instruction which John Lord called 'Stop Drill' which broke down or split up each different drill movement into even smaller parts than was shown in the *Drill Manual*. This method enabled the instructor to 'stop the camera' at any given moment to correct a fault or draw attention to a bad position. This method is now standard practice and is written into the present day *Drill Manual*, yet another example of how John Lord's instructional thoughts were years ahead of the accepted doctrine.

His attention to detail extended to other areas within the span and life style of the instructors at Sandhurst. He loved his Sergeants Mess, and our education continued even when we were relaxing within the portals of this holy of holies! Sergeants Mess meetings took place once a month, always in the evening and in No 1 Dress (Blues). We were all encouraged to take a full part in debating any proposal which came up for discussion, with due regard and respect for our seniors. The importance of conducting oneself with dignity and with due regard for the well being of other mess members was a strong feature urged by John Lord.

Other areas of instruction which he taught – not available to young Sergeants like myself elsewhere – were colour drill, pace sticking, stick orderlies procedures, company drill, and how to conduct and control a regimental boxing match as master of ceremonies. After a short period at Sandhurst under his direction, one felt nine feet tall, very confident, and light years ahead of one's equivalent rank outside Sandhurst.

It is interesting to reflect and note that a very large percentage of those Sergeant Instructors with whom I served during my tour of duty at Sandhurst, went on to become RSMs. Many also went on to be commissioned and are still serving today. Whenever we meet the topic of conversation turns to reflect upon our period of apprenticeship at the RMAS, something that money could never buy – to pass from one generation of soldiering to another. RSM Lord's thoughts, quotations and methods live on amongst instructors and are used throughout the British and Commonwealth Armies.

The extremely busy routine of the Academy continued and there is little doubt that RSM Lord drove himself very hard. In 1955 he was discovered to be suffering from TB and a long period of recovery was necessary. A magnificent gesture came when the Grenadier Guards, Parachute Regiment, and RMA Sandhurst combined funds to send him to Switzerland for a month in order to convalesce, and he was always to appreciate this kindness. RSM W. L. A. Nash, Grenadier Guards, came to the Academy as RSM and he was later to write to me:

I must readily admit that having established myself as RSM, I realised within a matter of days that John Lord had created a tremendous feeling and atmosphere. I felt a complete intruder. So my first move was to visit him at Hindhead hospital to have a chat. After that first talk I appreciated the need for me to become a caretaker for John rather than attempt to take over. *John was Sandhurst* and nothing else mattered.

In March 1956 RSM Lord intimated that he was ready to return and at a farewell dinner for RSM Bill Nash at the Sergeants Mess, the 'Wand of office' – A. J. Brand's pacestick – was handed back to John Lord.

On 30 November 1959, he was the subject of *This is your life* as mentioned earlier, but he had in fact appeared in an earlier programme when a former parachutist and POW at Fallingbostel, Andrew Milbourne, had been the subject. Now Andrew, who had been very badly wounded at Arnhem, returned the compliment by appearing to pay tribute, with many other guests, to RSM Lord.

In December 1960 John Lord's appointment was upgraded from RSM of the Academy to Academy Sergeant Major, possibly at that time to mark the fact that the recipient of the post would serve until retirement, foregoing the opportunity of a commission. This restriction has since been lifted. Until that time the RSM of the Academy had worn the small arm badge of rank below the right elbow, but now a splendid newly designed large badge was authorised to be worn above the elbow. Maj-Gen Sir Philip Ward KCVO CBE had taken a decisive role in designing the unique badge which has been worn by each successive AcSM.

In July 1963 AcSm Lord became the first Warrant Officer to give a lecture to officers attending the Imperial Staff College. WO1 Ian Birchall MBE, who was Superintending Clerk to Gen Sir Michael Gow, C-in-C of the British Army of the Rhine in 1982, advises me that when Gen Gow was on the College Directory Staff in 1963, he was instrumental in arranging for John Lord to present the lecture on the subject of Discipline. This has since become very well known for its content and is included in full in John Lord's earlier book.

Unusual in such a military setting, the officers actually gave AcSM Lord a standing ovation, and many who were present, including an old friend of the Parachute Regiment

and Stalag XIb days, RSM Alan Watson, confirmed how memorable the occasion had been.

The final rehearsal was well under way for the Sovereign's Parade to be held on 1 August 1963, in which AcSM Lord was himself to pass out in retirement from his long held appointment. Suddenly the rehearsal was halted and AcSM Lord was ordered to report to the grand entrance steps, where he was presented with gifts by the Director of Music of the RMAS Band, by a Sergeant representing the Sergeants Mess, and by the Senior Under Officer. A letter received by me in 1982 from Mr G. F. Burnand confirms:

I was the SUO who was privileged to present AcSM Lord with a gift from existing and past officer cadets. The present was a magnificent silver clock with a statuette of a cadet and a guardsman on either side. The guardsman had double buttons – and needless to say, the great man noticed immediately!

On the following day the Sovereign's parade was immaculate, and was inspected by The Earl Mountbatten, who then awarded the AcSM with the Meritorious Service Medal. As the officer cadets slow marched up the steps of the grand entrance of Old College, John Lord followed them, turned, and gave his last salute as a serving soldier.

John Lord had held the rank of WO1 for over 21 years when he retired and was the Senior RSM of the British Army. He continued to serve Sandhurst for a time in the sports and estate office, but his health continued to cause concern, and he was found less arduous work in the office of the Airborne Forces Security Fund, which concerns itself with the welfare of former airborne soldiers.

In 1967 his condition worsened until he required hospital treatment, and it was a great sadness to all to learn that he had died at his home on 21 January 1968. On Friday 16 February, a Memorial Service was held at the Royal Memorial Chapel RMAS, where almost 500 friends, colleagues, soldiers and former soldiers attended. Sixteen Generals numbered among the congregation.

John Lord's grave is situated in the small cemetery within the grounds and amongst the sounds of the Academy he served so well. There can be little better tribute to an RSM than that paid by one of his recruits of many years before. Jimmy Ashdown of Mortlake in London, was a recruit at the Parachute Regiment ITC at Aldershot in 1946-7. To mark the 40th anniversary of the Arnhem operation by laying a wreath upon the grave of his RSM, Jimmy decided to walk the 30 miles from his home to the RMA Sandhurst. A fine gesture when one appreciates that Jimmy was 55 years old at the time (in 1984) and had in the past suffered some heart trouble. As a product of the ITC however, Jimmy is quite indomitable as his recollections of the walk reveal.

I left Wimbledon at 7pm on Saturday 15 September, carrying a large umbrella in lieu of a tent which I had dispensed with as being unnecessarily unwieldy. My neighbours barely gave me a second glance – assuming that I was having one of my funny turns again.

Former parachutist Jimmy Ashdown places a wreath upon the grave of RSM John Lord to mark the anniversary of the Arnhem Operations. Mrs Audrey Lord, RSM Ferneaux Grenadier Guards, and WO2 Hallis of the Parachute Regt are also present at the Royal Military Cemetery, Sandhurst. Camberley News

I walked through New Malden, Kingston, alongside the waterworks at Sunbury, past Kempton Park racecourse and to the outskirts of Staines. Here at midnight I decided to stop, and making a fire, looked forward to a welcome meal. It was not to be however, as I discovered that in reducing the weight of my pack, I had left my tin opener behind. After a spartan meal I made myself comfortable on a sheet of polythene and slept until 5am.

I woke up to find a squirrel eyeing me as if stunned, I was probably the biggest nut he had seen. A cup of tea and half an hour later I was passing through Staines and Egham, and onto the A30. Dressed in my old Denison smock and red beret with pack and wireless aerial – I really looked the part, and played recorded marches by the Parachute Regiment Band to help myself along, and for the benefit of passers by.

I must admit that by now I was feeling my age and the weight of my pack, so I jettisoned my tins of food – after all I had no tin opener! Following a meal at a public house I walked on to Virginia Water and Bagshot before stopping at 2pm close to Camberley. Later I acquainted the security people at Sandhurst of my arrival and found a guest house for the night. The next morning my umbrella came into use as it poured with rain for three hours. I managed to collect the wreath and a spray of red roses from the local florists and then made my way to the RMAS at 2pm as arranged.

At the cemetery Capt D. T. Lynch, with several other officers including Capt MacKay of the Parachute Regiment were in attendance, and also WO1 Ferneaux, Grenadier Guards, and WO2 Hallis of the Parachute Regiment. Mrs Audrey Lord, her son and his wife also attended, and I was able to hand the roses to Mrs Lord. I then placed the wreath on AcSM Lord's grave, removed my beret, and remained standing to attention for one minute. One of the most emotionally charged moments of my life . . . but mission accomplished.

26 July 1985 marked an auspicious occasion at the Sergeants Mess RMAS, when the J. C. Lord Room was opened by Mrs Audrey Lord. The original idea had come from AcSM Denis Cleary, who over a period of months had a suitable area converted, carpeted and furnished, until an extremely attractive restaurant/function room was formed, complete with photographs of John Lord taken at various stages of his career. The opening of the room was attended by Mrs Audrey Lord and her family and an impressive number of guests which included many former soldiers who had served with or under RSM Lord.

Capt Alistair MacDonald concluded so well in his letter to me . . .

Our loss is that he is no longer with us, but perhaps the fact that our memories of him remain so vivid, is God's way of allowing him to be alive in the spirit, to continue to help us all on our way through life . . .

CHAPTER 14

Academy Sergeant Majors to 1989

W. L. A. Nash, Grenadier Guards, was appointed RSM of the RMA Sandhurst, from May 1955 to March 1956, a period during which RSM J. C. Lord was recuperating from TB. Bill Nash wrote of that period:

I had the privilege to be invited to stand in for John Lord during his first long illness in 1955-6, and I was soon aware that one was sitting in a seat belonging to no ordinary soldier, and when I visited him in hospital once each week for 'orders' and to keep him up to date, invariably his first question was, 'Are you giving your best to Sandhurst?'

This was a typically modest reflection on the part of Bill Nash, as had he become RSM of the Academy at any other time, he would have settled to become a great Academy Sergeant Major with an influence entirely of his own upon the British Army. His sense of duty and loyalty was absolute and no WO1 would have been willing to give more to the responsibility of training young officer cadets.

Bill Nash had served at Sandhurst as the Company Sergeant Major of Dettingen Company, Old College, in 1949, under the influence of RSM John Lord. It was with such loyalty and a sense of duty to the Academy, that Bill Nash opted to relinquish the appointment on the return to fitness of John Lord, and he accepted instead the appointment of RSM of the Eastern Command at Hounslow.

Bill Nash had joined the Grenadier Guards in 1938 and served through the Second World War in North Africa, Italy, North West Europe and Egypt. His medals show that he served in the 8th Army, and was mentioned in despatches. The period following the war years provided a great deal of competition between highly experienced Warrant Officers, and a measure of Bill Nash's calibre is reflected not only by his appointment in September 1951 as Guards Depot RSM, but also in his subsequent role at the RMA Sandhurst.

For a time Bill Nash was RSM of the 3rd Battalion, Grenadier Guards and was then commissioned to become Quartermaster, receiving the MBE for his outstanding service. In 1970, Maj (QM) Nash retired to become the first Guardsman to hold the title of Superintendent of Her Majesty's Castle at Windsor. He held this extremely responsible post for over 12 years, making a host of friends through his patient, caring and absolutely conscientious application.

I approached Bill Nash in relation to the previous book on the career of RSM John Lord and I received the most full and kind help from him, extending to a visit to Windsor Castle in order to discuss with him his memories of shared service with John Lord. One only had to meet and talk with him to appreciate his deep and enthusiastic interest in all matters military, and above all, a supportive desire to help and make sure that everything was done correctly. This quality is found in so many of the really great former Regimental Sergeant Majors, of which he was one.

Maj (QM) W. L. A. Nash MVO MBE, died at the King Edward VII Hospital, Windsor, on 10 October 1983, at the age of 63, following a heart attack.

RSM W. L. A. Nash, Grenadier Guards, RSM of the RMAS 1955-6. AcSM RMAS

Like John Lord, whom he held in such admiration and respect, Bill Nash died far too young, with much still before him. Had he been given the opportunity to write of his experiences, there would have been available for the the next generation a wonderful example of soldierly loyalty and Christian endeavour.

RSM Cyril H. Phillips took over as AcSM from John Lord in August 1963, having earlier served two tours at Sandhurst as CSM in the 1950s, and RSM of Old College. RSM Phillips had joined the Welsh Guards in 1934 and served with the 1st Bn in Gibraltar before going to France on the outbreak of war, as CQMS of the Prince of Wales's Company. He was captured in action just before Dunkirk and spent the following five years as a POW.

In September 1945 he rejoined the 1st Bn and was soon promoted as CSM of the Prince of Wales's Company, serving the next four years in Palestine. He returned home to be made Drill Sergeant, as the battalion commenced a tour of public duties. Later he served in Germany and took a prominent part in the organising of the battalion rugby team which succeeded in winning the BAOR Cup twice. At this stage he became college RSM at the RMA Sandhurst, and gained valuable experience in the training of officer cadets. A complete change came in 1958 with the appointment as RSM of the 11th Bn King's African Rifles, which at that time was very much a ceremonial battalion.

On appointment as AcSM in 1963, C. H. Phillips completed a period of seven years before handing over in December 1970 to RSM R. P. Huggins MBE. He then became a member of the Queen's Bodyguard of the Yeomen of the Guard, and crowned a distinguished career as Messenger Sergeant Major and Keeper of the Wardrobe at St James's Palace.

MSM C. H. Phillips RVO's last great parade was the 500th Anniversary Parade of the Yeoman of the Guard, when after over 50 years of service in uniform, he handed on his responsibilities to former GSM Tom Taylor MVO MBE.

RSM Raymond Pearse Huggins MBE became AcSM in December 1970, having earlier served as RSM of Old College from 1965-6. I was able to visit the RMA Sandhurst on more than one occasion to talk with him and observe parades which he was taking, and also to visit him at Blenheim Palace. The following absorbing details and comments resulted from our conversations.

Five generations of the Huggins family have served in the British Army. Ray's great grandfather, S. Huggins, served in the 90th Regiment of Foot, when it was the 90th Perthshire Light Infantry, during the Crimea and then India. His son, F. W. Huggins (Ray's grandfather) also served in the same regiment, by then named the Cameronians (Scottish Rifles). Ray's father, F. J. Huggins served as a Sergeant in the King's Liverpool Regiment in 1918, and then as a Sergeant in the RASC during the

Academy Sergeant Major C. H. Phillips, MBE, Welsh Guards.
AcSM RMAS

Second World War. As he left the army in September 1945, Ray was enlisting in the Grenadier Guards at Manchester. Ray's son entered the Duke of York's Royal Military School in the early 1980s and his daughter was more recently a Captain Instructor with Victory College RMAS.

Born on 22 March 1928 at Hazel Grove, Cheshire, Ray Huggins enlisted at the age of 17 in the Grenadier Guards in September 1945, only months after the end of the Second World War. He went through the Guards Depot at the time of RSM S. M. Hamilton and following further training at Windsor, was posted to the Westminster Garrison Battalion at Wellington Barracks. He was then posted to the 4th Bn, Grenadier Guards, in Hamburg, where the RSM was A. J. Spratley. Ray was always impressed by his standards.

Arthur Spratley was a 'giant' of 5ft 9ins. He had started in the regiment as a drummer boy and went on to become Lieutenant Colonel. He had a particularly fine parade voice – beautiful crystal clear tone. We called him 'Sir Arthur' and whatever he had as an RSM, it was just that sort of magic.

The 4th Bn was disbanded in 1946, as part of the army's reductions after the war and Ray Huggins was present at its final parade when he received credit from the inspecting officer, Maj-Gen Marriott. He was then transferred to the 1st Bn, Grenadier Guards, at Neuminster, Germany. In 1947 when the battalion returned home, Ray was made Lance Corporal and selected for the Guard of Honour attending Westminster Abbey for the marriage of HRH Princess Elizabeth and Prince Philip.

I took part in a Guard of Honour course of 96 men, and was selected number 96! I was the shortest man on parade at 6ft 1in and the right hand man of the guard was 6ft 8ins! We marched in khaki uniforms from Wellington Barracks to Westminster Abbey, through great crowds of people and as this was the first ceremonial parade after the war, it was a great occasion. Incredible to be part of it. The Household Cavalry wore ceremonial dress and the people loved it. A great parade which will always remain in my mind.

1948 found the 1st Bn in Palestine and Cpl Huggins became Lance Sergeant. I was serving in the 2nd-3rd Bn, the Parachute Regiment at that time, and I remember that as we and most of the other regiments left Palestine in May 1948, a Grenadier Guards battalion took over our barracks and Ray Huggins confirms that the 1st Bn was the last unit to leave.

He later moved with the battalion to Tripoli, where he was promoted to Gold Sergeant. Here the Queen's Birthday Parade was held, with two Foot Guards Battalions taking part. In 1952 Sgt Ray Huggins was posted to the Guards Depot as a Superintending Sergeant, where the depot RSM was W. L. A. Nash. He adds:

I suppose that Bill Nash was the first gentleman Sergeant Major. Make no mistake about it – there was right and there was wrong, but he had this magic, gentle manner. He later held the appointment of RSM of the RMA Sandhurst and was the same there, a super man. I noticed that in the book about John Lord, Bill Nash chose to mention a parade held at the Academy in which he made a mistake by giving an out of date order. It took a man of charm to select a memory like that, as many of us have made mistakes which we do not care to talk about.

Ray Huggins was a sportsman throughout his service, taking part in swimming and athletics, sabre fencing and rugby, and he was the light heavyweight boxing champion in his battalion for a time. In 1954 he returned to the 1st Bn in Berlin where he was made CQMS. He served under RSM A. Dickinson at this time and describes him as:

An RSM of the old school – the Mighty Dick – a pre-war soldier with a definite black or white outlook in relation to standards, no in betweens. A strict but magnificent RSM.

The battalion held a smart Queen's Birthday Parade in Berlin, when Sgt Huggins was elevated to Sergeant of the Escort to the Colour. In 1955 came promotion to CSM and one year later he went to 14 Company at the Guards Depot, which at that time trained over 600 recruits! He worked

under two great Grenadier RSMs during that period, RSM L. C. Drouet and RSM F. Clutton MM.

In 1958, CSM Huggins returned to the 1st Bn and three years later went to the British Southern Cameroons. On returning home, he was posted to the 2nd Bn Grenadier Guards, as Assistant Drill Sergeant to RSM Joe Randell, and then advanced to Drill Sergeant. The 2nd Bn then went on a duty tour to British Guyana.

In 1965 Ray Huggins was appointed RSM of Old College at the RMA Sandhurst, where AcSM C. H. Phillips had been in office for three years. His predecessor, John Lord, was working at the sports and estate office at that time. After a successful tour at the Academy, Ray Huggins was, in 1966, appointed Sergeant Major of the 2nd Bn, Grenadier Guards, at Wuppertal, and was the first post-war enlisted Grenadier to be made RSM.

In January 1968 the sad news was received that former AcSM John Lord had died, and RSMs Ray Huggins and Peter Lewis (from the 1st Bn) were flown home to England to attend the funeral at the RMAS Cemetery. The bearer party consisted of AcSM C. H. Phillips in command, GSM Tom Taylor, RSMs Peter Lewis, Jack Thomas and Ray Huggins from the Household Division and RSM A. Arnold with three colleagues from the Parachute Regiment. Following his sad and short visit to this country, RSM Huggins returned to the 2nd Bn, where he particularly remembers the following parades:

When we returned from Germany, we held a Farewell to Armour parade, in which the battalion handed over all of its armoured vehicles and reverted to Foot Guards. With our CO, Col P. G. A. Prescott MC, I devised a parade which would quite literally illustrate the battalion's change of role. The Divisional Commander, Gen Erskine-Crum (Scots Guards) was taken to the orderly room, and then to the saluting base – with the parade ground clear of troops. Then the vehicles were driven on to the ground with the men aboard and standing to attention, and the battalion was driven past in salute. As the armoured vehicles drove on in battalion formation the men removed their combat jackets, which had been donned over drill order, exchanged their berets for forage caps which were in the vehicles, and as the drummer sounded the form up the men quickly formed in ranks as the vehicles were slowly driven off. The battalion then marched past the saluting base – and we had reverted to Foot Guards. It was a super parade and was performed well.

The second parade remembered was the Presentation of New Colours to the 2nd Bn, Grenadier Guards, in the grounds of Buckingham Palace in 1969. As an RSM may only experience this parade once during his career, he makes sure that everyone rises to the occasion.

In December 1970, RSM Ray Huggins achieved his great ambition when he was appointed the Academy Sergeant Major, recognised as being the Senior Warrant Officer post in the British Army. At the time of writing, Grenadier Guards RSMs have held this distinguished appointment for 50 of the 89 years of this century.

When Ray Huggins took the post in 1970 very much of the old school remained and the training courses lasted for

RSM R. P. Huggins, shortly before becoming the Academy Sgt-Maj, is in conversation with HRH The Prince of Wales at the Royal Tournament. Ray Huggins (PRO HQ, London)

two years, with adequate time for drill and ceremonial, but there have been many changes since. With the amalgamation of Eaton Hall OCS with the Mons OCS in 1958, and the closure of Mons in 1972, the RMA Sandhurst became the only officer cadet training establishment. Ray Huggins now talks generally about his period as Academy Sergeant Major.

One of the outcomes of several of us attending the funeral of John Lord, was that we asked ourselves – why is it that we only meet at funerals? AcSM Cyril Phillips really took this conversation to heart with the result that he arranged an RSMs convention at the Guards Depot in May 1969, and then we arranged one in 1970 at the Academy. There had been conventions held in John Lord's time, but not for a number of years. Since 1970 however, conventions have been held at two yearly intervals. This is a learning, discussion situation, and Tom Taylor and I must have attended for ten years together, during which period we have seen a great many RSMs go through. There is a dual benefit, as the long service members are able to put over the knowledge and retain the standards, whilst new methods can also be thrashed out.

Not everyone likes change and at Sandhurst people would assure me, 'Oh, but that has always been done like that!' and I would reply 'Rubbish . . . there has been change ever since 1803!' They said that we couldn't have 2nd Lieutenants at Sandhurst as students, but look at the books in the library. It was not the first time that we had received 2nd Lieutenants, as all of these things had occurred before! The course had been lengthened or shortened.

The problem with everything in this day and age is that every emphasis is placed on money. My answer has always been the same – that one has to remember that Sandhurst is training the *Leaders*! This is the officer corps of the British Army, and if one trims away at that – the effect must be experienced later.

There were great changes during my periods as College RSM and Academy Sergeant Major. In 1965 the officer cadets were mainly from public schools with only a fifth from grammar schools. A comprehensive schoolboy was then accepted and with the junior officer cadets ruling their companies with rods of iron, he probably had a tough time, although he was very good. Now the ratio is probably 50:50 public school and comprehensive. Both

the type of student and the training has changed. One of my CSMs used to teach the officer cadets the order of cutlery, and the correct wine glasses to use at a table in preparation for dinner nights . . . just a small example of how things have changed over the years. Now these people are required to go straight to Northern Ireland service, or to the Falklands. Mind you, the Falkland Islands campaign proved the point, as no other country could have mounted an operation like that. We had the right spearhead units fully trained. Incredible!

The thing that upsets me here at Blenheim Palace is that people still say to me, 'You were an RSM for 20 years weren't you – will you shout for us?' I reply, 'Look, I'm sorry.' That's the problem with images, everybody imagines this great big guy, with great big boots and a big hat, shouting and bawling from 6am to 10pm.

One has to shout on occasions, because it is usually a large area in which one holds a parade, and that's the image they refer to as 'the voice'. I always said to people – especially those I was teaching to command – that I did not reckon to have a great parade ground voice, and I was the first to admit it. I used to point out that one had to use what one had to the best of one's ability, and that was the trick – to project the voice. Some were fortunate in having been born with a fine voice, such as Peter Lewis, Tom Pugh and John Lord. Myself, I had to develop a style which everyone could hear and with various tricks of moving about, always ensuring that I was in the right place and all that sort of thing, I could overcome it. Arthur Brand had a great voice, and I

Academy Sgt-Maj R. P. Huggins, Grenadier Guards.
Grenadier Gazette

aw him as RSM of the RMAS in 1948 when I was a Corporal. He vas one of the great shouters, but things have completely changed ow. One has to be a signals wizard, a watch keeper, a harbour naster, a public relations manager. One of my gimics was to say 'I nay not be the best Academy Sergeant Major they ever had, but 'm the best PR man!' In this day and age, keeping the Army in the ublic eye is absolutely essential.

Every Sovereign's parade was a public occasion, and I was ortunate enough to be on parade for three Presentations of New Colours, which must be unique. Once at Buckingham Palace, hen at the RMA Sandhurst as AcSM and lastly when HM The Queen presented a new banner to Sandhurst, which only occurs nce each 60 years!

Another fine parade at Sandhurst is the Royal British Legion Parade. I feel that this is a great occasion for officer cadets who are ntelligent people – the top seven per cent of the youth, according

Three distinguished Sergeant Majors salute the Colours at Buckingham Palace. (L to R) Academy Sgt-Maj Ray P. Huggins, Grenadier Guards, RMA Sandhurst. Command Sgt-Maj Frederick E. Darling, Academy Sgt-Maj at the United States Military Academy, West Point, 1971-3. (Sgt-Maj Darling served n the Pacific area 1941-45, Korea 1952, and Vietnam 1969-71, being awarded the Distinguished Flying Cross, 2 Bronze Stars, and 13 Air Medals.) Garrison Sgt-Major, London District, Tom Taylor, Grenadier Guards.   Ray Huggins (PRO HQ, London)

to one newspaper. On Saturday rehearsals I would explain matters and say that at this stage they would see coming up King's Walk, over 500 Standards of the British Legion, with 2,000 Legionaires, and I could see by their faces that they were thinking, 'Oh – here he goes again.' On the day, when I called them to attention however, and they saw the Standards being marched in by the Legionaires, I could see how impressed the officer cadets were. It made the whole thing worthwhile, a superb parade!

I enjoyed almost all drill, and considered myself an exponent of the number 4 rifle and rifle exercises. A favourite drill movement is the Sandhurst method of forming two ranks and three ranks, which was unique to the Academy, and the dressing was always so immaculate and appeared so good.

During my service I went on two duty tours to the West Point Military Academy in America, and as a AcSM went on a parade there. With 4,000 officer cadets on parade on 'the plain', it was very impressive. The parades are very different there however, as there are perhaps eight battalions on parade and each carries out its movements separately, whereas we have a whole parade moving together.

We exchange instructors with America and other countries for tours of duty, and those from West Point always enter well into the spirit of Sandhurst.

In 1973 AcSM R. P. Huggins was awarded the MBE and soon after the Meritorious Service Medal. In 1976 he

received the Cross of Recognition from the French Army. After ten years as AcSM, Ray Huggins retired on 11 September 1980, at the age of 52. He was presented with a solid silver five piece Georgian tea service, with an inscribed silver tray, by Gen Sir Robert Ford, Adjutant General, at a special ceremony at the MOD. The gift was paid for by contributions sent from his former cadets, then serving in different countries all over the world. He has since been employed by the Duke of Marlborough at Blenheim Palace.

Denis Cleary, Irish Guards, became the Academy Sergeant Major in 1980 and was the first Warrant Officer of his regiment to hold this appointment. Born in Dublin, he joined the Irish Guards on 2 July 1955 and completed his training at the Guards Depot under RSM D. Whyte, Scots Guards. A first close encounter with an RSM came when he and a fellow recruit decided to spend a few off duty hours in London, but then found that a sudden rail strike prevented their return to the depot. They decided to go and watch the guardmounting at Horse Guards and were standing amongst the crowds of spectators when an immaculate RSM suddenly confronted them, inspected them, and marched them off to the CLRD. They explained their presence as being due to the rail strike, but were promptly advised that this had ended several hours before! The RSM then obtained cups of tea for them and arranged transport back to the Guards Depot. The kindess of the RSM was legendary, and Denis Cleary remained a close friend of GSM George Stone for the following 30 years. He had for a time however, expected his trip to London to end in the guardroom.

Other RSMs to impress Denis as a young guardsman, were RSMs – Paddy Mercer, Arthur Bell and Maurice O'Brien who was RSM of the depot from 1960-1, and according to Denis, a marvellous soldier with a strong sense of humour. Checked by him in his office for an infringement of the regulations, a recuit would begin to explain why he had broken the rules. The RSM would listen patiently and then opening his door would invite others to, 'Just come and listen to *this*!' Later, in front of the CO, the recruit would reply in answer to the charge, simply, 'Nothing to say Sir.'

In October 1972, Denis Cleary went to the RMA Sandhurst as CSM of Rhine Company in New College, and served until November 1974 where he learned a great deal from AcSM R. P. Huggins. On promotion to Drill Sergeant he served in Germany under another distinguished Sergeant Major, RSM Tommy Corcoran, Irish Guards, who hailed from the same area of Dublin.

In March 1976, Denis Cleary returned to Sandhurst, but on this occasion as RSM of Old College, where he remained until October 1978. There then followed 16 months as RSM of the 1st Bn, Irish Guards, before in February 1980, he was appointed as Academy Sergeant Major to the RMA Sandhurst.

I visited AcSM Cleary in 1982, by which time he was well established, and during research upon this book our paths were to cross on numerous occasions. Indeed, a very proud occasion came on 26 July 1985, when with others I was invited to attend the opening of the J. C. Lord Room. Denis Cleary had worked extremely hard to prepare a splendid memorial room and to arrange a marvellous evening, which will always be remembered by the family of John Lord, and by the many former 'JC' men present.

On the following morning, a number of us attended a Saturday morning rehearsal for a coming Sovereign's parade, in which approximately 100 officer cadets and some 20 women officer cadets took part. The rehearsal was taken

Right: *Academy Sgt-Maj D. P. Cleary, Irish Guards.*   Jim Farrar

Academy Sgt-Maj D. P. Cleary and his wife Jackie in conversation with HM The Queen Mother at the RMAS, 1982
Denis Cleary

by the Old College Sergeant Major, RSM B. Everist and was observed by the Adjutant who was present on horseback.

RSM Everist first announced to the assembled cadets,

Last night a special room was opened in the Sergeants Mess, in the name of John Lord, a former Academy Sergeant Major. One of the guests was Mr Ray Sheriff, who is sat with his wife behind you. He was a close friend of J. C. Lord, and was captured with him after being wounded and blinded at Arnhem.

He has asked to be here this morning, and although he cannot see you, he can hear you and will know how good your drill is. Make sure that he hears how good it is, as you march around.

With the band of the 17th/21st Lancers positioned on the steps of the Old Building, the rehearsal commenced and Ray Sheriff, with his wife Betty, enjoyed with the rest of us, the marvellous sounds of Sandhurst, as the officer cadets, men and women, marched in line around the square in slow and quick time.

Sgt Ernest Barrable, with whom I attended the parade, suggested that I might step onto the square to obtain better photographs of the marching, but such was my anxiety that I hurried and ruined the shots. 35 years before at Aldershot, it had been a cardinal sin to step onto the square

Many new RSMs believe that upon being appointed they must change to become stern and solitary, but this is not necessary. They have been selected for their own personal qualities and so long as they maintain the standards and carry out their duties efficiently, there is no need for a change of personality. The aim should be to control by firmness and fairness and not to seek to rule by fear. It is wise to remember that the appointment is all about getting on with people.

At the Academy, one can initially miss the support of Drill Sergeants as, whilst serving in the Guards Regiments or at the Guards Depot, there is a full team of CSMs and Drill Sergeants, but this is not so at the Academy, where there are instead, College RSMs and CSMs. Once used to the different regime however, the new team is well appreciated. The setback then can be that the team is never static, as warrant officers and instructors are constantly completing their tours of duty and moving on to new responsibilities, often of course, to return later in higher rank.

With its strong links with other countries, the Academy draws enquiries from all over and when answering the phone, the Academy Sergeant Major never knows what will come, he has to become an authority on all matters military. He must always have the welfare of both staff and cadets in mind, as the cadets are high calibre volunteers, eager to learn and to question, and they represent what the Academy is all about. The instructors are the very best, and they need support to perform well and cope with the pressure. A good two year tour does a great deal for the instructor and he goes on to better things.

As with many changes at Sandhurst, even the tour of duty of the AcSM has altered from a permanent posting to become an optional period of service, and AcSM Denis Cleary decided to retire from the army on 31 December 1987, and although his links remain firm, he has already joined the multitude of officer cadets, instructors and staff, who belong to the history of the world's finest military academy.

unless on parade. Such was our training under RSM J. C. Lord that I remain almost totally unable to walk onto a square.

When I had previously visited Denis Cleary in 1982, I was to realise how hard the officer cadets and instructors had to work in order to fit in every aspect of the training. At 6pm I watched groups of officer cadets set off for runs around the grounds, and there was still a great deal of activity one hour later. At 7.45pm a drill session could be heard with the officer cadets calling out the time and the sounds echoed around the buildings in the evening sunshine. These cadets had then to commence a shining hour which would take them to 9pm. Every opportunity has obviously to be taken for a period of drill, and I could hear cadets calling out the time until late in the evening – and people suggest that the army is becoming easier!

The routine is just as long for the instructors and when I imagined that they would wish to be relaxing in the evening, I joined a group of weapon training instructors to find them eagerly enthusing over the trajectory of a certain weapon. During many conversations, both long and short, with AcSM Denis Cleary, he explained many absorbing points to me.

RSM Michael Nesbitt became AcSM on 1 January 1988, having served two earlier tours at the RMA Sandhurst, as Colour Sergeant Instructor in 1977 and as CSM in 1980. He enlisted in the Grenadier Guards in 1967, and went through his training at the Guards Depot during the period in office of RSM J. Grindley. As a Lance Corporal he took part in the Queen's Birthday Parade in 1969 and looks back upon this greatest of all ceremonial parades with pride. During his service he has been fortunate in working under excellent RSMs, including RSM John Holbrook at the Guards Depot, when serving there as a Lance Sergeant, RSM Gordon Whitehead during a period when he also remembers taking part in an extremely smart parade in Berlin for Allied Forces Day. Also under RSM Alex Dumon when serving as a Sergeant Instructor at the Depot, RSM Don Ashworth and RSM Ray Barnes and of course, during his tours at the RMA Sandhurst, under AcSM Ray Huggins. When a Drill Sergeant, he worked with RSM Dave Ling in the 1st Bn, Grenadier Guards, and in 1986 was appointed RSM of the same battalion.

As AcSM, Michael Nesbitt reveals all of the qualities necessary to conduct the present day regime at Sandhurst, with its short but dynamic and complex course of training.

There would appear to be a greater than ever requirement for the AcSM to appreciate and understand all of the needs of the specialist military and civilian staff of the Academy. The WOs and NCOs look particularly to him for example and career structure guidance.

There may be less drill content in the training programme, but when I witnessed a college parade recently, this did not reflect in the smartness of the officer cadets. The parade was incidentally taken by RSM A. Lord, Coldstream Guards, who follows in illustrious footsteps.

RSM D. P. Cleary, Irish Guards, introduces the Warrant Officers of the Irish Guards at Pirbright to HM The Queen Mother on St Patrick's Day. Denis Cleary

The Saturday morning parade at the Royal Military Academy Sandhurst. Officer Cadets slow march on the Old Building square on the day following the opening of the 'J. C. Lord Room'. Ray and Betty Sheriff can be seen seated by the famous steps of the Grand Entrance. Photo by the author

Mention has been made of the Pace Stick in this book, and several RSMs and former RSMs have produced papers on the subject, including RSM A. J. Brand, RSM J. C. Lord, and Maj (QM) W. J. Holbrook.

A booklet was produced by AcSM R. P. Huggins in July 1976, in which he sets out the history of the pace stick and illustrates the various drill movements.

A Pace Stick Competition has been held annually between the Guards Depot and the Royal Military Academy Sandhurst for 37 years, in which teams of four Sergeants with a Warrant Officer Team Captain, carry out the pace stick drill over a set course in slow and quick time. With the help of Ray Huggins, Denis Cleary and AcSM Michael Nesbitt, the following results have been compiled, which reveal in the early years how seriously RSM Lord took the competition, and how thoroughly he prepared his teams. There has been only one drawn match, in 1971, which seems to have marked a period of intense effort between the teams of AcSM Ray Huggins and those of RSM John Holbrook.

1952 RMAS	1971 Drawn Match
1953 RMAS	1972 GDS Depot
1954 RMAS Depot	1973 GDS Depot
1955 GDS Depot	1974 RMAS
1956 RMAS	1975 GDS Depot
1957 RMAS	1976 RMAS
1958 RMAS	1977 GDS Depot
1959 GDS Depot	1978 RMAS
1960 RMAS	1979 RMAS
1961 RMAS	1980 GDS Depot
1962 RMAS	1981 RMAS
1963 GDS Depot	1982 GDS Depot
1964 GDS Depot	1983 RMAS
1965 GDS Depot	1984 GDS Depot
1966 RMAS	1985 RMAS
1967 GDS Depot	1986 GDS Depot
1968 RMAS	1987 GDS Depot
1969 RMAS	1988 RMAS
1970 RMAS	

CHAPTER 15

The Garrison Sergeant Majors of Headquarters, London District

Garrison Sergeant Majors have been appointed to military districts in this country and abroad since the mid 1800s and we have read of Sgt-Maj T. Gowing serving as GSM of the Allahabad district in India from 1872-6. Because of the GSMs' of the London District association with ceremonial in London and in particular with the ceremony of Trooping the Colour, held on Her Majesty The Queen's Birthday, they have become increasingly prominent since the end of the Second World War.

The change from purely garrison administrational duties, which were naturally at their heaviest during wartime, to that of the present ceremonial specialist, has been gradual, but the greatest change came with the appointment of George Stone, Irish Guards, in 1952. Before his period in office, the duties of the GSM were mainly garrison based, but since his time, have been almost wholly associated with ceremonial.

The appointment must have carried great responsibility during the wars because of the enormous circulation of Allied troops through London, whether moving through as units or spending periods of leave there. Before the Second World War the work of the GSM was probably covered by the WO1 in charge of recruiters, based at the Central London Recruiting Depot, but when the duties increased with the declaration of war, his work separated although he remained based at the CLRD.

WO1 GSM Thomas Courtney, Coldstream Guards, held the appointment from 1940-50 and his must have been an interesting story, with so many Commonwealth and American troops spending time in London, during the Blitz and later, doodlebug and rocket attacks. Sadly this is a period about which little has been recorded and we can only speculate upon those dramatic years.

RSM George Howe, Irish Guards, took over and held the appointment for just over one year, before RSM Frederick Thomas Aylen of the Coldstream Guards was appointed for a further year. George Stone became GSM on 6 February 1952 and his first ceremonial task was the State Funeral of HM King George VI, followed by the Coronation of HM Queen Elizabeth II. His great friend Bill Rooney MBE MM, Irish Guards, a former RSM of the Guards Depot, tells us of George Stone's qualities:

Although his Christian name was Gerald, the initial G was inevitably interpreted as George in his early soldiering days, and so that name stuck throughout his long, distinguished and colourful career. A career which started when he enlisted into the regiment on 11 August 1927, at the age of 15.

I knew George from the first day I joined in 1936, when he was already an NCO in the drums. He was a Lance Sergeant when I was a Lance Corporal and we went to Egypt and Palestine together in the years before the war. During the war we first went to Norway, where he was mentioned in despatches for his work in action with the Intelligence Section, and then to North Africa.

He became a Drill Sergeant after the war, indeed, he was one of my Drill Sergeants at the Training Battalion in Lingfield. I remember marching up and down after a particularly heavy Friday night. Saturday morning – always a drill parade at eleven o'clock. I put it to the Drill Sergeant, 'George, haven't you laid on some rain?' 'I tried Sir,' he replied, 'but it was a Grenadier on the other end, and he wouldn't play.' Rich as the English language is in adjectives, it would be difficult to find one, or even a combination, to adequately define the many talents, qualities and gifts which George Stone possessed in such abundance. Behind a serious and conscientious approach to his work, he had a lightning wit and tremendous sense of fun, neither of which was ever unkind or offensive. A gifted impressionist, his impersonations of famous regimental figures were always a popular feature of many a Sergeants Mess party.

Of all my scores of wonderful memories of him, the one I treasure most is of a day in Hubbelrath, where he had a young NCOs course on the 1.30 parade in the drill shed. The CO, then Lt-Col B. O. P. Eugster, decided to visit the squad, and as he and I approached near the drill shed, George – who had his back to us – brought the squad to a halt. He hurried towards the right hand man, who was around 6ft 7in tall, and with whose performance he was obviously far from happy. He then spotted a set of steps a few feet away, left by an electrician and in a flash placed them by the offender, climbed up until he could speak face to face with him. The CO had by now changed direction, remarking with a huge smile, 'Sergeant Major . . . we won't spoil the Drill Sergeant's moment of fun.'

However, it was his long tour as GSM, London District, that had the greatest impact upon his life and on the whole field of ceremonial in the Household Brigade, as it then was. His appointment on 6 February 1952, in which I am pleased to have played a part, was probably the most appropriate and wisest ever made. He had excellent credentials, equipped with pre-war experience as a Sergeant in the Corps of Drums, then as Drum Major and later as a Drill Sergeant. He also had a wide knowledge and appreciation of martial, as well as other music, and his friendship and close association with bands and Directors of Music provided the ideal background. Indeed, if there were such a thing as a degree in ceremonial, George would have passed with honours.

I believe it is true to say that he was the first GSM to become totally involved with all aspects of ceremonial as well as attending to his other duties. He was without doubt, part of the great state occasions, and each time, George could be seen discreetly and tactfully checking on any possible last minute imperfections, because his standards and the example he set others was nothing less than perfection.

The Brigade Majors, like the great Gen Fitzalan-Howard and Erskine-Crum, thought the world of him because there was absolutely nothing that he didn't or couldn't do. The RSMs would come back from abroad, rusty in their ceremonial and George was there with a helping hand. All would, I am sure, endorse the assessment that he was one of the greatest authorities on ceremonial of our times. He was an encyclopedia of fun and a most lovable character. Not one of the old breed of RSMs who spat fire and brimstone, but a gentleman who got more out of people by his gentle approach.

Continuity is of vital importance in the appointment of the GSM of the London District and during his final six months in office, the GSM will always carefully train and ease in his successor. RSM Tom Taylor therefore, worked with George Stone for six months before becoming GSM in 1965.

When I first prepared for appointment as GSM, I read as much as I could of the *Household Divisional Standing Orders*, which is the great Bible of the GSM and which increases in information all the time, but when the time came I was extremely glad to join George Stone during his last six months of service. Little was done before the war to prepare detailed papers on the Queen's Birthday Parade, or the other ceremonial drill parades in London. George had been a pre-war Drum-Major and in that rank had been on the Birthday Parade many times, and knew the musical side and the role of the Drum-Major.

When he became GSM he really concentrated upon the ceremonial side of life and began to write or re-write the Brigade Standing Orders, and to measure up the ceremonial routes. He compiled a table of routes wherever it was necessary to mount street lines of troops. So many yards equalled so many men. He also, for the first time, got into the drilling of bands effectively. He would have a Drum-Majors' course with all five of them on the square and would make sure that the staff drill was absolutely right. Then he would go through with them the interior movements of the band, before going near the bands themselves.

There would follow six or seven massed band drills working through every phase of the parade. Marching on, forming up, each year a different format depending on many factors. Also, when George Stone took over he had a great deal of ceremonial work to contend with. His service culminated in the preparation for the funeral of Sir Winston Churchill. These state funerals have to be organised quite quickly, although much of the planning has to be completed in advance. This is named 'Exercise Hope Not'. Nevertheless, there is always a great deal to do and much midnight oil to burn.

Many phases had to be worked out for the Sir Winston Churchill state funeral; later I inherited this huge file and was able to adapt certain parts to suit other occasions. I was fortunate indeed to be able to work and learn side by side with George Stone from the Christmas of 1964 until he retired six months later.

We prepared for the Queen's Birthday Parade working together on the massed bands drills. One could not possibly pick this up alone by trying to translate the movements from 'The book' onto the ground. I actually took a 'staff' and by joining the Drum-Majors on parade learned the drill by doing it. I do not read music – but I learned the staff positions. I knew that when the Senior Drum-Major raised his staff mine also had to go up and that it went up on the left foot, and came down on the right foot, and that sort of thing. I also learned from George Stone the many periods of massed band drill and the intricacies of the interior movements of the spin wheel.

Garrison Sgt-Maj, London District, George Stone, MBE RVM, Irish Guards. A distinguished and very highly respected guardian of ceremonial 1952-65. Guards Magazine

Major Bill Rooney now concludes:

George had indeed prepared the way for those who were to follow and the appointment of Garrison Sergeant Major in its present form owes a great deal to his efforts. When George Stone laid aside his sword and pacestick in 1965, he took up employment in the Metropolitan Police College, Hendon, renewing friendships with many police officers from the old Scotland Yard, and making many more friends.

A staunch and loyal supporter of the Irish Guards Warrant Officers Club and the Irish Guards Association, he scarcely ever missed an annual dinner. It was at these that another of his gifts proved so popular, his own unique brand of after dinner fireside chats, so casually but eloquently delivered and which were always greeted with such uproarious applause.

I last saw him at the unveiling of F. M. Alexander's statue on 9 May 1985, when he and I had the honour of being presented to HM The Queen at the reception which followed. It was to be his last big occasion and how fitting that he was accorded this privilege to talk with the Sovereign whom he had served for so long and so loyally.

George's passing left a great vacuum in the lives of all who were privileged to have been his friends, and there were many.

Having shadowed George Stone for six months, the appointment of GSM now came to RSM Tom Taylor, but his service had commenced as a wartime Guardsman and when I talked with him about his career he gave me the following details.

I arrived at the Guards Depot late on the last day in December 1942, a rather odd night to arrive as everyone was of course whooping it up. I was just placed in the receiving room and left for a time until others came and we were taken to get a haircut and have the paperwork done.

The Depot Sergeant Major was at that time a Welshman, a fine figure of a man, RSM P. Dunne, MBE. To us recruits he was the epitome of a Sergeant Major. He always wore pre-war service dress and forage cap and amongst the khaki parade, stood out as a magnificent sight, being tall and slim. Anyone wanting to make the army a career would wish to emulate him. He was a very fair man, but at the same time, going back through my mind now, was quite remote from us. The trained soldier, the squad instructor and the CSM were the men who really moulded us into being Guardsmen.

The 14 week training course was rather hard and we very quickly realised what was required. There was a system of passing recruits out at various stages and you had to get yourself to standard, or be back-squadded. We covered all basic foot and rifle drill up to a high standard but did not go on to ceremonial work at that stage. The squad instructor taught us drill and came to talk to us in the barrack room about regimental intelligence. We had boards over our beds depicting the regiment's battle honours and we had to quickly learn the details.

The trained soldier also taught us battle history and these men were always well experienced, being selected to illustrate and supervise within the barrack rooms. They were an important part of the system and were often hard men, quite capable of making life difficult.

During the war each Regiment of Guards had its own training battalion and I went to Victoria Barracks at Windsor after the Depot. We went on to guard duties at Windsor Castle, but before the six weeks course was over a request came for volunteers for training with tanks and I went with others to the Guards Armoured Training Wing at Pirbright. In fact I had undertaken no ceremonial guard duties at Windsor and did not do any ceremonial work until after the war.

I completed the mechanical training and went on to gunnery. We had a variety of tanks and became familiar with many, but I trained particularly with Churchill tanks with which the 4th Bn were equipped, as opposed to the Sherman tanks of the 2nd Bn. I trained as a tank gunner, missing the signal wing altogether, and passed out as a gunner-mechanic. I remember that the driver-mechanic had most to learn. On completion of training I was posted to the 4th Bn, Grenadier Guards which was stationed at Welbeck Abbey. I was sent straight away to the Reconnaissance Troop which was equipped with Bren-gun-carriers.

We practised, and polished, and trained with these carriers for ages, draining the radiators at night in winter and filling them up again in the mornings. I thought that we were never going to take part in the war. Then came a large exercise in Yorkshire and finally we moved to Canterbury for what was clearly training for the invasion of Europe. D Day came on 6 June 1944 but we did not go to France until D 19, by which time Bayeux had been taken and there was something of a stalemate.

We were soon in action as the Guards Armoured Division, with a Scottish Division, were used to punch a hole through the German line. We gained only 1,000 yards on the first day, but then broke through and in only a few days raced through to Brussels. After the army became bogged down around Brussels, the battalion reformed at Geldrop and an attempt was made to push forward. Three of our squadrons went through very marshy ground and soon became clogged with mud. Our light unit rushed through under the cover of a huge smoke screen and took off the trapped crews, but the 14 tanks remained there until the area was captured, when they had to be cleaned up and refitted.

During the brief hold up, an NCO Cadre was held, and the local Dutch people must have thought us mad to be drilling at that time. Following the course I was promoted to Lance Corporal and although that represented the first rung of the ladder I cannot claim that I held any ambition to remain in the army and considered myself a purely wartime soldier.

Following the crossing of the Rhine the war was drawing to a close, but we lost men and tanks to German fanatics who would lay in wait in ditches, armed with Panzerfaust rocket weapons. Although the Churchill tank was said to be slow moving, it proved itself the opposite when the break through came after the Rhine and we rushed 400 miles to reach a position near Kiel, where we remained as the German Army surrendered.

Needless to say, Sgt-Maj Spratley arranged a training programme and a great clean up of equipment followed. It was then ordered that the whole division would regroup at Cologne. It was a wonderful sight to see all of our tanks moving along the autobahns. Soon the whole battalion was housed together in barracks and two battalion drill parades were held, before I was ordered to report to the School of Infantry at Warminster as an instructor.

With demobilisation taking place it was obvious that the army was going to lose many instructors, so a group of 180 experienced soldiers were sent from the Rhine army to go through a selection course for six weeks and I attended as a Lance Corporal. Almost half of us qualified and I met many men who became well known in their future careers. I went from Lance Corporal to Sergeant Instructor in six weeks, which stood me in good stead for the future. I was at the School of Infantry from October 1945 until March 1948.

I then went to the 2nd Bn, Grenadier Guards, when we were made jointly responsible with a Coldstream battalion, for the training of NCOs for the rest of the British Army. The Coldstream Guards ran their cadres at Aldershot, but we went to a very large training area in Germany. There we received intakes every six weeks from the basic training centres in England.

In 1950 I came home to our 3rd Battalion upon promotion to Colour Sergeant (pay sgt) and this was when I became involved for the first time in ceremonial work. In London we did all the normal duties for the King's Guard and I became responsible to the Quartermaster for accommodation, clothing and pay. I was detailed for King's Guard as the Senior Sergeant and had to prepare the pay sheets or equipment rolls between the times of posting guards and reliefs! One just had to do this as the time could not be spared from company work.

On the King's Birthday Parade in 1950, I was made Left Guide of Number 7 Guard – a key role in the guard as one is responsible for the dressing at the halt and for guiding the guard through the forming points. Then on the 1951 Parade, I was proud to be chosen to be the Left Guide of the Escort to the Colour. Although I had not previously carried out much ceremonial, everything is much rehearsed and I soon picked up the necessary drill. At Buckingham Palace one had to keep cool and calm and it was only if one began to flap about that mistakes occurred. The watching public wouldn't notice but of course minor mistakes do happen.

The Drill Sergeant would accompany the Palace Guard and closely supervise movements. He would carry out certain tasks such as dressing and later go with the St James's Palace detachment. He would correct any fault and see that the men stood still, also keep an eye out for any man becoming ill. He might notice a man beginning to sway about, and by walking ehind and speaking to him, urging him to get some air into his ungs, hold him on parade. If left alone the man would pass out. Many times I have encouraged a man to stand and grit his teeth. Much better to encourage and speak firmly to him than allow him to fall flat on his face and then to have to remove him.

Whilst I was with the 3rd Bn, Grenadier Guards, we went out to gypt, where we were involved in various troubles for three years nd then in 1953 I was promoted to CSM and posted to the RMA andhurst. I went to New College where I worked under the 'ollege RSM Dickinson. This was something new to me and I und in training officer cadets that one was certainly working ith willing material. I also found myself in company with CSM L. rouet and whilst he took Somme Company, I had Ypres ompany. We were both part of the great team of instructors nder RSM J. C. Lord. Such was his influence and example that nstructors gained as much from the Academy course as did the fficer cadets.

When RSM John Lord instigated the Pace Stick Competition, nis resulted in the pace stick becoming widely used, but before nat the Guards Depot issued them to Superintending Sergeants, 'SMs, Drill Sergeants and RSMs. At the RMA Sandhurst, pace ticks were so widely used that the hinges were breaking, so a nuch stronger metal hinge joint was produced. One became very exterous – using the stick in either hand – even the gloved hand in vinter.

For the competition the square was marked out in 20 pace boxes nd the teams were formed with three Sergeants, captained by a CSM. Normally, use of a pace stick is second nature, but verything had to be absolutely correctly carried out, such as the hange hand from right to left hand – and back. Each movement ould change at the 20 pace box mark, and all was judged arefully.

Occasionally the stick would be dropped and a lot of marks lost nd this could put your team out of the competition. That was the nain worry – the trick was to catch it before it reached the ground. ewer marks would be lost than if you had to run back and pick it

up! If in trouble with the stick slipping, one had to control and catch it – and take up sticking again – as smoothly as possible.

The Pace Stick Competition is now a world wide event with many teams entering, including some from other countries. The former AcSM Ray Huggins MBE wrote an excellent pamphlet on Pace Stick Drill, which is widely read.

As a Sergeant Major anywhere of course, the voice has to be trained to give orders regularly. If one does not shout correctly, from the diaphragm and not the throat, the voice will go quickly. At the RMA Sandhurst, with the officer cadets, we found that their confidence developed with an ability to give orders. We instructed them by conducted shouting. This was done by standing in a prominent position above the 60 cadets and conducting them with a pace stick.

We started by explaining what was required, in clarity – punch – and timing, and then got them to learn how to breath in fully – and keep them waiting – lots of laughs! Conducted shouting very quickly developed the art of shouting orders and breathing properly. The Guards Depot would use the same method with NCO Cadres and also of course, the All Arms Drill Wing.

We would place the cadets in two lines, 30 yards apart, with six paces between each man. One line would then shout orders to his partner opposite – all with different orders! Soon the man giving orders would try to assist by carrying out his own orders as a guide – but with confusion over left or right. Good fun for both cadets and the instructors.

Then on to squad drill when one soon realised whether cadets had learned some of the basic arts in shouting and of course, timing. The correct timing and position of the foot is absolutely essential. I always received more satisfaction from teaching rifle exercises, than drill. I enjoyed 'swank' parades with music,

Garrison Sgt-Maj, London District, Tom Taylor, Grenadier Guards, leading the Freedom of Windsor Parade, 23 July 1968.
Tom Taylor (PRO HQ, London. Mike Roberts)

When not on parade . . . The Garrison Sgt-Maj, Tom Taylor
W. Muir, MBE BEM, late Scots Guards

teaching cadets to march to music and pointing out the deliberate left beat. You get such style with music; correct tempo and pace, with someone regulating the pace, taking them around. Very nice.

In 1955 I went to the 2nd Bn in Egypt as Assistant Drill Sergeant, a rank peculiar to the Foot Guards. My old friend Lou Drouet was Drill Sergeant and the CO was the present Duke of Norfolk. We were stationed at the golf course camp until the army came out of Egypt and we returned to Pirbright, then Windsor, where we took over the duties of the 1st Bn on their departure to Cyprus. It was not long before I was made up to Drill Sergeant and on moving to the Guards Training Bn I came under the influence of another great RSM, Sgt-Maj Smith (Coldstream Guards). He was a large man with a large personality and he had been awarded the Distinguished Conduct Medal during the war. He was the kind of tremendous character you could not emulate in any way – a style all his own. He was strong and carried situations which some other Sergeant Majors could not have done. A large number of troops were going through that training and RSM Smith had to know his job. A feature was the large swank parade which he would take every Saturday, when the whole training battalion would be on parade.

In the Guards, the Drill Sergeants assist the RSMs and as they would often be the strict disciplinarians in order to get things moving, the Sergeant Major could sometimes stand back a little and advise and be the counsellor. I would be present on the square when squads were at drill and if I saw a sloppy squad I would pick up the step and move them along. Although strict, one could still be oneself, but the emphasis was on correct training: never condoning mistakes or allowing a sloppy turnout. One had to be hard and would appear to be always bawling and shouting.

Disciplining is not necessarily charging. I did not like the idea of charging as many men as I could in a day. The military law is there

to guide, but it is not ours to punish. We make a charge out and is a commissioned officer's task to punish. However, the Sergeant Major often has to be the judge of whether to charge or persuade man. Sometimes he will be able to put things right without charge. If conduct is against military law, a charge must follow an if a man was insubordinate or was fighting, I would always charge

In 1958 I transferred as Senior Drill Sergeant to the 1st Bn Chelsea Barracks, where I worked under RSM L. Drouet, doin the Queen's Guard and all the duties of a London battalion. Sg Maj Drouet then was chosen as RSM of the Guards Depot and course, he had also been moulded by the great J. C. Lord. As suc he was one of the 'gentlemen' RSMs. He could move a squa around however and knew how to chastise a man, which he coul do at length without ever repeating himself! His place was take by RSM R. Dobson who was very well known in the soccer wor as a referee and who later became a Major Quartermaster.

I then returned to the RMA Sandhurst in August 1959 as CSM of New College. I came to know John Lord well during tremendous three year period with him and our friendshi remained after he had retired.

Whilst at Sandhurst I went with a group of officer cadets durin one of the long recesses, to the Army Parachute Training Schoc and completed a course of jumps. John Lord also went o refresher courses to continue his parachuting from his days in th Parachute Regiment. On AcSM Lord's retirement, RSM C. F Phillips took over and I remained as Senior College RSM to assis I then became aware that the appointment of Garrison Sergean Major of the London District would become available in du course, as GSM George Stone had been in post for some 13 year and was approaching retirement.

My name was put forward to the Brigade Major, Sir Phili Ward, and it was agreed that I should remain until the pos became available. I therefore completed six years as College RSM at the RMA Sandhurst. In December 1965 I was proud to b appointed GSM London District.

The GSM rarely features in an actual parade, but when the fiv Regiments of Foot Guards received the freedom of Windsor enabling them to march through Windsor with bayonets fixed Colours flying and drums beating – I was given the privilege leading the parade from a position close behind the parad commander. I also took part in the parade on the occasion of th funeral of Field Marshal Montgomery, when I was required give the word of command starting the parade off.

My first State Funeral was in fact upon the death of the Duke Windsor and of course his lying in state was at St George's Chap at Windsor. I trained a team of Sergeants to do the sword drill an the slow march on to the catafalque as a demonstration for the 4 officers. We practised for hours until each officer had mastere the change of watch. The Funeral Drill is a particular parad which we in this country perform very well and we pride ourselve in doing it with dignity and without mistakes.

When planning a parade I would often use graph paper, wit the position of each man detailed in code and symbols. John Lor would always use symbols – a Sergeant was represented by a cros with a square under it – and he would explain that the Sergean would have to bear his cross. I had metal discs placed in positio for the Freedom of Windsor parade which involved all fiv regiments of the Foot Guards and these helped to indicate whe all of the prominent movements would take place.

For State visits at Windsor Castle it was initially decided tha there would be street lining troops all the way from Eton Windsor Castle and I paced out and marked the whole rout Later however, this was changed and street liners were used for shorter distance on the Long Walk at Windsor Castle. I needed t mark out the intervals at each 60 paces on grass and I wondere how to line these up properly. Eventually I enlisted the help of th Borough Surveyors Department and a surveyor with theodoli elped to guide me in line and after each 60 paces I placed a metal isc in position. It took some doing but eventually all the discs vere correctly in place on the afternoon before the parade.

Early next morning I thought that I would just check that all my iscs were in place, but I found to my shock, that many had been emoved by children who had enjoyed a game of skimming them! managed to line up some more discs quickly, but I had learned ny lesson and in future I took a Pioneer Sergeant with me to ring he discs in paint so that a guide remained.

At the Horse Guards parade ground there are permanent tones, placed before the war, which mark out the various ositions for the Queen's Birthday Parade. These mark the front anks, but we would actually scratch out other lines in the loose urface for other movements. Then came the day when they armaced the square and we could not scratch about on it! I then iad to obtain special chalk to make the necessary guide lines – this aking place from 6-7.15am before the permanent stones had to be wept to remove any loose grit. A battalion RSM saw me with nackintosh and yardbroom one very wet morning and said 'Well, rather fancied the job of Garrison Sergeant Major, but not now!'

One of my tasks as GSM was to suggest a change in the format of the Queen's Birthday Parade from that of pre-war days, purely n an attempt to shorten the length of time of the parade. I had to cratch my head and wonder how this might be done. As the person with all the timings and distances one could only work out possibilities, such as the cutting out of certain movements and dressings and eventually ideas were forwarded to the Brigade Major. He would report upon feasibility and then the matter would go before a meeting of all five Regimental Colonels for approval.

A large change that I became responsible for was in relation to a long standing complaint of the rear divisions on the march off, that they could not hear the bands clearly, as they were so far ahead around the Duke of York's steps, and echoes were making it difficult to maintain step. I worked on this and suggested a cut in the number of divisions by forming each guard into two divisions instead of three. This shortened the length of the parade and looked good with the large phalanx of men right across the width of The Mall – and they could hear the music.

During the last 20 years there has been an economy of movements, avoiding long hours of unnecessary drill. For instance, in the old days when guards were formed in barracks, the whole of a company would parade and many men would be called out for fatigues and various picquet duties as well as the guard. Now only the actual guard will be formed and this saves much time.

Actually the RSM of the battalion trooping the Colour rarely performs on the Queen's Birthday Parade more than once. It is his day and when the GSM has helped with the preparations for the parade, he hands over to the RSM. The Escort to the Colours, in which the battalion RSM takes part is the important feature of the parade and for the only time in his career he will draw his sword – with a world-wide television audience watching!

Once the Birthday Parade is started it has to go on and I suppose that only catastrophe would stop it, such as the Field Officer falling off his horse, or losing his voice. The weather can of

Former RSMs Tom and Neville Taylor. Tom was GSM of London District, and Neville was RSM of the 1st PWO Regt of Yorkshire. David Frogett

Ever watchful on parade. GSM Tom Taylor, Grenadier Guards, and RSM Alex Dumon, Coldstream Guards, working together, 1977. Tom Taylor (PRO HQ, London)

course delay or cancel the parade and the Major General has the responsibility of deciding if this is suitable. Only once in my 12 years was the parade cancelled and I believe that George Stone had only one cancellation.

As GSM I was directed to prepare the Royal Company of Archers for their Tercentenary Parade in Edinburgh. I anticipated a company of about 60 members but found that they had four detachments each of that number. I knew relatively little about the company before going to Edinburgh Castle, but on talking to their Adjutant on arrival I was handed a Long Bow and a book of drill and told, 'That is what I would like you to instruct upon tomorrow morning!' I took myself off to my quarters and standing in front of a mirror taught myself the correct drill movements. I stayed for five days in Edinburgh and managed to remain one lesson in front. Many former high ranking officers in the services were included in the Royal Company of Archers and I found it a most interesting assignment.

During my time as GSM a Quartermaster was required by the Guards Parachute Company and I seem to remember that applications were slow. I had earlier accompanied a group of officer cadets from Sandhurst to take the parachute course, so decided to express my interest. I was 47 years old when I went for interview and was advised that whilst London District HQ would not stand in my way, and I had admittedly completed the parachute course, I was really rather old for that sort of thing! I decided to remain as GSM. The successful candidate was the former Depot RSM Tom Pugh, a great character and athlete, who

was always selected for the cross-country team and middle distance running events.

RSM Alex Dumon spent six months with me before taking over as GSM and he and I did the Silver Jubilee parade together. We decided that the three services Guard of Honour outside Buckingham Palace had to have their positions absolutely correctly marked on the pavement, so RSM Dumon took charge of this whilst I went to St Pauls in order to mark out there. On that marvellous day I was at St Pauls and I knew by the television cameras exactly where HM The Queen was. The day in fact went extremely well for everyone.

Prior to my retirement from the army at the age of 54, I applied for the post of Doorkeeper to the Gentleman Usher of the Black Rod at the House of Lords. I was called forward for interview by Black Rod and was very happy to be accepted. Whilst still serving as GSM, I applied to be included on the roll for the Queen's Bodyguard of the Yeoman of the Guard and was accepted by the Ministry of Defence. The requirements for such selection being included in the Queen's Regulations.

The Queen's Bodyguard of the Yeoman of the Guard was originally formed by King Henry VII in 1485 and therefore with a continuous service of more than 500 years, is the oldest Military Corps in the world. Many former Warrant Officers are members of the Guard, and former Sgt-Maj C. H. Phillips MBE held the rank of Messenger Sergeant Major for 14 years until he retired. Former GSM Tom Taylor MVO MBE is now the Messenger Sergeant Major and carries out his responsibilities from the St James's Palace.

RSM Alex Dumon MBE, Coldstream Guards, was appointed Garrison Sergeant Major of the London District in 1977, having completed the usual six months experience with Tom Taylor. When I visited him at Headquarters Horse Guards in September 1986, he was within months of completing his service in the army, and between busy telephone calls and callers, he was able to talk about his career.

Alex Dumon was born in Leeds and enlisted in the Coldstream Guards on 1 March 1951, receiving his training at the Guards Depot during the period of RSM B. E. Hillier DCM. Few recruits at that stage, he stressed, had any aspirations of becoming an RSM, but concentrated wholly upon completing the course of training.

Within months of joining the regiment, he went abroad with his battalion, travelling the Medlock route to Tripoli. Three years later and back in England, he became associated for the first time with the Queen's Birthday Parade, when as a young Guardsman he was included in the Groundkeeping Party which lined the parade ground. He could have had no inkling of the great part which this most famous of parades would play in his future career.

He mentioned having been at a possible disadvantage for top promotion, being in the 3rd Bn, Coldstream Guards, as an Orderly Room Clerk, which was perhaps not the usual road to prominence as a ceremonial specialist. In 1955 however, he gained promotion to Lance Corporal and managed to take a more active part in the rehearsals for that year's Trooping of the Colour under GSM George Stone, only to experience the disappointment of the parade being cancelled because of a national rail strike.

In 1958 Alex Dumon was promoted to Sergeant and in the following year participated as a Sergeant of the Escort from the 3rd Battalion in the Queen's Birthday Parade, and was able to savour fully the unique atmosphere of this marvellous and colourful parade. This was in fact the last occasion upon which the Mark 4 SMLE rifle was used as 1960 saw the introduction of the SLR.

The next important step forward came in 1959, when a three year tour of duty commenced as an Instructor at the Guards Depot, and the RSM of the time, Johnnie Rodger, was to make a strong impression upon him. In the opinion of Alex Dumon:

He was one of the greatest RSMs. He demanded an extremely high standard and the depot really buzzed under him. The Saturday morning parade at Caterham was particularly impressive and the memory of RSM Rodger fully stands the test of time.

Handling a squad of his own revealed to Alex Dumon that it took time for the recruits to settle into the regiment. He enjoyed watching them develop with instruction and a little bit of fear, to become transformed into Guardsmen. He explained that half the squad would take to army life with barely a cross word and that others would make the grade with a lot of effort, but three recruits would not make it – and it was *better that they did not!*

Alex Dumon next went recruiting for two years, but then returned to the Depot as a CSM, where he found himself working with CSM John Holbrook. There followed appointments as Drill Sergeant, firstly under RSM Peter Clifford, and then RSM Norman Welch, before Alex Dumon was himself made RSM of the Guards Depot on 5 November 1972, following in the footsteps of John Holbrook.

In early 1975 Alex Dumon completed his period at the Depot and by 5 March was installed as GSM in Hong Kong, where he remained for two years. In 1977 he then took the

Garrison Sgt-Maj, London District, Alex Dumon, Coldstream Guards. Alex Dumon (PRO HQ London)

prestigeous appointment of GSM of the London District.

GSM Dumon confirmed that George Stone had, during his period in office, elevated the appointment from its former administrative role – of billeting, provision of escorts and the furnishing of fatigue parties – to the stage where the appointment could more accurately be termed Her Majesty's Ceremonial Warrant Officer. With Alex Dumon's service almost completed, he was coming to terms with yet more fundamental change in the world of ceremonial, with the introduction of the SA 80 rifle. He took into retirement with him many memories of the greatest parade.

There is nothing in the world like the Queen's Birthday Parade! A lot of blood, sweat and tears go into it. The parade has humanity, and to my mind the best drill movement ever is the Escort going forward in quick time, to receive the Colour.

'The Garrison Sergeant Major will always face change,' I was told, and whilst it might occasionally be necessary to pace out a new route in the early morning, before London's traffic begins, the real difficulty for the future will become that of finding sufficient men with which to line the routes – as soldiers are at an absolute premium now.

The practice parade of the Massed Bands of the Guards Brigade for the Queen's Birthday Parade in 1987, was held at Chelsea Barracks in May and with Alex Dumon's permission, I attended in order to take photographs of one of his last parades before retirement. I must admit that the spectacle of so many immaculately turned out bandsmen in scarlet and the magnificent sound of their music, at first reduced me to just walking parallel with them along the edge of the parade ground, and watching, but gradually I began to seek ways of portraying the instruction of GSM Alex Dumon.

RSM A. G. Mason, Coldstream Guards, was going through his six months preparation in readiness for taking over the appointment and both were busily supervising the complicated movements of the marvellous spin wheel. I shall always remember Alex Dumon standing at a distance from the huge massed band, giving the order, 'By the centre, quick march!' and then marching immaculately towards the band himself in order to illustrate the kind of style he wanted in the marching.

RSM A. G. 'Perry' Mason, Coldstream Guards, was appointed GSM, London District, in June 1987. He had joined the Coldstream Guards as a Boy Soldier in May 1962 and was one of two brothers serving in the army. His elder brother joined the Royal Corps of Signals and at one stage almost claimed him into the same corps. An uncle had also been commissioned in the Royal Corps of Signals.

In his early service GSM Mason was a Lance Sergeant Instructor at the Guards Depot and then a Colour Sergeant Instructor at the RMA Sandhurst from 1974-6. He was

Drill Sergeant to RSM Terry Nicholls and was appointed RSM of the 1st Bn, Coldstream Guards in 1986. He pays tribute to the examples of RSM John Holbrook, AcSM Ray Huggins and of course, GSM Alex Dumon, whom he holds in the highest esteem.

I was very fortunate in being allowed to attend the guardmounting on Horse Guards in May 1988, which is virtually a first rehearsal of the Trooping of the Colour. Prior to the parade, the Marker Party assembled under the famous centre arch of Horse Guards, which has such a long history of pageantry. The complex positioning of the

An historic photograph of three great Garrison Sergeant Majors of the London District: George Stone, Alex Dumon, and Tom Taylor. Outstanding in the world of ceremonial.   Alex Dumon

markers was carefully explained to them by GSM Mason, with only one minor explosion when one of the markers failed to come to attention when spoken to. The markers then marched smartly out to their positions on the huge parade ground, and the guardmounting commenced with the magnificent band marching across the square in slow, then in quick, time.

The Brigade Major was present on horseback and with the GSM in close attendance, they watched and carefully noted any points in the parade requiring improvement. GSM Mason had earlier commented that whilst he expected few difficulties with the more complicated movements, there would probably be faults in the basic drill which he would wish to improve. To me the whole parade was immaculate and I was particularly impressed with the arms drill with the SA 80 rifle.

I was very interested to meet and talk behind the scenes with GSM Mason's orderly and learned that Guardsman

Rifles taken into use during the last thirty years. (L to R) L/Sgt Tidswell, Grenadier Guards, with the Lee-Enfield. L/Sgt Allott, Coldstream Guards, with the SLR. L/Sgt Reagan, Irish Guards, with the SA 80. GSM A. G. Mason, Coldstream Guards (PRO HQ London)

Richard Curtis, Coldstream Guards, had served for six months as orderly to GSM Tom Taylor, no less than ten years as orderly to GSM Alex Dumon and now one year to GSM Mason. A very impressive orderly with the proud attitude that, 'If my RSM is going to check others, he must be the smartest of them all!'

Having later viewed the Queen's Birthday Parade, in which it was marvellous to see the 'Slope arms' so smartly carried out again. I asked GSM Perry Mason if the movements had been slowed down as the pauses were so well defined. He conceded that for this first parade with the SA 80, everyone wanted it to go just right and the drill movements were given a very adequate amount of pause. The result was extremely good, with very audible slapping of the rifle and precise movements with an obviously heavy and awkward drill weapon.

The following article by GSM A. G. Mason on Arms Drill for the SA 80, appeared in the *Guards Magazine* in 1988, and with the kind permission of the editor, is reproduced here because of the great interest it will foster in the memories of former soldiers who worked with earlier rifles.

The deployment of SA 80 to battalions in London District is now complete. The replacement of the 7.62mm SLR by a weapon of 5.56mm calibre follows the judgement that the SLR was overpowered and the bullet unnecessarily heavy. More 5.56mm ammunition can be carried and an optical sight (SUSAT) magnifies the target four times. The weapon is based on the 'bullpup' design with the magazine behind the trigger, and a sling allows the firer to carry it across his chest, thereby freeing both hands when required. The rifle is fed by a 30 round magazine and fires individual shots or automatic bursts. The Light Support Weapon (LSW) uses many of the same components and is half the weight of the GPMG. With the introduction of both weapons the infantry section is now organised into two fire teams, each under an NCO and with one LSW.

We in Horse Guards have been involved in the selection of the new arms drill. We have experienced some difficulty, mainly because of the weapon's weight, size and the number of protrusions on it.

We followed six basic principles in selecting our solution. We could not take a purely parochial view and thus the first principle was that the new drill had to be the same for the three services, excluding minor regimental variations. Second, the weapon had to be ready for use: for example the sight should not be removed except perhaps for ceremonial. Third, the drill had to be sustainable during long parades by all servicemen; hence positions adopted had to be comfortable and relieve the weight of the weapon at appropriate times. Fourth, the drill should cause as little damage to uniforms and medals as possible. Fifth, the drill should be smart and safe. Finally, no additional expenditure should be incurred.

Our first attempt tried to produce a solution that was as close to the current SLR drill as possible. On the march and at the position of attention the weapon was carried in the right shoulder. For the stand at ease the weapon was brought down into a horizontal position across the lower body and held by both hands. This produced a number of problems. The rifle was too heavy for the average man to carry for any significant time in the shoulder: Guardsmen had locked arms and numb fingers. The various protrusions caught on medals, uniforms (and, in the Scottish Division, sporrans) resulting in unnecessary expense and some of the damage to tunics after only a few guards was extensive. Finally, those units issued with the basic SA 80 with the iron, rather that SUSAT, sight (which includes most of the Army less the Infantry and most of the RN and RAF) would probably have to adopt a different drill because the weapon would not fit under the arm on the march. We also trialled the weapon across the body using its sling, but some basic movements, for example, the present arms, were not possible and it was dangerous, especially with bayonets fixed.

This was the unsatisfactory situation that faced us in the summer of 1987, made worse by the news that we could not procure a pistol grip which would have solved many of our problems. Further trials were conducted by the RMA Sandhurst, 2nd Battalion Coldstream Guards and the Guards Depot, to find a better solution. It was decided that the arms drill adopted for SA 80 should include the slope arms, especially when marching. In order to distribute the weight, the weapon should be sloped on the left or right shoulder (the left being the ceremonial position) thereby necessitating more frequent use of change arms. The

stand at ease and stand easy positions should be at the shoulder These positions suited both types of SA 80, the friction with the uniform was reduced, the body took much of the weight on the march, with one arm being given relief at all times, and of course there was historical precedent, with many of the movements the same as No 4 Rifle drill. Moreover, this new drill was easy to learn. Subsequently, the decision was made to adopt this form of arms drill for all three services.

The first parade using this new drill took place in December 1987 at The Sovereign's Parade at the RMA Sandhurst. Although the officer cadets had not had much time to practise, the result was pleasing to the eye. In particular, the carriage of the weapon at the slope encouraged the individual to stick his chest out and swing his arm. It is too much to expect the operational requirements for a new rifle to include any significant requirement for drill. Hence, we have had more than our fair share of problems in trying to adapt to SA 80. We are constantly reviewing our arms drill and some changes are possible before the final solution is adopted. We believe that we now have the best solutions in the circumstances and that it would be wrong for guardsmen to be issued with anything other than SA 80 for public duties and state ceremonial. As long as the possibility, however remote, exists that guardsmen may have to use their weapons, we must drill with the weapon currently on issue. Furthermore, we do not want to train with, store and clean two separate weapons.

London's pageantry is admired throughout the world and the magnificent Trooping of the Colour, to celebrate our monarch's birthday, forms a vital part of our national heritage. George Stone, Tom Taylor and Alex Dumon have played prominent roles in maintaining the unique ceremonial life of London and now 'Perry' Mason takes the post of 'HM Ceremonial Warrant Officer' towards the 21st century, with the certainty that he will, like those before him, face challenge and change.

CHAPTER 16

RSMs of Eaton Hall and Mons Officer Cadet Schools

Following the departure of the Royal Navy from Eaton Hall in 1947, the army leased the 350 acre estate near Chester and the establishment became a training school for national service officer cadets. In addition to academic and infantry training, the cadets experienced what was described as an extremely hard assault course and they also came under the discipline of Brigade of Guards RSMs.

The first RSM to enter through the famous golden gates of Eaton Hall was RSM C. Copp, Coldstream Guards, and after his four years in appointment to retirement, RSM A. E. Tomlinson, Coldstream Guards, took over. He served for four years until in 1955 RSM D. T. Lynch DCM, Irish Guards, came to the school, but he was to be there for only three years before the decision was taken to close Eaton Hall and amalgamate the training with the Mons Officer Cadet School in Aldershot. Some 15,000 army officer cadets had trained at the Eaton Hall establishment and all of them will carry memories of the beautiful old hall with its magnificent gates – and a stiff course of strict training.

Mons Barracks had accommodated the Royal Signals OCTU during the war, but then became a basic OCTU and in 1948 the Mons Officer Cadet School. For some of those years, Ronald Brittain MBE, Coldstream Guards, was the RSM of the establishment. He had by now gained the reputation for having the loudest word of command in the British army and for maintaining the most strict regime of discipline. Former officer cadet John Passingham wrote to me in 1989 to describe his memories of Mons OCTU in 1947 under RSM R. Brittain.

I volunteered for the Hampshire Regiment in 1945 and after service in Austria and Italy was posted to Mons Barracks OCTU at the end of 1947. The cadets were a mixed bunch coming from a wide variety of regiments with a preponderance of infantrymen. The majority had been posted to Mons soon after their corps training; others coming from many units where they had held easy jobs – this latter group found training at Mons a very hard experience.

We were taught tactics, military law etc, but my main memory is of the barrack square, bull and discipline. Discipline could be swift when RSM R. Brittain was involved as we found on one of our early parades. One man in my platoon was actually guilty of dumb insolence towards the RSM, deliberately marching in a slovenly and silly manner. He was of course, rushed to the guardroom, but when we returned to our barrack room it was as if he had never existed. He was gone and his kit was gone; all that remained was an empty bed. He had been placed under close arrest, appeared before the CO and returned to his parent unit in less than two hours!

RSM C. Copp, Coldstream Guards, instructs Officer Cadets at Eaton Hall OCS, 1951.   RMAS Collection

RSM Brittain could certainly make his presence felt as on one occasion he was walking, or rather marching, through the camp when he saluted a rather small second lieutenant in the ACC who did not return the salute. RSM Brittain stopped, waited until the officer was about 50 yards away and shouted in his best parade ground voice, 'I saluted you, Sir!' I have seldom seen a man so flattened as that officer was by one simple sentence.

Brittain had a very powerful personality as well as a powerful voice. One man in my platoon had an irritating cough which medicine had failed to cure, but RSM Brittain cured him. We were gathered around him in a group and the sound of coughing came from the centre of the group. Brittain was talking about the importance of smartness and said, 'When we were in the Maginot Line in 1940, we blancoed and we polished and we pressed and it was good for us, good for morale. Stop coughing, that cadet!' The man stopped coughing and did not cough again.

Also, he could do slightly odd things. On one occasion we were preparing for the passing out parade and RSM Brittain announced that the band for the parade would be the regimental band of the RASC. Brittain: 'We shall march past to the regimental march of the Royal Army Service Corps. What's their regimental march, cadet?' (Pointing to a cadet in the RASC.) Cadet: 'Wait for the Waggon, Sir.' Brittain: 'No, no, no. I don't want to know what it's called. I want to know the tune.' So the cadet, a rather shy man, had to stand on the parade ground in front of about 600 other men and sing his regimental march!

From Mons I was posted to the RASC OCTU at Buller

Lt-Gen Sir Colin B. Callander, KBE CB MC in conversation with RSM Ronald Brittain, Coldstream Guards, at Mons OCS, 2 Oct 1952. RMAS Collection

Barracks, Aldershot where I encountered some fine Warrant Officers and NCOs on the technical side and I sometimes think that too little attention has been paid to this group of people who were the backbone of many branches of the army.

The best RSM I ever encountered was the RSM of my first unit, the 27th Training Battalion, a splendid unit for volunteers and potential officers. In no other unit did I experience such a high standard of drill, discipline and enthusiasm. The RSM played a major part in bringing this about, and I can remember him very clearly as an older man, very slim, who seemed to be made of bone and sinew, with a typical Guardsman's walk.

The first time I saw him in action was the evening of my first day in the army. It so happened that the day we joined was the day of the battalion boxing championships and we were taken to watch it. Under amateur rules there was, of course, no cheering or noise allowed during the rounds, but during one particularly exciting bout a lot of cheering broke out in one part of the hall. Immediately a slim grey-haired man, the RSM, stood up and looked towards the noise. He did not shout or even glare but simply looked. It took about two seconds for the noise to stop. I thought then and I still think, that to enforce discipline without saying a word requires a great personality. I believe that his name was RSM Charlie Yardley.

When in 1954 Ronald Brittain reached retirement he received a great send off from Mons, but also an unusual and kind gesture from RSM Ronald J. S. Tyacke of the 1st Bn, Coldstream Guards, which was based at Windsor. RSM Brittain had invited many friends and colleagues to Mons for a farewell function and in return the Sergeants Mess of the 1st Bn invited him to spend his last day in the army with his old battalion. RSM Tyacke allowed Ronald Brittain to take all orders and parades for that day, which must have been a distinct shock for some Guardsmen one would imagine! Tibby Brittain thoroughly enjoyed his last day.

His place was taken by another long serving Coldstream Guards RSM – RSM C. L. Smy MBE DCM, who had worked with RSM Brittain for three months prior to taking appointment. He had incidentally, trained under Ronald Brittain at the Guards Depot in 1935 upon enlistment. Most of his service was with the 3rd Bn, Coldstream Guards, in the Middle East, as the battalion moved to Egypt in 1937 and did not return until 1944, during which time it fought in the North African, Sicilian and Italian campaigns. Charles Smy was awarded the Distinguished Conduct Medal as a CSM at Salerno, in company with Acting CSM Peter Wright, of subsequent VC fame.

In 1946 he became RSM of the 3rd Bn, taking the place of RSM Solly Joel, who later had strong connections with the Parachute Regiment. The two RSMs who had earlier influenced Charles Smy were Len Rawlinson, who was RSM of the 3rd Bn in 1943 and Solly Joel, from whom he took over.

After the war Charles could count only 21 surviving comrades of the battalion, from those who had originally set off for Egypt with him in 1937. He went as RSM of the battalion to Palestine where it remained until the British Forces left in 1948. He had in fact, served there before in 1936 and for a time in 1938. RSM Charles Smy remained at Mons OCS from 1953-8 during which time he made his own impressive reputation with the approximately 500 officer cadets trained. He retired from the army in 1958.

An indication of the respect with which he is received by those with whom he served in the 3rd Bn, came recently when Peter Horsfall was instrumental in arranging a reunion dinner for past members of the battalion. Over 380 former members attended and when RSM Charles Smy entered he received a standing ovation, the sure sign from former soldiers, of warm appreciation for one of the great wartime RSMs.

In 1957, upon the closure of Eaton Hall, RSM Desmond Lynch DCM, came to Mons and a further chapter in its history was about to be written.

When Capt Desmond Lynch MBE DCM, retired from the RMA Sandhurst at the end of term in 1985, he had given a lifetime of service to the British army, and his influence will remain for many years to come, as the thousands of officer cadets trained by him continue to achieve high rank and pass on their standards. A great exponent of drill and ceremonial, he had also been very much a fighting soldier and was awarded the DCM and promoted in the field to CSM during the Second World War, when only 22 years old.

I have known Desmond Lynch since 1979, when I first went to Sandhurst to talk with him about a fellow sergeant instructor, who served with him at the RMC Sandhurst in 1941 – John Lord. I have been tremendously impressed by Desmond's standards, which remain so high that only the very best efforts of those working with him will suffice. He is a great Irish Guardsman, an enthusiast in all he does, and a true soldier's soldier. I am very proud to write of his service.

Born in Dublin, Desmond Lynch's father Tom Lynch served in the 1914-18 War, and was for many years the president of the British Legion of the Republic of Ireland, based in Dublin. Desmond enlisted in the Irish Guards in 1937 and went through the Guards Depot at the time of RSM W. J. Dorman, Scots Guards. A 6ft 3in tall and straight young Guardsman, Desmond, by his positive and confident attitude, immediately made it clear that he intended to get on in his chosen career. He was fortunate to find himself going abroad within his first year when, with the 1st Bn, Irish Guards, he went to Egypt and Palestine.

In 1939 he returned to the Guards Depot at Caterham and in that extremely short period had revealed sufficient qualities to be made a Squad Instructor and Superintendent Sergeant. He assimilated some of the strengths of the then Depot RSM, J. Stack MC, Irish Guards, whom he greatly admired.

An indication of his obvious promise came when he was transferred to the RMCS in 1941 as a Sergeant Instructor, and although only 21 he helped to train and prepare many officer cadets for their prominent role in the war. The photograph of Sgt Lynch taken with a happy group of cadets, suggests already the stature and bearing of an experienced instructor.

Sgt John Lord, Grenadier Guards, was a fellow instructor at the college and one can only imagine the high quality of such training and his influence upon the young, keen cadets. RSM A. J. Brand MBE, was the RSM of the RMC Sandhurst at that time, and both Desmond Lynch and John Lord would always maintain a great respect for him. Sgts Lynch and Lord wished for more action however, and they were soon to find this as Desmond Lynch was posted back to the 1st Bn, Irish Guards and John Lord went off to become RSM of a Parachute Battalion.

The History of the Irish Guards in the Second World War by Maj D. J. L. Fitzgerald MC makes prominent mention of Desmond Lynch in the fighting of the 1st Bn in Tunisia in 1943, describing how a platoon of No 4 Coy attacked and destroyed an observation post on Hill 212, Sgt Lynch disposing of a number of the enemy and bringing back an artillery officer and two Sergeant Majors as prisoners.

Sgt Desmond Lynch with Officer Cadets at the Royal Military College Sandhurst, 1941.   Desmond Lynch

Later when No 4 Coy advanced through olive groves, the only surviving officer was wounded in company with CSM Kiely. Sgt Lynch placed the officer in cover, stood to attention and saluted, still under fire, and asked, 'Leave to carry on Sir?' He then went on to lead the company in its advance. As the surviving senior NCO of 4 Coy, he took part in the desperate close quarter fighting on Hills 212 and 214 when 173 men of the Irish Guards held their positions against five strong attacks by the enemy. At the end of the action only 80 Guardsmen emerged.

In June 1943 HM King George VI visited the battalion and after finding an extremely smart guard of honour, the battalion presented four surviving medallists to the King. Sgt Lynch DCM, L-Sgt Ashton DCM, L-Sgt Pearson MM and Guardsman Nicholson DCM. The citation for the award of the Distinguished Conduct Medal to 2718820 Sgt Desmond Lynch reads as follows:

In the attack on points 212 and 214 on 27 April to 1 May 1943, Sgt Lynch was Platoon Sergeant in the leading company, which came under very heavy fire at the start line and had considerable casualties inflicted upon it. The Company Commander and two Platoon Commanders were wounded or killed and the CSM killed. Sgt Lynch looked after his wounded Platoon Commander and then took charge of the company, or what was left of it. When the advance continued he organised his company and assaulted and gained his objective.

Throughout the period 28-30 April, when the force was being continually attacked, Sgt Lynch remained in command of the company except for a brief period. He was throughout an outstanding figure, and his smart soldierly appearance under the most difficult circumstances created an impression amongst the men, equalled only by his constant calm and bravery. The company held the west of the ridge forward towards point 214, and was continually under shell and mortar fire even when infantry attacks were not in progress. That the men never wavered under fire was largely due to his example.

At 11.00 hours on Wednesday 28 April enemy 88mm guns opened up on the west of the ridge with unexpected violence. Casualties were caused and some of the men badly shaken. Sgt Lynch, who was at Force HQ at the time, without hesitation, ran up through the heavy fire to his company, held the men steady in their positions, moved a bren gun forward at great personal risk, to meet the first infantry assault and gave the first fire order. The initial success gained by Sgt Lynch in beating back the first German assault raised the morale to the highest peak, proving conclusively by his own example that the fiercest fire could be endured and a determined attack broken by small arms fire.

Sgt Lynch consistently showed the greatest devotion to duty and even when half-blinded by blast he continued to command and encourage his rapidly dwindling company.

In 1988 Col Sir William Mahon Bt wrote to me the following interesting story.

I took a tour of veterans to North Africa in 1987 and in Tunisia we stood on the famous Hill 212 of 1943 (The Bou). After John P. Kenneally VC had quietly and modestly described his exploits, Maj Brian Synge suddenly exclaimed, 'You remember that fellow Sgt Lynch?' (Who could not, for he had a reputation for ferocity unequalled in the Micks.) 'Well, the regimental history states that I was wounded gallantly going down the hill to collect ammunition. It's not correct. What really happened was that Sgt Lynch had a tin of peaches. It was open and we were having it pretty rough, and it was very hot. When after 20 minutes he didn't return from one of his patrolling expeditions, I feared for the worst and thought he would not return, a not unreasonable thought in the circumstances, so I took half a tinned peach and popped it into my mouth. Nectar! At that moment the angry bull returned wiping his bayonet. So enraged was he that in order to pacify him I promised to go and find a loaf of bread from the dump at the bottom of the hill. It was on the way down to get the loaf that a sniper got me. All I can say is thank God Sgt Lynch was on our side!'

The 1st Bn, Irish Guards, went on to the Italian campaign where at Carroceto the Nos 1 and 4 Companies fought in further costly close quarter actions almost to extinction, before the survivors were captured by German Parachute troops. Desmond Lynch was wounded and was taken to a hospital in Rome where he was cared for by nuns until he was fit enough to be transferred to a POW camp in Florence three months later. He was to spend the last year of the war at Stalag 7A.

When liberation came and the Second World War ended, welcome home leave allowed some recuperation before Desmond found himself posted to the 2nd Bn, Irish Guards. After one year however, he was promoted as Drill Sergeant and was entrusted with an historic task when he was made the first Drill Sergeant of the All Arms Drill Wing at Caterham in February 1948. Indeed, he even suggested the title of the new wing. A vast number of NCOs and Warrant Officers would go through the drill course, which raised the standard of drill throughout the whole army. Courses were run regularly for RSMs of all regiments. Warrant Officers and NCOs were taken back to their days as recruits, but this time to be fully instructed in the basic mechanics of foot and arms drill. Not a few would find themselves on show clean parade. The majority would revel in the high standard of the course, and return to their units as well trained experts in the field of drill, to the mutual benefit of both the NCO and the unit.

Many people will remember the film *They were not divided*, in which in 1949, RSM Ronald Brittain made such a memorable impact. Desmond Lynch had already featured in a film made in 1940, entitled *Unpublished Story*, and now he also appeared in the second film which revealed so graphically the life of the Guardsman in war-time.

In 1951 after 22 courses had passed through the All Arms Drill Wing, the school was moved to Pirbright, where Desmond Lynch continued to take the courses in the rank of Drill Sergeant – only rarely did a Regimental Sergeant

Major seek to question his authority.

Prior to moving from Caterham, the Drill Wing had received a visit from the Commander-in-Chief of the Indian Army, Gen Carrippa, who before leaving had enquired of the Commandant of the Guards Depot if he might speak with the Drill Sergeant. There on the side of the square, when Desmond Lynch marched off from drilling a course, the Commander explained that he was seeking an RSM for the Indian Military Academy at Dehra Dun, and asked if he would accept the appointment. Desmond did so with alacrity and this led to a very happy three year secondment at the Indian Academy in the foothills of the Himalayas, where he passed on the Guards' methods of training to the officer cadets of the Indian army. RSM Lynch was the last

RSM D. T. Lynch, DCM RSM of Eaton Hall OCS, 1956.
Desmond Lynch

British Warrant Officer to instruct at the Dehra Dun Military Academy, although two WOs from the Household Division remained in an advisory capacity. He returned to Britain in 1954. His work as an RSM was from then on to be associated with the training of his own country's officer cadets.

Eaton Hall Officer Cadet School, close to Chester, had since 1947 trained many thousands of national service officers, and two RSMs from the Guards Division had gained high reputation in charge of drill and discipline there: RSM C. Copp MBE, Coldstream Guards, who served from 1947 until retirement when he was replaced by RSM A. E. Tomlinson, Coldstream Guards.

Through the golden gates of Eaton Hall in 1955 now strode RSM D. T. Lynch DCM Irish Guards, to fulfil a short but memorable appointment and leave his mark upon many a keen officer cadet. Maj E. J. A. Vaughan was the Adjutant at Eaton Hall prior to Desmond Lynch's arrival, and he wrote to me of those days:

The Coldstream Guards RSM who had been there for a few years reached retirement age, and I stressed to Household Brigade the

very high calibre man required for what was the national service Sandhurst. Desmond Lynch was provided and filled the post admirably. He had the benefits of stature, bearing, high standard and character.

At a farewell party for me at the Sergeants Mess, I added to my speech of thanks my surprise, that driving in from 15 miles away had never been late for 08.15 Wednesday Adjutant's Parade always being there when the clock struck. Uproarious laughter ensued, and Lynch explained that at some expense they had persuaded the estate clock winder to stop the clock as necessary!

In the spring of 1958 the establishment of Eaton Hall was amalgamated with the Mons Officer Cadet School in Aldershot. Mons Barracks had accommodated many regiments in its time, but in 1942 had come RSM Ronald Brittain, Coldstream Guards, who influenced a great many officer cadets at the then 161 (RMC) OCTU, followed by the Basic OCTU, and finally the Mons Officer Cadet School. After 12 legendary years he had retired from the army, and RSM C. L. Smy DCM, Coldstream Guards, had

Field Marshal Sir Bernard Montgomery inspects Officer Cadets at the Mons OCS in 1958, followed by Colonel Eugster and RSM D. T. Lynch. Desmond Lynch

taken his place. Now in 1958 RSM Smy had left, and two of the most prominent officer training establishments amalgamated to become one, retaining the name Mons OCS.

The appointment of RSM was filled by RSM Desmond Lynch DCM, and he went on to spend three impressive years there passing on his inimitable style and bearing to large numbers of officer cadets. Brig R. J. S. Corbett, Director Defence Programme at the Ministry of Defence, was one of the cadets of that period, and he wrote to me in 1988:

I know Desmond Lynch very well. I first met him (encountered might be a better word) when he was RSM of Mons OCS and I was a cadet there in late 1958, early '59. As an Irish Guardsman I had been a recruit in the Guards Depot Squad at Caterham beforehand – I and my Mick companions (including Brian Alexander, the second son of FM Alexander) particularly came under his eagle eye. It was, I can tell you, a terrifying experience to be inspected by him. He demanded even higher standards of us young men who were to be commissioned into his own regiment than he did of everyone else. He was a powerful and towering figure, immacutely smart and with a pronounced Irish accent which could be detected even in his words of command.

He gave the cadets occasional lectures amongst which was one on dress and general deportment when off duty. I can remember to this day the way he admonished us as young officers to never wear shoes with 'excessively t'ick soles'. I can also remember the explosion, almost nuclear in its proportions, when a cadet asked him at the same lecture whether it was in order for officers to carry umbrellas when in uniform. We were all in awe of him and quite rightly so; I think that all the Mick cadets were secretly proud of him too.

Col Sir William Mahon Bt was also a cadet at Mons in the year 1960, and he remembers the following incident:

RSM Lynch was a terror to us, but there were lighter moments too. The morning of our Passing Out Parade (on April Fool's Day appropriately I think) we were up with the lark. Fatigue parties rushed hither and thither and the leaves on the edge of the square were swept into tidy piles, awaiting the handcart to take them away. All had to be immaculate.

We cadets did not know that this was not the RSM Lynch plan, but a bright idea of one of his accolites. The Sergeant Major swanked his way patronisingly around the barracks early that bright chilly morning – and seeing us sweeping leaves (and knowing that no hand cart actually existed) gripped us in true Sergeant Major fashion. 'Scatter those leaves' says he 'Natural ike . . .' So we then scattered them, but they never really looked natural like'. Leaves don't once they've been swept, do they?

Maj (Retd) L. H. J. Tollemache, Coldstream Guards, also writes of that period:

While I was Adjutant at Mons OCS Desmond Lynch was the RSM. We worked very closely together over the years we were here. He was a splendid example to the cadets and to the other members of the Sergeants Mess both on and off parade. When asked to get something done it was done as soon as possible, usually much sooner than I thought possible, and to the highest standard. He had a delightful sense of humour, probably not often apparent to cadets, and was a great pleasure to work with.

RSM Desmond T. Lynch, DCM, when RSM of Mons OCS, 1959.   Desmond Lynch

Mons carried a Sergeants Mess of some 150 members, perhaps one of the largest of its kind, and the initial tasks were for RSM Lynch to integrate not only the training programmes of the two establishments but the two Sergeants Mess'. An extremely active and busy mess developed with frequent functions involving many regiments – not the least of which was to be the annual St Patrick's Day Ball.

In addition to the heavy training programme at Mons, he was to be the Parade RSM for the Queen's Birthday Parade, held in 1959 and 1960, under the command of the GOC Aldershot District. Desmond also took part in a tableaux presented by the Mons OCS at the Aldershot Tattoo in 1960. A very busy year ended with RSM Lynch, his wife and two young sons, travelling proudly to Buckingham Palace where he was presented with the MBE by The Queen.

As Christmas approached in 1961 and Mons prepared itself for change with the ending of national service, the Passing Out Parade as usual ended with the commissioning detachment slow marching off the parade ground to the accompaniment of *Auld Lang Syne*, and behind them marched RSM Desmond Lynch who was passing out with them. He was leaving to take a commission as Captain with the 28th Commonwealth Brigade. He received a moving send off from the Sergeants Mess, and was presented with an inscribed gold watch and Albert and a silver coffee set by which to remember a great period of his service.

Commissioning Parade, 24 Jan 1963, held in cold conditions at Mons OCS. RSM S. A. J. Blake, Coldstream Guards (centre).
RMAS Collection

Within a short time, Capt Lynch was serving with the 28th Commonwealth Brigade in Malaya and then after two years of active service, became Adjutant of the Singapore Guard Regiment, with which he remained until 1969. 1970 found him appointed as a Staff Captain with the Ministry of Defence, and he held this post until retirement from the army in 1973, but this was far from the end of his busy career.

As a retired officer Desmond Lynch worked first at the Joint Service Mountain Training Centre in Wales, before returning to what in 1947 had become the RMA Sandhurst, as Assistant Adjutant. The Adjutant was one of his former cadets at Mons, now Brig R. J. S. Corbett:

Desmond's main responsibility lay in ensuring the security of Sandhurst, a most important task by that time. We shared an office. Luckily for my eardrums it was a very long one with him at one end and myself at the other, since he had lost none of the remarkable vigour and volume in giving out the detail that I remember of him as a RSM. I sometimes wondered whether he actually needed a telephone at all to get his message across!

He was exceptionally thorough, greatly respected by the Regimental Police who were his main task force, and not averse to 'gripping' anyone, regardless of rank or station, in the cause of security. Not surprisingly, there were ruffled feathers about the place from time to time, but I certainly never had to worry about gaps in the security of Sandhurst in the 24 months we worked together. Perhaps the years had mellowed him but I also discovered what a kind and thoughtful man there was behind his upright and rather bristling exterior. He was also marvellously supported by his wife, Betty. I will never forget Desmond striding about the grounds of Sandhurst, in his tweed civilian suit and hat or cap, but unmistakeably for what he was – a former RSM of the Foot Guards – a formidable man in any circumstances and one who has certainly made a lasting impression on me.

Lt-Col (Retd) J. R. Innes served at the RMA Sandhurst as Adjutant from 1982-84, and he writes of his memories of working with Desmond:

Desmond has a firm belief that orders are meant to be obeyed; people who disobey regulations deserve to be punished. He does not subscribe to the fashionable view that rules are merely guidelines to be ignored if they are inconvenient. While I agree with Desmond's philosophy, the rigid way he applied it at Sandhurst sometimes caused me the odd hiccup.

Of course there was no problem with the students. It was just too bad if they felt they had received a raw deal from Desmond; anyway they did not dare complain. Some of the staff and more particularly their wives, had grander ideas. As the Security Officer, Desmond was in charge of the Regimental Police, and one of their many duties was to control traffic within the Academy grounds. The speed limit was 25 miles per hour but some cadets and rather more members of the staff had cars which preferred to travel faster. There were therefore plenty of customers for Desmond's radar gun.

One morning I was telephoned by a Colonel who was beside himself with fury. His wife had been caught in a speed trap, accused of doing 30mph and ordered by Desmond to remove her car from the Academy grounds for 14 days. 'Totally unreasonable and quite impossible' said the Colonel. 'How can my wife take the children to school? Anyway by whose authority does Capt Lynch have the power to punish my wife?' I sympathised with the distraught Colonel, explained that Desmond was only trying to uphold the Commandant's directive: that drivers caught speeding must be taught a lesson. I also explained, as tactfully as I could, that his wife was not the only person to suffer Desmond Lynch's wrath. As a matter of fact, the Commandant's wife too had been caught speeding and she was planning to celebrate the return of her car in three days' time.

At least Desmond was fair. He treated the highest in the land just the same as the humblest officer cadet. There are many stories about Desmond; I have no doubt they improve with the telling, but the one I have given is actually true. I hope it gives an example of Desmond's firm belief in the rule of law and his high moral courage. It mattered not one jot to him if he upset senior officers. His priority was to see that orders were scrupulously obeyed.

Desmond Lynch held the post of Staff Officer Security from 1978-85 and whilst he made his influence felt by his diligent attention to detail, the security of Sandhurst was in very good hands. His staff of Regimental Police were seconded from all Cavalry Regiments of the British Army, and it was a credit to them that such a high degree of security was maintained within a very large area.

In early 1985 Desmond Lynch received one of his greatest honours when as the founder of the All Arms Drill Wing at the Guards Depot at Caterham, he was asked to personally open the D. T. Lynch Room at the Sergeants Mess. A large photograph of him is displayed in the room with full details of his service. The 40th anniversary of the opening of the wing was celebrated on 17 September 1988, when many former RSMs, Drill Sergeants, and Instructors attended as honoured guests.

Thankfully there are many worthy people with a sense of history anxious to remember the achievements of the past, and regimental reunions have always represented a way of keeping in touch with valuable former members. There have been four reunion dinners of the Eaton Hall OCS held bi-annually, to which former officers, instructors, and Royal Naval and Army officer cadets have been invited. Why Royal Naval officer cadets? Well – the Royal Navy occupied Eaton Hall from 1943-47 before the army moved in, and so they also marched through those magnificent golden gates.

At the last reunion dinner in March 1988, the Patron, His Grace the Duke of Westminster, DL, attended, and a former Adjutant of the School, Maj-Gen Sir Philip Ward, KCVO CBE DL, presided. There were several very high ranking officers present at the top table – and a very proud former RSM of the school – Capt Desmond Lynch. Long

may reunions of such great establishments be held.

As a holder of the Distinguished Conduct Medal, Desmond is a member of the DCM League which musters as many of its members as possible each year. In 1987 the League mustered at Winchester where the Lord Mayor was a DCM holder. Desmond Lynch laid the league wreath at the memorial in Winchester Cathedral. The year before had witnessed a particularly auspicious occasion at Windsor Castle, when HM The Queen had taken the salute of DCM holders attending from all over the world. The present President of the DCM League is Maj (Retd) J. C. Cowley, DCM, who was a prominent RSM in the Coldstream Guards. I met Desmond Lynch in July 1985 on another great occasion, when we attended the opening of the J. C. Lord Room at the Sergeants Mess at the RMAS.

As 1985 drew to a close, official farewells were made to Desmond at the RMA Sandhurst, as his service as Staff Captain Security ended. He retired on 1 January 1986 after 48 years of distinguished work with the British Army; work and service linked with some of the greatest and most influential military establishments in the world.

The name of Desmond Lynch, DCM, Irish Guards, will always be synonymous with the All Arms Drill Wing. He also featured most prominently in the history of Eaton Hall and Mons Officer Cadet Schools. The Indian Army Academy will always remember him and he has a special place in the history of the RMA Sandhurst. These 'men of spirit' never really retire, of course. Desmond remains very busily involved with the work of his county's victim support scheme, in which he provides help and advice to the victims of crime, and he also works with Age Concern.

1961 saw the arrival of RSM S. A. J. Blake, Coldstream Guards, at the Mons OCS, followed in 1964 by RSM T. B. John of the same regiment. RSM F. D. E. Harrod, Irish Guards, came in 1967. Fred Harrod enlisted in 1944, and most of his service was with the 1st Bn Irish Guards, in Palestine, Tripoli, Egypt and Cyprus. He particularly remembers a tour as CSM of New College at the RMAS from 1963 to 1964 under RSM L. C. Lord, when his College RSM was Tom Taylor.

The last RSM to serve at Mons from 1969-72 was RSM F. P. Horsfall MBE of the Coldstream Guards. Peter Horsfall enlisted in the regiment in 1946 as a Drummer Boy, and after being kitted out went straight to the Training Battalion at Pirbright, where his first RSM was 'Nippy' Kirke.

Posted to the 2nd Bn, he came under RSM Arthur Ramsden MBE MC who he describes as 'a fabulous Sergeant Major'. In 1961 he was selected for the RMAS and went as a Sergeant under RSM J. C. Lord MBE, indeed, was employed as his Superintending Sergeant for two years. He assimilated many of RSM Lord's methods of instruction and took them with him to Mons, where he served for a time as Drill Sergeant to both RSMs T. B.

John, and F. D. E. Harrod, before completing three memorable years as RSM.

A strict and experienced disciplinarian, it was no problem in relation to the regime of the school which was remembered by Peter Horsfall when I talked with him about his period as RSM of Mons – but one probably faced rarely by a Coldstream Guards RSM. Among his office staff was a young member of the WRAC and there came a day when he had to admonish her for some minor matter, but before he could begin she broke into tears. Trained and prepared for every eventuality he could not cope with that and saying 'No – please don't do that' he quickly collected his pace stick and left the office to walk around the barracks. Returning shortly afterwards he found the girl recovered and RSM Horsfall simply reminded her to take more care in future and dismissed her.

Progressing to Quartermaster before retirement from the army, Maj Peter Horsfall MBE now holds the distinguished post of Staff Superintendent of the House of Lords.

Eaton Hall

RSM C. Copp	Coldstream Guards	1947-51
RSM A. E. Tomlinson	Coldstream Guards	1951-55
RSM D. T. Lynch	Irish Guards	1955-57

Mons Officer Cadet Schools

RSM Ronald Brittain	Coldstream Guards	1948-54
RSM C. L. Smy	Coldstream Guards	1953-58
RSM Desmond Lynch	Irish Guards	1957-61
RSM S. A. J. Blake	Coldstream Guards	1961-64
RSM T. B. John	Coldstream Guards	1964-67
RSM F. D. E. Harrod	Irish Guards	1967-69
RSM F. P. Horsfall	Coldstream Guards	1969-72

Commissioning Parade, 4 Aug 1972, Mons OCS. Gen Sir Michael Carver, GCB CBE DSO MC, is the inspecting Officer, and RSM F. P. Horsfall, MBE is in attendance. RMAS Collection

CHAPTER 17

Regimental Sergeant Majors of The Guards Depot to 1957

The Guards Depot was first established in 1832 at Warley Barracks, Brentwood, which had earlier been the Recruit Depot for the East India Company. Within a year the recruits of the Coldstream Guards, and the Scots Fusilier Guards moved to Croydon, where in 1835 the recruits of the Grenadier Guards joined them. The Depot remained there for the following 30 years until in 1854 the Grenadier Guards moved to St John's Wood Barracks, where they remained until the Crimean War. But by 1865, all recruits of the Guards Brigade were again housed at Warley Barracks.

In 1870, a permanent Commandant was appointed with a small staff, but so far as the Depot Sergeant Major was concerned, an acting rank held by the Senior Drill Sergeant of the Brigade, operated until 1881. The Guards Depot moved into new barracks built on farm land at Caterham in October 1877, and it was four years later in July 1881 that the first substantive Sergeant Major was appointed, H. Darrell of the Coldstream Guards, and the roll commenced of some of the greatest RSMs of the British Army.

This prestigious appointment has at the time of writing (1989) been held by 58 RSMs, 19 having been Coldstream Guardsmen, 14 Grenadier Guardsmen, 12 Scots Guardsmen, eight Irish Guardsmen, and five Welsh Guardsmen. An early roll of names was destroyed by fire, but a new roll was researched and produced in June 1982 by Maj (QM) W. J. Holbrook, and this now stands in the entrance of the Sergeants Mess at the Guards Depot. This distinguished roll forms the basis of the following story of the RSMs of the Guards Depot. In some instances it has been possible to gain additional information of an RSM's service record. Such known details are included in either photograph captions, or in the following text.

One of the great Grenadier Guardsmen, George Frederick Godwin Turner, was awarded the DCM as a Corporal in the 2nd Bn in 1918. He had enlisted on 17 November 1915, serving in France as a L-Cpl, Cpl, and Lance Sgt. Within five years he progressed to CSM, and in 1929 served under RSM W. E. Hawkins as Drill Sgt. In 1934 he became RSM of the Depot, but nine months later was appointed RSM of the 3rd Bn upon the retirement of RSM Hawkins. George Kirby was a Sergeant in the regiment, and has fond memories of RSM Turner:

My first brush with RSM G. F. Turner was during a drill parade in my first week at the Depot Caterham in 1934. I felt a sharp prod in

RSM A. Telfer, Scots Guards Depot RSM for two months in 1891. Sgt-Maj Telfer enlisted in the Scots Fusilier Guards 3 March 1877, when the Depot was first established at Caterham Barracks. He was made 2nd Drill Sgt 1 March 1887, and 1st Drill Sgt 24 April 1888. Promoted RSM 18 March 1891, he was transferred to the 1st Bn in May of that year.   Guards Magazine

the back and he ordered me to 'Strike your rifle harder lad, as though you mean it!' He had a much different tone however, from some of the abusive remarks I received from the Trained Soldiers or Squad Instructors and I gradually developed a respect for him.

During my later service at Chelsea Barracks, I was walking past the RSMs office when I heard the call, 'Guardsman Kirby!' I halted, turned about and faced the RSM, expecting the worst. 'Would you like to become my batman?' he asked, to my surprise. 'With pleasure Sir,' I replied, and I was to take great pride in keeping all of his equipment in shining condition for a time.

When the 3rd Bn was at Kasr-el-nil barracks in Cairo on

Left: *RSM J. Sparkes, Coldstream Guards Depot RSM 1891-3. Sgt-Maj Sparkes enlisted in the Coldstream Guards 11 Aug 1876 at Warley Barracks. Promoted Drill Sgt 22 Dec 1886, he was made RSM of the Depot 13 May 1891. He became Garrison Sergeant Major of London in April 1895. He had earlier served in Egypt and was present at the battle of Tel-el-Kebir.* Guards Magazine

Right: *Quartermasters 1905. Included in this marvellous group are former RSMs mentioned elsewhere in this book, and two former Depot RSMs. (Standing): (1st left) F. W. Walker, Scots Guards. (4th from left) G. Gooding, Coldstream Guards, Depot RSM 1897. (5th from left) J. W. Sibary, Scots Guards (see DCM Roll). (6th from left) W. J. Cook, Grenadier Guards, Depot RSM 1897 (see DCM Roll). Sitting: (1st left) J. Fowles, Irish Guards. (4th from left) W. Garton, Grenadier Guards.* Guards Magazine

Below right: *1st Bn Irish Guards, Wellington Barracks, 1908. (L to R) Drill Sgt J. Foley, Lt & Adj P. I. Reid, RSM C. Baylis. Sgt-Maj Baylis enlisted in the Grenadier Guards at Windsor in 1886. He was promoted RSM of the Irish Guards and posted to the Guards Depot in 1903. Discharged after 22 years' service in May 1908, he became Acting Sergeant Major at the Dulwich College RVC. In 1912 he was appointed Assistant Secretary, Guards Unemployment Society and of the Household Brigade Magazine. During WW1 he trained the 1st Bn Surrey (Croydon) National Reserve. At the end of the war a great load fell upon Charles Atkin Baylis, owing to the number of men for whom work had to be found, and he is said to have worked all hours. This may have contributed to his early death at the age of 63 years. On the right stands Dril Sgt K. Kirk, who was RSM of the Depot in 1913.* Guards Magazine

Below: *The Colours of the 3rd Bn Coldstream Guards, Cairo 1907. Drill Sgt Beacham, RSM J. Boyd (Depot RSM 1901-2), Drill Sgt Gray. Drum Major Maskell (sitting centre).* Guards Magazine

RSM Harry Wood, Grenadier Guards Depot RSM 1913-15. Sgt-Maj Harry Wood enlisted in the Grenadier Guards in March 1895, going through the Depot during the period of RSM W. Stewart. He served throughout the South African War as Gold Sgt in the 1st Bn, and by 1911 was a Drill Sgt. In this appointment he was the Warrant Officer of the Bearer party at the funeral of King Edward VII. At the outbreak of WW1 he was the RSM of the Depot, but in 1915 was posted to the 2nd Bn in France. He remained in action for the following two years until commissioned 2/Lt in the Guards Machine Gun Regt. He was awarded the DCM 13 Feb 1917. Just before the end of the war he was made Quartermaster and remained in this appointment until 1931, when he retired from the army after 36 years' service. Harry Wood was a greatly respected RSM and when dealing with NCOs and men was a firm believer in allowing warnings, always ending by saying: 'You understand?' He never threatened or lost his temper, and was much admired for this. Guards Magazine

RSMs of the Guards Division in May 1919, taken at Chelsea Barracks. (L to R) RSMs E. T. Cutler, MC, Scots Guards, J. Cahill, DCM, Irish Guards (see DCM Roll).

J. Capper, MC, Grenadier Guards; J. Barwick, MC, Scots Guards Depot RSM. G. Ellis, Coldstream Guards; F. Speller, MC, Grenadier Guards; A. M. Hill, MC DCM, Grenadier Guards (see DCM Roll); E. J. Wadham, Scots Guards; W. Cook, MC, Coldstream Guards; J. Littler, MC, DCM, Grenadier Guards; A. Gray, MC, Coldstream Guards; and W. Stevenson, DCM MM, Welsh Guards (see DCM Roll).
Guards Magazine

RSM J. Barwick, MC, at the Guards Depot in 1918 with the Commandant, Adjutant, and Drill Sgts. As CSM in the 1st Bn Scots Guards, Joseph Barwick was awarded the Military Cross in 1915 for numerous courageous acts when under heavy fire, during which he was wounded many times. He was Depot RSM 1916-19 and at the time of this photograph the strength of the Depot was said to have been 14,500.

Curator, The Guards Museum

HM King George V in conversation with RSM J. Barwick, MC, when inspecting the 1st Bn Scots Guards, in 1921.

Guards Magazine

Right: *Officers of the Guards, including Capt J. Wood, DCM, Grenadier Guards Quartermaster; also RSM W. E. Hawkins, Depot RSM 1922-5. Sgt-Maj Walter Edward (Chef) Hawkins enlisted in the Grenadier Guards in 1909, going through the training of the Depot under RSM J. Teece. He progressed to Sergeant by the time of the WW1 serving in France and being mentioned in despatches. Promoted CSM in 1916 and Drill Sgt in 1918, he served in the 5th and 3rd Bns before being appointed RSM of the Depot. 'Chef' Hawkins then returned to the 3rd Bn as RSM, and later served in Egypt for three years, two of his young NCOs at that time being John Lord and Arthur Spratley. RSM W. E. Hawkins, MBE MSM, retired from the army in 1934, and remained a greatly respected old soldier for many years. He died on 9 Aug 1975 aged 85 yrs.* Curator, The Guards Museum

Left: *RSM R. Brittain, Grenadier Guards, Depot RSM 1934-5. (Taken with visitor RSM Tantum, Rhodesian Police.) Sgt-Maj Ronald Brittain became perhaps the most widely known and recognised RSM, following his appearance in the film 'They were not divided', and in many news films and periodicals of the time. His stature and mighty voice were easily recognisable, and his brand of discipline well remembered. His story is included in the chapter dealing with 'RSMs of the Eaton Hall and Mons Officer Cadet Schools'.* Curator, The Guards Museum

Below right: *Guards Brigade representatives on HQ Staff at the Guards Depot, Aug 1934. (centre) RSM G. F. G. Turner, DCM Grenadier Guards, RSM of the Depot, 1934.*
Curator, The Guards Museum

Christmas Day 1935, RSM Turner visited our mess room and the lads were merry with food and drink. Two of the stalwarts – I believe they were John Lord and Joe Flanagan – picked him up and chaired him across the square with the intention of ducking him in the Nile! All of the assembled men clapped and cheered, singing *For he's a jolly good fellow*. He took it in good spirit and did not get the ducking.

Later in 1936, when I was on sentry duty at the main gate of the barracks on a very hot day, I saw the CO Lt-Col C. R. Britten approaching in company with the RSM. My mind went back to Caterham as I said to myself, 'I've got to get this just right!' and I presented arms striking my rifle hard. Later the RSM walked back into the guardroom and I feared that I was in the book, but all was well as I found that I had been awarded a credit for smartness on sentry.

Fred Turner had been commissioned Lieutenant QM in 1939 and during the retreat to Dunkirk never failed to supply his battalion until he was – with his transport – cut off by enemy action. He then organised the evacuation of many men from the beaches. In 1943 he was made Camp Commandant of 2nd Army HQ and was mentioned in despatches in 1943 and in 1945. He ended the war as a Major, but in 1946 was promoted Lieutenant Colonel, and remained so until retirement from the army in 1948. His

many medals included the OBE, DCM, MSM and the French Croix de Guerre. After the war Lt-Col Fred Turner became Secretary of the Grenadier Guards Association and of the Household Brigade Employment Society, for 1 years and is remembered by a vast number of former Grenadiers for his kindness and help.

He was appointed a Military Knight of Windsor and was to grace many colourful parades with his splendid bearing and smart appearance. Fred Turner died on 12 October 1968 at the age of 70.

Maj (Retd) William Rooney, MBE MM, Irish Guards, was the RSM of the Guards Depot from 13 August 1946 to 1 December 1949. It was a pleasure indeed to talk to him about his period as RSM at the Guards Depot and other events in his long career.

I was born and brought up on a small farm in Co Monaghan but because of the world wide depression in the 1930s came over to London and enlisted into the Irish Guards in March 1936. Such difficult times, together with a recruiting campaign, brought many fine young men from both North and South over to join the regiment. Many of these had trained for the priesthood, teaching and other professions and all were attracted by the prospect of tour of duty in Egypt with the 1st Battalion. The recruiting campaign was designed to bring the battalion up to strength before embarking.

I went to the Guards Depot with other recruits, where I was to hear for the first time the penetrating voice and see the magnificent figure of the great RSM Arthur Brand, Grenadier Guards. It was a frightening experience for any new recruit, but one soon got used to the continuous barking of commands, not only from the RSM but from 20 or more squad instructors.

Guards Depot 1935. Lt/Adj L. R. C. Stucley, Grenadier Guards. Lt QM T.D. McCarthy, MBE, Irish Guards. Commandant Major W. L. Faulkner, MC, Irish Guards, and RSM A. J. Brand, MBE, Grenadier Guards. (Black armbands were worn for the death of King George V.) Sgt-Maj Arthur Brand completed a period of eleven years at Sandhurst and saw it develop from an OCTU unit to the Royal Military Academy. His story is detailed in the chapter dealing with the 'RSMs and AcSMs of the RM College and Academy Sandhurst'.
Curator, The Guards Museum

In August 1936 with training completed, I joined the 1st Bn at Pirbright where it was carrying out annual training and where NCOs and Guardsmen fired their course, as it was then known, in order to qualify for additional pay. From there we returned in September to our permanent station at Chelsea Barracks and shortly afterwards proceeded on embarkation leave prior to preparing to leave for Egypt.

We sailed from Southampton in November, on the Troopship *Neuralia* and for the next ten days, after surviving the notorious Bay of Biscay, thoroughly enjoyed the Mediterranean sunshine. There was much recreation on board to relieve the boredom, such as boxing, tug of war, PT and so on. We arrived at Kasr-el-Nil Barracks, Cairo, where we were to stay for the next two years, apart from a three month period in Palestine in July 1938, during the Arab troubles. I was appointed L-Cpl in 1937, the first small step on what was to prove a very long ladder indeed. While in Palestine I was fortunate enough to be awarded the Military Medal resulting from an action in which my section was involved.

A search however, through Regimental Intelligence reveals rather more:

For conspicuous gallantry in action at Asira Ash Shamaliya, on 22 September 1938, L-Cpl W. Rooney was awarded the Military Medal. His section was advancing throught the olive groves when they were fired upon at 30 yards range by a small gang of well-armed enemy. This NCO promptly got the Lewis gun into action, but owing to the thick trees, had to change his section's position several times under heavy and close range fire. He eventually succeeded in obtaining a field of fire and both bandits were killed. If L-Cpl Rooney had been less energetic, these men – one of whom was well known – would have escaped and it was due to his dashing leadership and disregard for danger that the very important papers found in the bandits' possession were captured.

Major Rooney continues:

We left Palestine in October 1938, sailing from Haifa to Alexandria, where we were held aboard ship to await the outcome of Prime Minister Chamberlain's visit to Hitler in Munich. We had visions of the battalion having to go to Mersa Matruh to prevent the Italians from advancing on Alexandria from Libya, but following a day of much speculation the news came of peace in our time and we began to disembark.

The battalion later left for home, arriving at Southampton on 16 December 1938 to a welcome by our Regimental Band, and a group of officers led by Maj-Gen Alexander, came aboard to greet us. The next morning we travelled by special train to Waterloo, where a great reception awaited us and we formed up to march past the Colonel of the Regiment and on to the Tower. Soon

The Depot Guard being mounted at the Main Gate at Caterham, 1936. RSM A. J. Brand, MBE, takes the parade. He was the Depot RSM 1935-6. Guards Magazine

afterwards we were sent on disembarkation leave to spend Christmas at home.

We returned in January 1939 to find the international situation getting more serious, the German army occupied Czechoslovakia in March and Britain began calling up reservists for training. Our 2nd Battalion reformed, along with other Guards battalions which had been in suspended animation since the end of the First World War.

We left the Tower in February to move to Pirbright for training and then back to Wellington Barracks for a tour of public duties just before Easter. I had previously been on public duties for only a brief time in September 1936 when I did guard duty at St James's Palace, but now as a L-Cpl I did the whole round of London duties.

With the calling up of reservists for our 2nd Battalion, promotion began to build up and in July I was promoted to Lance Sergeant. Then came a very important parade for me, when a Guards detachment of 400 men – 80 from each regiment – was sent to Paris to take part in the Bastille celebrations. We marched down the Champs Elysees and of course the Parisians had never seen anything like it. The Band of the Grenadier Guards and the CO, mounted, led the Parade. The pavements were so packed with admiring, cheering crowds, the route had to be twice closed – such was the enthusiasm and fervour sparked off by the Guardsmen in their red tunics and bearskins, not to mention their traditional marching precision and bearing.

Back in London, I was only three weeks a Lance Sergeant before being promoted to Sergeant, and I had been very fortunate to reach that rank in just over four years. I was posted to the battalion's new Carrier Platoon which was thought at that time to be the Infantry Tank. In September the Germans invaded Poland, and the Second World War began.

We left Wellington Barracks, London, in April 1940 on the ill fated expedition to Norway. We were to go up the Narvik fiord in a lightly armoured repair ship converted from an old cruiser, but it was learned just in time that the Germans had mounted guns overlooking the fiord, so the plan was wisely abandoned and we returned to base. We were then moved further south aboard a Polish liner, but the ship was bombed and set on fire. All our senior officers who were accommodated on the upper deck were killed, the CO, Second in Command and all four Company Commanders. The battalion was commanded by a Lieutenant for a time. Our RSM was Sgt-Maj J. A. Stack, who was later awarded the Military Cross for conspicuous gallantry in Norway.

We returned to Scotland and from there to Northwood, where we remained training until October 1940, when the battalion moved to Sanderstead. RSM Stack MC had meanwhile gone to the Guards Depot in July, to change places with RSM Hugh McKinney, Irish Guards, who now came to the 1st Battalion. In November I went to the Training Battalion on promotion to CQMS and again was fortunate in being in that rank for only three weeks before being promoted to Company Sergeant Major.

I went back to No 1 Company of the 1st Battalion and remained for exactly a year, until October 1942. Just before Montgomery's offensive at El Alamein, I was told that I would be going to Achnacarry, the Army Commando Training Centre, as one of two Guards Drill Sergeants to train a large intake of Police Reservists. Nat Turton, Grenadier Guards, was the other. These mature men whose call up had been delayed, were in deferred categories and the War Office decided that they should be trained initially by Warrant Officers with the rank of Drill Sergeant, so that happy duty fell to us. We were at Euston Station starting our journey when news broke of the El Alamein Offensive.

We were at Achnacarry for three months training these marvellous young former policemen in drill, whilst Commando instructors took them through the numerous assault courses built over the mountains and rivers in the area. It was a tremendous course and the men were fit for battle after completing it. I can still remember them as fine, well motivated volunteers from Police Forces all over the country.

The 1st Bn Irish Guards had meanwhile moved up to Ayr with 24th Guards Independent Brigade to prepare for overseas. The CO was now Lt-Col C. A. Montagu-Douglas-Scott, the new RSM was Sgt-Maj McLoughlin and I was the senior Drill Sergeant. RSM McKinney had become the Quartermaster. McLoughlin, however, injured his ankle in our last exercise in Ayr and RQMS Peilow was appointed Acting RSM.

The battalion sailed for Algiers on 1 February 1943 to join the 1st Army, and soon found itself in the fighting at Medjez El Bab and right through the North African campaign until May when the 1st and 8th Armies met and Tunis was liberated. The battalion was heavily involved in action on the The Bou and I was close to A-RSM Peilow when he was killed. During the advance I had been standing with him under a tree and as we were the senior Warrant Officers I mentioned to him that we should not be together under fire. He agreed and told me to move to a German dug out vacated only hours before. When the time came to continue advancing A-RSM Peilow was not around and I learned later that he and several other men had been killed when a shell hit the tree. I was the only WO to reach Hill 212, but was not long there as I suffered a badly sprained ankle when I stumbled over a boulder in the darkness and had to be evacuated. It was in the

RSM W. I. Rooney, MM, Irish Guards, Depot RSM 1946-9.
Bill Rooney

ensuing battle of The Bou (Hill 212) that L-Sgt Kenneally won his Victoria Cross.

After the battle we remained at Hammamet throughout the summer and autumn of 1943 and then just before Christmas moved to Italy, where initially we were in reserve at Canosa on the east coast, then to Gragnano, close to Naples just beneath Mt Vesuvius. The 8th Army was bogged down on the River Garigliano, but on 21 January 1944 we marched down to the local docks where we boarded landing craft, sailing overnight, past the Isle of Capri, and at first light the following morning, landed at Anzio. As we came ashore unopposed I remember seeing Gen Alexander and Admiral Trowbridge talking together on the beach. Within a short time however, the Germans were in position and heavy fighting ensued.

RSM McLoughlin had now rejoined us but within three days was badly wounded and had to return to the UK, so with less than eight years' service in the regiment I was promoted RSM of the 1st Battalion. It was during some of the bitter battles that followed that our Battalion HQ was surrounded and as we tried to break out through a deep gully I, together with another stalwart Guardsman, was captured. A German Officer left us in the gully guarded by two soldiers but eventually, by sharing our haversack rations with them, they were persuaded to come back to our lines, by which time the situation had somewhat stabilised.

However, within three weeks I too was wounded by an 88mm shell which landed in the truck in which I was escorting ten German prisoners back behind our lines, killing them all and injuring me in the hand and lung and perforating my left ear irrepairably. This meant that I was evacuated to the UK, back via Naples, Sicily and Algiers. Nevertheless, I was able to rejoin the battalion when it was ordered back from Italy in April, having suffered such heavy casualties that it was unable to continue in action and reinforcements could not be sent from the 2nd or 3rd Battalions, which were preparing for the invasion of Europe.

The 1st Battalion came to Hawick via Chelsea Barracks, where by that time many men from the RAF Regiment were transferring to Infantry as their role at airfields diminished. Scores of these excellent men received additional training, some later going to reinforce our 3rd Battalion.

After about three months at Hawick, I exchanged duties with RSM Tom Kelly of the Training Battalion and remained near Edinburgh until November 1944 when we returned to Lingfield, having moved out to make room for those taking part in D Day operations. I stayed with the Training Battalion until the end of the war and into 1946 when, with many other war establishments, the Training Battalion was disbanded at Aldershot in June of that year. In common with many RSMs, some 20 or so from all five regiments, whose battalions had been also disbanded, I found myself redundant.

I then went to Paris to marry Jacqueline who I'd met before the war and was married on 13 July, before reporting back to Windsor where sadly there was no appointment for me. I was asked if I wished to go to the Indian Military Academy, but having just got married and with no guarantee that my wife would be able to accompany me, I declined the appointment. As it happened an old friend, John McGarrity, went there and made a great name for himself.

I went home to Ireland hoping that something would turn up and after only a few days I received a telegram ordering me to report back to Windsor immediately. I returned on a Sunday night not knowing what was awaiting me, and when the Chief Clerk, Dickie Bird, advised me that I was to go as RSM to the Guards Depot at Caterham, I just could not believe my good fortune because there were so many others senior to me, available at the time.

On 13 August 1946 however, I took over the appointment from RSM S. M. Hamilton MBE at the Depot, just ten years after

RSM W. I. Rooney, MM, approves the progress of one of the squads on the square at Caterham, with his Drill Sergeants Moran (left) and B. E. Hillier, DCM, Welsh Guards (right) who was Depot RSM 1949-51.   Bill Rooney

eaving it as a recruit. It was the most challenging experience in my career so far, to have become the Regimental Sergeant Major of the Guards Depot. Not only that, the Commandant, Lt-Col J. C. Windsor-Lewis DSO MC, Welsh Guards, one of the most decorated and distinguished officers of the Second World War, was one who demanded nothing less than the highest standards so, from the first day I set foot there, I knew exactly what was required of me. It was a return to traditional peacetime soldiering, with its Ceremonial, Colour, Sword and Company drill. The war was over and while Col Windsor-Lewis liked good war soldiers, there was never any doubt about what would happen if one was not prepared to get back to pre-war standards.

Everyone wanted to improve his military knowledge, none more than those seeking promotion, and the Guards Depot was the centre of knowledge. Someone there would always know the answer to a problem. As RSM of the Guards Depot one had to be familiar with the customs and traditions of all five regiments of Foot Guards. This took time but much had been learned during recruit days. Before the war we had trained at the Depot for 16 weeks and a lot of regimental knowledge went into that. Our battle honours in the Irish Guards do not go back as far as some but one learned a great deal as a recruit about the history of each regiment and its customs.

I always liked drill and in particular enjoyed moving companies around the square, manoeuvering them, getting them into line or column, forming them on the march, a marvellous experience. About half way through my tour came the formation of the All Arms Drill Wing. Pre-war, each regiment and corps had its own code of drill and this differed in timing and detail. Now it was time to standardise it throughout the army and it was realised that the only way to do this was to train all WOs and senior NCOs, who

had a responsibility for drill in their units, on one specialised course. Where could that course – sponsored and controlled by the War-Office – be better placed than at the Guards Depot?

The first WO to take charge of the course was D-Sgt Desmond Lynch DCM, and it really was a case of cometh the hour, cometh the man. He gave the course 120 per cent efficiency and made it a splendid success, as the drill in the British and Commonwealth armies testifies to this day.

Close to the end of my tour in 1949, when Guardsmen were becoming thin on the ground due to overseas commitments, it was necessary for recruits from the Depot who were beyond their twelfth week of training to line part of the route for the Queen's Birthday Parade. This was an unusual, if not unique occasion. At about this time, the first drill book was written and many of us were on the production committee headed by Col Dick Gooch, Coldstream Guards, the Sergeant Majors being Arthur Ramsden, John Lord, 'Dusty' Smith and myself.

I had several very good Drill Sergeants working with me at the Depot, Jim Cowley DCM, Coldstream Guards, 'Tomo' Tomlinson MM, Scots Guards, Mickey Moran MM, Irish Guards and Bert Hillier DCM, Welsh Guards.

After three and a half happy and rewarding years as RSM of the Depot, at first under Col Windsor-Lewis, who incidentally insisted that his RSM be dressed in pre-war service dress and puttees, and then under Col J. Chandos-Pole, Coldstream Guards, I returned to the 1st Bn Irish Guards in January 1950 as

RSM, taking over from RSM George Howe who went to London District as GSM.

What a moment it was to come back after five years at the Training Battalion and Guards Depot. It was the fiftieth anniversary of the formation of the regiment and celebrations were soon under way. The most historic and memorable of these was when King George VI accompanied by Queen Elizabeth, presented shamrock to the Irish Guards on St Patrick's Day at Chelsea Barracks. Field Marshal Alexander, our Colonel who was Governor General of Canada at the time, flew home with Lady Alexander, for the Parade and attended the Sergeants Mess Grand Ball in the evening. This was a momentous occasion and the Parade is one that will live with me forever.

It was in 1952 when the battalion was in Germany that the vacancy for GSM again came up and, as I was by that time the senior RSM in Household Division, I was offered the post. The CO asked me to consider the appointment over the weekend. The post of GSM, although held by Guardsmen, did not involve them in any responsibility for major ceremonial at the time. On the following Monday morning when asked by the Adjutant during his Orders what my decision was, I replied that I had not made my mind up but if the regiment wanted me to take the appointment I would, although I was perfectly happy where I was. His answer provided the decision when he said, 'The Regiment does not want you to go.' My problem was therefore solved and when I later spoke to the CO I asked if I could recommend D-Sgt G. Stone for the appointment because his vast knowledge of ceremonial would bring a new dimension to the post and be of enormous assistance to the Brigade Major. To my delight George was selected and as we all know, for 15 years was an outstanding success as GSM, making a huge contribution to every aspect of ceremonial.

I continued for a short time as RSM and the last big parade in which I took part was the occasion of the Queen's Birthday held at the Rhine Centre, Dusseldorf, when the salute was taken by the then High Commissioner, Sir Ivone Kirkpatrick. I was commissioned in 1952 and became Camp Commandant HQ, 32 Guards Brigade in the Canal Zone Egypt. It was Coronation year in 1953 and as an ex-RSM I was asked to prepare a parade which we held at El Ballah, a quiet location, miles from anywhere, in June 1953.

The 1st Battalion had come to Egypt following the Coronation and was now stationed in Moascar. In January 1955 the Quartermaster George Howe MBE, went to 1st Guards Brigade as Camp Commandant and I took his place as Quartermaster in March. I was made an MBE in the New Year's Honours 1955 and received the insignia from Gen Sir Charles Keightley, C-in-C Middle East Land Forces, in September of that year.

The battalion returned from the Canal Zone to Lydd early in 1956, then in 1958 went on an emergency tour to Cyprus for four months. From Cyprus we returned to Victoria Barracks, Windsor, from where I was posted to the Guards Depot, this time as the Quartermaster. My tour there coincided with one of those rare periods when all the senior staff happened to be drawn from the five Regiments of Foot Guards – the Commandant from the Welsh Guards, Second in Command Coldstream, Adjutant Scots, Quartermaster Irish and the Regimental Sergeant Major Grenadiers. By now I had completed the double having been RSM of the battalion and the Guards Depot and Quartermaster of both.

In 1963 I left the Depot to take up the appointment of Company Commander HQ Wing RMA Sandhurst, where I had an absorbing four years until retiring in 1967, at the age of 53. I was then extremely fortunate to be re-employed as a Retired Officer at Headquarters London District, where I was on the staff with those I had known and often served with during previous years, until finally retiring in 1980. So, after almost 45 years of public service, eight of these as a RSM, I have memories in abundance.

I have known many splendid RSMs and Jack Stack was one of those, not of great physique but you were not long in his presence before realising that here was a humane, gentle but extremely firm and fair man. Hugh McKinney too was all of these things, as well as being a humorous and entertaining friend. John Lord was an extremely able and distinguished Sergeant Major who brought credit to the army, his regiment and to the rank itself. These were just three of many.

I have never modelled myself on any of my predecessors but tried to be myself. I took the view that if you place yourself in a mould or straight jacket you run the risk of not remaining adaptable as one must be to meet often changing requirements. There is only one Regimental Sergeant Major in a battalion. That in itself gives the post enormous prestige and in turn enormous responsibility falls on the incumbent. He is in fact, that single link between other ranks and command, which calls for close liaison, co-operation, tact, sounding out the mood and morale, monitoring the temperature, in short doing everything necessary to ensure a happy unit.

He must of course be familiar with regulations, use discretion wisely when dealing with men and above all be scrupulously fair and be seen to be. A mild sense of humour, provided it is not

W. L. A. 'Bill' Nash, Grenadier Guards, Depot RSM 1951-3. Sgt-Maj Nash was of the few to hold the appointment of both RSM of the Guards Depot and of the RMA Sandhurst. For his service details see the chapter on 'RSMs and AcSMs of the Royal Military College and Academy, Sandhurst. Grenadier Gazette

arcastic or offensive, can be a great help. It has been a great privilege living among and working with outstanding soldiers and friends for nearly half my life. The loyalty, comradeship and mutual respect achieved by training and discipline cannot possibly be equalled in any other walk of life and I would not have wanted it otherwise.

Finally, the rank I enjoyed most serving in was that of Regimental Sergeant Major, not because of any power it brought but because of, among many other reasons, the wide discretion one could exercise, more often than not with sympathy and humility.

Sgt-Maj Ronald J. S. Tyacke, enlisted in the Coldstream Guards on 18 November 1932 and went through the Guards Depot during the time of RSM J. D. Hughes, Welsh Guards. Having been selected for the Depot Boxing Team, he was back squadded and joined the 3rd Battalion after training in a draft of one recruit! In June 1935 he was made Lance Corporal and went with the 3rd Bn to Palestine in 1936 and then to Egypt one year later when he became a Lance Sergeant. He was to remain for seven years in the Middle East, being promoted to Sergeant in the Signal Section in August 1939 and CQMS in June 1941.

In April 1942, Ronald Tyacke was promoted as CSM and a few months later left the 3rd Bn on being posted to the No 2 Infantry Training Depot, Middle East. For six months he served as Senior Drill Instructor in charge of two Cadet Companies at the ME OCTU in Palestine. At that time he played very prominently in rugby in the Middle East command. On 15 May 1944 he left Port Said for England and was placed on the strength of the Guards Armoured Training Wing, serving as the CSM of the Wireless Squadron.

In 1945 he was posted to the BAOR School of Infantry Training at Sennelager, as the Senior Drill Instructor, where he again took his place in the BAOR rugby team. One year later he was transferred to the 5th Bn at Cologne and then the 4th Bn as Drill Sergeant.

His ability as an Instructor having been well established, D-Sgt Tyacke was attached firstly to the Guards Depot, then to the 3rd Bn, which was at that time a Junior NCOs cadre battalion, and where he also took part in the 1950 Tercentenary Parade. Finally he went to Tripoli where at one stage he was flown to Geneifa to organise and instruct a special drill course for NCOs of the 17th Infantry Brigade.

As the RSM of the 3rd Bn was away, he stood in to supervise the training of the Battalion Coronation detachment and it was then that news came that he was to be the RSM of the Guards Depot. Disappointingly he was unable to attend the Coronation Day Parade, as a tunic large enough for him was not available! Instead, he installed the first large screen TV set in the Sergeants Mess, and invited all of the families and available Depot staff to watch the Coronation of HM Queen Elizabeth II.

Following an active seven month tour as RSM of the Depot, RSM Tyacke was posted to the 1st Bn Coldstream Guards, where he remained for the final two years of his service. During that period in 1954, the battalion formed

RSM R. J. S. Tyacke, Coldstream Guards, Depot RSM in 1953.
Ronald Tyacke

the Escort to the Colour on the occasion of the Queen's Birthday Parade – a very proud day for him.

RSM Ronald Tyacke was discharged from the army on 17 November 1955, after 23 years Colour service. His service to his country was far from over however, as he was sworn in as a Yeoman-in-Ordinary, of her Majesty's Bodyguard, on 8 March 1960. He took part in many Royal ceremonial events during the following 20 years, and was awarded the Royal Victoria Medal (Silver) on 31 December 1980. He was then promoted Messenger Sergeant Major in 1982.

On reaching his 70th year, MSM Tyacke was placed on the Supernumerary List of the Queen's Bodyguard. He remains a very active former Coldstreamer, with a fund of memories about his service.

I first had the pleasure of meeting Maj Lou Drouet at the Guards Depot, Pirbright, in 1979, where I went to discuss with him his former service at the RMA Sandhurst, under the late AcSM J. C. Lord. This resulted in the absorbing details of his tour as CSM there, being included in the story of RSM J. C. Lord MVO MBE.

We met again at a rather special dinner held at the Sergeants Mess of the Guards Depot in September 1982. Now in retirement, Maj Drouet lives only a short distance away, and I have the benefit of his tremendous enthusiasm and knowledge for all matters military, but in particular regarding his regiment, for which he retains such a firm loyalty and spends so much of his time in support of its functions.

I was being shown through his extensive collection of photographs, contained in a beautiful album presented to him by the Household Division Shooting Team in 1983, when he talked with me about his experiences.

I am a Guernseyman and my parents were Guernsey people of French extraction. We left when I was about nine years old to live in Jersey where prospects were better in my father's work as a carpenter. He had fought in France during the First World War in the Guernsey Light Infantry. Guernsey's war efforts should never be forgotten, particularly the very heavy cost they paid in lives, which considering the size of the population, proved to be the

RSM D. M. Whyte, Scots Guards, Depot RSM 1953-6. (left) Capt/Adj P. J. C. Ratcliffe. (right) Sgt. J. Edwards.

heaviest loss in the British Empire. They produced some fine soldiers, many of whom were highly decorated. Likewise, in the Second World War, many Guernseymen served their country and we had the distinction of a Guernseyman gaining the first Victoria Cross of the Tunisian campaign, Maj J. Le Paturel of the Hampshire Regiment, in the fearful battle for Tebourba.

I first joined the Royal Militia, Island of Jersey, in about 1935 and although this was very much a territorial unit, it was staffed by some very fine British army instructors. RSM MacLean was from the Cameronians and an extremely smart soldier whom we all much admired. The CSM of our rifle company was George Coe of the KOYLI, a marvellous man who went on to become Quartermaster of his regiment. The Adjutant was Capt Smythe of the 11th Hussars, also a very good officer. Then I remember a quite brilliant instructor named Fields, from the Northamptonshire Regiment, who taught us in the machine-gun company.

I enlisted in the Grenadier Guards in July 1939, and found myself at the Caterham Guards Depot. There was a marvellous Depot RSM in post at the time, RSM Hugh McKinney of the Irish Guards, the acme of perfection, tall and slim with a swarthy complexion and very clear white teeth. With his green band around his forage cap and Irish Guards cap badge, he looked absolutely immaculate. We watched him as he marched along the flank at the Depot and he looked like a military machine. A very hard RSM, but with a lovely style and a lot of Irish wit with a demeanour for all occassions, whether it be squad drill or the great Depot swank parade.

At the Depot we recruits were mainly concerned with surviving the course, but first impressions are lasting ones and when one sees that kind of personality one never forgets. I used to say to myself, 'one day I will come back here, and will be the Regimental Sergeant Major myself.' I tried to model myself upon him and he was a great influence on a young soldier.

When war came in September 1939 we immediately handed in our home service clothing and those of us in the Grenadier Guards who had completed 12 of the 18 weeks course, were taken off to form our Training Battalion at Windsor. Those who were fully trained went to form the Grenadier Depot at Chelsea. I remained with the Training Battalion for quite a time as I completed a signals course, but then we progressed to the Holding Battalion at Wellington Barracks, from which the overseas battalions were fed with drafts of men. It was whilst we had been at Windsor that we heard the news of the award of the VC to Cpl Harry Nicholls of the 3rd Battalion on the River Schelte. How proud we were to be Grenadiers.

The Dunkirk evacuation occurred whilst we were at Windsor and with the threat of a German invasion we went over to our scare stations. It was stand to all the time, with a careful watch being kept for German parachutists. When the 3rd Battalion came back through Dunkirk, it was temporarily placed at Wakefield and it was whilst there that we were sent in a draft to join it from the Holding Battalion.

Soon after, the 3rd Battalion was moved to take over and guard a section of the East coast from invasion, but eventually we went to Inveraray in the Scottish Highlands, for special training in preparation for landing operations in Madagascar and the Channel Islands, but these were cancelled at the last moment. Further large exercises took place until we went aboard troopships in November 1942, bound for the invasion of North Africa.

We disembarked at Algiers and then travelled in trucks for 500 miles over the Algerian mountains into Tunisia. I shall never forget those magnificent RASC drivers, who drove all day and at night carried out their maintenance before attempting to refresh or rest. The Germans were heavily reinforced by air, of which they had command, and also by sea, and when the rainy season

RSM L. C. Drouet, Grenadier Guards, Depot RSM 1956-7.
Major Lou Drouet

commenced we could not use our tanks and armour, so the campaign bogged down for the winter, and into 1943. We were committed mainly to patrol activities in the Tunisian mountains, but also took part in battles such as Bou Arada, Jebel Mansour, Kasserine, Long Stop, Medjez el Bab, to name but a few.

Our battalion RSM was Bill Hagell, who certainly knew how to handle us, whether in or out of the line. Out of the line however, the first thing to be organised would be a drill parade and even on short rest periods the order would come to blanco up and clean up. A good deal of chasing about would follow of course, but it was in fact, a great morale booster to clean oneself up and the discipline was a most necessary thing. I still believe that the finest remedy in the world to shake people out of their lethargy is to get them cleaned up and out on a drill parade.

RSM Bill Hagell practised the philosophy that one should work

hard and play hard, and he also had the knack of being able to get the best out of the worst. After a testing time in the line we came out for a short rest and the word promptly came around – 'Battalion drill parade tomorrow morning – equipment to be fully blancoed'. One company refused to do so, but instead of placing every man under close arrest, RSM Hagell ordered them on parade carrying their webbing equipment. He appeared in front carrying his own webbing and said, 'I will now show you how to blanco your equipment far more quickly than you do. Get your belts off, we are going to blanco together! Now, with blanco held so . . .' he demonstrated and the company followed and so he humoured and chatted up the men and soon the equipment was blancoed. He had avoided an unnecessary showdown by leadership and example.

He could also play hard in the Sergeants Mess and would socialise with the junior Sergeants until the early hours, but in the morning would be as sharp as ever on parade, and woe betide the junior Sergeant who was not up to it. Another of his strengths was that he would always make sure that any member of the battalion in hospital was visited and that the necessary creature comforts were taken to maintain spirits.

In February 1943 the battalion, in company with the 3rd Parachute Battalion and a Foreign Legion unit, attempted to assault and take high ground which would give us control of the lower country. The Germans had a similar plan unfortunately and in some desperate fighting our units were decimated. The battle of Jebel Mansour developed in which our Company attacked at 1400hrs 80 strong, but by 1630hrs was down to 15 men. The German firepower was tremendous compared with our own and when, as a Platoon Sergeant, I was crawling up towards a rocky feature, I was hit by fire from a machine-gun. I owe my life to three comrades with whom I had served since joining the regiment. Jackie Byrne was a Lance Corporal Stretcher Bearer and was awarded the DCM for getting me off that hill, and Wally Kershaw and Tommy Higginson were mentioned in dispatches for their part. They carried me for nine hours to get off the mountain top and then I was evacuated to a casualty clearing station. I had been shot through a kidney and across the spine and was out of the campaign for six months while I recovered.

I was medically downgraded and as the 3rd Bn sailed off to Italy and the Naples battles, I was posted to Staff HQ in Algiers as a Sergeant. I remained in FM Wilson's HQ until Gen Alexander took over in Italy and he was subsequently followed by Gen Harding. I ended the war as an administrative Company Sergeant Major in Padua and it was whilst there that I met my wife Pat, as she was also serving there in the ATS.

After Italy I came home to the 1st Battalion in London, and had a short period of public duties under a very fine soldier – RSM Arthur Spratley. This included all of the main ceremonial guard duties, so I had to read up on all the drill to go on parade as CSM – a vast change from my earlier experience as a Guardsman – and it was quite a test of strength and character to deal with it. Practice was the thing, if only one could get it!

Many of us held war substantive ranks and as the army came down to peace time establishment, the acting rank could quickly be taken away. In my case I would have gone from CSM to Colour Sergeant, but at that time a College was formed at Harrogate for Army Apprentices, and several of us went as WOs to instruct them in regimental training. I had three good years there before being posted to the 2nd Bn, Grenadier Guards, at Krefeld, as CSM of No 1 Company, where I learned a great deal from D-Sgt Alf Dickinson and RSM George Hackett.

In 1952 I was posted to the RMA Sandhurst as CSM and it was there that I came under the influence of the great RSM John Lord, who militarily speaking, taught me almost everything I know. I was proud to be appointed CSM of Somme Company under RSM Alf Dickinson, who had by now been appointed RSM of New

College. I remember an occasion when the officer cadets of the college decided upon a prank. During the night they made a mock grave in the centre of the college square, placing a head-post fashioned from a pace stick and forage cap, marked with the inscription 'RIP – AD.1952' in which they 'buried' Alf Dickinson. RSM Dickinson saw the joke, but later had the last word.

On completion of my tour at Sandhurst, I returned to the 2nd Bn in Egypt as CSM of Support Company, but then received promotion to Assistant Drill Sergeant in the 3rd Bn, stationed at Chelsea. RSM Bill Nash was in post and the other Drill Sergeant was Sammy Lowe MM, although Fred Clutton MM soon took over. We carried out public duties for most of the year, until I returned to the 2nd Bn as a full Drill Sergeant. Tom Taylor was Assistant Drill Sergeant with me in Egypt and we worked well together in the 2nd Bn.

I became the Depot RSM at Caterham in 1956, following RSM Donald Whyte of the Scots Guards, and initially found it quite a challenge. At that time one had to serve as RSM of the Depot, or as a College RSM at the RMAS, before one could become RSM of a battalion. Of the two appointments the Guards Depot post carried the heavier responsibility in my opinion, as a large Sergeants Mess was included.

At the Guards Depot, the RSMs life revolved around discipline and drill – drill – and more drill. National Service was then in full swing and with some 3,000 men on the strength, we often had as many as 60 or 70 squads on the square at one time.

I used to enjoy getting in amongst the men in a squad, giving them a good chasing, then settle them down and standing them at ease, have a good talk with them. To build up their knowledge we would discuss the various customs, traditions and rivalries between the regiments and I found that it paid off tremendously to bring out their regimental spirit.

The Commandant at that time, was Col J. Bowes-Lyon, who later became Major General of the Household Division. He was, I believe, instrumental in seeking more useful ways of dealing with men serving periods of punishment. The Commandant would often send for me afterwards to enquire, 'Besides chasing these people around on drill, Sergeant Major, what can we do to teach them something worthwhile?' I replied on one occasion that we might allow them to extend the pig and turkey farms, so it became part of the detention men's duties – following drill parades – to get changed into denims and do some useful practical work.

As RSM at the Depot, one attended to most of the regimental functions, St Andrew's Day with the Scots Guards, St Patrick's Day with the Irish Guards, St David's Day with the Welsh and St George's Day with the Coldstream Guards. The Grenadiers, of course, do not need a patron saint.

My Drill Sergeants at the Depot were Leo Johnson, Grenadier Guards, and Norman Morse, Coldstream Guards. Both went on to become RSMs, Leo Johnson of the Malaya Regiment – a great privilege in those days – and Norman Morse of the 2nd Battalion, and subsequently Major QM. Ray Huggins, who was destined to become Academy Sergeant Major at the RMA Sandhurst, was one of my CSMs and I always feel that I owed him and the other CSMs a great deal, as they were extremely efficient and were of course the pick of their regiments.

One tried to apply strictness and sharpness with some humour and laughter, a knack which eventually came naturally – humour that is without being frivolous. Charging goes with any rank of course, as one cannot overlook any indiscipline or dishonesty. If these things are not stopped quickly small matters will become large ones. Faults must be registered and one must be seen to be in command. The training programmes of the day at the Guards Depot ensured that everyone worked at full stretch and there was no latitude for idle hands to make mischief.

After a period of some 13 months at the Depot, I was appointed RSM, of the 1st Bn, Grenadier Guards and Fred Clutton MM took over the Depot. He was a distinguished Sergeant Major, who could not have been better for the establishment and he went on to a great commissioned career in the regiment. I went out to Germany to join the 1st Battalion and I particularly remember the happy working relationship which developed between the CO, the Adjutant and myself as RSM.

I had taken over from RSM Alf Dickinson, and had two excellent Drill Sergeants, George Kirkham, who later became an RSM and is now a smart member of the Queen's Bodyguard, The Yeoman of the Guard, and Barney Owens, who went on to become RSM of the West African Rifles. I was again fortunate in having such high calibre Drill Sergeants.

On completing its tour of duty with the Rhine Army, I well remember the battalion returning home and marching through the City of London with bayonets fixed, drums beating, and Colours flying. A magnificent sight. The full battalion of 900 men, in ranks six abreast, the CO on horseback leading, the Adjutant close behind on horseback, followed by the RSM on foot. The Queen's Company and the rest of the battalion followed, with the Colours in the centre. When we arrived at Blackfriars Bridge, the battalion was halted whilst the Colours were cased and then we marched on to Waterloo Station for entrainment to Pirbright to prepare for public duties.

I was commissioned in 1958, firstly as Lieutenant MTO of the 1st Bn and later as Quartermaster of the 2nd Bn. In 1966 I returned to the Guards Depot as Transport and Messing Officer, in my view two of the largest responsibilities; the wheels to keep everything moving and the messing to keep everyone content.

I was destined to remain at the Guards Depot at Pirbright, firstly as Camp Staff Officer and then on retirement from the regiment, as Range Officer. I moved from one chair to another, but the next 12 years were to see great changes. The change of rifles made a great deal of difference to the ranges because of the much greater muzzle velocities. Improved ranges had to come to deal with the greater rapidity of fire, as faster heavier weapons cause greater wear and tear upon the system and safety has to be a constant factor. Such sophisticated weapons are used ceremonially and there will always be argument over whether weapons like the SA80 are suitable for arms drill.

The question of which RSM particularly impressed me is a tough one, because one knew so many during long service. My personal choice might sound rather strange, but I hope not. I will always remember our RSM of the Jersey Militia from the Cameronians, RSM MacLean, as he was my first. He was extremely smart and efficient and was a magnificent example of a professional RSM. Another was RSM Hugh McKinney, Irish Guards; I suppose it is only natural that one's first RSMs will stand out the most. I never forget that when I attended a Scottish Command Physical Training School, on a three month course in 1941, there was a former Olympic gymnast in the APTC, an RSM 'Jock' White, who I admired as being one of the finest Warrant Officer's bred in the British army!

Another all rounder was GSM George Stone, Irish Guards, and when as a young Drill Sergeant in London, taking a Guard of Honour to Victoria Station, or on some ceremonial occasion elsewhere, one would be aware that George was standing unobtrusively nearby ready to help if necessary. Not for him the attitude that one should know the drill by now. He was there to support and to see that everything went well. The hallmark of a great GSM in London.

As Quartermaster at the Guards Depot, I also saw others go through as Depot RSM and I particularly remember two fine examples. RSM John Holbrook was in my opinion a classic, and then there was Ray Barnes. RSM Barnes went on from the Depot to become a College RSM at the RMA Sandhurst, with a view to him taking over from AcSM Ray Huggins, but he tragically collapsed and died following a jogging session. He was a very articulate and extremely smart soldier. Then of course there was AcSM John Lord, but it required a whole book to pay tribute to him.

When Lou Drouet finally retired, the Pirbright ranges were described as being the finest ranges in the United Kingdom and for his contribution to Army shooting he was honoured by the Chief of the General Staff in 1980, by being made an Honorary Life Member of the Army Rifle Association. In 1984 Gen Kitson presented him with a plaque in recognition of his contribution to service markmanship from 1972-84.

Maj Drouet was awarded the MBE in 1960. He has many absorbing interests and strongly supports the work of the Commonwealth War Graves Commission. Above all, he has a tremendous loyalty to the Grenadier Guards, in which he has the distinction of having served in the 1st, 2nd and 3rd Battalions. As a student of British Army history, Lou Drouet finds great enjoyment in participating in battlefield tours of the First and Second World Wars and supports all that is humanly possible in the affairs of the Regimental Associations and its many and various functions. He states how fortunate he is to be able to do so, and adds that this is attributable to the good health he enjoys, which he feels is a by-product of the good regimental training and life he has undergone.

'AD 1952' College RSM Alf Dickinson, RMAS, and CSM Lou Drouet pay due respect to the overnight 'grave'. Note the boots!
Lou Drouet

CHAPTER 18

Regimental Sergeant Majors of the Guards Depot 1958 to 1989

The greatest pleasure from researching this work has undoubtedly come from meeting so many of the former great Regimental Sergeant Majors, and following years of correspondence with John Holbrook, it was a marvellous experience to meet him when he was Major QM at the Guards Depot in September 1982. He has been associated with the earlier book dealing with the career of AcSM John Lord, of whom he retains such admiration, and John Holbrook has guided this work throughout. A measure of his steadfast support is revealed not only by the number of items listed to him in the acknowledgements, but from the time factor, that his vastly informative letters date back to 1979, when he was Captain QM of the 2nd Battalion, Coldstream Guards.

John Holbrook had served as RSM of the Guards Depot only seven years earlier, but has just retired as Lieutenant Colonel (QM) to bring his experience and enthusiasm to bear on the recruiting of the next generation of soldiers into the British army. Having been so instrumental in the production of this book, it is of particular pleasure to present the following details of John Holbrook's career in the Coldstream Guards.

My first experience of military life was when in 1946 at the age of 14 I decided to join the Army Cadet Force. The unit at my home town of Sutton in Surrey was D Company, the East Surrey Regiment, and it was with them whilst attending the many weekend training and instruction camps at the Guards Depot, Caterham, that I formed my first impressions of the Brigade of Guards.

The pace of life within the walls of 'The barracks' Caterham was always much sharper, more alive and to me, full of interest, when compared with what I thought was a very dull civilian world. The turnout and bearing of the recruits I saw undergoing training and the rigid no nonsense, but fair, attitude of the staff, left me in no doubt that I wanted to join this breed of military supermen.

As soon as I reached the minimum adult enlistment age of 17½, I went along to the nearest recruiting office at Croydon and was attested into Her Majesty's Coldstream Regiment of Foot Guards. I reported to the Guards Depot Caterham on 10 October 1950 and started my recruit training along with 25 other young men, as a member of Sergeant Blood's squad. I must admit that I found life a great deal more spartan and the training harder than I imagined. Being under training full-time, 24 hours a day, was vastly different to my weekend visits, when I was able to return to the comforts of home at Sunday tea time.

Whilst under training, everything a recruit did was explained and where necessary, demonstrated in great detail by the instructors, who were usually seasoned veterans with lots of campaign medal ribbons. All the sweat and tears were planned almost to perfection as if to give one more nerve and a breaking point far higher than soldiers in other regiments. The basic training in drill, PT, weapons, education and regimental history, lasted for 16 weeks at Caterham, before moving on to another phase of training at the Guards Training Battalion at Pirbright, near Woking in Surrey.

At Pirbright we continued our military education, but were now allowed to refer to ourselves by the rank of Trainee Guardsman, having successfully passed our basic recruit training. It was then the turn of NCOs using the wide open heathlands and ranges to teach us the finer points of musketry, fieldcraft, endurance marching, assault course and obstacle crossing techniques. All our training seemed to move up a gear and was presented to us under realistic tactical settings and conditions, both by day and

RSM T. Pugh, Grenadier Guards, Depot RSM 1961-4.

RSM E. J. R. Rose, Grenadier Guards, Depot RSM 1964-6. When kindly assisting with permission from the MOD for this photograph of RSM Rose to be reproduced, the Commander of the Household Division, Maj-Gen Christopher Airy, CBE, added a brief note in his reply, 'Ted Rose was my Company Sergeant Major when I was a Cadet at Sandhurst. I was well taught!' Leaving the RMAS in 1954, Ted Rose returned as RSM of Victory College in 1959, and although leaving to become RSM of the Guards Depot, his service at the Academy was not ended, as he subsequently returned as Major, Officer Commanding Headquarter Wing. During his period as RSM of the Depot, the Household Cavalry Training Squadron joined the Depot in 1966, and since that time all seven regiments of the Household Division have trained at the Depot. MOD London

Corporal on 28 January 1952. Hardly had the two chevrons been sewn on to my sleeves before we departed to reinforce the military garrisons in Egypt, where there had been riots resulting in the killing of a number of Europeans.

We were to oppose and seek out groups which went under such grand sounding names as 'the daughters of the Nile'. We travelled, a single company at a time, by sea, on a landing craft tank (LCT), landed at Port Suez, then on to a tented camp named Port Louis at Tel-el-Kebir. There I was to see at first hand the area of a regimental battle honour in 1882, about which, as a recruit at the Guards Depot, I had been made to recite in great detail on shining parade in the barrack room.

We remained guarding and protecting the stores in this vast ordnance depot for some weeks, before moving to a signal station on the side of the Suez Canal, known as Wolseley Camp, El Ballah. I then returned to the Guards Depot as a Squad Instructor in July 1952.

My first task at Caterham was to attend a course of instruction with other potential instructors, where I very soon realised that I would have to study hard if I was to qualify to teach recruits. The men responsible for our higher education were RSM Donald Whyte, Scots Guards, D-Sgt Ernie Osborne, Irish Guards and Sgt Pinto Price, Grenadier Guards, and it was under the eagle eyes of this fearsome trio that I learned how to drill and excercise a squad on a sixpence.

When not on the barrack square we were in the classroom giving lecturettes. Here we became so confident that we were able to stand up and instruct or talk on almost any subject – from a matchstick to a battleship – given a short period in which to research some background facts and figures.

Having successfully passed my course, I was to spend just over two very happy and rewarding years as an Instructor at the Guards Depot. I took six squads through their basic training, producing 123 men for my regiment. After my second squad I was promoted as Lance Sergeant on 29 August 1953 and entry to the Sergeants Mess opened up a whole new dimension in my military life.

My tour at the Depot ended in October 1954, when I was posted back to the 1st Battalion, which had returned from the Middle East to Victoria Barracks, Windsor. We then moved to Chelsea Barracks in early 1955, to carry out public duties in London. I married my wife Patricia, whom I had met whilst at the Depot, on 12 March 1955, at Caxton Hall, Westminster. I was promoted to Sergeant on 4 November and moved with the battalion to Krefeld in Germany, as part of 32nd Guards Brigade.

As a Platoon Sergeant in BAOR, I concentrated my efforts on perfecting the basic infantry battle field skills of both myself and the men under my control. I was by now well settled into Sergeants Mess life and was beginning to note and register various points from my conversations with seniors during social moments. I also began to realise that the RSM had a great influence upon the lifestyle of mess members, even in off duty hours and that one looked to him for example and advice in so many things.

night, very often using live ammunition. The final two weeks were spent at a Battle Camp at Pickering, in North Yorkshire, putting all our training and battle tactics to the test under field conditions against a skilled 'enemy'.

On completion of training I was posted on 23 May 1951 – Festival of Britain Day – to the 1st Bn, Coldstream Guards, stationed at Victoria Barracks, Windsor, where the battalion's role was to carry out ceremonial duties both in London and Windsor. I found myself involved in such events as the Queen's Birthday Parade, Guards of Honour for Heads of State, Windsor Castle Guard, the State Opening of Parliament and various other public duties.

In November 1951, due to unrest in the Middle East, the battalion was moved at short notice to Cyprus, along with other units forming the 32nd Brigade. We entrained for Portsmouth where we boarded the Aircraft Carrier *HMS Illustrious*.

We took up residence in south-west Cyprus at Polemidhia Camp in the hills just above Limassol and found a camp partly tented and hutted with electric light and other very basic amenities. Whilst stationed here I was selected to attend a ten day course of instruction for potential Lance Corporals. The course was supervised by the formidable D-Sgt Leslie Trimming, a man who accepted nothing less than excellence and could by his mere presence send shivers up and down one's spine. His stare left one frozen to the spot, speechless just like a stone statue!

Along with some other successful students, I was made a Lance

In the summer of 1956 I was selected for a tour of duty as a Sergeant Instructor at the RMA Sandhurst where I spent three wonderful years training officer cadets. I found later, as RSM, that I was able to draw upon a great deal of the experience I had gained during this period; it provided a well of knowledge and information that I could tap when ever I needed it.

I returned to the 1st Battalion in 1959 where I was employed as a Police Sergeant, which required me to work under direct control of the RSM and Drill Sergeants. Here again, I gained a grounding in military law and the rules and regulations for soldiers under sentence. I then moved to Support Company to become the Mortar Sergeant, an appointment I enjoyed, bringing into use the new concept of a Support Platoon – of two mortars and two anti-tank guns – within a rifle company.

The battalion went on operational tours in Kenya and British Guyana, which were carried out straight from our public duties role and base at Windsor. The RSM of the battalion throughout this period, was RSM Dennis Wilkinson, a man who had a great influence upon many of my thoughts, decisions and actions when I later became an RSM myself.

RSM Wilkinson controlled the battalion for six years through a whole range of events and roles, from public duties, Trooping the Colour, a BAOR mechanised role, HM The Queen's review of the British Army of the Rhine, plus emergency tours in Aden and British Guyana. I was very impressed with his tremendous adaptability. He also made many sweeping changes in the Sergeants Mess, setting aside many of the out dated practices, without loss of any mess etiquette or dignity. He set out to cater

more for the young Sergeants, wives and children and th Sergeants Mess became an even more fun place to attend, ver much the centre and hub of life within the battalion.

During this period I gained promotion to Compan Quartermaster Sergeant, now turning my mind to stores an ration accounting. It was just prior to moving to Aden that I wa informed of promotion to CSM of HQ Company, and this prove to be a tremendous experience, controlling and dealing with man departments within the company.

Midway through the Aden tour, I returned via Germany t collect my family, then on to the Guards Depot, which was now a Pirbright, as CSM. I was posted to 13 Company, Coldstrea Guards, to control recruit training for my regiment. Here I gaine valuable experience from two fine WOs, RSM Ted Rose an RSM Jim Grindley. Both men were very approachable and alway ready and willing to give sound advice or offer a guiding hand. I was during this period that I now realise I was receiving that fina grooming and I have much to be grateful for to these two fin Coldstream Sergeant Majors.

After 18 months at Pirbright I returned to Chelsea Barracks as Drill Sergeant and was fortunate to have a fine Sergeant Majo RSM Tom Forrest, plus a first class friend and fellow Dri Sergeant, Kiwi Clements. I was now being tasked under the eagl eye of RSM Tom Forrest with much more responsibility for majc ceremonial events. I was sufficiently qualified and confident t stand in for the Sergeant Major on Queen's Guard Mounting whilst he went on leave, and I felt that I had now finally won m spurs. When such men accepted one as being almost equal, smile

RSM D. Nicholson, Welsh Guards, Depot RSM, 1966-7.
MOD, London

RSM W. J. Holbrook, Coldstream Guards, Depot RSM 1969-72.
Lt-Col W. J. Holbrook

Maj-Gen Sir John Swinton KCVO OBE, Academy Sgt-Maj R. P. Huggins, and Depot RSM W. J. Holbrook reflect upon a drawn match, following the Annual Pace Stick Competition, 1971.
Guards Magazine

and with a pat on the back said, 'Well done,' after a big parade or major event, it was a great moment, and I often felt nine feet tall!

In August 1968 I moved back to the Guards Depot as Drill Sergeant, once again working under RSM Jim Grindley, who was due to finish his military career in November 1969, when I was to be appointed as his successor. Looking back on my time as RSM of the Guards Depot, I still regard it as the most rewarding and happiest period of my military service and in terms of job satisfaction and achievement, it was a truly wonderful appointment.

From the very start I gave a great deal of thought to the following directive, which is taken from Standing Orders of the Guards Depot.

The regularity of the daily routine, the tone, behaviour of the Non Commissioned Officers and their knowledge of their duty, the soldier-like bearing of all ranks, of Non Commissioned Officers and men on and off parade, and in and out of barracks, mainly depend on the actual supervision, the example, the power of giving instructions and thorough knowledge of the regulations of the service by the Sergeant Major.

I was also conscious of the fact that I was now the custodian of seven sets of regimental customs, not just those of my own regiment. It was very important that I should not only know and understand these customs, but be able to teach them, giving historical origins and the reason for their present day retention in a modern professional army. I found myself at the end of any day, or month, able to look back with a real sense of achievement and quiet satisfaction. On average, at any time, I was responsible for 300 staff, 600 adult recruits, plus 1,500 junior soliders, musicians, drummers and pipers under training at the Depot.

It was my task to ensure that the doctrine was taught and drill and discipline properly administered. This doctrine has been in continuous practice within regiments of the Household Division for over 300 years. Anyone who has experienced battle knows

that there is no such thing as a discipline that takes the place of individual effort, that indeed, all military discipline is simply a method of uniting individual effort. It is important throughout a recruit's instruction to overcome the shambling habits of nature and prove that the Guardsman's style of carrying himself is the only proper way of moving over the ground.

There was also the All Arms Drill Wing, which ran drill and ceremonial courses of instruction for WOs and Sergeants of British, Commonwealth and some pro-Western foreign armies. The Wing was self contained but came under Guards Depot control for administration and discipline.

The Depot Charter also contained responsibility for running and staffing Household Division Centralised Courses. I was also at the head of a very large and happy Sergeants Mess, which contained – like many other training establishments – many very young, keen and ambitious WOs and NCOs. It was important to remind myself that the Mess was the married man's club, and the single man's home, which maintained very high standards of hospitality for those old comrades and visitors who would cross the threshold.

I handed over my appointment at the Depot in November 1973, on being commissioned as a Lieutenant, to carry out the duties of Families Officer with my regiment in Berlin. I was then promoted to Captain and took on the task of Mechanical Transport Officer, which was a complete change that involved on occasions, rolling up the sleeves and getting stuck in.

After controlling this aspect of battalion life for a few years, both in England and abroad, I moved on to become Technical Quartermaster. I was then appointed Quartermaster in both service battalion and at the Guards Depot, and once again found myself enjoying every moment of my soldiering. It gave great satisfaction to be regarded as the father figure of the regiment, my advice or opinion often being sought by all ranks from CO to Guardsman, on a variety of matters both military and personal.

I considered myself very fortunate indeed to receive promotion

RSM W. J. Holbrook in attendance during Maj-Gen James Bowes-Lyon's Annual Inspection of the Guards Depot.
Guards Magazine

to Lieutenant Colonel Quartermaster in September 1984 and felt I'd come a long way since first walking through the gates at Caterham. A great moment came in 1981 when I was made a Member of the Most Excellent Order of the British Empire, in the Queen's New Year Honours List. My investiture took place at Buckingham Palace on 21 July 1982, a memorable day in the lives of myself and my family. My youngest son Mark, then a Lance Corporal with the 2nd Bn, The Parachute Regiment, had just returned to England having been wounded in the battle for Goose Green, during the Falklands campaign. My eldest son Jeffrey, serving in the Life Guards, with the Household Cavalry Mounted Regiment at Knightsbridge, had just dismounted Queen's Guard after the horrific bomb attack by the IRA on the Troopers and horses at Hyde Park on the 19 July 1982. It was also a wonderful reward for my dear wife, for all the devotion and support she had given, both as a soldier's wife and as the mother of a future generation of soldiers.

At the conclusion of the Investiture, we were asked by the Equerry in Waiting to remain and were then quickly taken to a side room off the State Ballroom where we were to have the privilege of a short informal meeting with Her Majesty The Queen. A moment that will be treasured and never forgotten.

Every young soldier has heard the words, 'Things are not what they used to be,' from his seniors and from the older soldier and very often it is a good job they are not! Since I joined in 1950, there have been many changes in the army and in the Household Division and this is really not surprising as good organisations learn from past experience. Whilst still retaining regimental

customs and ceremonial standards, it is a mistake not to progress with the times.

One of the main areas of change has been in the system of applying military discipline. It is not so rigid now as in the past and much more attention is given to explaining the reason behind an order. The results are just as good and maybe even better than when under the old system.

Air Trooping has changed the life of UK based batallions, especially those stationed in London. One has now to be ready to move at a few hours notice, complete with vehicles and equipment, to any possible trouble spot in the world. This demands greater fitness and an awareness of world events, plus a constantly high level of training and maintenance of equipment. The steady voyage by sea, which allowed some time to shake out, has gone and it is now possible to step off an aircraft within hours of leaving home base and be deployed into an operational situation, which can range from winter warfare in Norway to patrolling the hills of the Radfan.

The ever present terrorist threat has also affected the whole atmosphere of public and ceremonial occasions and this has also changed other parts of what used to be normal practice within military life. Soldiers can no longer walk out in uniform and the pride of walking about in town, or visiting a public house to swap tories with old soldiers, has gone, as the emphasis is now on laying down the fact that one has military connections.

The Recruit Training content of the programme of the Guards Depot has also undergone many changes and at the end of training, larger emphasis is placed upon a sense of achievement, there now being a Passing Out Parade attended by parents, plus guests. The parade takes the form of a miniature Troop, after which parents then meet the officers, Sergeants and staff, have lunch, followed by a tour of the training complex. The immediate family of the new Guardsman is made to feel part of a large but very caring, Household Division community.

The Sergeants Mess has also undergone many changes and it is a fact that they are often more formal in character now, than are some Officers Messes. Mess Dinner Nights take place with great regularity; gone are the days when to present this kind of occasion cutlery, crockery, candelabra and place settings had to be borrowed from the Officers Mess. Sergeants Messes now own all of this kind of equipment, which is well controlled by a Steward, supported by a first class team of waiters.

This has all been made possible by the forethought, flexibility, dedication, planning and pride of the RSMs of the Household Division, many of whom I have mentioned in this article. In the standards of our Sergeants Messes we are now the envy of many armies of the world.

My military career has now sadly run its full course and I am retired in an appointment as Army Careers Officer-In-Charge at an Army Careers Information Office in South Yorkshire. I am however, grateful that it is a uniformed post and that I will now have the opportunity to counsel and advise young men wishing to follow the noble profession of taking up and bearing arms in the service and support of their Queen and Country.

As AcSM Ray Huggins approached retirement in 1980, he must have been both proud and delighted to have learned that his successor was to be a fellow Grenadier Guardsman, an RSM who was already established at the RMA Sandhurst as RSM of New College. It was all the more sad therefore, when RSM Raymond Osborne Barnes collapsed and died on 23 December 1979, just three months before taking up the ultimate appointment in the British army.

Ray Barnes had joined the Grenadier Guards in January 1952 and went through his training at the Guards Depot under RSM W. L. A. Nash, Grenadier Guards. Within three years he had risen to the rank of Lance Sergeant, but he decided to leave the army to pursue a career in the Stockport Police Force. AcSM Ray Huggins, in a splendid obituary to Ray Barnes, wrote of those days:

Whilst on leave and passing the Stockport Town Hall crossroads, I watched a large crowd gathering to await the arrival of PC Barnes to carry out point duty. This was no ordinary session of police traffic control. Into the centre of the crossroads marched the immaculate figure of a policeman, glittering from his highly polished (Guards Depot type) boots to the top of his gleaming helmet, arms encased in brilliant white (starched, of course) traffic duty sleeves. Need I say, it was a display of traffic control and drill such as only an expert could perform. I am told that people drove miles out of their way to be stopped by PC Barnes.

In his police and detective duties he also excelled. When you tackle three burglars at dead of night and, though injured in the affray, still manage to arrest two of them – yes, Raymond gave as much to the Police Force as he could.

After seven years Ray Barnes rejoined the Grenadier

A shared occasion. Jeffrey (Life Guards) John, Pat, and Mark Holbrook (Parachute Regiment) attend John's investiture, July 1982.   Lt-Col John Holbrook

RSM R. O. Barnes, Grenadier Guards, Depot RSM 1975-8.
Grenadier Guards

RSM W. A. Davis, Irish Guards, Depot RSM 1978-81. Sgt-Maj Bill Davis enlisted in the Irish Guards in April 1957, training at the Depot during the time of RSM L. C. Drouet. During his service of 24 years, he was impressed by numerous Sergeant Majors, but none more than Garrison Sergeant-Majors George Stone, MVO MBE RVM, and Tom Taylor, MVO MBE, whom he states were: 'Gentlemen of the highest order – respected by all'. For a sense of humour, he considers that one could look no further than Tommy Corcoran, who was RSM of the Irish Guards 1974-6, and who retired from the army as a Major. Bill Davis spent over four years as a WO1, firstly in Hong Kong for two years as GSM, having taken over from Alex Dumon, and then at the Guards Depot, taking over from the late Ray Barnes.
Capt W. A. Davis

Right:
RSM W. A. Davis, Irish Guards (centre) with Drill Sgt A. O. Bowen, Welsh Guards (left) who went on to become the Depot RSM 1981-3. Sgt-Maj Tony Bowen was in charge of the Depot when the author was able to visit in 1982, to talk with him, Maj John Holbrook, and RSM B. Veitch, who was at that time in charge of the All Arms Drill Wing. There followed a unique occasion at the Sergeants' Mess, as RSM Bowen had invited a number of serving and former RSMs to lunch, including Maj L. Adams (RTO) Maj L. C. Drouet, Maj QM John Holbrook, Maj Gordon Whitehead, Capt Peter Richardson, Capt Albert Smith, Lt Derek Rossi, RSMs Tony Fox, B. Veitch, and J. Pheasant. It was marvellous to talk with such a distinguished group, whose combined service in the army totalled 298 years! The Drill Sgt on the right of the photograph is W. Fullerton who later became GSM of Hong Kong.   Capt W. A. Davis (PRO HQ, London)

Guards in 1962 as a Lance Corporal, and progressed durin the following years, to become RSM of the Guards Depo from 4 February 1975 to 20 April 1978. Ray Huggins write further:

When he was appointed Sergeant Major of the Guards Depo everyone in the Guards Division applauded the choice. His tour a Pirbright will long be remembered as one of the great highlights c the Depot's history. Raymond was a man of many parts, a man fo all seasons. The appearance of that immaculate figure has struc terror into the heart of many a soldier and officer alike. A Raymond said, 'A little terror never hurt anyone.'

But this big, firm disciplinarian, this exterior of oak, was insid a super softie. Nothing was too much trouble for Raymond to do to help other people; he loved people and life. He was a man c many talents – expert gardener, painter in water colour an military poet. And now, as he has joined those other warriors i Valhalla, I know that the turnout, drill, discipline and humou will, in that final resting place, be as it always was with Raymond of the highest order.

A Memorial Service for RSM Raymond Barnes was hel at the Royal Military Chapel, Sandhurst, on 28 Januar 1980. Ray Barnes would have been one of the very fev Warrant Officers to serve as RSM of the Guards Depot anc AcSM at the RMA Sandhurst. As a tribute to his memory the Warrant Officers and Sergeants of the Sergeants Mes at the Guards Depot, have retained a Raymond Osborn Barnes Room.

I was allowed to visit Sgt-Maj David Gibson in Septembe 1986, in relation to his duties both as RSM of the Depot anc of the Junior Infantry Soldiers and Leaders. I was no surprised to find that he was a former Oswestry man having trained as a Junior Leader in 1962. He impressed a an excellent example of that two and a half year course which produced so many of the present day Warran Officers and Senior NCOs.

During his service, in which he held every NCO rank, including RQMS, David Gibson mentioned having been influenced and guided by many distinguished RSMs, including RSM 'Dusty' Smith, RSM Ted Rose and RSM John Holbrook. He particularly remembered the Queen's Birthday Parade of 1979, which was his first and only Trooping of the Colour, in which he took part as the CSM Right Guide to No 7 Guard. In 1980 he was made Drill Sergeant and worked with RSM R. Watson for a time, before being promoted RQMS in December 1981, which in his view completed a long apprenticeship. In November 1983 he took over from RSM A. O. Bowen as RSM of the Depot.

I was told by David Gibson that he had sought, during his period as RSM of the Depot, to get beyond being seen only on the square in dress uniform with pace stick and made a point of meeting recruits on field and weapon training. Prior to each passing out parade, he also invited recruits to visit and look around the Sergeants Mess, pointing out the paintings of their regimental history. He had, during his tour, obtained many paintings to add to what is an excellent regimental museum.

We talked of the Junior Company, the Parachute Regiment, which resides and trains alongside the Junior Guardsmen at the Depot. I learned that NCOs of the Parachute Regiment were seconded to the Depot in order to train their Juniors, Corporals becoming Lance Sergeants for that time. RSM Gibson was impressed with them and assured me that, 'Some cracking good NCOs are received from the Parachute Regiment!'

Like all previous Depot RSMs, he took very seriously, the customs and traditions of the Household Regiments and advised the recruits – 'If I know the customs of all the regiments, you should know those of your own regiment!' To encourage this he had arranged for orders to be given on certain days by fife and drum, pipes, cavalry trumpet, in addition to the normal bugle calls.

I was very impressed with David Gibson's modernistic attitude and also his determination to retain good sound traditional strengths, such as the practice for double sentry drill and the duties of Stick-man for the best turned out man on guardmounting. As fellow railway enthusiasts, we also talked about the *Flying Scotsman*. RSM David Gibson was commissioned within the regiment two months after our conversation.

Sgt-Maj L. Winter enlisted in the Coldstream Guards in November 1966 and trained at the Depot under RSM D. Nicholson. He adds:

RSM Nicholson always seemed to be a kindly man – with a powerful voice. I vividly remember him speaking with my parents on the day of my passing out parade, and they commented upon his obviously deep interest in the recruits and I think this was very genuine. I never came across him again, but I will always remember him.

Alex Dumon was one of my first CSMs and he went on to become one of the great GSMs of London District. He was a superb drill man and I felt the lash of Alex's tongue a few times in my career from being a Guardsman to when I was a Drill Sergeant. He had a quaint way of telling lesser mortals their shortcomings. When I was appointed RSM I found him to be a pillar of strength and a fountain of knowledge.

My Squad Instructor was Lance Sergeant C. Pratt, Coldstream Guards, who is now a Captain QM and my Platoon Sergeant was D. Rossi, Grenadier Guards, who has just retired as Captain QM, so one could say that I was instructed by the best of the best. I do not believe that I was influenced by any single RSM, but have assimilated much from several. These were Alex Dumon, Ray Barnes, John Holbrook and Tom Taylor. All had the ability to reveal both sides of the coin; the strict, no nonsense, with the approachable human side. Above all they were their own men, the philosophy being to do it, do it quick, to ponder is to bring unnecessary pressure upon the soldier.

When I became Drill Sergeant, the outgoing D-Sgt left me a pencil, a rubber, a copy of *Household Division Standing Orders, Her Majesty's Regulations for the Household Division* and two aspirins. I still have the aspirins, and a fair amount of the two publications in my head.

I was made Drill Sergeant of the 1st Bn Coldstream Guards on 14 May 1984. I think that the most memorable parades are Presentation of Colours Parades, maybe because they are family parades, but I had the good fortune to help to organise, to some degree, the last one in 1985. I carried the unconsecrated Queen's Colour to Horse Guards, and felt privileged to do so. To uncase a flag – and within minutes see it become the Queen's Colour – is a very moving experience, especially when one thinks of the history and tradition that surrounds the Colours that represents the heart of any regiment.

I have been a Coldstreamer for 22 years and have thoroughly enjoyed my service and would do it all again. People may change – but the regiment will live for ever.

On 20 May 1988, I attended a Passing Out Parade of recruits at the Guards Depot to talk to, and photograph Sgt-Maj Winter. This was a very busy day to talk to him as he wished to meet as many of the relatives of those recruits passing out as he could. I was able to talk with Sgt Ian Buckwell, Steward of one of the busiest and well attended Sergeants Mess' in the British army. He has a wealth of experience in arranging the many functions and explained to me that it is usual for recruits to assist as there is always a shortage of staff on special occasions. This is good for the recruits as they observe what goes on in the Sergeants Mess and also see their own Instructors in a different setting.

Whoever holds the appointment of RSM of the Guards Depot, will be handling the training of a recruit who will in 20 years hence, himself be RSM of the Depot. It has always been so, and it is difficult to envisage anyone holding the appointment who has not completed his own training at the Guards Depot.

Regimental Sergeant Majors of the Guards Depot

RSM H. Darrell	C. Gds	1. 7.1881 – 30. 8.1881
RSM S. White	C. Gds	31. 8.1881 – 30. 6.1883
RSM E. Dickerson	C. Gds	1. 7.1883 – 1. 4.1885
RSM J. Jones	G. Gds	19. 8.1885 – 27.11.1887
RSM H. Martin	C. Gds	23. 1.1888 – 17. 3.1891

RSM A. Telfer	S. Gds	18. 3.1891 – 12. 5.1891
RSM J. Sparkes	C. Gds	13. 5.1891 – 31. 1.1893
RSM W. Stewart	S. Gds	1. 2.1893 – 9. 5.1896
RSM W. J. Cock	G. Gds	30. 3.1897 – 30. 4.1897
RSM G. Gooding	C. Gds	1. 5.1897 – 30.11.1897
RSM J. C. Mant	S. Gds	1.12.1897 – 1.12.1899
RSM J. Skidmore	G. Gds	11. 9.1900 – 26. 2.1901
RSM J. Boyd	C. Gds	27. 2.1901 – 3. 9.1902
RSM J. Mitchell	S. Gds	3.12.1902 – 28. 2.1903
RSM C. A. Baylis	I. Gds	1. 3.1903 – 3. 1.1905
RSM J. Teece	G. Gds	14. 1.1905 – 12.12.1909
RSM F. J. Caunell	C. Gds	13.12.1909 – 1. 4.1911
RSM J. Tate	S. Gds	2. 4.1911 – 3. 5.1913
RSM J. Kirk	I. Gds	4. 5.1913 – 17.12.1913
RSM H. Wood	G. Gds	18.12.1913 – 13. 8.1915
RSM E. Ellis	C. Gds	14. 8.1915 – 28. 4.1916
RSM J. Barwick MC	S. Gds	29. 4.1916 – 3. 7.1919
RSM A. E. Pettit MC	S. Gds	4. 7.1919 – 31.12.1920
RSM C. Harradine DCM	I. Gds	5. 1.1921 – 24. 4.1922
RSM W. E. Hawkins	G. Gds	19. 5.1922 – 15.10.1925
RSM F. Gill	C. Gds	16.10.1925 – 14. 4.1930

This period was significant for an outbreak of diptheria at the Depot in 1927, which caused a temporary evacuation of the Caterham Barracks.

RSM W. A. Blakeley	S. Gds	1. 7.1930 – 2. 7.1931
RSM J. D. Hughes	W. Gds	3. 7.1931 – 1. 2.1934
RSM G. F. G. Turner	G. Gds	2. 2.1934 – 15.11.1934
RSM R. Brittain	C. Gds	23.12.1934 – 8.10.1935
RSM A. J. Brand	G. Gds	19.10.1935 – 31. 8.1936
RSM M. Jones	C. Gds	1. 9.1936 – 5. 2.1937
RSM W. J. Dorman	S. Gds	6. 2.1937 – 15. 5.1939
RSM J. Hastings	I. Gds	16. 5.1939 – 17. 5.1939
RSM H. McKinney	I. Gds	18. 5.1939 – 6. 7.1940
RSM J. A. Stack MC	I. Gds	7. 7.1940 – 30. 9.1940
RSM P. Dunne	W. Gds	1.10.1940 – 13. 7.1944
RSM D. Hobbs MBE	G. Gds	20. 7.1944 – 12. 8.1945
RSM S. M. Hamilton MBE	S. Gds	13. 8.1945 – 12. 8.1946
RSM W. Rooney MM	I. Gds	13. 8.1946 – 15.12.1949

RSM B. E. Hillier DCM	W. Gds	16.12.1949 – 10. 9.195
RSM W. L. A. Nash	G. Gds	11. 9.1951 – 23. 3.195
RSM R. J. S. Tyacke	C. Gds	24. 3.1953 – 7.10.195
RSM D. Whyte	S. Gds	8.10.1953 – 4. 4.195
RSM L. C. Drouet	G. Gds	5. 4.1956 – 30. 5.195
RSM F. Clutton MM	G. Gds	31. 5.1957 – 6. 3.195
RSM W. Rodger	S. Gds	7. 3.1958 – 3.10.196
RSM P. O'Brien	I. Gds	3.10.1960 – 21.11.196
RSM T. Pugh	G. Gds	22.11.1961 – 25. 7.196
RSM E. J. R. Rose	C. Gds	26. 7.1964 – 6. 4.196
RSM D. Nicholson	W. Gds	7. 4.1966 – 28. 2.196
RSM J. Grindley	C. Gds	3.10.1967 – 2.11.196

Shortly before RSM Grindley completed his tour at the Depot, th establishment moved from Caterham to the newly built Alexandr Barracks at Pirbright, which was officially opened by Counte Alexander of Tunis, on 25 September 1969.

RSM W. J. Holbrook	C. Gds	3.11.1969 – 4.11.197
RSM A. Dumon	C. Gds	5.11.1972 – 3. 2.197
RSM R. O. Barnes	G. Gds	4. 2.1975 – 20. 4.197
RSM W. A. Davis	I. Gds	21. 4.1978 – 21. 1.198
RSM A. O. Bowen	W. Gds	22. 1.1981 – 13.11.198
RSM D. Gibson	C. Gds	14.11.1983 – 7.11.198
RSM L. Winter	C. Gds	8.11.1986 – 3.11.198
RSM R. A. D. Phasey	G. Gds	4.11.1988 –

At the time of publication the RSM of the Guards Depot is R. A. D. Phasey, BEM, Grenadier Guards (3rd from left). Sgt-Maj Phasey enlisted in the Grenadier Guards in 1968, going through training at the Depot under RSMs J. Grindley and W. J. Holbrook. He has also been influenced during service by RSM Ray Barnes and, when serving as Drill Sgt in Germany, by RSM Michael Nesbitt. Prior to becoming the Depot RSM on 4 Nov 1988, he served as RSM of the Multi-Nationality Peace Keeping Force, and this included contingents from eleven nations. CSM J. Rankin, Scots Guards, Drill Sgt M. Burns, Irish Guards, and Sgt C. Noble, Irish Guards, complete the group on parade, April 1989. Jim Farrar

CHAPTER 19

RSM W. G. Clarke, King's Troop, RHA and RSM P. Westrope, RA
RSMs of the Honourable Artillery Company

As in most regiments of the British Army, the senior NCO of the Royal Regiment of Artillery was long known as the Sergeant Major until the First World War, when the Warrant Officer (Class One and Two) was established. Brig (Rtd) R. J. Lewendon, Historical Secretary of the Royal Artillery Institution, advised me in 1984:

In contemporary accounts of the Boer War, I have seen both the Brigade Sergeant Major and the Battery Sergeant Major, abbreviated to BSM, which must have confused matters, but later the Brigade SM became WOI and the Battery SM a WOII.

The First World War also saw the adoption of the title Regimental Sergeant Major instead of Brigade Sergeant Major. It was not until 1938 that Artillery Brigades were retitled Artillery Regiments and the title RSM vis-a-vis BSM has some rationale.

As regards Royal Artillery Depots, there were many in the 19th Century, but in the 20th Century the Depot was at Woolwich, except during the two World Wars, when again there were several. One has to appreciate the size of the Royal Artillery in the wars, for example 850,000 plus in August 1945, and larger than the Royal Navy at the time!

When at the kind suggestion of Brig Lewendon, I wrote to two former RSMs regarding memories of their service, Capt W. G. Clarke RA replied to me mentioning an earlier serving RSM named Arthur Leonard Clarke MBE DCM (not related) whose photograph was hanging on the wall of the Sergeants Mess of the 4th Field Regiment RA. With the help of Capt W. G. Clarke and Brig R. J. Lewendon, it was possible to obtain the following service details of a gallant wartime RSM of the 1st Regiment, Royal Horse Artillery.

Arthur Leonard Clarke came from Guildford and enlisted in the Royal Artillery on 19 February 1925, being posted after training to the 1st Regiment RHA in May 1925. He served in Egypt from 1931, then returning home went with the BEF to France in October 1939. He came back through the Dunkirk evacuation, and for a brief period was placed in the Lancashire Fusiliers before rejoining the 1st RHA in June 1940. There are no details of his promotions, but he was sent back to the Middle East in September 1940, and fought at Tobruk where his guns were so effective that they were known as 'Clarke's guns'.

Sadly, the records of the 1st Regt RHA reveal:

On 25 October 1942, RSM A. L. Clarke MBE DCM, was killed by a sniper during the day. He had been with the Adjutant, Capt A. Chichester, arranging for the collection of two of B Battery's 25 pounders which had been knocked out on the Miteriya Ridge on the first morning. The death of this Warrant Officer who had served in the regiment for such a long time was a very great loss.

RSM A. L. Clarke, MBE DCM, Royal Horse Artillery, 1942.
RSM 1st RHA

The second former RSM suggested by Brig Lewendon was Maj (Retd) Peter Westrope of the Ministry of Defence, and when I contacted him he replied with the following details of his earlier career:

I joined the Army in September 1944, going initially to the No. 5 Primary Training Centre at Winston Barracks, Lanark, Scotland, for eight weeks basic infantry training. This was in the General Service Corps, where the permanent staff were mainly infantrymen drawn from the Scottish regiments. I cannot remember the RSM there and do not even know what his regiment was, for when one was a recruit one was in dread of ever meeting the RSM. The only time that I did see him was on the Saturday Drill Parade, when my one hope was that I would not let the platoon down or be awarded an extra drill.

I later came to know RSM D. J. Ward MBE MM who was well known in the Royal Artillery, having served under many COs. A small dapper man with a strong personality and hard discipline, he

RSM P. Westrope, MBE, Royal Artillery.   Peter Westrope

served in the desert campaign during the war and was awarded his Military Medal for saving the lives of soldiers in a burning truck – his body bore the scars for the rest of his life. RSM Ward served in the 45th Field Regiment RA taking part in the Korean campaign where he was awarded the MBE. He subsequently worked in army recruiting in Whitehall before becoming a GSM, firstly at Blackdown, then finally at Dusseldorf.

During my own career I served two tours as RSM; the first as RSM of the 12th Light Ack Ack Regiment RA from March 1963, when I joined the unit at Delmonhorst, Germany. A farewell parade was about to be held as the unit was to be the last British unit to be stationed there, and I had only a short time in which to organise the parade. It was to be a foot parade with no weapons, but the officers were to carry swords, so I worked with them before breakfast on sword drill, and then held battery drill and finally regimental rehearsals. All of the practice was within the confines of the barracks, but one final rehearsal was held in the town. The actual parade results were good.

The regiment went on active service to Malaya, Singapore, and Borneo, and was equipped with the L40-70 Bofor Gun, radar fire control equipment and generators. The only training in which I was involved during my tour with the 12th Regiment was the junior NCOs cadre courses and adventure training. I worked as Safety Officer at practice camps where I made it my job to know all of the equipment in use by the regiment and how it was operated.

I was also very involved in all activities of the regiment, sports, social and welfare – particularly important during the period in which the unit was on active service. Two batteries were deployed with part of RHQ at Tampin, and there were 250 families to be cared for. With one battery at Singapore and another at Kuching,

the state of operational readiness had to be at a high standard.

During the sixties the gunner regiments did not get too involved with parade drill as the main training was in gun drill and fir control. Regimental parades might be held only once or twice each year, for Administration Parade and Remembrance Day and when these parades were due there were concentrated periods of practice.

As an RSM, my tasks were many and one of prime importance was concerned with the maintaining of morale of the families. A Tampin we were the only unit and were self contained, so that self help was the order of the day. My own private venture and contribution was in relation to cine newsreels, and as a keen cine cameraman I would take films of the activities of the families develop and edit the films and on my trips to the deployed batteries would show them to the husbands. On the same trip would film the men on the gun sites at work and at play, and on return to Tampin show the results to the families.

My tour of duty with 12th Regiment ended in March 1966, and although the regiment had been widely deployed for some of the time, I found it a very interesting tour of duty. My second tour was as RSM to the Junior Leaders Regiment RA, where I had earlier served as Battery Sergeant Major. The training of the junior leaders was divided into education, military, adventure, sports and extra mural activities, and for both junior leaders and permanent staff it was a full day. This tour from 1966-9 was the most interesting and enjoyable period of my Army service, as there was always a challenge and a belated satisfaction.

I was very involved and had plenty of contact with all concerned. My main task was maintaining discipline and taking foot and arms drill parades and competitions. There were three terms to the year, and the climax of each term was the Goschen Parade, which was also the passing out of the Mustering Gunners – junior leaders who had completed their training – and whom were to be posted to adult regiments of the Royal Artillery Training for these parades took place throughout the term by means of troop drill, and culminating in the end of term drill competitions, and weekly RSM's drill parades.

The Goschen Parade was a grand spectacle to watch, a full parade with all movements based upon the Sandhurst style Mustering Gunners carried small arms whilst the remainder of the parade did not, and the parade was unique in that it was conducted by the junior RSM, who was himself a junior leader. I was wholly commanded by the juniors, whose parents were included in the crowds of people watching. The climax of the parade was the March Off of the Mustering Gunners in slow time to the music of *Auld Lang Syne*, and as they disappeared behind a wall, the throwing of their hats into the air!

Of course drill and discipline were not the only feature of the RSM's job. It was necessary to have an interest in everything that was going on, to be seen, to be approachable and to set a good standard. It was important to know what was going on and to have a feel for the regiment, and of course to keep the CO fully in the picture.

I was interested in sport and was a qualified judge and referee, and also assisted with adventure training in the Lake District. I was fortunate in having a very loyal Regimental Provost Sergeant, who helped me to keep a finger on the pulse of the regiment. I ended my tour of the Junior Leaders Regiment RA, on being commissioned to Quartermaster, and was very happy to be awarded the MBE in the New Year's Honours List in 1969. A very satisfying end to my appointments as Regimental Sergeant Major.

It has been particularly pleasing to meet former junior leaders in the succeeding years, and to see their progress through the ranks and on commissioning.

The prominent features of London's ceremonial centre around the Trooping of the Colour, Changing of the

Guard, the firing of salutes by the King's Troop, Royal Horse Artillery and the Queen's Life Guard in Whitehall. Capt W. G. Clarke RA served with the King's Troop RHA through the ranks from Trumpeter to RSM, and he describes the years of training and preparation behind the glittering ceremonial of London.

The King's Troop, Royal Horse Artillery, is the saluting battery of the Queen's Household Troops, and as such takes its place in the order of precedence of batteries and formations of the Royal Regiment of Artillery, from the 'Riding House Department of His Majesty's Ordnance' which was formed in 1803. The troop crest today is the original crest of that establishment.

During the 19th century the name of this establishment varied between Riding Horse Troop, RA, and Riding Troop, RHA, and it was finally disbanded as the Riding Troop, RHA, at Woolwich in 1939 on the outbreak of World War Two. During its existence its prime task had been as a training establishment, teaching gentlemen cadets from the RMA Woolwich, and the boys from the Boys Battery, to ride. It also supplied horses for general officers to use on large parades and for the use of escorts.

Until 1939 successive RHA Batteries had been stationed at St John's Wood for periods of up to three years, as the saluting battery of the Household Troops. This practise had been in effect since 1880 when the first Battery, A Battery of A Brigade (which is now A Battery, The Chestnut Troop) moved into the barracks. The last battery was K Battery RHA, which was mobilized at St John's Wood in 1939.

After the war, King George VI expressed the wish that he could again see a horse artillery battery dressed and equipped in the traditional manner, taking part in the ceremonies of State. This was no easy task as after six years of war all RHA Batteries were mechanised and horses and 13 pounders were not easily obtainable. After much work and preparation however, the first salute was fired in full dress by the Riding Troop RHA for the King's birthday on 13 June 1946.

On 24 October 1947, the King visited the troop at St John's Wood Barracks, and asked during a pre-lunch drink if the troop would like to be called 'The King's Battery'? The Superintendent at this time, Maj J. A. Norman, asked if it could be 'The King's Troop' to which His Majesty agreed with the words 'All right, so long as it's mine I don't mind what you call it!'

The King's Troop has been at St John's Wood ever since. On the death of King George VI, HM The Queen decreed that to mark her father's special interest in the troop, it should continue to be known during her reign as the King's Troop. The Queen visited the troop on two occasions, once in 1962, and again in 1972 following the rebuilding of the barracks.

St John's Wood Barracks has a fascinating history, being used first of all, when still St John's Wood Farm, by the Corps of Gunner Drivers in 1802. After the cavalry riding establishment, the Foot Guards, and the 1st Life Guards, the barracks came back to the Gunners in 1880. It is now one of the oldest establishments in the Royal Regiment of Artillery. The strength of the King's Troop RHA is 187 officers and men. (Seven officers, including one RAVC Veterinary Surgeon. Approximately 21 senior NCOs, and 159 junior NCOs and men.)

The troop is equipped with the QF 13 pounder MK1 Gun, as used during the First World War and in service with the RHA Horse Batteries until 1939. This was the last gun designed specifically for the Royal Horse Artillery. The Troop has ten 13 pounders, all of which were fired in anger during the First World War. The full dress worn by the troop today was the last one to be designed for the Royal Horse Artillery in 1914, and apart from changes to the body lines which now hang on the right breast instead of the left, and the introduction of the Butcher Boot in

1964, to replace the Jack Boot, the uniform is otherwise the same. The braiding on the uniform is of various materials according to rank, and most of the busbys in the present day are made from synthetic material.

I joined the Junior Leaders Regiment, Royal Artillery, at Bramcote in Warwickshire, on 2 January 1961. Part of the new regular army – known as 'soldiers of the sixties'! The regiment had only recently moved from Hereford to Gamecock Barracks in Bramcote, and this was an ex Fleet Air Arm airfield (*HMS Gamecock*). Rather stark and typical of the period, as although it had been brick built in the 1930s, no modernisation had taken place. The Boys Regiment at this time was only about 350 strong, but discipline was hard and at times harsh! Standards were very high, and we had a most distinguished CO in Lt-Col P. A. Porteous VC RA, who was awarded his Victoria Cross following the Dieppe operation in 1942. The most notable RSM during this period was WO1 RSM Taylor, who was later to become Lt-Col (QM) with the 1st RHA.

The Boys Regiment was still wearing the old high collar service dress c1944, and one custom of the RA Boys was to press an inverted crease down the centre of the back of the jacket from nape of neck to tail! Very impressive. Most of my memories of Boys service are happy ones, although it was hard work and we were kept very busy.

I qualified from the regiment in August 1962 as a Battery Surveyor, and went with the rest of my squad to the 6th Field Regiment RA at Larkhill, which at that time was responsible for Fox Troop – the Boys continuation training troop. Fox Troop was separate from the regiment in its own accommodation, and was run by an officer, a WO2, and SNCOs of the regiment. Our officer at that time was Capt The Hon V. Brooke RA. Son of Field Marshal The Viscount Alanbrooke.

When Gunners, Signallers and Battery Surveyors had re-qualified, we were posted to batteries of the regiment to carry out training with them on range days, and I went to V Battery RA. Our general training still continued however, and every Saturday morning was given over to company drill in preparation for our passing out parade in December. In the late November there was the buzz of excitement in the troop, when posting orders were published. I had been a trumpeter in the boys band, and had also been pressed into being the Quarterguard Trumpeter for the 6th Field Regiment whilst with Fox Troop, so it was no surprise to me to find my name on the posting list to the King's Troop, Royal Horse Artillery. How I envied those going off to Malaya, Hong Kong, Cyprus, Singapore, Kenya and all the other exotic places still left in our empire.

I arrived at St John's Wood Barracks on 2 January 1963, during one of the worst winters this century, as a bright new Trumpeter, albeit a highly qualified Battery Surveyor as well, to begin my mans service. On arrival at the King's Troop I was posted to D Sub-Section and was of course employed primarily as a Trumpeter. There was a troop establishment for 12 Trumpeters, all of whom normally came from the Junior Leaders Regiment, RA, and this tradition went back many years, indeed, all boy soldiers recruited into the RA before the war were initially trained and posted to their regiments as Trumpeters.

All Trumpeters carry out the duties of Orderly Trumpeter in barracks, or wherever the troop is camped. These duties last for 24 hours, and there are some 31 set daily trumpet calls to be sounded, plus a number of field calls when required. I attended my recruits ride in February, and was fortunate enough to have as my instructor Sgt Ben Jones, who later was to represent Britain at the Olympics in the three day event team, winning a team gold medal at Mexico in 1968. He was a superb instructor and one could not fail to learn a great deal from him.

At this time the King's Troop and the Household Cavalry

Regiment were still wearing old service dress and knee puttees with ammo boots and learning how best to put on the puttees was a test in itself! Dressing ourselves for guard and piquet mounting was a real art, especially as best puttees were twice the length of second best. This uniform and the puttees were finally dispensed with at the end of 1963, with the issue of Number Two dress and the Butcher boots. There are still many old tales of men being dressed for guard mounting by the Sub-Section, and then being wheeled down to the Guard Room on a barrow, all this in the hope of being selected as stickman.

FM Viscount Lord Alanbrooke died in 1963, and his funeral took place at Windsor. Having been a Gunner Field Marshal, the King's Troop was heavily involved, with gun carriage, gun salutes and Trumpeters, and I had the honour of being one of the eight Trumpeters to sound the last post and reveille at his service in St George's Chapel, Windsor.

Our RSM at this time was WO1 RSM G. F. Stirling, the very epitome of the RSM with large black moustache. He had joined the army as a boy Trumpeter before the war, and had served with the airborne forces during the war. He then served with the King's Troop as a Bdr and Sgt No. 1 before returning later as BSM, and then after a further year, as RSM. He was an excellent RSM and was made MBE at the end of his tour. A great influence upon young soldiers, and I learned a lot from him.

At the end of my first year in early 1964, in order to further my career, I changed my job from Trumpeter to normal Linesman and became a member of the Gun Detachment. I completed my detachment ride, and the fact that I had been able to ride fairly well prior to joining was a help to me when later in the year I was trained as a centre driver for the gun team. 1964 also saw the King's Troop perform the first musical drive abroad in its history, when we flew to Copenhagen to perform at a tattoo in aid of the British Trade Week, and fired to accompany a performance of the 1812 Overture.

In 1965 I moved to become the centre driver of D Sub Section, all novice drivers starting in this position. We had a sad start to the year when Sir Winston Churchill died in January, and the troop was required to fire the bulk of the minute guns for the state funeral. We came into action at the walk in St James's Park, just opposite Wellington Barracks, and were in cloak order, which can make things a little difficult for the gun detachments on mounting and dismounting. Funeral minute guns fire one round each minute for every year of the deceased's life, and in this instance the King's Troop fired the first 60 rounds, and the Honourable Artillery Company fired the remaining 30 rounds from the Tower.

This year also saw an outbreak of equine flu during the spring, which meant that we could not perform the musical drive until late June, and although all of the salutes were still carried out, these were only at the walk. This was an idyllic period for us as the horses could not be ridden properly so we were walking them to Regents Park. Each man would lead two horses to graze on the lush green grass of spring, all in the bright May sunshine and it really was super from our point of view. Once the horses had recovered however all of the shows started in earnest again, and we went abroad again, this time to Milan, for another British Trade Week.

RSM Stirling departed at about this time and RSM Hough came to the troop. He was also a very good man having been a pre-war boy soldier, and had served with the troop before as Bdr, Sgt and RQMS. During the last war, in the Western desert and after the decimation of his own unit, he volunteered for the SAS, where he remained until the end of the war. RSM Hough took me on my JNCOs Cadre, and was a very fair and firm RSM who had a very good style – a most important ingredient. Unfortunately, RSM Hough suffered a heart attack after only six months in post and his death was a very great loss to everyone.

There was difficulty over a replacement and as an interim measure RSM Stirling was brought back. This was in the summer of 1966, and I was by this time a LBdr wheel driver. I will never forget the day that RSM Stirling returned. We were at the Aldershot Tattoo and formed up in full dress ready for inspection before going into the arena, when out from a tent on the other side of our camp strode this large figure – with an even larger moustache! Immediately the whisper went through our ranks – 'Christ . . . Jerry is back!!' He had an electrifying effect upon the whole parade, such was his bearing and presence. RSM Stirling remained with the troop for almost six months until RSM W. Pearson arrived.

A notable thing for me in 1966 was my season as wheel driver of a gun team. The wheel driver is the man positioned closest to the limber, and he is responsible for the brakes. There are no brakes actually as it is the action of the wheel horses sitting in the breeching that in fact slows the team down. Naturally this is a very important job, and dire consequences can arise if one gets things wrong. One of the most common things to get wrong as the wheel driver – certainly during the musical drive – is to allow the gun and limber to be dragged around a corner at speed, instead of the team coming around in a nice half moon effect from lead horses to gun. The usual result of this happening is for the gun to hit a rut and turn over . . . which obviously stops everything! Sometimes the driver and one or other of the horses is hurt, but rarely very seriously.

It was a mistake such as this that sticks in my mind. We were performing at Acton West on a lovely summer afternoon, and the drive was going well until my team came around the top corner to start the scissor movement. We were travelling at great speed and I just could not get the wheelers to keep up and bring the gun round myself. Almost immediately as we started to come out of the corner I heard a great Ooooh! from the spectators as my gun hit a rut, went straight up into the air, turned turtle with the limber, and with a thundering crash came back to earth again. We came to a shuddering halt but fortunately neither horse went down or was hurt, and I escaped with nothing more than damaged pride!

The arrival of RSM Pearson was in fact quite a break from the tradition of the King's Troop. Prior to his arrival all previous RSMs and BSMs had either served with a pre-war horsed Artillery Battery, or had served with the troop as a senior NCO. Unfortunately, with the sad death of RSM Hough, there was no-one available with immediate horse experience. RSM Pearson was an RHA through and through however, having been BSM of A Battery, The Chestnut Troop, and RSM of the Honourable Artillery Company, so he was well qualified and experienced in the ways and standards of the Royal Horse Artillery.

He helped me a great deal by educating me during annual JNCOs courses, and by constantly guiding and advising me. He was an excellent man manager and had the strongest influence of any RSM upon me. Unfortunately RSM Pearson was prevented by illness from going further than RSM, but with six years subsequent service, he remains the longest serving RSM ever to remain with the King's Troop. I should mention that in my first year serving with him, I was not in his good books at all, being rather too cocky as a young LBdr and tending to try and burn the candle at both ends. Once the error of my ways had been made clear to me by him however, I never looked back.

1967 found me as the Lead driver of D Sub Section, and then in 1968 I became Battery Leader for the musical drive, responsible for the pace and movement of the drive, for me the ultimate position. The troop travelled abroad again in 1967, this time to Montreal for EXPO 67, which was a truly marvellous tour lasting for most of us for just over one month. I had earlier been selected to attend the Army Equitation Instructors Course at Melton Mowbray, and on return from Canada, went straight to begin the six month course.

Once again I was lucky so far as the Chief Instructor was

concerned, as Maj Tommy Thompson MBE DCM of the Life Guards was from the old school. He had been a Corporal at Weedon in 1936, which was then the Army School of Equitation, and had gained his DCM during the Second World War. Prior to taking the position as Chief Instructor, he had held the post of Riding Master of the Household Cavalry Regiment in London for many years. One of his favourite sayings was the term 'Line Cavalry!' which we would use frequently to describe someone's standard of riding. Such rivalry between the Household Cavalry and the Cavalry Regiments of the Line has been quite common for a great number of years, and I should add that as members of the Royal Horse Artillery we also came in for quite an amount of flak. Tommy Thompson retired in 1968 and went on to work at the Royal Mews at Windsor.

My career from 1968 continued in much the same way, and I became in turn Lead driver of B and then A Sub Sections, collecting another stripe on the way. In 1971 I was promoted as Sergeant, and posted back to where I had started as trumpeter, but this time as No. 1 of D Sub Section. I remained there until September 1973, and was fortunate in what was virtually my last three weeks duty with the troop, to be one of the first three Sergeant Guard Commanders to go on the Queen's Life Guard at Horse Guards. My Guard was in fact the last on duty that year as the King's Troop for the first time in its history relieved the Household Cavalry Regiment to perform this most public of ceremonial Guard duties. On completion I handed over to a Guard from the Blues and Royals.

Returning with my Guard to St John's Wood Barracks, I handed over my Sub Section that afternoon, and left for Larkhill, where I was to spend a few months on conversion training, before joining the 1st Regiment, Royal Horse Artillery, in Detmold BAOR. So ended over ten years of very happy and rewarding service with the King's Troop.

January 1981 found me as Battery Sergeant Major with my B Battery RHA preparing and training for a six month emergency tour in Belize, Central America. At this time I was informed that I had passed the WO1 (RSM) Board, and that I would depart in due course to take up an appointment as Regimental Sergeant Major. Two months later all 11 successful WOs were informed of their appointments, and I learned that I had been selected as the next RSM of the King's Troop, Royal Horse Artillery.

I went with B Battery to Belize in April, but departed in June 1981 to take up my new appointment. What a contrast! The jungle and heat of Belize on 2 June and the hustle and bustle of London on the 3rd! My takeover period lasted for one week, and by 14 June I was firmly established as RSM of the troop, and now came my chance to put into practice all I had learned from earlier RSMs, and from my previous experience.

The duties of BSM and RSM are similar albeit on different scales of responsibilities. The Battery Sergeant Major is limited to the discipline and smooth running of his Battery, and he organises the Battery Office and clerks. He also guides and advises junior officers in the Battery, and of course the senior and junior NCOs. Operationally he is also responsible for the supply of ammunition, and the defence of the wagon lines under the command of the Battery Captain.

The RSM is responsible to the CO for the tone and conduct of the Sergeants Mess, which is important in any unit. With the aid of the BSMs he maintains discipline throughout the regiment, and enforces the regulations and standards of dress, turnout bearing and general conduct. He is the COs right hand man in these subjects, and in the planning of the WOs and SNCOs careers. He must know all of his NCOs well, and be able to advise the CO and the Battery Commanders of the NCOs progress.

I have always believed and lived by the motto 'by example we lead' and feel it to be extremely important that WOs and SNCOs possess integrity and belief in their regiment. I have always preached this when instructing young soldiers on cadre and promotion courses, indeed, I have pushed it at every opportunity on parade and at mess meetings, as I feel that such an education of soldiers and NCOs is an ongoing thing.

During my tour as RSM the troop again went abroad to the Berlin Tattoo, and then to Atlantic City USA in 1982, where our display was a great success. I was sent as RSM on a three week exchange visit to the US Field Artillery Centre, Fort Sill, Oklahoma. They have a gun team and horses for outriders there, and the unit is managed by a Sergeant First Class, the equivalent I believe of our Staff Sergeant. This was a tremendous experience, their Half Section as it is called, being dressed in World War One uniforms, and being equipped with French 75mm guns. In due course the Sergeant First Class came to visit the King's Troop for three weeks in London.

For three consecutive years during autumn, I trained the Guards from my unit for the duties of Queen's Life Guard, and I must admit that this was when I found some of my favourite drill movements, both mounted and dismounted. Basic cavalry drills have always been carried out by the Royal Horse Artillery to a certain extent, but we vary most when carrying out battery drill movements with the gun teams. One of my favourite drill movements is sword drill when mounted, especially the 'draw swords' which is an impressive sight whether carried out by a single soldier or by a body of men.

I have always enjoyed taking part in and instructing in gun drill, as this is a good lively activity which sharpens up the gun detachments, and is particularly enjoyable when carried out with towed equipment such as the 13 or 25 pounder guns. I remember one rehearsal at Chelsea Barracks for the Cenotaph Parade on Remembrance Sunday when things were not going too well, as the Household Cavalry Regiment was having a small problem with the pace. GSM Alex Dumon halted the parade halfway through the march on, and turning to the Household Cavalry Regiment said, 'The King's Troop here – can be excused for not marching properly, as they were not trained at the Guards Depot Pirbright . . . but you people have no excuse, *so get a grip of yourselves!!*' Quite a double edged comment I thought.

My tour of duty as RSM of the King's Troop came to an end in 1984, and I had enjoyed it all immensely. I was the first since the war to have risen through the ranks from Trumpeter to Lead Driver, to Equitation Instructor, and to return as RSM. Others have of course been Trumpeters and have gone on to become RSMs in other units, but it is with some pride that I was first to go through the full house and return as RSM.

I handed over my appointment to WO1 (RSM) G. P. Bailey on 15 February 1984 upon being commissioned. I have since held the appointments of Battery Captain with a Field Battery RA, and then became Quartermaster at the end of 1985. This was a very different life from anything I had known in the past, but it had its lighter moments. I became the Technical Quartermaster of the 3rd Regiment, Royal Horse Artillery, in 1988, and this marked my 28th year since joining the Junior Leaders Regiment as a boy.

The Honourable Artillery Company also fulfils a major ceremonial role within the City of London, and their RSMs have long been found from the Foot Guards. Capt David D. Horn, Grenadier Guards, MISM of the Guards Museum, writes of the period during which he served as RSM of the Company:

The position of RSM in a territorial regiment tends to require a Warrant Officer with great flexibility. This must be so because in most regiments although drill now takes a much lower profile, there are still numerous guards and parades and other events which require some form of ceremonial. In addition there are the normal duties associated with the RSM which are often made more difficult by having companies of the regiment in several locations. Much of the organisation of training also falls within the compass of this Warrant Officer as so many units have such a small regular staff.

Nowhere is this combination more evident than in the Honourable Artillery Company, formed by Royal Charter during the reign of Henry VIII in 1537. This ancient regiment not only has an operational role within the Royal Regiment of Artillery, but also forms a major part of the City of London's ceremonial. The regiment is made up of gentlemen who in the main have their occupations within the square mile of The City, and who on various evenings in the week and at weekends exchange their bowler hats and umbrellas for Number One Dress or combat suits. It is organised into three Sabre Squadrons and a Headquarter Squadron, and has in addition a Gun Troop armed with 25 pounder guns, whose members carry on the customs and traditions of the Royal Horse Artillery. It also has a Band and Corps of Drums who often parade dressed in tunics and bearskins similar to those of the Grenadier Guards, except that any lace is of silver and not gold.

It is the responsibility of the RSM HAC to supervise and co-ordinate the individual drills of all these sub-units. Large guards of honour are found when required at St Paul's Cathedral, on great state occasions, and at Guildhall or Mansion House for visiting Heads of State and distinguished visitors. A saluting battery from the regiment fires traditional gun salutes at HM Tower of London on royal anniversaries and state occasions. These tasks are not made easier by the limited time available for rehearsal and often the unavoidable absence of many members from practices.

There are also within the HAC several other military sub-units which parade on occasions either separately, or with the regiment. The Company of Pikemen and Musketeers, who are dressed and drill as they did in the seventeenth century, and a troop of Light Cavalry who parade, both mounted and dismounted, dressed in Victorian uniforms. These two units whilst not directly the RSM's responsibility, often seek and are guided by his knowledge and experience in matters ceremonial. Another city responsibility of the RSM is the role of a Military Marshal for the Lord Mayor's Show, which with its many military detachments is one of the worlds largest unrehearsed pageants and requires perfect timing.

The post of Sergeant Major has been for many years filled by an RSM from the Foot Guards, and has since 1973 been a tied post for the Grenadier Guards. It could be said that the position of the RSM in the HAC is in many ways similar to that of a college RSM at the Royal Military Academy. For those Sergeant Majors who have had the privilege of serving with the HAC, it has been a most challenging and unique experience. Totally rewarding, never dull, and always fun.

During my tenure I had the honour of preparing the regiment for a Presentation of New Colours by HM The Captain General, a parade which encompassed all the sub-units on a unique parade – a gunner regiment with Colours and guns.

During its long history the Honourable Artillery Company has enjoyed the attentions of many prominent RSMs, and who better to present them than three former COs of the Company. Col B. Kay, TD HAC recalls:

At the end of the Battalion Supper, much beer was drunk in the sutling room, and through a smoky haze Doug Mann clambered onto the top of the bar, then jumped and grabbed the centre chandelier. At the top of his swing it came away from the ceiling fixture and the whole lot fell to the floor. Next morning Lord Freyberge was holding his enquiry trying to apportion the blame when WO1 (RSM) Dick Fletcher (Welsh Guards) said 'Well Sir in my view, it was simply a case of bad Mann management.' The sequel to this was that Peter Oakden at breakfast was recounting the event with great glee to his family. When he had finished telling in exaggerated detail the yarn, his father lowered his newspaper and said in a frosty voice . . . 'Your uncle and I presented that to the HAC before the war . . .'

On another occasion RSM Dick Fletcher was putting the Guard of Honour through its paces. The Guard had a coffee break and then came back on parade, when the RSM said in a very stern voice, 'Gentlemen of the Honourable Artillery Company . . . Pte Brown has reported to me that someone this morning has stolen his best boots. Let him have them back please gentlemen . . . for several reasons, firstly it's not very honourable – the man who took them can't be a gentleman, and most important – they were bloody awful boots and *I don't want anyone wearing them on my parades*!

Col C. H. Martin OBE TD HAC writes:

The Honourable Artillery Company has always been keen to acknowledge the support received from the Guards Division and the Grenadier Guards in particular. The posting of Guards Sergeant Majors and drill instructors to Armoury House has been essential to assist the HAC meet its many commitments, not least the ceremonial duties in the City of London.

WO1 (RSM) W. E. Grimley arrived at the HAC in good time to prepare the regiment for the ceremonial associated with Her Majesty's Silver Jubilee on 7 June 1977. Possessed of that wonderful sense of humour and style reminiscent of an officer cadet school, Bill Grimley soon had the young men of the City responding to his every wish and command. Without his tireless efforts it is doubtful whether the regiment would have met the required standard to mount a guard of honour at St Paul's Cathedral (a comment by the then Senior Major HAC).

On one rehearsal which involved a march around the artillery garden, a game of cricket was in progress. Inevitably, a ball on its way to the boundary went straight through the marching column. Was it the look in the RSM's eye – or the sound like thunder which stopped the fielder in his tracks? – a fielder who had clearly every intention of nipping through between the band and drums and the guard itself!

Away from the ceremonial, Bill was always keen to visit training in the field and to participate in some of the more bizarre activities. As an ex-miner, no-one should have been surprised to see him arrive at the selection course location at the end of an abseil rope dangling from a disused railway viaduct at Merthyr Tydfil.

Probably the most bizarre event of Bill Grimley's tour with the HAC must have been his trip to Boston Massachusetts. A sizeable delegation set off from Armoury House to assist the Ancient and Honorable Artillery Company of Massachusetts (one of the oldest chartered bodies in the US) to celebrate its 1978 June Day Parade on Boston Common. If Bill was taken aback by some of the remarks of the crowd, for example – 'Why has he a cat on his head?' He did not show it, and the overwhelming hospitality of the Ancients made a lasting impression.

It was not surprising therefore that Bill was to be seen at Heathrow early on Sunday 9 July 1978, part of a welcoming party for a small group of Ancients visiting London. It was later that day that Bill suffered a sudden and severe heart attack and died. The HAC was stunned to lose such a good friend, a man of humour and stature, a Guards Sergeant Major who seemed to grasp the concept of civilians spending their spare time soldiering, from the first moment he stepped over the threshold of Armoury House.

With the prospect of new Colours being presented by the

Captain General in June 1980, considerable concern existed about the availability of a Sergeant Major who had the experience and ability to prepare the HAC for such an event. WO1 (RSM) D. D. Horn filled that requirement exactly, making his presence felt in all corners of the regiment, guards of honour, salutes, squadron parades, NCOs' cadres, recruits and selection courses, all of these benefited from his influence. Here was an RSM quite different from Bill Grimley, Bill with his chiselled facial features, every inch the stalwart from the Nottinghamshire mining district. By contrast, David Horn was tall, youthful looking, and would have surprised no-one had he admitted to being a senior executive in one of the leading City merchant banks in his spare time!

Whilst the HAC would never admit it, the task presented to David Horn was immense, trying to train part time soldiers to a standard of drill appropriate for the Captain General. There were difficulties which, in being resolved, served to underline the great ability of David to keep his eye and his mind on the objective. This Sergeant Major had every detail of the parade at his fingertips, having produced within days of arriving at Armoury House a lengthy and detailed instruction on the minutiae of the proceedings, only the COs reply to Her Majesty remained to be included on the day.

If RSM Grimley and the Senior Major had entertained the gentlemen of the HAC in the Artillery Garden by shouting at each other across the wide expanse of turf, Clive Martin, now the CO, and RSM Horn could be heard shouting at each other in the MT shed. No opera singer could have received better tuition!

Col M. S. H. Ring TD HAC writes:

Sgt-Maj Dann served for two years at Armoury House and in that time he had both the distinction of being our Sergeant Major at the time of our 450th Parade through the City of London, and the doubtful experience of being locked up for 12 hours in a cattle truck! The cattle truck incident occurred during the regiment's Camp in 1986; the scenario of the exercise was such that the regiment needed to be taken from Wales to Cumbria as, in effect, prisoners. An escape and evasion exercise would then start over the Cumbrian hills. DS were, as ever, in short supply so Sgt-Maj Dann had to volunteer, becoming I believe, the first Sergeant Major to be locked up!

After that Camp, preparations began for our 450th Parade which was to take place the following May. Sgt-Maj Dann was in his element and, happily, the regiment and its veterans,

comprising some 1,200 men in all, responded for both the rehearsals and the Parade went off very smoothly. On the day itself, it was too good to be true for, having got into my stride with the various words of command, I was about to step the regiment off, only to find Sgt-Maj Dann approaching me. This was not according to his well laid plan; nor was the fact that, after an immaculate halt and salute, I was informed that we were seven minutes early. Another immaculate salute followed and away he went, leaving, as he rightly should, the CO to sort the problem out – it would have helped however if I had had a watch!

Sgt-Maj Ridley replaced RSM Dann at about the time of our Camp in September 1987 and kindly volunteered to spend part of his holiday period with us at Camp in Germany. He too found himself doing something rather unusual. A check point was needed to be manned for 12 hours or so through the night. The scenario was a five day escape and evasion exercise and 48 hours had elapsed. Weary teams of four, somewhat harassed by an aggressive enemy, were extracting themselves from the heights of Hartz Mountains, with the task of meeting up with a Frenchman (Sgt-Maj Ridley) who was wearing shorts and was to be found fishing in a stream. On arrival the fisherman was to be asked 'Do you come here often?' when the reply was to be 'Only in the mushroom season.' Sgt-Maj Ridley kept this up all night, though by 4am, the cold got the better of his shorts and long trousers appeared. Needless to say, the whole regiment was most impressed with their new Sergeant Major's performance and his name was made.

Having had the regiment's 450th Parade in London in 1987, in 1988 the regiment, on a voluntary basis, took a substantial contingent to Boston, USA where the regiment's counterpart, The Ancient and Honorable Artillery Company of Boston Massachusetts, were having their 350th Anniversary. Once again, a parade was required, this time through Boston, and as only one rehearsal was permitted this demonstrated that flexibility was going to be the cry. The route and timings were vague in the extreme and Sgt-Maj Ridley, together with our Adjutant, wisely decided that they would patrol as recce parties in order that some sort of warning could be given to me as to what was likely to happen next. It worked and indeed, so far as Sgt-Maj Ridley was concerned, it worked so well that he ended up with an ardent female admirer as well!

Both 'my' Sergeant Majors were quite different in character but were a pleasure to know and work with – and indeed they had to cope with much the same wide variety of tasks that now confronts an HAC Sergeant Major.

CHAPTER 20

Regimental Corporal Major B. Lane, The Blues and Royals

It is very unusual for three generations of a family to produce a Regimental Sergeant Major or Regimental Corporal Major, or for the regiments in which the family has served to include such a diversity of arms – Line regiment, Artillery unit, Guards regiment and Household cavalry regiment. Maj Brian W. Lane, The Blues and Royals, is now retired from the regular army, but remains closely connected by his work with the careers office of the Household Cavalry. He served through the ranks from Drummer Boy, and has allowed me the following fascinating record of not only his own service, which included a period as Regimental Corporal Major, but that of his father and of his grandparents who had a strong military background.

Within a period of 55 years my family have produced two Regimental Sergeant Majors and a Regimental Corporal Major!

My grandfather, William Lane, served in the 2nd Bn, Royal Irish Rifles, from 16 July 1883 to 15 July 1904, progressing through the ranks to CSM. He married my grandmother, who was the daughter of a Sergeant in the Bengal Sappers and Miners, in Malta in 1894, and she subsequently taught in school as a member of the Corps of Army School Mistresses.

For two years between 1896-8 my grandfather served on detachment with the Scind Volunter Rifle Corps. On the outbreak of war he re-enlisted on 14 September 1914, and serving throughout was appointed RSM on 28 November 1917. His army service ended when he was transferred to the reserve on 7 February 1919.

My father, George Lane, served in the 6th TA Bn Royal Warwickshire Regiment before the Second World War, and remained throughout the war with the regiment, which was converted to become the 122 Anti-Tank Regiment RA (Royal Warwickshire Regiment) – the unit retaining its original regimental badge. My father was eventually appointed RSM of the battalion, and was discharged from the army on 11 August 1945.

My own service commenced when I enlisted as a Drummer Boy in the Grenadier Guards on 3 December 1949. My attestation went through the same recruitment office as had my grandfather's. I reported to the 3rd Bn Grenadier Guards, at Chelsea Barracks two days later, and walking along the Ebury Bridge Road side of the barracks, arrived just as the COs memoranda was about to start. The RSM, who was Reg Butler, stopped and had a word with me. He was a tall man of six foot two inches, but to me appeared to be seven feet tall! Throughout his period as RSM I can never remember him becoming ruffled or resorting to the shouting, swearing, threatening image of the RSM so often portrayed.

When 34 years later I attended the annual dinner of the Riding Masters, Quartermasters, and Directors of Music Association (a most illustrious body), Lt-Col (QM) retired, Reg Butler was the President, and he made my night by recognising me after so many years. He still addressed me as Boy Lane however!

When reading of boys serving in the army in my grandparents time, I realise that little had changed between then and my time in 1949. Our pay was 3/6d per week, no smoking or drinking, not allowed to go out with girls, no walking out except on Saturdays or Sundays (after six months service) and then in full battledress with boots and anklets. We had to be in by 2100hrs with lights out every night at 2130hrs. Reveille sounded daily at 0600hrs, there was church parade every Sunday, school every day until we obtained our certificates of education. Above all else, musical practice was held every night until 1930hrs.

Hard, firm but fair discipline was the order of the day, but never maliciously imposed, indeed my barrack room Lance Corporal of those days, George Higgins, who had enlisted in 1936, is today the godfather of my twin daughters, and has been a friend for 35 years. All was not work of course and we managed to get into scrapes, but RSM Reg Butler always seemed able to treat these for what they were, provided they were not too serious. Whatever happened would invariably be sorted out in his office and not go before the Adjutant.

One year the battalion Christmas cake was removed by the boys, and although there were 25 of us, we managed to make it last until the following March! Some of the WOs who were destined not to make RSM, would lean on the Boys a little, and one in particular, a Drill Sergeant, had a wife who always got up before reveille to check that the Duty Drummer was on time – a second late and the Boy would lose his name!

Overseas service was the norm, with the battalion moving to Tripoli in 1951, and from there to the Canal Zone and Jordan, before returning to the UK in 1954.

RSM Bill Nash took over from Reg Butler, and ran the battalion through the latter days of the Canal Zone, and the return to Chelsea and Victoria Barracks. He was responsible for all the arrangements for the tercentenary year (1956) when all three battalions were involved. Bill Nash had a distinct sense of humour and was well liked. He later retired as Quartermaster, and eventually of course, became the Superintendent of Windsor Castle.

In 1956 the 3rd Bn was mobilized for the Suez operation, and the arrival overnight of the reservists brought our strength up to 1,000 men. We embarked on the *New Australia* for Malta, where we were encamped on the old wartime airstrip from which the three famous old Gloster Gladiators – Faith, Hope and Charity, operated.

By the time the Suez operation ended, Cyprus and the EOKA terror gangs were under way, so the 3rd Bn went to a camp just

William Lane, Brian Lane's grandfather, stands at the rear of the group next to the blackboard, and his grandmother is the schoolmistress sitting on the left. The Regimental School of the 2nd Royal Irish Rifles, Poona, 1897. Brian Lane

Brian Lane's father, RSM George Lane, Royal Warwickshire Regt 1943. Brian Lane

outside Nicosia, where we were to remain on internal security duties for the next three years. Bill Nash had been replaced by RSM 'Knocker' White, but in Cyprus we suffered a tragedy when the next RSM to come to the battalion, unfortunately took his own life. He was succeeded by an RSM whom I personally rate the greatest; RSM Arthur Stevens was to me the very epitome of the RSM, a smart approachable man who led from the front in everything which the battalion did, whether in ceremonial or in the field.

We were also very fortunate in our CO, Col A. G. Way, and the battalion fairly hummed along for a time, but in 1958 we received word that the 3rd Bn would eventually be placed in suspended animation as a result of the defence cuts. I was by now the Drums Sergeant of the battalion, and when we returned home in August 1959 to Wellington Barracks, there followed a year of ceremonial and farewell functions, before in December 1960, the men of the 3rd Bn were dispersed to the 1st and 2nd Bns. Many of us had served in the battalion since being Boys and had been brought up in its ways to become Sergeants or Lance Sergeants, and to us it represented the end of an era. I was eventually to serve with both 2nd and 1st Bns, but they were never quite the same for me.

I was transferred to the 2nd Bn Grenadier Guards at Hubberath, near Dusseldorf, where the RSM was Fred Clutton MM, a picture-book RSM who was well respected by all who knew him, and whom like so many, went on to become Major

The Band of the Royal Horse Guards, 1967. Corporal of Horse Brian Lane as Drum Major.   Thelma Lane

QM. On return to the UK I was ordered to the Guards Depot at Pirbright, to take up the appointment of Drums Sergeant and Demonstration Platoon Sergeant. There was no Drum Major on establishment at the time. There was in post, in my opinion, one of the great RSMs at the Depot, RSM Tom Pugh, affectionately known as 'Puggy' or 'Pug H'. A parachutsist and a great motivator – his presence on the square or in the Sergeants Mess was something to behold. Stories about him are legion within the Grenadier Guards.

In 1964 I was posted to the 1st Bn in West Germany as Drum Major, again serving under RSM Tom Pugh, who was later commissioned as QM. In addition to Drum Major I was employed as the Reconnaissance Platoon Sergeant, and in 1965 began to seriously consider my future career. Whilst we had been stationed in Cyprus, the RHG (The Blues) had been camped only half a mile away, and having got to know them very well and studied their ways, and now having gained a good deal of recce experience, I decided to seek a transfer to The Blues. I had 15 years of accountable service plus two years as a Boy Soldier to my credit. I took part in the birthday parade of 1966 as Drum Major, then in August transferred to the Royal Horse Guards.

I am often asked the reason for my transfer, but can honestly say that I left with no ill feeling towards the Grenadier Guards. I maintain all my links with former friends via associations, and consider myself in many ways still a Grenadier. Probably above all I think of myself as an ex-Boy Soldier who was taught, instructed, pushed, chased and encouraged, by some of the army's finest RSMs.

I left the 1st Bn with a host of fond memories, and awaited the return of The Blues from West Germany to Combermere Barracks at Windsor. The RCM at that time was George E. Martin, who had not long before taken over from RCM W. A. Stringer, who was a real regimental character. The regiment at the time was an Armoured Reconnaissance Regiment, with A Squadron detached in Malaya, B Squadron an Armoured Car Squadron (Saladins and Ferrets), and C Squadron – to which I was posted – was an Air Portable Squadron (Ferrets only), and had an operational role in support of the 16th Parachute Brigade.

I was initially kept busy attending armoured courses in order to retain my rank as Corporal of Horse, and was successful in these, being promoted to Squadron Quartermaster Corporal within 12 months. During this period the Blues band did not have a Drum Major as such, and whenever they appeared on parade a senior NCO was detailed by the RCM to do the job. Needless to say with my past experience, I was a dead sitter for the task!

In March 1968, RCM George Martin was relieved by RCM D. L. Godfrey-Cass, who had been the Garrison Regimental Corporal Major in Hong Kong. He made a great impact upon both the regiment and the NCOs Mess, demanding the highest standards on parade, and really bringing the Mess from its rather old-fashioned ways into the present day. During his time standards were raised in such things as performance, food, decor, and the type of functions held in the Mess.

By 1968 I was made Squadron Corporal Major of C Squadron, and remember that we were gathered together to be advised that in March 1969 The Blues would be amalgamated with the 1st

Royal Dragoons in Detmold, and that we would first be moving to carry out conversion training to chieftain tanks.

HM The Queen visited the regiment in September 1968 to bid us farewell, and such was the influence of RCM Godfrey-Cass that Her Majesty not only agreed to sit for a photograph with the NCOs Mess, but also presented Long Service and Good Conduct Medals to SCM W. Clarke and myself. From what I can ascertain, although not having fully checked, these may be the only medals of this kind to have been presented by the Sovereign.

The next six months were shrouded in diesel fumes and dust, but March 1969 found the two regiments in Germany busily preparing for the Amalgamation Parade. I was to be the SCM of A Squadron, and having driven to Detmold with my family, discovered that there was to be a drill parade the following morning. As my wife got down to the pots and pans, I got into the buff, boots and pressing. In retrospect the years 1969-71 as

years. On the ceremonial side, we had the presentation of a new guidon coming in the great park in 1972, in which the combined Mounted Squadron RHQ and Sabre Squadrons of the Armoured Regiment and Regimental Association would take part. The parade was to conclude with a regimental ride/drive Escort for HM The Queen down the Longwalk and into the quadrangle at Windsor Castle.

The following year was to see the Presentation of New Standards to the Household Cavalry on Horse Guards Parade, again combining both regiments' Mounted Squadrons with an armoured squadron from each regiment in a wide variety of wheeled and tracked vehicles. Neither of these parades had been attempted before, and there was nothing available to read up! Needless to say I committed all to paper and worked out a complete format.

In addition to the ceremonial side, I was very fortunate to be

Brian Lane when Squadron Corporal Major of A Squadron, Blues and Royals. The Tank Park, 1968. Brian Lane

Squadron Corporal Major were probably the most rewarding to me as WOII, as during this period we had to set and establish standards for all successors, and at the same time face the flak from other quarters. We were fortunate in the choice of our first CO Lt-Col (later General) Sir Richard Vickers, and RCM D. L. Godfrey-Cass.

My Squadron was selected to take over the Arctic role from the Life Guards, and in January 1971 we moved to Norway for a six week introductory period. On return to Germany we were told that we were going to Windsor in March, prior to undertaking a four month tour in Belfast. I was advised that on our eventual return in October 1971, I would be promoted as RCM in place of RCM T. W. Tucker, who had replaced RCM Godfrey-Cass in May 1970.

When in September 1971 I became RCM of the Blues and Royals, I began to fill in my diary. We had a permanent squadron in Cyprus, a Squadron also there on UN duties and a Squadron presence in Northern Ireland which we were to maintain for three

able to accompany my CO when he went to visit our squadrons in Northern Ireland and Cyprus. We were poised so delicately in the early 1970s that as we drove in to the barrack gates after the Guidon Parade, there was an order awaiting our B Squadron to move to Northern Ireland for 'Operation Motorman' and the move was achieved that same night.

I was the RCM with a couple of years to go, and my personal opinion was that I had probably reached my zenith and did not really expect to go any further. My belief that one of today's failings is that WOs expect to be the RSM and also to achieve a commission. In consequence some of them may not put 100 per cent into the appointment.

One is in a position as RCM or RSM to assess the thrusters from the coasters, and it is important at this stage to groom and prepare those with adequate ability for eventual promotion to RCM. This process obviously begins at SCM/CSM level, and although all promotions are gained on merit, one always likes to believe that one's talent spotting led to the promotion of men through the ranks.

It is very important to maintain contact with the Trooper at all times, and to have one's finger on the pulse of the regiment. I used to make a firm point of going at 1000hrs around the regiment visiting all departments, tank parks, offices, NAAFI, in order to talk with all ranks. In this way communication was maintained, and if on return to my office I had picked up some minor problems, they could be attended to with the minimum delay.

At some time in mid 1973 I was asked by my CO if I would accept a commission in the regiment which would require me to become a Platoon Commander at the Guards Depot. I was delighted to accept, and left The Blues and Royals in December 1973 to be commissioned on 7 January 1974.

Someone had previously said to me that as RCM one never knew one's value until one left. This point was brought out when having been given a splendid farewell by the Officers Mess, and the NCOs Mess, my wife and I were invited to the Troopers Mess for their Christmas dance. We were enjoying ourselves when during a break in the proceedings, the Troopers presented us with six cut glass sherry glasses on a silver tray. This in itself was a splendid gift, however, as we later left the function, all of the Troopers lined the route from the dining room and gave us a marvellous but moving farewell. I might add that there were a few tears shed that night. I was succeeded as RCM by J. M. Heath who came from the Royal Dragoons.

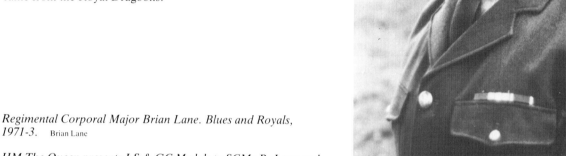

Regimental Corporal Major Brian Lane. Blues and Royals, 1971-3.   Brian Lane

HM The Queen presents LS & GC Medals to SCMs B. Lane and W. Clarke, 1968.   Brian Lane

CHAPTER 21

RSM N. D. Taylor, Prince of Wales's Regiment of Yorkshire

When I first met the former Garrison Sergeant Major of London District, Tom Taylor, in March 1983, to talk with him about his service, he mentioned that his elder brother Neville had also served as a Regimental Sergeant Major in the Prince of Wales's Own West Yorkshire Regiment. I was very happy four months later to meet Neville Taylor at the Regimental Museum at Beverley, where he worked as Assistant Secretary of the Regimental Association, when he not only talked with me about his service life, but was able to help my research into the 18th Bn POWO West Yorkshire Regiment (Bradford Pals) which fought in the First World War.

The stories of Neville and Tom Taylor provide most interesting comparisons of service as RSMs at similar periods, but in different regiments and settings. Neville Taylor told me that he had joined the 5th Bn POWO West Yorkshire Regiment, on 31 August 1939, three days before war was declared, and during the following months was stationed at York, Catterick, and Malton. He continues:

We then set off in 1940 on the abortive Norway mission, but turned back before going ashore. We returned to Scotland but in May 1940 re-embarked on a troopship and four days later were surprised to find ourselves at Reykjavik in Iceland! We remained there for two years to guard against a possible German invasion, then returned home in April 1942. We were based at St Donats Castle at Llantwit Major for a time.

I was married in November 1942, having made application to the CO for permission. I well remember his reply . . . 'Certainly Corporal! but two things . . . firstly you will be a soldier – then a husband. Secondly, you are on the next draft for India!' I arrived in India in February 1943, expecting to go to either our 1st or 2nd Battalion, but was instead posted to the East Yorkshire Regiment, at that time stationed at Bombay. After a while the battalion moved to Burma for operations, by which time I had been promoted to Sergeant. We were later positioned in the Shan hills where I was appointed Provost Sergeant. Following a period of leave I reported back ready to return to my duties as Provost Sergeant, but was ordered to report to HQ Company as Company Sergeant Major. Within a few days I was claimed by D Company, so with six years service I was made CSM of D Company.

The war ended at this stage, and a party of 36 of us travelled home via India, arriving at the old Depot at Victoria Barracks, Beverley, in March 1946. After a short period we went out to Naples in company with a large number of Italian ex POWs who were going home. Following ten days in transit there we moved on to Austria, where the 5th Bn were already stationed under canvas. Overnight the battalion was redesignated the 1st Bn East Yorkshire Regt, and my A Company took over guard duties at Graz POW Camp, which housed mainly war criminals – former SS men and women. I particularly remember when walking around the camp, how scrupulously clean the SS kept their quarters.

We were then moved into barracks at Bruck, where training got under way. The RSM at that time was Freddie Gibson MBE MC, who was an ex Light Infantryman. He had served in the 5th Battalion in the desert where he gained his MC. Following the Armistice Parade in November 1947, I was in the Sergeants Mess when I looked round to see an old friend from India RSM 'Jock' Riches. He was to become a close friend and I learned a great deal from him, as with his vast experience he was to me an expert. Although quite small in stature, everyone respected him and when he left us in 1949 he must have completed 27 years of service.

I was then selected to attend the first drill course at the new All Arms Drill Wing at the Guards Depot Caterham in May 1948. I arrived from Austria on a Thursday and the course was due to begin on the following Sunday. I took a bus to the Depot and found my way to the Drill Wing square, where not a soul was in sight. Then I heard someone behind me and a large Warrant Officer from the Irish Guards came into view pacing in slow time. He asked me who I was and then introduced himself as Drill Sgt D. T. Lynch DCM, WO in charge of the All Arms Drill Wing. He asked why I was there so early and I explained that due to the boat times etc. He promptly told me to go away until Sunday! He called to a Sergeant, 'Take this Warrant Officer – feed him – pay him – and get him out!' Ten minutes later I was out of the back door of the Depot and on my way to visit my mother-in-law.

There were about 90 WOs and Sergeants on the course, three of whom were RSMs, and one, Lew Borrett, was an RSM from my regiment. We formed three squads and our squad Instructor was a CSM from the Welsh Guards, whilst others irrespective of our ranks, were Sergeant Instructors. I thoroughly enjoyed the course as I was keen on drill and ceremonial. Admittedly it was a bit hard as it was held during one of the hot spells in the summer of 1948. One just had to maintain a sense of humour as in the heat of the moment one could easily lose one's temper and foul things up.

Drill Sgt Lynch was taking a drill session, and pulled out an Irish Sergeant from the squad to take over. During this the Sergeant shouted – 'Number two man in the front rank – pull on your rifle butt!!' The Drill Sergeant immediately interrupted to advise '– ask the man his name – so that you can check him in future.' The Sergeant continued 'You there . . . Sgt Alexander! . . . What's your name?' It was little things like that that got us by.

It was drill, drill and more drill, from 0800 to 1600hrs and back to living in barrack rooms with kit laid out and fire buckets highly polished! Strictly back to square one. I met some excellent chaps on the course however and we all mucked in. Royal Scots – Irish regiments, all sorts of units. The whole point was of course to teach a standard form of drill throughout the British Army, which in my mind was a good thing. It made life a lot easier on parade if everyone was going to perform the same drill movements on the word of command.

We were taught basic drill from the correct position of attention, and also all of the arms drill movements. Above all we were taught how to instruct, which I found absolutely marvellous as I hoped to become an RSM in the future. It taught me drill confidence and when I demonstrated a movement I knew that it was correct.

When I returned to Gras in Austria, I was appointed the Battalion Drill Instructor, working with RSM Riches who ran all of the cadres. In April 1950, I took over as CSM of B Company, and this remained my company for the next six years. We remained in Austria for a further four and a half years, doing spit and polish guard duties in Vienna, including some international 'Four Power' duties which were very interesting.

We left Austria in 1951 to move near Hamburg, where a very busy nine months of mainly field training followed with the 7th Armoured Division. Then in November the battalion moved to Montgomery Barracks in Berlin, which bordered on the Russian sector. Our range stop butts were in fact in Russia to all intents and purposes. Again we provided part of the Four Power guard duties, this time at Spandau where several prominent German prisoners were being held. We could in fact wander more freely at that time, indeed, could go into East Berlin.

In December 1952 the battalion returned home to England, but not for long however, as in January 1953 we were off again, this time to Malaya for a tour of three years. There followed a long period of bandit chasing with much jungle patrolling. In my Company I had a man employed as sanitary man, and one day I had reason to check him and tell him to get one of the toilets clean. When going around later I found a notice which stated 'Out of bounds' – and the man had signed it – adding *CSM*! I got him in sharp and asked 'what's this CSM stuff?' and he replied 'Company Sanitary Man – Sir!'

On 24 December 1955, we sailed from Singapore for home and spent a nice Christmas and New Year on the Indian Ocean. We later came through the Suez Canal, where to my delight my brother Tom, who was at that time Drill Sergeant with the 3rd Bn Grenadier Guards stationed nearby, came aboard for drinks. The battalion arrived home again in mid January 1956, but then in April we were moved to Osnabruck, where we joined the British Army of the Rhine. The big event at Osnabruck was the Presentation of New Colours by the Lord Lieutenant of the East Riding, Lord Middleton. It was an excellent parade, and I had a lot to do in company with the RSM but the only thing I did not like was the extremely cold November weather.

I was also PMC of the Sergeants Mess at that time and a lot of old comrades came out to see the parade. We went down to the station in coaches to meet them, and the RSM tasked me with looking out for Bill Chafer one of our regimental holders of the Victoria Cross. I expected a large, tough man, but seeing nobody likely I eventually asked a quiet looking old gentleman, 'Excuse me – do you know which one is Bill Chafer VC?' 'Yes' he replied, 'that's me!' He was a very nice old gentleman, and I much enjoyed looking after him. He had been awarded the VC during the First World War.

I left Osnabruck on 6 December 1956, having served for 13 years with the 1st Battalion, and made many friends in the East Yorkshire Regt. I was appointed RSM at the Newcastle University Officer Training Corps, where the students could train for TA or Regular Army Commissions. There really was not sufficient for me to do as I found myself mainly sitting at a desk writing memos, and whilst I enjoyed it, I needed more activity. I heard in June 1957 of the pending amalgamations of the regiments, and it was patently obvious to me that the East and West Yorkshire Regiments would be among the first to be affected. This soon happened and the two regiments were amalgamated to become the Prince of Wales's Own Regiment of Yorkshire. I was rather anxious that having been promoted RSM so recently, I would never be made RSM of the 1st Battalion.

One morning I was advised by the Chief Clerk that the Adjutant wished to see me at 1000hrs. I reported, and he stated simply 'You are posted.' As I had been there for only 15 months I wondered where I had gone wrong. He placed the posting order in my hand and invited me to read it. I read that I had been selected to become RSM upon the amalgamation of the East and West Yorkshire Regiments! It was arranged that RSM Maddocks of the 1st Bn West Yorks Regt would change duties with me prior to the amalgamation, so I was able to join the battalion in Colchester in order to get the feel of things.

The battalion then moved to Connaught Barracks at Dover where the 1st Bn East Yorkshire Regt arrived direct from Germany on 24 April 1958. The next morning at reveille I went along with two policemen, and we raised the flag of the Prince of Wales's Own Regiment of Yorkshire, for the first time. I had CSMs, Colour Sergeants and Sergeants from both East and West Yorkshire Regiments, but we all had to forget the past and accept that we were now one new unit.

My great memory of Dover was of course the Inauguration Parade of the Regiment, in which the salute was taken by HRH The Princess Royal, who was our Colonel in Chief. This took place on the Crabble, the Kent County Cricket ground. I first sorted everything out with the Adjutant, and then the drills got under way. I remember starting one rehearsal on the football field behind the barracks (there was not a suitable parade ground in the barracks) and it became so thick with fog that I could not see what was going on, so we had to end the practice.

We held the full dress rehearsal on the Crabble in Number One dress but wearing canvas PT shoes! It really was a fine cricket ground and as it had rained a great deal, we were worried in case we ruined it; I had of course marked out the area so as to avoid the wicket, so we did not trample on that. On the day of the parade the sun thankfully shone and it was a glorious event. The actual act of amalgamation started with the Colours of the West Yorkshire Regt on the right flank and the Colours of the East Yorkshire Regt on the left. Each then marched in slow time into the centre closing up, then formed so that they faced HRH The Princess Royal. From that point the parade took the form of the normal Trooping of the Colour and Her Royal Highness inspected the new battalion.

It was a tremendous weekend, and the Mess was teeming with old comrades and guests who came from all over the country. Lots of old friends came, Capt Tommy Bowden former RSM of the old East Yorkshire Regt, and also former RSM H. Savidge of the West Yorkshire Regt. HRH The Princess Royal visited the Mess, and I had the pleasure of greeting her officially and then taking her around to meet various WOs and Sgts.

Prior to the amalgamation parade, I remember walking through the barracks and spotting an old gentleman walking around, I went across to enquire where he was going. 'I am just looking at my old battalion Sir' he explained. I asked when he had enlisted in the West Yorks, 'I joined in 1895 Sir!' he replied, and went on to introduce himself as ex CSM Arthur Hole DCM – 31 years service! So I took him to the Mess for a drink.

Soon afterwards, when I was in my office, there came a knock on the door and another little old gentleman came in and explained 'I have driven from Ashford to Dover, and was in the West Yorkshire Regiment – my name is Arthur Kenyon, ex Company Sergeant Major!' I told him that we had received a visit from another old soldier of the regiment named Arthur Hole. 'Ah' he commented, 'a young soldier.' I asked him when he had joined, and he replied '1893 Sir, two years senior!' With the COs permission, I invited the two old soldiers to the amalgamation parade and at the reception in the Mess, introduced them to Her Royal Highness, explaining that they had enlisted in 1893 and 1895. Those two old gentlemen were immaculate in lounge suits with regimental ties, and I was very proud of them. The parade was a tremendous success and it gave me a lot of confidence.

We were due to go to Cyprus on a six month tour, but in August 1958 we instead found ourselves on the way to Aden, where there

RSM N. D. Taylor when RSM of the Prince of Wales's Own Regt of Yorkshire. Neville Taylor

was a bit of trouble. We were sent out by troopship and soon had our companies dotted about in the desert. It was an interesting period, we had no families with us just the battalion, and shots were fired in anger near the Yemen border. I am sure that the CO Col Garside, would agree that it was a very useful period in the development of the battalion, coming so soon after the amalgamation. I well remember doing a tour around the battalion positions with the CO, by flying up to visit one company, then coming back by Land Rover across the desert to visit another.

We had HQ Company and Support Company in the battalion area, and so guard duties were necessary. When I could get half a dozen men together on a sandy patch we would have a spot of drill, but I had mainly administrational work to do whilst the companies were so spread out. I was able to get my 'dhobi' done and keep my kit reasonably clean, so looked fairly smart in starched KD shorts and shirt with SD cap and Sam Browne belt. One day the CO popped his head around my door and shouted 'Come on RSM!' I grabbed my pace stick and shot out after him – climbed into a Land Rover and the next thing I knew we were down to an RAF base and aboard a beaver aircraft.

We landed at Mukieras where C Company was positioned, and the Company Commander, Maj Bill Robinson, grabbed my pace stick from me and thrust a rifle and a bandolier of 50 rounds at me. We mounted another Land Rover and were soon up into the hills where there was a racket going on with the Yemeni firing at us. There was I in best KD, SD cap and Sam Browne belt, trying to appear calm and collected behind a great big rock! I often chuckle about it now . . . of course everyone was highly amused at the RSM being stuck out there being fired at. Needless to say, with my prominent dress, I kept a low profile.

In April 1959, the Border Regiment took over from us, and we

sailed to Gibraltar, where we were initially housed in the old Casements Barracks. This was a very old barracks with a small parade ground, and the main guardroom was situated on the other side of a main road. Then there were 180 steps up to the Moorish Castle, which was our Battalion HQ! On Monday mornings we held a formal guard mounting on the Casements Square, normally watched by a number of tourists. I mounted the guard with the Adjutant and then the band of drums led the parade for the full length of Main Street. On the Convent Square would then follow the changing of the guard. Although the appropriate drill was always recorded in the *Manual of Ceremonial*, one had to compromise a great deal at times, to fit in with the limitations of the ground.

After about three weeks in Gibraltar, the CO sent for me, and advised that an ex Governor of the Rock, much loved by the community, was very ill and could not be expected to live for long. We were to make preparations for the military funeral, the lying in state, the catafalque, bearer party and gun carriage. We were attending a lecture one day when someone placed a note in my hand which said that the former Governor had just died, and we were therefore to get busy. I hurried to the cathedral and arranged the catafalque for the lying in state, and completed all of the other arrangements. The military funeral went very well, and we completed our part, marching down to the North Front Cemetery, where we were met by GSM Rob Roy, who took over. He was the former 'Piper of Tobruk' and I got to know him well.

That was my first introduction to ceremonial work, but all sorts of parades followed. At Christmas 1959 we moved down to

Europa Point, which was a much nicer place at the base of the Rock, and had a large flat sand area which could be used as a parade ground. The Rock above could be covered by a sultry mist for days, which would turn clean brasses 'gold' in no time, but our new lower point overlooked the bay and remained clear, indeed, the coast of Africa could easily be seen.

In June 1960 the battalion was due to have its first Presentation of Colours by the Colonel in Chief, HRH The Princess Royal, and our CO again ordered preparations to be made in good time. I sat down and wrote out the whole parade from the *Manual of Ceremonial*, and then paced out and marked the square. We set off with the basic drills, and gradually worked up to the rehearsals, the size of our area allowing us to have four complete guards. It was a very good parade and went like a charm, the open setting keeping everyone cool.

Within a few days the Adjutant called me in and advised me, 'I have news for you Sergeant Major, we are Trooping the Colour for The Queen's Birthday.' 'Where are we doing that Sir?' I asked. 'On the Naval ground down in Gibraltar, and His Excellency The Governor will be taking the salute.' This was one parade in which I did have to make alterations, and after looking around I had a fence removed so as to gain a little extra space. The ground was really only the size of a soccer pitch, but I paced it out and returning to our Europa Point parade ground marked out a similar area on the sandy ground with the help of the Provost Sergeant and fatigue men. The rehearsals were held within that area, and I had to reduce the strength of the guards for the parade from the normal 72 men to 48 men. The Trooping of the Colour was a success, and we had a glorious day.

I also produced Guards of Honour for HRH The Duke of Kent, and HRH The Queen Mother. Also we found a Guard of Honour for the Opening of Parliament in MacDonald Square, where one could only just fit in a Guard within the restricted space, so the drill had to be very precise. We were in Number Three Dress, and after the salute had been taken by the Governor of Gibraltar, he went in to the official building. We stood at ease while the speeches were being made, but were there for one hour, and I allowed myself a roving commission as one or two of the men were beginning to sway in the ranks due to the heat. I stood behind them encouraging 'brace yourself boy . . . get up on your toes . . . take the weight off your heels!' I had a couple of men fall out, which was not bad considering there was little or no breeze.

We left Gibraltar in August 1961, after experiencing a lot of ceremonial, but then that *was* Gib! I had almost completed my tour of duty and on the boat sailing home I was called into the first class lounge where all of the Warrant Officers were assembled, and to my delight, the CO presented me with a very beautiful silver mounted pace stick. The plaque was engraved *Presented to RSM N. D. Taylor on completion of his tour of duty, as the first RSM of the 1st Battalion Prince of Wales's Own Regiment of Yorkshire, by the Officers.* I have the stick at home, and it remains one of my treasured possessions.

Having completed four years, my next appointment was as RSM to the Berlin Brigade, where I soon commenced a lot of ceremonial work. There were guards of honour for visiting Generals and Allied Staff, and one of the big parades was The Queen's Birthday Parade, which I would place second only to the Horse Guards Parade in London. I marked out the area in Berlin for the six guards on parade, two from each battalion. I was also RSM for the 1962 and 1963 parades, and in the latter the Welsh Regiment was Trooping the Colour with two guards, whilst the others were from the Durham Light Infantry, and the Somerset Light Infantry. It had been my experience in the past that when the Light Infantry was on parade with us, the pace marched would

Above:
Laying up the Colours of the East Yorkshire Regt (Duke of York's Own) at Beverley Minster in Sept 1961. RSM Neville Taylor at rear of Colour Party.   Hull Daily Mail

Left:
1st Bn (PWO) Regt of Yorkshire. Trooping the Colour on the Queen's Birthday Parade, Gibraltar, June 1961. RSM N. D. Taylor marches behind the Escort for the Colour.   Neville Taylor

be ours, but on this occasion the Brigadier required that each regiment would assume its own pace, so on the march past the Welsh Regiment marched in slower time to the end of the passing line and halted, followed by the Light Infantry at 140 paces to the minute. The whole parade then had to return to the inspection line *at the same pace* – so the Welsh Regiment's Goat went past like a greyhound!

I enjoyed the Berlin appointment although it was largely administrative and entailed helping the Brigade Senior Staff Officer. I was commissioned as Quartermaster on 4 July 1964, and went to the 3rd Bn Federal Regular Army in Aden. On retirement from the Regular Army I was commissioned in the TA as a Non Regular Permanent Staff Officer, and served as Quartermaster in the 3rd Bn Yorkshire Volunteers until 30 June 1980.

So far as drill movements were concerned, I enjoyed all movements if properly carried out. The Advance in Review Order was marvellous if carried out absolutely correctly, but otherwise could look awful. If we got that right the first time in practice I was always happy, but I used to believe that things could go too well in practice – and often a poor rehearsal results in a fine actual parade.

CHAPTER 22

RSM R. Hopton, King's Own Royal Border Regiment, RSMs of the Parachute Regiment and Glider Pilot Regiment

During 1980 The 1st King's Own Royal Border Regiment held a number of marches through towns in Cumbria, to display New Colours which had been presented to them. When the Colour Party with Escort and Band marched through Cockermouth, my son Jeremy Alford took a series of photographs, from which the quality of marching of the Number One Guard in particular, was so apparent that I determined to contact the CSM in charge in order to discuss with him the training of the men for the parade. It was not until 1986 that I actually met the CSM, who was by then Capt R. Hopton, of the Junior Infantry Battalion (Scottish and King's Division) stationed at Albermarle Barracks, and learned that he had not only been the CSM on parade, but had taken a prominent role in the training of the No. 1 Guard.

When I also discovered that he had originally trained with the marvellous Oswestry Junior Leaders Regiment, had served as an Instructor at the RMA Sandhurst, and had gone on to serve as RSM with the UDR and the 1st Bn King's Own Royal Border Regiment, I invited him to contribute his thoughts and memories, and the following absorbing comments are the result.

The aim of the Oswestry Junior Leaders Regiment was to train young men to be the future WOs and NCOs of the Infantry, and when one looks back over the last ten years and sees how many RSMs were ex-juniors from Oswestry, the regiment clearly did so. What the officer cadets have at Sandhurst we had at Oswestry. Since it closed down many have tried to emulate the system, but no establishment has achieved the same standard of excellence as did Oswestry. Most boys spent between two and two and a half years there, and the training was divided into two parts. All of the drill was taught by the Brigade of Guards, whilst the skill at arms, signals, and tactics was taken by the Infantry of the Line. All of the instructors were Sergeants or above. Jan Hooper, Coldstream Guards, was the Drill Sergeant, and he became RSM when 'Dusty' Smith left.

Drill Sgt Jan Hooper was the man to stay away from, and he had that frightening husky voice which made one shake from head to toe! He was not considered by us to be approachable, but about six months before I was due to leave, and when I was a junior CSM, Jan stopped me as I was walking up to the Battalion HQ building. He spoke normally and I was so overcome and shocked that I couldn't reply, or at least don't remember making any reply. In such awe was he held. From that time onwards until the end of my training at Oswestry, and after joining my battalion, I realised that his performance on the square was just a game. A serious game admittedly, but a game to motivate men into doing what he wanted, whereas off the square he was a different man altogether. Later I was to use that philosophy myself, and was to learn that one needed to have not only a dual – but a triple personality!

Two other things have remained with me from my junior leader days – boxing and climbing, but while I still climb today, I had enough sense to give up boxing when I left Oswestry, although remain a keen observer of all novice boxing. My one regret was that I was not made junior RSM, as RSM 'Dusty' Smith selected a boy from the Guards Company. I must admit that he looked the part, and believe that he left the army to become a policeman.

RSM 'Dusty' Smith was like a second father to me, and I never knew him to lose his temper in all the time I was there. You always knew when he was not pleased with your performance however and he had the ability to give a thorough dressing down without shouting. It may have been because we were so young and impressionable, but 'Dusty' Smith could send a tingle down one's spine when addressing the senior boys on one of his favourite subjects such as 'leadership'. Every Saturday morning there was a battalion drill parade, and Dusty would stand in front towering over us. He was very much an old school RSM, and his drill was immaculate. A gentleman in every way, he was feared and respected for all of the right reasons and we would have done anything for him. The final feature I remember about him was his English bull dog which, like his master, played out his role to the full.

When I later was posted as Sergeant Instructor to the RMA Sandhurst, I enjoyed my tour but at the same time found it a little frustrating. My main purpose was to teach the officer cadets skill at arms, range work, and tactics. The working relationship between Guards Regiments and the Line Regiments was not always the best, but I must say that I got on with them all very well. Most of my fellow instructors were appointed as RSMs at about the time I was, and it proved very useful to know them when visiting barracks or taking over new camps.

AcSM Ray Huggins was in charge during my time, and his successor, RSM Denis Cleary, was the Old College RSM. I was posted for most of my time with the New College, where the RSM was Dave Elliot. Two RSMs will always stand out in my memory, the first of whom, 'Dusty' Smith, I have already mentioned. The second was AcSM Ray Huggins, a totally unflappable soldier whose drill and turnout was always immaculate. He created a remarkably optimistic atmosphere in which all felt that they were destined to go places and I think that most of us did. My tour at the RMA Sandhurst provided me with an insight into the officer corps, which I would not have otherwise gained, and it was possible to see the results of one's efforts to steer and mould the young cadets into soldiers. It also gave me the confidence to work with junior officers when later I was appointed as RSM.

When appointed as RSM of the Ulster Defence Regiment, I must admit to feeling a little apprehensive, but needn't have been. They were some of the best people I have ever worked with and they accepted me, with my family, as their own. My tour with them was one of the happiest and busiest I have had. Having said happiest – it was also at times the saddest, as I buried eight men during my 18 months with them, the first after only two days in post. I found that I had to temper my approach a great deal as the

RSM R. Hopton and RQMS G. Prince on duty, Cyprus, May 1985. Capt R. Hopton

unit was fully operational, and the last thing these people needed was to be chased by the RSM when completing a patrol. During the second half of my tour, the CO appointed me as the Battalion Operations Officer, in addition to my duties as RSM.

At the very end of my tour I lost four men in one explosion, and during the next two days we buried them. The same escort of eight men worked on all four funerals, and after the last one I took the eight men into my Mess, at two o'clock in the afternoon, still in full uniform – locked all the doors – and we stayed there until my wife came for me at two o'clock the next morning. By then all our grief had come out and we were ready for work the next day. I was proud to have soldiered with them as they are dedicated professional men and women, and I have a great admiration for them, yet also a great sadness knowing how much of a difficult task they have before them.

From being a Lance Corporal in Honiton, Devon, the appointment of RSM of our 1st Bn was the job I most dreamed about. There is nothing in the army to compare with it, no other rank can provide as much satisfaction. To improve the standards, maintain the regimental traditions, and to keep a hold on the discipline. I was the eleventh RSM since the formation of the regiment in 1959, and the day I took over the appointment was without doubt the proudest of my life. I must have been one of the only RSMs to go back to the All Arms Drill Wing at Pirbright, to sharpen myself up with a drill course before taking up my post with the 1st Bn – and I enjoyed the course even more than the first time I had attended.

Soon after taking appointment, I took a large company of men to London on public duties for six weeks. We took a great pride in our turnout and drill, in company with a detachment of Guards, we practiced on the square at Chelsea Barracks and the Guards RSM later took both of the companies on a rehearsal. After about one hour he stood down my company but kept his guard working for the rest of the morning. The air was blue around Chelsea for the remainder of the day. In my opinion the way to judge the standard of our guard, other than by its arms drill, was to watch their arms swinging, and it was not only that they swung their arms to the correct height, but that they reached that height in absolute unison. GSM Alex Dumon made some very kind comments about the standard of the guard, and we came away from London having made a name for ourselves.

I was fortunate enough to help the 1st Bn to prepare for its 25th Anniversary Parade at Catterick, which was attended by Princess Anne, Colonel in Chief of the regiment. It was a great privilege for me to introduce some of the members of the regiment to her, a task made easy by her charm and personality.

Also whilst the battalion was at Catterick, I held – for the first time in the regiment's history – an Inter-Company Pace Stick Competition, and then sent the winning team to Pirbright in order to compete in the Guards Competition. Our finishing position was not so important as the fact that we were the first Infantry of the

Line Regiment to enter, and the Guards Division couldn't do enough for us. We sent a team the following year from Holywood NI, and very nearly split the Guards teams. AcSM Denis Cleary wrote to me complimenting the performance of the team.

We had as a battalion been to Northern Ireland many times, and so going to Holywood was like going home. The Border Regiment had been there in the 1930s and there was a photograph of them in the HQ building. I was RSM there for the first year and of all the camps in NI, Holywood is the best. We were operational, with one company deployed in West Belfast, and each of the other companies were at different states of readiness. Even so we were still able in the battalion to celebrate Arroyo, and St George's Day.

When the Border Regiment left in the 1930s, they donated a cup for the local football league, and this is still competed for – indeed they still call it the Border Cup. Fred Grimshaw and the rest of the old battalion must have left a lasting impression, and I would bet that they took a few wives back to England with them too. It was a great pleasure for me to take a British Legion Parade in one of the local towns one weekend, and I don't know who was the more thrilled, them seeing a regular RSM with his pace stick open marching on parade, or me being able to drill all of the old Burma Star men, and other veterans from both wars. The party after the parade was good too.

I well remember the training and preparation of the Number One Guard depicted in the photograph of them marching through Cockermouth in 1980. My company had just returned from a five month tour in Crossmaglen NI, and the morale was very high – and went even higher when it was decided that Arnhem Company would make up the bulk of No. 1 Guard. One of the main reasons why I remember it so well is that I broke three pace sticks . . . two during the first week when brushing off the cobwebs of five months in NI, and the third during the last week of preparation. The whole thing took three weeks, the first of which was left to the CSM, the second to a Drill Sergeant from the Welsh Guards (WOII Tony Bowen, who was later to become RSM of the Guards Depot), and the third week to RSM John MacCartney (later Quartermaster of the 1st Bn).

The first week was hell, even though the lads were keen. I started with 80 men but soon whittled it down to 60. Half of the time on the course was spent on drill, a quarter on PT and the remaining quarter on kit cleaning. When Drill Sgt Bowen took over in the second week, he concentrated on the finer points, passing on tips about marching in line, forming, and lots of other things taught only in the Guards Division. This was a much better week as the men were beginning to work as a team. The third and final week with the RSM went like clockwork, except for the officers. A full parade rehearsal was held in the morning, with PT afterwards, and a full parade after lunch with sports afterwards. On the day of Presentation of New Colours, the whole battalion went for a two mile run, had a good breakfast, went on parade and performed like Guardsmen! Later of course, parades were held in towns in Cumbria in order to display the New Colours.

'A ceremonial parade provides an occasion for men to express pride in their performance, pride in their regiment, and pride in the profession of arms.' So said Field Marshal Alexander of Tunis, and I am certain that this is true. The men will always give 100 per cent on a ceremonial occasion, but their actual performance will depend upon the qualities and abilities of their instructors.

I am now a commissioned officer, but make no apology for saying that the WOs and senior NCOs of a regiment represent its backbone. The Regimental Sergeant Major is the kingpin and should be able to provide the motivation to keep the men absolutely on their toes. If there is a good RSM there is a good regiment – a bad one and life becomes hell! Over the years his job has changed little, but what has changed is the army in which the

RSM R. Hopton, King's Own Royal Border Regt, on the drill square at Holywood NI, Oct 1985. Capt R. Hopton

RSM has to work.

I earlier spoke of a triple personality, and the third one is of course the persona required at home. Without the support of our wives such appointments would be unbearable. My wife has looked after the wives of the battalion when the menfolk are posted away, and has looked after the widows when my task has been to bury their husbands. On some occasions she has visited a soldier's house to say that I had just placed him under close arrest . . . Those tasks require a special kind of lady.

The Parachute Regiment has produced some fine Regimental Sergeant Majors, one of the first, John Lord, coming from the Grenadier Guards. He not only trained and served with the original 3rd Battalion through the war, but trained the post war volunteers when the regiment could still produce a full Division. He trained men for the many battalions with an extremely high standard of drill, even though many would serve for only two years under the 'duration of emergency' call-up scheme which later became National Service.

John Alcock replaced John Lord at the Infantry Training Centre, but by then reductions in the army were taking place, and the regiment quickly came down to brigade size. Alan Watson ran the Depot at Aldershot, but went on to become RSM at the RM Staff College at Camberley. RSM Sam McGeever took over the Depot, and was in fact the last person to address many of us completing our short period of service in 1948. His words at the time reflected the tension between east and west. 'I will not say goodbye – because you will all be back soon.' I believe that most of us thought the same, but he was to be proved wrong.

Many excellent RSMs followed in the regiment, RSM Tom Duffy who had been appointed in the field during the war, and served continuously as RSM for over 21 years. RSMs Brian Fehilly, 'Spike' Davis, 'Paddy' Pestell, Jim Aitken, Pete Kelly, John Williams – the youngest RSM in the army at 31 years during the latter 1960s, RSM Tony Arnold whom I was proud to meet at the opening of the J. C. Lord Room at the RMAS, and many others.

My meeting with RSM Peter Longley in 1974, when he trained and prepared the three regular battalions of the regiment, and the 4th Territorial Battalion, for the Presentation of New Colours by HM The Queen, was the first occasion upon which I had spoken to an RSM socially. This led indirectly to the book about RSM J. C. Lord, and to the research upon this book. I had worked with David Longley, a former Sergeant in the regiment, and younger brother of RSM P. Longley, for some years in social work, and when he mentioned his intention of attending the parade in Aldershot, had very gladly accepted his invitation to accompany him. He knew and had served with many of the men on parade that day, whereas I was visiting the regiment for the first time in 26 years. It was a marvellous occasion, and we were all extremely proud to see the regiment perform so brilliantly in the very wet conditions.

National Service was in operation when Peter Longley signed on for three years, initially to make sure of direct entry into the Parachute Regiment. He trained with 56 Platoon, and the Depot RSM was 'Paddy' Pestell formerly of the Irish Guards. Posted to the 2nd Battalion, Peter Longley moved quickly through the ranks, and remembers that his NCO Cadre to become Lance Corporal was almost wholly drill based. Due to a good education he became Sergeant by 1956. His RSM in the 2nd Bn at that time was RSM Jim Davis, later RSM Bob Hill and RSM Geoff Banks.

As a young Sergeant he was delighted to be selected to represent the regiment as an instructor at the RMAS, but had to qualify in the six weeks selection course under RSM J. C. Lord. Having qualified, he was given the choice of the posting to the RMAS, or to the USA under an exchange scheme. Peter Longley opted for the USA, and became a Platoon Commander in the 187th Infantry Battalion, of the US 82nd Airborne Division. He subsequently worked with their Operations Headquarters.

Following this interesting secondment, he was posted as CSM to D Company of the 1st Bn Parachute Regiment, where he worked under RSM Pete Kelly, in his opinion – a great RSM. Posted later to the Recruit Company at the Depot, he became School Sergeant Major at the regiment's Battle School at Brecon. Recruits at that time went twice to

RSM A. Arnold, Parachute Regt Depot, Aldershot, 1970.
Tony Arnold

Brecon, initially on a one week fieldcraft course, then later on a longer tactical training course.

After two years as School Sergeant Major, Peter Longley was made Drill Sergeant in 1968, where in the 3rd Bn, his main task was in training the Junior NCO Cadres. His RSM was RSM Tony Arnold who subsequently became RSM of the Depot. In 1969 Peter Longley was made RQMS at the Depot, where he served under RSM Jim Winter until 1971. He was then made RSM of the Brecon School, and he remained there for 18 months until taking over the appointment as RSM of the Depot. The highlight of his career came in 1974 when he trained the 1st, 2nd, 3rd Battalions, and the 4th TA Battalion for the Presentation of New Colours. Peter Longley was commissioned in September 1974, and when I visited him in December 1988, was still serving as an officer in the British Army.

Another regiment to be formed with the help of RSMs from the Guards Division was the Glider Pilot Regiment, and Bill Higgs, former Sergeant Pilot wrote to me:

The RSM who sticks in my mind is the one selected to knock us into shape following our acceptance into the Glider Pilot Regiment. His name was RSM J. C. Cowley, DCM Coldstream Guards, and he was one of several guards senior NCOs who were there to make or break us. 'There' was Tilshead Camp on Salisbury Plain where we were to complete our ground training before moving to EFTS for flying training.

RSM Cowley struck fear into us from the moment we stepped down from the transport which brought us from the little railway station (long since closed). Both officers and men were under his eagle eye and he didn't miss a trick. More than one mistake meant RTU (return to parent unit) a fate worse than death at that time. We dreaded his charge of 'Idle button' or 'Idle bootlace', in fact the only consolation was that he treated the officers the same, and referred to them as 'slovenly gentlemen'. I remember him on parade striding over the square towards me – and I thought my time had come! Fortunately he stopped in front of the man next to me, and described very luridly what he would do with this pace stick if my neighbour did not stand still on parade.

One cold Christmas morning RSM Cowley, like the Guardsman he was, made a terrific halt on the square, turned right, pace stick exactly level with the ground, and gave the order 'Battalion . . . A Merry Christmas!' No one answered as it was easy to lose one's name for speaking on parade. He repeated his shout – looked around – and added in a dark brown voice, 'Say *something* you unsociable lot!' Realising that we were safe to reply, we started bleating like a lot of sheep 'A Merry Christmas Sir.' Jim Cowley smiled like one who is at last loved and then quickly got on with the parade.

RSM Cowley was super in the Sergeants Mess off duty, and you couldn't believe that he was the same man who struck such fear on parade. I had the nerve to sing a song at a concert, entitled *Jim*, the lines of which went something like:

> Jim never buys me pretty flowers . . .
> never while's away the hours . . .
> I don't know why I am so crazy . . .
> about Jim . . . etc etc.

He enjoyed it, and every time he noticed me in the mess, I had to sing it again, and was never brave enough to refuse. I also had to repeat my Max Miller act. They were really great days, and although RSM Cowley did not fly with us, he did create a strong backbone to the regiment.

Gen Sir Geoffrey Howlett and Defence Secretary John Nott share conversation with Falkland Campaign RSMs Malcolm Simpson and Laurie Ashbridge of the Parachute Regt. MOD, London

Bill Higgs was badly wounded at Arnhem, and was with many others captured and imprisoned at Stalag X1b at Fallingbostel.

When I contacted Maj J. C. Cowley DCM Military Knight of Windsor, and President of the Distinguished Conduct Medal League, he remembered well his time with the Glider Pilot Regiment, but explained:

I was only with the regiment for nine months, and was at the time a War Substantive Sergeant, acting WOII, acting WOI! and was only just 23 years old – with under five years Colour service. I was privileged to help train them in 1942, but would point out that RSM Mick Briody MBE, went on active service with them. He was senior to me and eventually transferred to the Royal Army Pay Corps, and was the Major Paymaster at the Airborne Forces Depot at Aldershot.

RSM P. D. Longley, Depot RSM of the Parachute Regt, on parade at the Presentation of New Colours by HM The Queen, 1974.   Ken J. Upton

CHAPTER 23

RSMs of the Grenadier Guards

When I visited the Royal Hospital Chelsea in 1982, I was introduced to a tall, rather fierce looking old Coldstreamer, former RSM Joe Patterson, who in brief conversation talked of his regiment in extremely loyal terms, but conceded at one point that the Grenadier Guards had produced a few good RSMs who had not served as either Depot or Academy Sergeant Majors. Perhaps he had in mind some of the following.

Arthur Spratley was born in 1910 and joined the Grenadier Guards as a Drummer Boy in 1926. There is a beautiful little story included in the *Grenadier Gazette* related by Lt-Col G. H. Ealden, MBE MC about Drummer A. J. Spratley:

The time was 8.15am on a morning many years ago, at the Guardroom of Windsor Castle. The Warrant Officer of the Guard addresses Drummer Spratley. 'Now Drummer, as you know, or ought to know, today is an Honour Day. Your job is to take this gleaming bucket, proceed in a direction which should already be known to you, collect the very finest specimens of Laurel leaves, return here, make a wreath, polish it and produce it to me for inspection prior to it being placed on the Colour in time for the Guard to dismount. Get going lad!'

Drummer Spratley is next seen, complete with burnished bucket, proceeding 'in the direction known to him', which was somewhere in the area of the Round Tower. He selects his spot and begins to choose nothing but the very best specimens of leaves when he finds a bearded, regal looking figure at his side. This regal figure is no less a person than HM King George V, who demands to know what the Drummer is doing. The Drummer explains the tradition and His Majesty enters into the spirit of things by saying that on this particular day he, personally, will choose the leaves. The Drummer empties his partially filled bucket and the whole process of selection begins again. HM is very meticulous in his selection, but eventually the bucket is again partially filled with sufficient of the 'King's Laurels'.

Drummer Spratley salutes His Majesty and begins his journey back to the Guardroom. Halfway down Lower Ward he is met by the Sergeant of the Guard who tells him that the Warrant Officer is 'blowing his top' at the length of time he has been away from the Guardroom. The Drummer explains what happened. They enter the Guardroom together and the Warrant Officer addresses them as follows. 'Drummer, where the ... hell have you been! and where (glancing into the bucket) did you get that bloody mangy looking lot of leaves from?' Drummer Spratley explained 'But Sir, they were all picked personally by His Majesty the King.'

The Warrant Officer exploded, 'I thought I had heard every excuse in the British Army, but I haven't heard that one before. Let me tell you, Drummer, His Imperial Majesty wouldn't no more go round helping idle Drummers to pick leaves than he would go round picking his nose. Sergeant, put him in the book!' 'But Sir,' explained the Sergeant, 'He is telling the truth. What do

Lt-Col Arthur J. Spratley, MBE MM, former RSM of the 4th Bn Grenadier Guards.   Grenadier Gazette

I put him in the book for?' The Warrant Officer glared 'I dunno. That's your worry. You think of something.' The Sergeant admitted 'But Sir, I can't think of anything.' 'That always was your trouble Sergeant!' exploded the Warrant Officer, 'Can't think in a crisis. Well – I've thought of something . . . put *yourself* in the book – BLOODY IDLE!!'

Arthur Spratley went on to serve in the 3rd Battalion in the 1930s spending three years in Egypt under two great RSMs, Hawkins and Turner. He was an excellent runner and represented his battalion many times. In 1940 he served with the BEF in France and eventually became RSM of the 4th Battalion, fighting from Normandy to the Baltic in his Churchill tank appropriately named *Windsor*. So many former Grenadiers speak of his example, and one young Guardsman to be strongly influenced by him was the future AcSM, Ray Huggins.

Commissioned as Quartermaster in 1949 with the 3rd Battalion, and later the Guards Depot, he eventually became HQ Company Commander at the RMAS, with the rank of Lieutenant Colonel. As a result of his service he held the MBE, MM, and the Croix de Guerre, with numerous campaign medals. He was then General Secretary of the Grenadier Guards Association for ten years, and was finally appointed a Military Knight of Windsor.

RSM Randolph Beard was spoken of with admiration and respect by Brig C. R. Britten OBE MC, whom I visited when researching the career of John Lord. He remembered an occasion when both he and Randolph Beard were getting rather old for marching with the Old Comrades on parade, and he had asked the former RSM if he was really going to march with the Comrades that day . . . and Randolph Beard had quickly retorted 'I *am* if *you* are Sir!'

Randolph Beard enlisted in 1906 and was a Sergeant before the First World War. He was wounded twice in France and was awarded the MM, and mentioned in despatches in 1916, and awarded the DCM in 1919. When the war ended he was serving as Drill Sergeant, and then in 1920 became RSM. He distinguished himself as Regimental Sergeant Major for seven years before being commissioned Quartermaster. Retiring from the army in 1939 as Captain QM, he quickly returned on the outbreak of the Second World War and served throughout as Major QM. Randolph Beard left the army for the second time in 1945, and lived to enjoy a long retirement. He died on the 10 February 1975 at the age of 86 years.

Richard S. Walker is remembered as a distinguished RSM of the 1st Bn Grenadier Guards, from 1929-36, and he had earlier served at the Royal Military College as CQMS and Company Sergeant Major. He was with the 5th and 4th Battalions during the First World War in France, and with the 1st Battalion and Guards Armoured Division as Commissioned QM in the Second World War. He became Major in 1946 serving with the 201 Guards Brigade until retirement from the army in 1947. He held the MBE, RVM, LS and GC medal, and many campaign medals of both World Wars. Major Walker died on 25 October 1976, but his memory lives on with a great many Grenadiers.

Bernard H. Pratt was another RSM of great note who joined the regiment in 1924. He was an instructor at both the Guards Depot and the RMC Sandhurst, before becoming RSM, and had served in all three battalions of the regiment. On the outbreak of war he served with the BEF as RSM of the 2nd Battalion, and was badly wounded by Belgian Fifth Columnists during the retreat to Dunkirk.

Although demanding the very highest of standards, he also had a well remembered sense of humour. He went on to become Quartermaster of the 6th Battalion in 1941, and then of the 2nd Battalion in Germany, finally serving as Camp Commandant at the Eastern Command HQ until retirement as a Lieutenant Colonel.

RSM George Kirkham MBE, enlisted in the regiment in 1941, and served under such fine RSMs as Lou Drouet, GSM Tom Taylor, and AcSM Ray Huggins. He wrote to me:

The rank of RSM is one of great responsibility and like every other walk of life, the mantle is carried better by some than others. I always feel sad when talking to former servicemen from all arms, to find that they cannot remember the name of their old RSM. Either they have a poor memory or someone has failed to make an adequate impression.

When I joined the Guards Depot in February 1941, my CSM was Harry Muckett, my Corporal Squad Instructor was John Sheldon, and the Sergeant Major was Mickey Dunne of the Welsh Guards. He was a man of about 6ft 5in and most impressive to a recruit of 19. All three were excellent NCOs and I was delighted to meet John Sheldon in recent years. My initial training and instruction therefore came from some first class people who placed me on the right track of a career. They transformed me from someone who was going to leave the army after the war – and was not over keen, to a person striving to reach the very pinnacle of appointments.

I joined the Sergeants Mess in 1946, where both Tom Taylor and Ray Huggins were serving as Sergeants. In 1958 I was made Drill Sergeant of the 1st Battalion, when Lou Drouet was the RSM. Soon after this I was made RSM of the Army Apprenticeship College at Chepstow, where there were 930 Apprentices, plus a Sergeants Mess of 110 members, including five other WO1s. The Staff were from most regiments and corps, mainly REME at the time, but later REs. What a different ball game from one's own regiment! The last thing they wanted was to be told how we did things in the Grenadier Guards, but by example one tried to win them over.

When one has served 18 years in a parent unit and is suddenly placed into a mixed organisation, it is certainly a challenge, but I served at the Army Apprentices College at Chepstow for six years, and enjoyed it to the end. I still have the privilege of belonging as an honorary member of the Mess, and also the CLRD Mess, so I remain in what is always considered the finest club in the world – the Sergeants Mess.

I retired from the army in 1964 having been a very fortunate man, and I continue to be so, for I am now a member of The Queen's Bodyguard of the Yeomen of the Guard, and still have Sergeant Majors looking after me.

During 1984 I was delighted to receive several letters from Crispin Keightley, who served in both the Grenadier Guards and the Parachute Regiment, and I am proud to include extracts of his memories of training and service in the regiment.

I enjoyed every moment in the regiment, but having a keen sense of humour and being able to laugh at even the ridiculous, I was in trouble many times for laughing on parade, particularly during my training. My late father served with the regiment during, and for a short time after, the First World War. I was 'family first reserve' for the replay 21 years later, and it follows that I knew a great deal about the brigade long before I joined. Nothing came as a surprise yet I frequently could not restrain a smile – so I lost my name once more.

We had been drilling at the customary 140 paces to the minute of the Guards Depot, when our Squad Sergeant, Walker, whom he said, spelled his name BASTARD, gave us a brief spell of rest standing properly at ease. Some, perhaps all, were breathing through the mouth as well as the nose, and the RSM F. M. Dowling MC, walked over and approached one recruit who was revealing his teeth. The RSM fairly gently tapped the trainee on his front teeth with the tip of his pace stick 'Close your mouth lad' he growled, 'I don't want to see your rabbit teeth. Can't you breathe through your nose?' and in the same breath he added, 'Put that man in the book for smiling on parade!' That was me of course, then I was confronted by this severe mien and he asked, 'Do you find me funny?' I tried so hard to control my pent up laughter that my eyes began to water. I won the first round and murmured 'No Sir', but the fight wasn't yet over for he looked into my moist eyes and groaned 'My God Sergeant, he's actually crying! where do we get these horrible little men – from Hilda's Academy for dancing?' That finished my self control and laughter burst out – and I was ordered to double around the square. As I set out I heard the RSM saying to the Sergeant, 'We must watch that insolent man. Let's not misjudge him, but watch him.'

Directly next to the RSM we had those other formidable men – Senior Drill Sergeants, and I found them more awe-inspiring than the RSM. Even more severe perhaps, because they were next in line for RSM rank. Ours, D Sgts Ripton and G. C. Hackett, appeared to be everywhere at once, never apparently needing sleep.

One day during foot drill – we were not yet considered capable of handling a rifle – D Sgt Ripton had the squad halted, and marching through the ranks until he stood close to the recruit next to me, he asked, 'Were you a sailor laddie – before we got stuck with you?' 'No Sir' replied the recruit. 'Then why do you roll like a sailor!' roared the Drill Sergeant. As the lad began to answer he was shut up by the traditional command, 'Stop talking!!' Then the Drill Sergeant added to the Squad Corporal totally poker faced. 'Corporal, after parade break this man's legs and reset them straight – he may march properly then.'

When I arrived at the Depot I was sporting a moustache, not particularly small – but not fully grown. One day when the entire intake was on parade, RSM Dowling standing on the other side of the parade ground, pointed his pace stick in my general direction and roared, 'That man there . . . Come here. Dress up!' I was not sure that he meant me so I stood fast, the pace stick could have been directed at any man on my immediate right or left. The RSMs tone rose to a penetrating pitch as he used all of the expertise gained by years of controlled shouting, and it left me in no further doubt. 'YOU, you idle man, Yes you, Clark Gable . . . the man with his nose running! Double here.' I doubled with my rifle at the trail but was ordered back to double at the slope. When I reached the RSM, he looked at my upper lip with disgust in his eyes for what seemed to be minutes, probably no more than 30 seconds, touched his own luxuriant full moustache and said 'THAT'S a moustache . . . but what's that under your nose! Whatever it is – get rid of it lad. Report to me this evening clean shaven, then do not shave your upper lip again without special permission!' I have had a more or less large moustache ever since.

An incident which reduced me to uncontrollable mirth – and gained me extra drills for a week, was created by D Sgt Allibone, when on parade he stared in horror at the trousers of the man next to me. Why did they have to pick on people so close to me! D Sgt Allibone said, 'Look at those trousers! – not a vestige of a crease. Not a vestige!' In point of fact the offending trousers would have passed muster on most occasions, but the wearer had obviously

over dampened them when placing them under his mattress the night before. With the warmth of his legs the creases had now become a little less than knife edged. The Drill Sergeant went on at the Squad Sergeant. 'Have *you* seen anything so disgusting and slovenly?' He nagged for almost two minutes or more which was a great trial for my control, but when he finally told the Sergeant to put the man in the book for 'IDLE WHILE SLEEPING' I exploded.

Being a mere six feet in height I was frequently told that I was a little man; squaring off, tallest on the right, shortest on the left, this time in the 2nd Battalion in Germany, RSM Hector Young asked me if I was standing in a hole, and how did I get into the Guards anyway?

My final recollection concerns a superb Company Sergeant Major of 2 Company, 3rd Bn Grenadier Guards, Sammy Lowe MM. He was my CSM and, like most WOs, a mainstay. During an attack in the few last weeks of the campaign in Italy, we were crossing a canal in north east Italy, the Fosso Cembalina. A burning house on the bank of the canal was illuminating the scene beautifully, and the canvas bridge which those lovely lads, the sappers, had managed to sling across the water made an excellent target.

The 'Tedeschi' were mortaring the area, and as they could always be counted upon for regularlity, we were able to take the calculated risk of doubling over the canvas strip in between stonks. The banks and the pontoon were expertly registered by spandaus too, and things were a little hectic. I was about to make the dash with a small group when Sammy Lowe noticed that my battledress collar was unhooked. Quietly, but with the authority born of long practice, he hissed in my ear, 'Where do you think you are Keightley! You're slovenly dressed and idle too. Do your collar up you horrible man. What do you think the 'Teds' would think if they could see you as I can see you! Do it up and double over that bridge.' I fastened my tunic.

Weeks later, we were in Austria clearing up the remnants of the organised resistance, but the war in Europe was all but over. Semi-peace time standards were being enforced. Sammy Lowe was lecturing us on the state of our general appearance, and glancing around in disgust, he said, 'There are enough sideboards (sideburns) around here to stock Times Furnishing over and over again. GET EM OFF!'

One and all – Warrant Officers and NCOs – they were lovely men, and the backbone of the regiment. I would not have missed my time in the Guards Brigade.

Maj P. A. Lewis MBE was RSM of the 1st Bn Grenadier Guards from 1967-69, and retains the reputation as having been the epitome of a regimental soldier. He joined the regiment in 1945 and trained at the Guards Depot under RSM S. M. Hamilton MBE Scots Guards.

Posted to the 3rd Battalion in Palestine, he progressed to Lance Sergeant in Support Company in 1947. Upon the withdrawal of British Forces in 1948, Peter Lewis celebrated his 21st birthday aboard the *Empress of Australia* as Troop Deck Sergeant in charge of some 600 members of the 6th Airborne Division, one of whom was the author. Many were 'duration of emergency' men whose service was reaching completion and Peter Lewis' task was not made easy. Four months later he was on his way to the jungles of Malaya.

L Sgt Lewis had already served under two Grenadier RSMs, 'Spot' Baker, whose drill square was known as 'Spot's plot', and RSM Timber Wood DCM, who was

Laying up the Colour of the 1st Bn, Grenadier Guards. RSM P. A. Lewis and Major H. S. Hanning at the head of the first detachment marching to Lincoln Cathedral. Guards Magazine

subsequently to serve at the RMAS. Entry into the Sergeants Mess had brought with it much experience and the RSMs had been met for the first time in a situation where their unique influence could be observed.

Peter Lewis was promoted Gold Sergeant in 1951, serving as the School of Infantry Anti-Tank Platoon Sergeant. He obtained an A (oustanding) grade during educational tests, in which he was one of only two of the candidates at the time to pass, and with this qualification he progressed to CQMS and Pay Sergeant of Support Company. There followed service in North Africa, Egypt and Cyprus, before promotion came as Company Sergeant Major and a tour at the RMA Sandhurst under RSM J. C. Lord. As with many WOs of promise, this period had a marked influence upon CSM Lewis and he assimilated the teaching methods and high standards of RSM Lord.

The appointment as CSM of 14 Company at the Guards Depot followed, where Peter Lewis used the methods taught by RSM Lord. He remembers working extremely long hours with the recruits and had the satisfaction of not only improving the standards, but of reducing the numbers of recruits seeking discharge by purchase. He also cultivated a good team of Sergeant Instructors to serve in the company, and was instrumental in the introduction of Passing Out Parades to which parents and visitors were invited to attend.

Promoted to Drill Sergeant in the 1st Battalion, he served with RSM J. Bing, and also with RSM T. Pugh in Germany. He remembers taking part in the Presentation of New Colours to the 1st Battalion in 1966, and also the unique duty as Drill Sergeant of being appointed to prepare the Royal Company of Archers, The Queen's Bodyguard of Scotland for a parade. At one stage when he was asked why a Grenadier should be training them – and not a Scots Guardsman, he replied 'Gentlemen, you are the best, you need the best – and I am the best!'

In 1967 and having served for 21 years, Peter Lewis was appointed Regimental Sergeant Major of the 1st Battalion and in addition to setting the battalion an extremely high standard of public duties, he served with them in a nine month tour in the Persian Gulf. RSM Peter Lewis prepared the Queen's Company for inspection by Her Majesty, at Buckingham Palace. Here it was necessary for him to devise a drill which would enable the company to form from column of divisions into line, and from three ranks into two

– simultaneously, for the march past in the restricted space available. Drawing on the experience of John Lord's training, he practiced the movement which on the day brought an exclamation from HM The Queen 'My Goodness, that was impressive . . .'

Commissioned to Captain Quartermaster of the 2nd Battalion, he went on to serve tours in Northern Ireland, British Honduras and Hong Kong. In 1974 he was given the responsible task of briefing Her Majesty upon her coming visit to the battalion, with the result that the Queen met the whole battalion and their wives in groups, and was able to discuss the forthcoming tour of Hong Kong with them.

Peter Lewis enjoyed drill and would have very much liked to complete a tour as the Drill Sergeant of the All Arms Drill Wing. His 'party piece' was to drill two squads at the same time, one in slow time and the other in quick time – with his back turned to both! Upon being commissioned an assessment was prepared by Col David Gordon-Lennox which stated:

Peter Lewis has had an outstanding career in the regiment, which culminated in the appointment of Regimental Sergeant Major of the 1st Battalion, Grenadier Guards.

He has always made an outstanding success of anything he has done, because he has that ability, determination and sense of loyalty and responsibility, which is given only to those who reach the very highest levels of leadership. The regiment will always be grateful for what he has achieved.

RSM B. T. Jim Eastwood enlisted in the Grenadier Guards in 1952 at Canterbury, and had a prompt

Top:
RSM B. T. 'Jim' Eastwood, Grenadier Guards. RSM of the 1st Mechanised Bn, Grenadier Guards, 1972-4. Bryan Poupard

Below:
A group of Coldstream Guards RSMs of 1969-70. (L to R) RSMs S. Williams, D. Cessford, N. Welch, W. Pickles, K. Mursell, J. Hook, W. J. Holbrook and P. Horsfall.
Col N. Welch

introduction to ceremonial when his first public duty was to line the route with the 1st Battalion upon the State Funeral of Queen Mary in 1953. His second duty was at the Coronation of HM The Queen in the same year, when he had already become a Lance Corporal. In 1954 he became an Instructor at the Guards Depot, and took eight squads through training during the time of Depot RSM D. Whyte.

In 1955 Jim Eastwood left the army to become a British Transport Commission Police Constable in London, but not for long, as the following year saw him re-enlist in the regiment, and he progressed through the ranks quickly. In 1958 he became a Recruiting Sergeant, and successfully recruited and married Sheila in November of that year. He went on to serve in North Africa, the Cameroons and Cyprus, before becoming CSM of Waterloo Company, Old College, RMAS, in 1968.

There followed three tours in Northern Ireland as Drill Sergeant of the 2nd Battalion, then RSM of the 1st Bn, and MTO of the 2nd Bn. His period of two years as RSM of the 1st Mechanised Battalion commenced in 1972, and was in the BAOR. His commissioned service covered Families Officer of the 2nd Bn in Hong Kong, Technical QM in BAOR, before becoming Quartermaster of the 1st Bn in Berlin in 1979. In 1983 he became Staff QM and Adjutant at the Royal Military School of Music. Jim Eastwood then in 1984 became the second Guardsman to hold the prestigious appointment of Superintendent of Windsor Castle.

Right:
'Studs-n-socks'.
Nothing changes!
Coldstream Guards
kit inspection
c1903.   R.G. Harris
Coldstream Guards
kit inspection 1946.
Guards Magazine.

CHAPTER 24

RSMs of the Junior Infantry Battalions

How better to conclude a work on the Regimental Sergeant Major than to write of the young soldiers of the Junior Infantry Battalions, who are not only the RSMs of the future, but in the case of a few, serve as Junior RSMs for the final weeks of their training, and actually command their own Passing Out Parade. Junior Leaders and Junior Soldiers are trained for Queen's and Prince of Wales's Divisions and the Royal Pioneer Corps at Shorncliffe, for the Light Division at Winchester, for the Guards Regiments and the Parachute Regiment at Pirbright and for the Scottish and King's Divisions at Harlow Hill, near Hexham.

I was allowed to visit all four establishments during 1986, and count it a privilege to have been able to observe such keen and well motivated young men in training. It did me a power of good to watch them responding to some of the most exciting training in the world, and especially to witness one of the Passing Out Parades, at Harlow Hill in December 1987, when the Junior RSM commanded such a smart and impressive parade.

The staff at Junior Infantry Battalions are carefully selected and I was very impressed with the attitudes of everyone I spoke to, in relation to both the obvious care of young men who commence their training at little over 16 years old, and the positive advice and guidance given. Training at the four establishments appears to differ only in relation to the needs of the adult regiment to which the junior soldiers will eventually be posted, but the early emphasis is on improving fitness and teaching basic military skills. Next comes tactical training for work in a section, and the final stage develops leadership qualities and improves military skills including shooting. There are also many aspects of educational, sporting and adventure training.

Lt-Col D. A. B. Williams (RGJ) at the JLR at Shorncliffe, advised me that former Army Cadet Force candidates often settled down to training quickly and performed particularly well, as they had already absorbed many of the basic requirements. Also that a high proportion of those who successfully completed the course of training later reached NCO rank in the adult army. This was not surprising when one realised that the final standard produced junior soldiers capable of performing so confidently on a Passing Out Parade commanded entirely by Junior NCOs.

I was most interested to discover how the present day instructors teach such young candidates, bearing in mind that they are two years younger than the former national service age of 18 years. Outwardly, discipline on the drill square appears to differ little, but the background regime of support and encouragement is very different, and the subjects taught and methods of teaching are much advanced. I found RSM R. W. Potter (Royal Anglian Regiment) an ideal mixture of a highly professional and positive soldier, tall and extremely smart, but with the additional qualities of patience and understanding with which to deal with very young soldiers. Obviously he was sharp, but was very approachable with a friendly manner and a ready grin. I was not at all surprised to learn that he had received his training at the Oswestry Junior Leader Regiment in 1965, nor that most of the young men on his course are now serving as RSMs. There could hardly be a clearer demonstration of the value of the Oswestry training.

He well remembered his training under RSM John Bing (Grenadier Guards) and had also been influenced during later training by RSM Stan Bullock of the Royal Anglian Regiment. In 1974 he had taken part as a Corporal of the Escort when the 3rd Battalion of the regiment had been presented with New Colours.

With such a busy programme of varied activities at the Junior Infantry Battalion, there is not an emphasis on drill, but RSM Bob Potter advised me that there is a battalion muster parade on Wednesdays and a Saturday morning drill parade. Preparations build up gradually for the Passing Out Parade throughout the course, and become extensive during the final weeks. All Platoon Sergeant Instructors had attended the All Arms Drill Wing, and Weapon Training Instructors the Skill at Arms at Warminster.

I was allowed to talk with CSM Peter Tatum (Royal Regiment of Wales), who was serving his third tour at Shorncliffe, the first being as a junior soldier from 1969-71, and the second as a Sergeant from 1982-84. He impressed as an extremely smart and positive CSM, with a kindly attitude towards the juniors. He explained that there is an element of counselling work necessary as some of the juniors have problems to solve. The standard expected is very high, and a failure rate of some 25 per cent is expected. There are defaulters as in the old days . . . and young men awarded extra duties complete these during the evenings, but the emphasis is on training and fatigues are not allowed to interfere with the programme.

I also enjoyed talking with Section Commanders, Sgt K. Bloodworth (Gloucestershires), Sgt S. Guy (Royal Fusiliers) and Cpl A. Hunter (Queen's) all of whom would be remembered by their juniors as having valuable experience to pass on. I was particularly pleased to be able to talk also with two Junior Leaders, J-Ldr S. Horder (R. Hampshire Regt) and J-Ldr A. Lavery (Queen's Regt). Both impressed me as being confident in the presence of the RSM – much more so than would have been the recruits of my day. Both had joined the army with the intention of following in their respective fathers' footsteps and were settling down well on the course. In national service days they would have been considered well above average. When I enquired a few weeks later, one of the young men had already received promotion as Junior Corporal. Both candidates passed out in August '87 and will now be well settled in to adult service life.

In June of that year, a unique occasion took place when the Senior Junior Leaders passed out. As the Junior RSM, Julian Davies commanded the parade of some 200 Infantry Junior Leaders, whilst watched by his father, RSM Davies of the 1st Bn, Royal Welch Fusiliers, who was amongst the spectators.

At Winchester I met RSM Derek Brennan (Light Infantry) who hails from Gateshead and was formerly in the Durham Light Infantry. He had seen service in many countries, since enlisting in 1964. His own training RSM came from the King's Shropshire LI, RSM Ben Dunster, and also RSM Ian Harding of the 1st Light Infantry Bn had influenced him as CSM. In describing the training programme of the Junior Infantry Battalion at Winchester, RSM Brennan mentioned that the junior soldiers wore camouflage caps until passing a drill test which carried as a reward and qualification the wearing of berets.

I was interested to note that RSM Brennan carried a cane instead of the usual pace stick. He mentioned that the

RSM Robert W. Potter, Royal Anglian Regt, inspects Burma Company at the Junior Infantry Bn, Shorncliffe, Nov 1986. Having been in the battalion for six weeks, the Junior Soldiers are being inspected prior to Passing Off the Square. Brian Pearson

Junior RSM Julian Davies with his father RSM Davies, 1st Royal Welch Fusiliers. JRSM Davies had just passed out into Adult service by commanding a parade of over 235 Junior Leaders at the JIB, Shorncliffe, June 1987. Brian Pearson

Training Battalion was at that time making preparations for the change from SLR to SA80 rifle. When discussing drill, RSM Brennan described the two drill movements which he particularly enjoys watching when they are well performed, the light infantry present arms and the advance in review order. He also recalled taking part as a rifleman in '68, in a fine parade when Laying up the Colours of the 1st Bn, Durham Light Infantry.

When I visited RSM David Gibson (Coldstream Guards) at the Guards Depot, it was in relation to his general duties, but he also had responsibility for the Junior Leaders and Junior Soldiers of the Guards Regiments and for those of the Parachute Regiment. Whilst the training regime is similar to that of other junior soldier establishments, the location of the battalion within the Guards Depot complex, and the combined Guards and Parachute Regiment Instructors provides an extremely disciplined setting.

Historically, the Guards have provided the basic regimental training for several of the regiments formed during the Second World War, including the Parachute Regiment, the Glider Pilot Regiment and the Army

Commando Units. The Infantry Training Centres were organised on the lines of the Guards Depot. Couple this with the fact that the 1st Bn of the Parachute Regiment was at one time the Guards Parachute Battalion (before reducing to an independent company) and there is every reason why the combined training of the junior soldiers should be successful.

Living within a reasonable distance of the Junior Infantry Battalion at Harlow Hill, I was able to visit them on two occasions in 1986, the first being to meet the CO, RSM and two Junior Leaders and the second to attend a Passing Out Parade.

Lt-Col J. C. Charteries MC received my enquiries with the utmost cordiality and talked with me about the present day training and its implications for the future. Again the qualities of the former Oswestry men were mentioned as so many of the senior NCOs were trained there. Col Charteries advised me of the selection procedures and of the future problems in relation to this country's lower birthrate, which will cause difficulties in maintaining the numbers of properly motivated young men able and willing to accept the present standards of training.

I was to meet Capt R. Hopton (King's Own Royal Border Regt) and learn that he trained the Number 1 Guard of the Regiment for the Presentation of Colours and the subsequent marches through several towns in Cumbria. I also met the Adjutant Capt Charles Gray, of the same regiment, who at 6ft 4in was a most impressive soldier. I then met RSM L. Larson (King's Regt) a tall and immaculate soldier whose appearance alone formed an excellent example to the junior soldiers. RSM Les Larson joined the army in 1969 and was appointed RSM on being posted to Harlow Hill in 1985. He particularly remembered training under RSM J. Weir (King's Regt) whom he described as a 'ball of fire' but was so correct in dress and manner.

RSM Larson had enjoyed a tour at the RMA Sandhurst during the late 1970s, where he served as a Colour Sergeant Instructor, Old College and subsequently as a CQMS. This had been during the time of AcSM R. P. Huggins MBE of whom RSM Larson spoke very highly. I was reminded that the duties of the AcSM, as Senior RSM in the army, includes visits to other establishments as AcSM Dennis Cleary was due to visit Harlow Hill JIB.

In general, RSM Larson believed that young men are now more questioning and would not put up with some of the attitudes and regimes of the past. As courses are so much shorter the emphasis has to be wholly upon training, with no time to spend on wasteful activities. He also makes a point of showing the junior soldiers around the excellent Sergeants Mess and in particular the many paintings of their regiments, so that they learn about their regiments' battle honours. Also by seeing the surroundings they may take the prospects of promotion more seriously and seek to share the facilities later in their careers.

I was allowed to talk with two Junior Leaders and was most impressed by their attitudes. Jun-Sgt John Allan (Black Watch) came from a military family and intended to make his career in the Black Watch. His training was hard but he was confident that all was going well and I have rarely experienced such mature enthusiasm in a young soldier.

Jun-Sgt Harry Tymon (Royal Irish Rangers) also came from a military family, in which his grandfather had served in the Royal Irish Fusiliers, and his father a Colour Sergeant in the Royal Irish Rangers (now composed of the Royal Irish Fusiliers, the Royal Ulster Rifles and the Royal Inniskilling Fusiliers). Sadly, his father had died soon after leaving the army after 22 years service. Now at a late stage of his training Jun-Sgt Tymon was preparing for the final tests and passing out parade. A lot of pressure was on for the pending selection of Junior CSMs and Junior RSM and both junior soldiers spoken to were much involved in the process.

On 13 December 1986 I went back to attend the Passing Out Parade of the two platoons of the Scottish Junior Leaders Company and one platoon of the King's Junior Leaders Company and was pleased to see John Allan on parade as a Junior Colour Sergeant and Harry Tymon standing alone in the centre of the parade ground, commanding the whole parade as Junior RSM. What an unforgettable experience for a young man and his watching relatives.

Maj-Gen C. R. L. Guthrie LVO OBE inspected the parade and then took the salute as the three platoons marched past in slow and quick time. The Advance in Review Order followed and then the Oath of Allegiance and Prayers. The Senior Division then marched off in slow time, their training as juniors now completed, whilst the Junior Division followed in quick time – their day still to come.

I later watched Jun RSM H. J. Tymon receive the Director of Infantry's Prize for Best Overall Junior Leader, Jun CSM S. R. Marriott (Black Watch) the prize for Best Scottish Division Junior Leader and Jun CSM S. L. Mullen (Royal Irish Rangers) the prize for the Best King's Division Junior Leader. I could not help thinking that Sgt-Maj Masterton MacIntosh of the old 79th Cameron Highlanders would have been proud to see the calibre of the ten Junior Leaders passing out to join their adult regiment – the Queen's Own Highlanders. For every junior

on parade, it must have been a great experience to march to the music of the Light Infantry Burma Band TA and Bugles of the 7th Bn Light Infantry, under WO M. A. Jacques. RSM L. Larson had also watched the parade with a great deal of pride.

During my visits to the Junior Infantry Battalions, I talked to young men in training who were smart, alert and fit, with enthusiasm and interest shining from them. One Junior Sergeant admitted to me, 'Yes – you get very tired when the pressure's on – but you try not to show it because you have to give a good example as a Sergeant.' This was not said with any sense of elitism, but with a modest grin, and I thought what a pleasure it must be to teach and guide such young men of quality.

The instructors are well selected and in my opinion need to be because it is as much a privilege to work with these young soldiers as it is to train officer cadets at the RMA

The CSM marches a platoon off the square watched by the RSM – but all are Junior Soldiers! Junior RSM H. Tymon and Junior CSM S. R. Marriott at the Harlow Hill JIB on 13 Dec 1986.
Photo by the author

Sandhurst. The attitude of the staff must be vitally important in such training, to achieve just the right balance, and this book is full of comment by men who have experienced this – from the NCOs and WOs they have chosen to remember and mention.

The Oswestry type of training, the Junior Soldiers and Junior Leaders establishments are worth every penny. It really is true that what we put in towards such training is returned with enormous profit in the quality of soldiers, NCOs and WOs of the future. Just look at the former Oswestry men. How we prepare and train our young soldiers has tremendous implications for the future and quality never comes cheap.

Junior RSM H. Tymon, Royal Irish Rangers, takes the Passing Out Parade at Harlow Hill JIB 13 Dec 1986. Photo by the author

A closing message from the current Senior Regimental Sergeant Major of the British Army, AcSM Michael Nesbitt, The RMA Sandhurst:

My conclusion to this story of the Regimental Sergeant Major is inevitably aimed at the young soldier of today, who faces the ever increasing responsibilities of tomorrow which are more professionally demanding than ever before.

The factors emanating from the experiences of those whose careers have been detailed in this work are, predominently, their determination to hold on to the standards and traditions of the army but at the same time retain the ability to prepare for and adapt to changes rather than to resist them.

The preparation for the unique responsibility of the Regimental Sergeant Major has always been the same in one important respect – a steady progression through the ranks; learning and accepting the implications of each rank in preparation for the next. Recognised in this way, the duties of the Lance Corporal are as necessary and important in the full apprenticeship as any other rank and, in that sense, the old arm badge of rank of four chevrons illustrates very clearly the gradual accumulation of knowledge and experience to be gained with each chevron.

One of the effects of a book such as this might be to blow away some of the mystery and charisma of the office of Regimental Sergeant Major. Some may regret this but when the result is to reveal so clearly how that necessary experience is gained and why such a depth of knowledge is necessay, the young soldier can feel some relief that the standards and the rank are clearly attainable with effort on his part.

There is surely comfort, not only in the fact that many of the great RSMs had no inkling of their ability until well advanced in service, but also that the holders of the rank differed so much in their methods and approach in seeking the necessary response. It is said that one of the greatest RSMs of recent years, John Lord, always warmed to the 'man of spirit', and I can probably give no clearer guide to the young soldier of today, and in years to come, seeking his way through the ranks.

RSMs' Military Awards

British RSMs awarded The Victoria Cross

The Victoria Cross was founded by Royal Warrant on 29 January 1856, but actions dating back to June 1854 were included in the first awards. The first Investiture ceremony was held by Queen Victoria on 26 June 1857.

The following holders of the Victoria Cross were serving as Sergeant Majors at the time of award:

John Grieve	
2nd Dragoons (Royal Scots Greys)	5.11.1854
Andrew Henry	
Royal Artillery	5.11.1854
George Lambert	
84th Regt (later York & Lancaster R)	1857
Ambrose Madden	
41st Regt (later The Welch R)	5.11.1854
Charles Colquhoun Pye	
53rd Regt (later King's Shropshire LI)	17.11.1857
William Robertson	
Gordon Highlanders	21.10.1899

British Sergeant Majors serving in the Indian Army when awarded the VC:

Peter Gill	4. .6.1857
James Miller	28.10.1857
Matthew Rosamund	4. 6.1857

British Sergeant Majors serving in the South African Forces:

Alexander Young	13. 8.1901

British RSMs awarded The Distinguished Conduct Medal

The following holders of the Distinguished Conduct Medal were serving as Regimental Sergeant Majors (or equivalent earlier rank of Sergeant Major) when awarded the medal or bar to the medal. The roll includes those acting or in temporary appointment in the rank. Bracketed dates are approximate.

Cavalry

2LG	F. Howard	16. 1.1915
HHD	C. Wright	6. 2.1918
2DG	G. F. W. Smith	17. 4.1918
DG	A. Allison	13. 2.1917
DG	L. F. Barrett MM	3. 9.1918
3DG	W. Buxton	31.10.1902
4DG	T. Urell	31.10.1902
5DG	Erasmus Green	(21. 1.1855)
5DG	William Manning	19. 4.1901
5DG	A. E. Hurst	23. 4.1901
6DG	William Lyons	(30. 4.1856)
6DG	J. H. Blaney	19. 4.1901
6DG	Henry Edgar Varley	31.10.1902
1DR	S. J. Oxford	14. 4.1920
2DR	W. J. Reeves	21. 6.1916
RSG	W. Cowell	14.10.1943
3H	W. Derrett	31.10.1902
3H	H. Smith	11. 3.1916
4H	A. J. Medley Bar	9. 8.1945
	Awarded DCM as Sgt 15.10.1942	
5L	W. D. Coldridge	21.10.1918
6DR	T. Wood	27. 9.1901
6DR	G. Johnson	21.10.1918
7H	E. Welch	25. 2.1920
8H	Samuel Williams	(9. 2.1855)
8H	William Mountford	11. 9.1901
8H	R. P. Pitchforth	11. 3.1920
9L	Robert Young	(11.12.1879)
9L	Walter Grant	27. 9.1901
10RH	T. Davis	23. 4.1942
11H	George Chadburn	31.10.1902
11H	T. G. Upton	17. 4.1918
12L	A. Morgan	3. 9.1919
14LD	Thomas Howell Clark	(14. 1.1859)
	Attached RWF	
14H	Alexander Fletcher Pridgeon	27. 9.1901
15H	W. Harris	27. 9.1901
17L	Frank Taylor	27. 9.1901
18H	H. Simmonds	31.10.1902
18H	L. Darch	21.10.1918
21L	E. N. Ryder	15. 3.1916
H	J. Jackson	18. 2.1918
H	W. G. White	1. 5.1918
H	W. J. C. Huxley	3. 9.1918

Yeomanry

H. D. Reid	13. 2.1917
H. Heath	18. 2.1918
H. H. Haines	28. 3.1918
E. E. Bond	3. 9.1919

Artillery

RHA	William Paton	(5. 3.1881)
RHA	C. McStocker	31.10.1902
RHA	L. Cook MM	11. 3.1920
RHA	A. L. Clarke MBE	9. 9.1942
RFA	Robert Elliot	(28. 3.1861)
	Peter Hamilton	19. 2.1864
	Michael Beverley	27. 9.1901
	E. J. Ellard	27. 9.1901
	J. G. Gordon	27. 9.1901
	William Marsden	27. 9.1901
	Fred Shepherd	27. 9.1901
	Thomas Stoyle	27. 9.1901
	J. T. Hood	21. 6.1916
	A. G. Moss	13. 2.1917
	A. Thompson	13. 2.1917
	W. Coombs	26. 4.1917
	J. H. Young	9. 7.1917
	J. Johnson	29. 8.1917
	A. L. Polk	18. 2.1918
	S. W. S. Randall	28. 3.1918
	G. Chappell	17. 4.1918
	F. A. J. Knight	17. 4.1918
	W. J. Pye	17. 4.1918
	A. C. Thorpe	17. 4.1918
	J. Banner	21.10.1918
	A. S. Fisher	21.10.1918
	H. O. Withers	30.10.1918
	W. Parker	3. 9.1919
	T. Burton	11. 3.1920
	C. Byart	11. 3.1920
	E. G. J. Hone	11. 3.1920
	L. A. Jolly	11. 3.1920
	J. E. W. Marshall	11. 3.1920
	G. McGhie	11. 3.1920
	C. Turrell	11. 3.1920
	S. E. Firth	10. 6.1920
	E. A. K. Martin	11. 7.1940
	J. Shelton	11. 7.1940
RGA	C. J. Chaundy	11. 3.1916
	W. Miller	21. 6.1916
	J. Mercer	21.12.1916
	J. Rankine	11. 5.1917
	W. E. Brown	9. 7.1917
	A. H. Annear	17. 4.1918
	W. Heath	17. 4.1918
	F. G. Webster	3. 9.1918
	H. F. Cuthbert	21.10.1918
	P. A. Taber	21.10.1918
	J. Isden	11. 3.1920
	W. May	11. 3.1920
	G. Watson	11. 3.1920

Corps of Royal Engineers

C. H. Ruiddock	11. 3.1916
W. G. Self	21. 6.1916
J. Robinson	19. 8.1916
H. Sinclair	13. 2.1917
W. Best	3. 3.1917
G. W. Brown	9. 7.1917
F. J. Sowray	26. 7.1917

M. A. Sprinks	29. 8.1917
C. J. Whitehead	28. 3.1918
J. B. Pearce	17. 4.1918
T. Curtis	3. 9.1918
A. E. W. F. Easterbrook	21.10.1918
H. C. Ellis	21.10.1918
J. J. Power	11. 3.1920
P. H. Smith	11. 3.1920
O. Davies	21.12.1944

Grenadier Guards

William Thomas	(9. 2.1855)
John Henry Hall	23. 2.1886
William John Cook	27. 9.1901
James Rolinson	27. 9.1901
Augustus Thomas	27. 9.1901
William Edward Acraman	31.10.1902
H. Wood	13. 2.1917
E. Jones	3. 3.1917
Serving with Ox & Bucks LI	
A. M. Hill MC	21.10.1918

Coldstream Guards

F. Dickinson	25.11.1885
Alfred Best	27. 9.1901
Stephen Wright	31.10.1902
C. E. White	21. 6.1916
Serving with RWF	
G. F. Dent	13. 2.1917
E. Irving	17. 4.1918
G. H. Cozens	30.10.1918

Scots Guards

Edward Edwards	1854-5
George Sharp	(14. 5.1862)
Peter Smith	13. 3.1885
Charles Livesay	23. 2.1886
Thomas Ross MC	27. 9.1901
J. W. Sibary	27. 9.1901
D. McKenzie	11. 3.1920

Irish Guards

T. Cahill	3. 9.1919

Welsh Guards

W. Stevenson MM	11. 3.1920

Royal Scots

William Johnson		27. 9.1901
Alexander Smith		31.10.1902
A. A. West		9. 7.1917
P. Darroch		17. 4.1918
G. Edwards		21.10.1918
A. Gourlay	Bar	2.12.1919
Earlier awarded DCM		
W. A. Harrison		11. 3.1920

The Queen's (R. West Surrey Regt)

R. Dormand	27. 9.1901
John Woulds	27. 9.1901
C. J. M. Elliot	16. 1.1915
W. Routley	22. 9.1916
W. G. Lockwood	24. 8.1944

The Buffs (E. Kent Regt)

Thomas Cheal	27. 9.1901
D. W. Dines	11. 3.1916
A. W. Andrews	21.10.1918

The King's Own (Royal Lancaster Regt)
Herbert Charles Bacon		27. 9.1901
R. Disley		27. 9.1901
E. Heaysman		21. 6.1916
S. Gibson		29. 8.1917
W. E. Smith		21.10.1918
T. D. Mashiter		11. 3.1920

The Northumberland Fusiliers
W. Myers		21. 6.1916
J. Weldon		9. 7.1917
G. Pullan		17. 4.1918
C. Finch MC MM		3. 9.1918
A. Richardson MM		3.10.1918
F. Burton		21.10.1918
A. M. Marr		21.10.1918
G. Eastham	Bar	30.10.1918
Earlier awarded DCM		
W. Henderson		30.10.1918
A. S. Harie	Bar	31. 1.1920
Awarded DCM 21.10.1918		

R. Warwickshire Regt
Thomas Henry Harwood		27. 9.1901
G. Beck		11. 3.1916
J. J. Dawkins	Bar	11. 3.1916
Awarded DCM 30.6.1915		
W. Callow		21. 6.1916
G. F. Downes		9. 7.1917
J. H. Foley		17. 4.1918
J. W. Windmill		17. 4.1918
G. H. Henderson		21.10.1918
C. S. Clarke		30.10.1918
F. M. C. Townley		30.10.1918

R. Fusiliers (City of London)
William Bacon		(9. 2.1855)
F. J. Kirkwell		31.10.1902
Harry Francis Metcalfe		31.10.1902
G. Oliver		31.10.1902
F. Sharpington		1. 4.1915
H. Rowbotham		13. 2.1917
H. E. Saunders		13. 2.1917
H. Savill		13. 2.1917
H. F. D. Dockrill		26. 7.1917
J. O'Brien		17. 4.1918
H. Weedon		17. 4.1918
A. Haines	Bar	1. 5.1918
Awarded DCM 11.12.1916		
W. A. Rumble		1. 5.1918
T. Brunton		3. 9.1918
F. Huband	Bar	3. 9.1918
Awarded DCM 22.1.1916		
G. W. Taylor	Bar	3. 9.1918
Awarded DCM as CSM 25.11.1916		
G. F. Healy		21.10.1918
S. H. Franey		3. 9.1919
G. Hollings MM		13. 1.1944

The King's Liverpool Regt
William Walker		(29.10.1859)
James Henry Robinson		(6. 3.1860)
J. Mackie		21. 6.1916
F. Connell		25.11.1916
W. T. Cain ·		6. 2.1918
W. Neale		6. 2.1918
Attached to E. Lancs Regt		

J. McDonnough		1. 5.1918
J. G. Geller		15.11.1918
T. Adams	Bar	5.12.1918
Awarded DCM 3.9.1918		
G. C. Stevens		30. 1.1920

R. Norfolk Regt
Arthur Turnell		27. 9.1901
A. F. Raven MM	Bar	3.10.1918
Awarded DCM as CSM 13.2.1917		

R. Lincolnshire Regt
Walter Church		(8. 3.1899)
R. Parish		11. 3.1916
H. A. Jackson		21. 6.1916
E. Whiting		22. 9.1916
F. Moore		6. 2.1918
W. Coldwell		17. 4.1918
T. A. Stuart		17. 4.1918
J. Wallis		17. 4.1918
G. L. Jarman		3. 9.1918
C. J. King		3. 9.1918
W. Shaw		1. 3.1945

The Devonshire Regt
Henry Connett		27. 9.1901
W. G. Hudson	Bar	20.10.1916
Awarded DCM as Sgt 27.9.1901		
F. H. Radford	Bar	3. 9.1918
Awarded DCM 26.1.1918		
W. Manley		11. 3.1920

The Suffolk Regt
C. W. Macey		9. 7.1917
J. J. French		26. 1.1918
J. Crissall		3. 9.1918

The Somerset LI
Patrick Callaghan		(7. 7.1856)
Thomas Tobias		27. 9.1901
E. Paul		22. 9.1916

The POWs West Yorkshire Regt
John Henry		27. 9.1901
G. J. Smith		27. 9.1901
H. Fenton		13. 2.1917
F. Raynor		13. 2.1917
A. Brough		16. 8.1917
A. Allerton		28. 3.1918
J. R. Tose		17. 4.1918
H. Barker		22. 9.1918
F. Stembridge	Bar	25. 2.1920
Awarded DCM 3.9.1919		
A. Sugden		25. 2.1920
A. Foster		11. 3.1920
J. D. Hayley MC		11. 3.1920
J. Maloney		22. 6.1944

The East Yorkshire Regt
John Winchester Springhall		27. 9.1901
A. Utton		17. 4.1918
P. Grieve	Bar	3.10.1918
Awarded DCM 9.7.1917		
J. W. Denton		11. 3.1920

The Bedfordshire & Hertfordshire Regt
William Bond		27. 9.1901

Hugh Cressingham DSO		27. 9.1901
A. Milton		21. 6.1916
F. Antcliffe		25.11.1916
S. Armstrong		13. 2.1917
E. E. Amos		26. 1.1918
G. Hott MM		15.11.1918

R. Leicestershire Regt

R. E. Small		11. 3.1916
H. Cox		11. 5.1917
G. H. Lovett		3. 9.1919
J. T. Meredith		13.12.1945

R. Irish Regt

J. Bergin		27. 9.1901
J. F. Plunkett		17.12.1914
H. Wells		30. 1.1920
J. J. Craigie		11. 3.1920

The Green Howards

John Magner		(7. 2.1855)
Patrick Campion		(20.12.1855)
John Walker		31.10.1902
J. T. Colver		17. 4.1918
J. Brammall	Bar	3. 9.1918
Awarded the DCM earlier		
A. Robson MC		3. 9.1919

The Lancashire Fusiliers

William Robertson		(9. 2.1855)
Andrew McGarry		27. 9.1901
William Moss		27. 9.1901
Percy Pilkington		31.10.1902
H. Brown		9. 7.1917
J. LeHuray		6. 2.1918
C. Murphy		6. 2.1918
R. A. Hoyle		17. 4.1918
E. McGarry		17. 4.1918
W. Garner		3. 9.1918
W. Lund		3. 9.1918
W. Watkins		3. 9.1918
G. Cocks		21.10.1918
W. A. Girling		10. 1.1920
R. Alexander		15. 6.1943
J. Arrowsmith		13.12.1945
D. O'Donnell MM		13.12.1945

R. Scots Fusiliers

John Steele		19. 4.1901
E. C. Titmas		1. 4.1915
E. Bennett		15. 4.1916
J. Brass		21. 6.1916
J. Young		26. 1.1918
J. McLean		17. 4.1918
G. J. Davis		3. 9.1918
R. Gilmour		24. 1.1946

The Cheshire Regt

Michael Foley		27. 9.1901
John Gaunt Willis		27. 9.1901
J. H. Holland		31.10.1901
S. Harvey		9. 7.1917
T. Lloyd		1. 5.1918
A. Greenhalgh	Bar	3.10.1918
Awarded DCM 3.9.1918		
J. Trobridge	Bar	3.10.1918
Awarded DCM 3.9.1918		

H. Brand	21.10.1918
A. P. Gough	21.10.1918
J. E. Bright	3. 9.1919
F. Howard	30. 1.1920

R. Welch Fusiliers

William Honey Smith	(15. 1.1855)
William Handley (or Hanley)	(7.10.1858)
R. Evans	5. 8.1915
E. J. Glazebrook	21. 6.1916
T. Hannon	21. 6.1916
R. H. White	26. 1.1918
S. Watkins	28. 3.1918
J. R. Jones MC	17. 4.1918
A. E. Waller	3. 9.1918
R. Cawley	21.10.1918
E. Branch	3. 9.1919
J. Crinyion	11. 3.1920

South Wales B

Edward George Busby	27. 9.1901
H. Westlake	11. 3.1916
W. Murray	29. 8.1917
P. Hall	18. 2.1918
W. Davies	17. 4.1918
G. Lockie	17. 4.1918

King's Own Scottish B

William Smith	27. 9.1901
C. Johnson	11. 3.1916
G. Murray	11. 3.1916
T. Geggie	21. 6.1916
T. C. Graham	3. 9.1919
G. McLean	3. 9.1919

The Cameronians

T. Slattery	26. 4.1901
Patrick William Carroll	31.10.1902
James Graham	31.10.1902
James Hardie	31.10.1902
D. A. Rigby	30. 6.1915
P. Docherty MM	11. 3.1920
P. Drummond	27. 8.1940

R. Inniskilling Fusiliers

William Martin	19. 4.1901

The Gloucestershire Regt

Thomas Lumsden	(14.12.1855)
Henry Baker	(29.11.1858)
J. Averies	31.10.1902
H. H. Say	31.10.1902
James Trevelyan	31.10.1902
J. H. Wagner	21. 6.1916
W. Portlock	13. 2.1917
F. Sabatella	29. 8.1917
F. H. Taylor	21.10.1918

The Worcestershire Regt

Charles Henson	31.10.1902
W. H. Tolley	21. 6.1916
C. Felix	3. 7.1915
D. G. L. Morgan	6. 2.1918
J. Chance	17. 4.1918
S. Mills	17. 4.1918
G. Samson	17. 4.1918
H. J. Farley	21.10.1918

East Lancs Regt

Richard Nagle		(31.12.1855)
William Hunn		(21. 8.1875)
J. T. Mathewson		27. 9.1901
J. P. Lydon		31.10.1902
H. Carrington		20.10.1916
J. A. Christie		26. 7.1917
W. Price MC		26. 1.1918
E. Bancroft		12. 2.1918
W. Welford		1. 5.1918
J. Haslam		3. 9.1919

East Surrey Regt

J. Anderton		27. 9.1901
Henry Clay		31.10.1902
G. E. Hyson		17.12.1914
E. Seymour		9. 7.1917
G. F. Hyde		3. 9.1918
E. E. W. Baker		21.10.1918
A. Lee	Bar	21.10.1918
Awarded the DCM 3.9.1918		
H. Morgan		21.10.1918
A. H. Adams		11. 2.1943

Duke of Cornwall's LI

John Kelly		(19. 4.1866)
George Carr		(25. 8.1885)
C. Powers		31.10.1902
J. Bonham		10. 1.1917
A. J. S. Piddington		21.10.1918
C. W. Willis		3. 9.1919
A. Hill		11. 7.1940

Duke of Wellington's Regt

George Tomlinson		(5.11.1854)
Lawrence Bellew		27. 9.1901
George Kerns		27. 9.1901
A. Butterworth		31.10.1902
R. Baxter		21. 6.1916
G. P. Bennett		21. 6.1916
C. Shepherd		22. 9.1916
J. Lynn MM		3.10.1918
T. Richardson		3.10.1918

Border Regt

V. H. S. Davenport	Bar	5. 8.1915
Awarded DCM as CSM 1.4.1915		
J. Duke		9. 7.1917
J. Malia	Bar	21.10.1918
Awarded DCM 3.9.1918		
C. Clarke	Bar	3. 9.1919
Awarded DCM as A-Sgt 3.10.1918		
A. Windeler		11. 3.1920

R. Sussex Regt

S. Thwaites		27. 9.1901
Charles Amos		31.10.1902
L. Bonney		21. 6.1916
H. Page		21. 6.1916
W. F. Rainsford		21. 6.1916
E. Haines		11.12.1916
H. M. Bird		3. 9.1918
H. A. Coles		21.10.1918
J. McClymont		11. 3.1920
G. Manvell		14. 4.1920

R. Hampshire Regt

T. Holdway	3. 7.1915
B. Clark	3. 9.1919
A. R. Hubbert	3. 9.1919
J. E. Palmer MC	11. 3.1920

South Staffordshire Regt

William Brown	27. 9.1901
Frederick Henry White	27. 9.1901
Albert Cooper	31.10.1902
R. Baker	17.12.1914
A. Burgoyne	13. 2.1917
W. S. Neale	18. 7.1917
Attached to London Regt	
G. Purchas	17. 4.1918
F. Howse	11. 3.1920

The Dorset Regt

Joseph Jobberns	(30.12.1856)
Alexander Brown	27. 9.1901
G. Delara	1. 4.1915
C. Wells	21. 6.1916
J. W. Boddie	3. 9.1919

South Lancs Regt

John Adam Altman		27. 9.1901
G. Devlin		27. 9.1901
A. Barnes		16. 8.1917
J. M. C. Harrison		3. 9.1918
T. Widd MM	Bar	3.10.1918
Awarded DCM as CSM 21.12.1916		
A. S. Ryan		11. 3.1920

The Welch Regt

John Harris	(9. 2.1855)
John Alfred Bryant	27. 9.1901
W. L. Heycock	13. 2.1917
C. Lewis	9. 7.1917
J. Jones	16. 8.1917
J. C. Davidge	17. 4.1918
J. W. Milson	11. 3.1920

The Black Watch R. Highlanders

John Granger	(20. 7.1855)
John Barclay	(26. 5.1874)
James Anderson	31.10.1902
A. Ferrier	17. 4.1918
D. C. Christie	21.10.1918
D. Sinclair	11. 3.1920
T. Vercoe	11. 3.1920

Oxfordshire & Buckinghamshire LI

H. Dempsey	(9. 7.1898)
G. Dancey	20.10.1916
T. A. Love	12.12.1917
G. T. Arlett	21.10.1918
W. Hedley	11. 3.1920
G. Futter MM	4. 5.1944
C. T. Briggs	15. 6.1944

The Essex Regt

William Hart	(5. 3.1855)
E. Lawrence	13. 2.1917
F. Bailey	4. 3.1918
H. Larkman	17. 4.1918
J. F. Knights	1. 5.1918
W. Cockrain	21.10.1918

F. James		3. 9.1919
F. Walker		3. 9.1919
W. Young		11. 3.1920
A. F. Sutton		11. 7.1940
C. J. Rose	Bar	24. 8.1944

Awarded DCM 25.11.1943

Sherwood Foresters Notts & Derbyshire Regt

H. G. Crummey	27. 9.1901
Henry Taylor	27. 9.1901
S. Poston	11. 3.1916
T. Cumming	3. 3.1917
J. Lacey	3. 3.1917
A. Lawrence	17. 4.1918
B. Maddock	17. 4.1918
W. Mounteney	11. 3.1920

Loyal Regt North Lancs

Ernest Cecil Mudge	11. 9.1901
Richard Rowley	31.10.1902
A. Watts	11. 3.1916
J. Farnworth	21. 6.1916
J. Anderson	13. 2.1917
A. Wileman	17. 4.1918
T. Butterworth	21.10.1918
W. G. Newton	21.10.1918
C. H. Edisbury	3. 9.1919
J. T. Dew	11. 3.1920

The Northamptonshire Regt

Charles Murray	13. 5.1882
G. Lee MC	11. 5.1917
J. Pennyfather	9. 7.1917

R. Berkshire Regt

William Thomas Mathieson	(22.10.1887)
Arthur William Rouse	27. 9.1901
W. King	16.11.1915
G. Lainsbury	16.11.1915
H. J. Bartholomew	20.10.1916
E. Addicott	3. 9.1919
A. H. Laidler	3. 9.1919

Queen's Own R. West Kent Regt

John Cusack		(14. 1.1855)
R. Rankin	Bar	3. 9.1918

Awarded DCM as CSM 13.2.1917

W. T. Skeer	3. 9.1919
P. Byrne	20. 7.1944

King's Own Yorkshire LI

H. G. Trott		11. 3.1916
G. E. E. Hewes		21. 6.1916
W. Moorhouse		13. 2.1917
J. Helliwell		17. 4.1918
H. Smart		17. 4.1918
O. Maltby	Bar	30.10.1918

Awarded DCM as CSM 13.2.1917

W. H. Ledger	16. 1.1919
H. D. Duncan MM	10. 1.1920

King's Shropshire LI

Robert Lindsay	(7. 1.1861)
J. Farthing	26. 4.1917

Attached Manchester Regt

G. Millington	3. 9.1919

Attached Hereford Regt

G. H. Wilson	3. 9.1919
G. Wilde	15. 6.1944

The Middlesex Regt

John Bergin	(5. 7.1855)
Henry Borret	(14. 1.1856)
W. Woollett	27. 9.1901
Frederick Sherman Steed	31.10.1902
G. A. McDonald	22. 9.1916
J. Webb	25.11.1916
W. G. Rice	28. 3.1918
A. Ambrose	3. 9.1918
C. Clark	3. 9.1918
W. J. Longley	21.10.1918
W. A. Manning	11. 3.1920

Attached London Regt

King's R. Rifle Corps

Robert Duncan		(30. 6.1858)
James Wilkins		(12. 6.1882)
D. Connoll		27. 9.1901
G. H. Gordon		27. 9.1901
A. H. Hill		25. 7.1901
A. H. Davis		11. 3.1916

Attached London Regt

J. Adams		9. 7.1917
G. H. Floater		9. 7.1917
H. Oxley	Bar	4. 3.1918

Awarded DCM as CSM 21.6.1916

W. Archer	21.10.1918
J. Horton MM	11. 3.1920
S. G. Cooper	14.10.1943

The Wiltshire Regt

Joseph Young	(31. 1.1889)
Sidney Grant	31.10.1902
S. J. Parker	3. 6.1915
A. J. Hill	21. 6.1916

The Manchester Regt

John Thomas Haddon	27. 9.1901
George Thomas Prosser	27. 9.1901
J. Parker	1. 4.1915
C. MacDonald	21. 6.1916
J. Morrison	21. 6.1916
J. Knott	18. 6.1917
W. J. Potter	17. 4.1918
J. A. Stewart	21.10.1918
R. F. Wilson	21.10.1918
F. W. Wise	21.10.1918
W. A. Kent	3. 9.1919

North Staffordshire Regt

Robert Katon	27. 9.1901
J. Brough	11. 3.1916
C. Hazlehurst	21. 6.1916
G. Parker	21. 6.1916
O. Lead	17. 4.1918
H. Dorrington	1. 5.1918
A. Shelley	3. 9.1918
G. Clement	3. 9.1919
B. J. Croney	11. 3.1920

The York & Lancaster Regt

Henry Jenkins	(24. 8.1860)
S. C. Nowlan	13. 2.1917
H. Walker	4. 3.1918

| T. H. Head | | 3. 9.1919 |
| W. T. Ottaway | | 2.12.1919 |

Durham LI

John Tudor		(23. 8.1866)
Joseph Freel		27. 9.1901
E. Crouch		11. 3.1916
A. Noble	Bar	11. 3.1916

Awarded DCM as C-Sgt 27.9.1901

W. Thew		11. 3.1916
J. Watson		11. 3.1916
J. J. Atkinson		13. 2.1917
R. G. Coghlan		13. 2.1917
W. Howes		17. 4.1918
T. J. Craggs		3. 9.1918
E. Wise		3.10.1918
E. Oldridge	Bar	21.10.1918

Awarded DCM 3.9.1918

W. E. Holmes		30.10.1918
S. Hunter		15.11.1918
J. Cresswell		3. 9.1919
W. Johnstone		3. 9.1919
W. C. Mason		3. 9.1919
F. W. Ogden		11. 3.1920
A. Jennings		24. 9.1942

Highland LI

John Pyle		(26. 2.1859)
John Blackwood		(8.10.1864)
A. Stevens		27. 9.1901
A. G. House		3. 6.1915
P. McNally		11. 3.1916
J. Patterson		11. 3.1916
D. Christie		19. 8.1916
J. Mathieson		19. 8.1916
J. McMenemy		14.11.1916
W. C. Shepherd		13. 2.1917
R. Rowan		17. 4.1918
J. Donnelly		21.10.1918
G. J. Taylor MC		11. 3.1920
W. H. G. Francombe		11. 7.1940
J. H. Chambers		24. 1.1946

Seaforth Highlanders

James Hart		(28.10.1858)
A. Farquhar		31.10.1902
Sinclair Gair		31.10.1902
Norman Reid		14. 8.1908
A. Sutherland		30. 6.1915
D. Sutherland		11. 3.1916
J. Forbes		14.11.1916
J. W. Pierce		6. 2.1918

Gordon Highlanders

F. McKay		27. 9.1901
John McLennan		27. 9.1901
J. Jefferson		3. 6.1915
R. Fleming		5. 8.1915
W. Henderson		11. 3.1916
J. Mathew		10. 1.1917
R. Inglis MM		11. 3.1920
W. Watt		11. 3.1920
L. L. Tevendale		21.10.1941

Queen's Own Cameron Highlanders

| Thomas Bunyan | | (1855) |
| John Emslie | | (18.11.1886) |

Joseph Campbell		(11.12.1886)
Donald McLeod		2. 9.1898
A. McKinnon	Bar	11. 3.1916

Awarded DCM as Sgt 27.9.1901

P. N. Scotland		11. 3.1916
A. K. Scott		21. 6.1916
J. W. Christie		18. 2.1918
J. Shiels MC MM		3. 9.1918
W. Vass		11. 3.1920

R. Irish Rifles

Alleyne Wolfe		(14. 1.1859)
Robert Gardiner		31.10.1902
P. Mulholland		26. 7.1917
D. Millar	Bar	16. 1.1919

Awarded DCM 21.10.1918

R. Irish Fusiliers

| H. Hamilton | | 14. 4.1920 |

Connaught Rangers

Patrick Cooney		(21. 1.1855)
R. Hart		27. 9.1901
J. Hudson	Bar	11. 3.1916

Awarded DCM as C-Sgt Irish Guards 31.10.1902

Argyll & Sutherland Highlanders

R. Bertram		21. 6.1916
D. Gilchrist		21.10.1918
J. H. Markey		11. 3.1920
C. Phimister		11. 3.1920
W. S. I. Lockie		11.10.1945

POWs Leinster Regt

W. J. Casey		27. 9.1901
Richard Joseph Haddick		27. 9.1901
H. Knight (8763)		3. 9.1918

R. Munster Fusiliers

G. Harrison		27. 9.1901
F. Bennett		31.10.1902
J. Ring MC	Bar	3. 9.1918

Awarded DCM 1.4.1915

| P. Cullinan | | 30. 1.1920 |

R. Dublin Fusiliers

Frederick Adrian Whalen		27. 9.1901
John Burke		31.10.1902
A. Guest		11. 3.1916
E. Murphy		26. 1.1918
K. Knight (10515)		3. 9.1919

The Rifle Brigade

Richard Cornelious		(7. 2.1855)
Roger Connor		(7.10.1858)
Edward Bull		(2. 9.1898)
W. E. N. Morrish		19. 4.1901
Walter Turner		31.10.1902
W. Miller		11. 3.1916
H. Wilkins		11. 3.1916
P. Witheridge		21. 6.1916
A. W. Barker		26. 7.1917
J. Furey		26. 1.1918
H. Harwood	Bar	26. 1.1918

Awarded DCM as CSM 11.3.1916

| W. J. Marsh | | 21.10.1918 |
| E. C. Goodey | | 20. 9.1945 |

Army Cyclist Corps

A. W. Clarke	17. 4.1918
H. Anderson	21.10.1918

Machine Gun Corps

C. Carr	21.10.1918
T. J. Gudge	3. 9.1919
J. McAra	11. 3.1920

Tank Corps

G. F. Bennett	17. 4.1918
D. Robertson	3. 9.1919

Labour Corps

J. H. Broom	21.10.1918

Army Service Corps & R. Army Service Corps

Ernest Urbane Hallett	31.10.1902
G. B. Vanderwerff	6. 6.1946

R. Army Medical Corps

F. B. Bowyer	27. 9.1901
D. Roberts	27. 9.1901
A. R. Titchener	27. 9.1901
Robert Watson	27. 9.1901
Edward William Newland	31.10.1902
James John Saunders	31.10.1902
F. W. Sharpe	11. 3.1916
R. C. Blair	21. 6.1916
H. Underwood	21. 6.1916
C. Kingston	26. 9.1916
C. W. Tapson	13. 2.1917
E. G. Gray	3. 3.1917
B. L. Aldhous	26. 1.1918
L. Gosley	6. 2.1918
J. E. Pritchard	18. 2.1918
T. R. Wilson	28. 3.1918
W. Lamkin	17. 4.1918
R. G. Leggett	17. 4.1918
T. McNicol	17. 4.1918
P. Bullough	22. 8.1918
F. B. Challis	3. 9.1918
J. Clough	3. 9.1918
E. Ratcliffe	3. 9.1918
W. B. Stedman	3. 9.1918
H. E. Bevans	21.10.1918
G. F. Lyon	21.10.1918
J. McKay	21.10.1918
J. Moore	21.10.1918
T. Moore	30.10.1918
G. T. Davies	3. 9.1919
G. W. Langford	3. 9.1919
D. G. Martin	3. 9.1919
C. E. Bull	11. 3.1920
W. Jarman	11. 3.1920
F. A. Philbrook	11. 3.1920
W. A. Winter	17. 1.1946

R. Army Ornance Corps

P. A. Hadland	21. 6.1916
D. Murray	21. 6.1916
G. Parkin	27. 7.1916
P. F. Hale	3. 9.1918
F. E. Peake	3.10.1918

R. Army Veterinary Corps

W. H. A. Field	11. 3.1916
S. Salt	11. 3.1916
J. E. Trevor	11. 3.1916
S. Harman	21. 6.1916

R. Corps Military Police

John Lyndas Burke	(23. 5.1884)
Also known as Emerson	
A. W. Bray	13. 2.1917
F. Lundy	13. 2.1917
A. M. Scott	9. 7.1917
H. Gaff	11. 3.1920

The Monmouthshire Regt

G. A. Gravenor	11. 3.1916

The Cambridgeshire Regt

B. H. Matthews	17. 4.1918

The London Regt

W. J. King	11. 3.1916
W. A. Muir	11. 3.1916
F. F. Bailey	21. 6.1916
J. E. Hawkes	21. 6.1916
C. H. Parrott	9. 7.1917
F. Neale	26. 1.1918
C. Bottomley	6. 2.1918
C. D. Schermuly	1. 5.1918
J. O. C. Laing MC	3. 9.1918
P. H. Avey	21.10.1918
S. C. Budd	30.10.1918
J. R. Danson	15.11.1918
H. Bush	16. 1.1918
H. Chesney	3. 9.1919
A. Oakham	3. 9.1919
E. C. Pittam	3. 9.1919
E. Fox	11. 3.1920
T. O'Connell	11. 3.1920

The Hertfordshire Regt

S. G. Tite	26. 1.1918

R. Corps of Signals

P. W. Phillip	11. 7.1940

The Parachute Regt

R. D. Gay	20. 9.1944

R. Marine LI

A. J. Banks	26. 1.1917
H. Evans	13. 2.1917

Acknowledgements

A project of this nature cannot be undertaken without a great deal of valuable help from those who have been actively involved with the rank of WO1 Regimental Sergeant Major. Lt-Col John Holbrook has been closely associated with the venture throughout and the work on the RSMs of the Guards Depot could not have been started without his personally researched roll of names. Other chapters also reflect his work, such as the service details and photographs of Stephen Wright.

Whilst part two of the book is not intended to portray the 'Guards Regimental Sergeant Major' it may appear to be the case, as the military posts at the establishments dealt with have so often traditionally been filled by RSMs of the guards regiments. In this respect the *Guards Magazine* has represented a major source of research and my sincere thanks go to the editor, Lt-Col Sir Julian Paget Bt CVO, and to Maj H. W. Schofield MBE, who have met my many and varied requests with patience and kindness.

The *Grenadier Gazette* has also proved to be a valuable source of information and thanks are due to Lt-Col H. S. Hanning and to Maj (Retd) E. C. Weaver MBE, regimental archivist, who has researched much of the detail on the early RSMs of the RMC Sandhurst.

Help and advice has always been willingly extended by Lt-Col R. K. May, curator of the Regimental Museum, King's Own Royal Border Regt, Carlisle, Maj (Retd) L. C. Drouet, Grenadier Guards, Mr Allen Percival, Deputy Director of Public Relations (Army) MOD London, and Terry Wise of Athena Books in Doncaster.

The strength of the book lies of course, within the many personally produced recollections of service and ceremonial by the RSMs, former RSMs and soldiers themselves, and I can only state, in thanking them, that it has been an honour and a marvellous experience to meet and talk with them in order to record their reminiscences.

The Royal Coat of Arms Badge of rank of the Regimental Sergeant Major is portrayed on the front cover by courtesy of the Director of Public Relations (Army) MOD London.

My further specific thanks are extended to the following:

To Gen Sir Geoffrey Howlett KBE MC, former Commander-in-Chief, Allied Forces Northern Europe, and Colonel Commandant of the Parachute Regiment, for his kind association with the venture and splendid foreword.

To Mr Hugh Davies, grandson of Lt F. J. Davies, Grenadier Guards, who wrote the booklet *The Sergeant Major – the origin and history of his rank with notes on Military customs and habits* for so kindly allowing extracts to be included in this work. Lt Francis J. Davies went on to command the 1st Guards Brig before the First World War and was director of staff duties at the War Office in 1914. He then commanded the 8th Div in France and the VIII Corps in Gallipoli. His post, on retirement, was Commander-in-Chief, Scottish Command.

Gen Davies' father had served as a General and also his father before him and therefore the command of armies had featured within this prominent military family for generations, indeed, they can trace their military origins back to the 1690s. Gen Sir Francis J. Davies KCB KCMG KCVO DL died in 1948. It is very

fitting that his early studies as a Lieutenant in relation to the Sergeant Major should form the historic foundation of this work on the subject.

Lt-Col (Retd) A. A. Fairrie, curator, and his staff at the Regimental Museum of the Queen's Own Highlanders (Seaforth and Camerons) at Fort George. Firstly for Col Fairrie's kind reading of the Masterton MacIntosh draft and helpful suggestions, and then for his help with the historical records of the 79th Regt Cameron Highlanders and permission to reproduce parts.

John M. MacIntosh of Forres, who kindly allowed me the help of his studies into the life of Masterton MacIntosh.

The main sources of reference for the Waterloo campaign were *A History of the British Army* by The Hon J. W. Forescue, the historical records of the 79th Regt Cameron Highlanders and Sgt-Maj Edward Cotton's *A voice from Waterloo* who, although providing a graphic account of the battle, stated very little about his own part in the 7th Hussars.

The Viscount Gough for his kind permission to reproduce extracts from *The life and campaigns of Hugh 1st Viscount Gough* by Robert S. Rait (who died in 1936), and the photograph of the painting of Sir Hugh Gough.

Service details of the Sergeant Majors concerned were traced and gained with the help of Lt-Col R. K. May, The Public Record Office, and the following Regimental Museums:

Maj (Retd) M. K. Beedle MBE, The Staffordshire Regt (Prince of Wales's)

Lt-Col P. Burdick OBE, The Devonshire & Dorset Regt

Maj (Retd) J. H. Peters MBE, The Duke of Edinburgh's Royal Regt, (Berkshire and Wiltshire)

J. G. Woodruff Esq, Curator, The Queen's Royal Surrey Regt

Lt-Col (Retd) K. G. Allen, The Worcester & Sherwood Foresters Regt

Col H. B. H. Waring OBE, Chairman, Queen's Own Royal West Kent Regt

Lt-Col A. W. J. Turnbull MC, The Royal Norfolk Regt Association

S. Manion Esq, Asst Keeper of Social Hist, Nat Museums & Galleries on Merseyside

Maj (Retd) J. S. Knight, Regtl Sec, The Queen's Own Hussars

Extracts from *A soldiers experience, or Voice from the ranks* by Sgt-Maj T. Gowing and photograph, reproduced with the knowledge of Kerry Draycott, Thos Forman & Sons.

The service details of Sgt-Maj Stephen Wright were obtained by John Holbrook with the help of the Staff of Regtl HQ Coldstream Guards. Reference to the 'Marshals of the Court' is by kind permission of the *Guards Magazine* from an article by Maj A. Douglas and E. C. Weaver MBE.

Ralph N. Hudson, author of *The Bradford Pals* for kind permission to use his book for background information on the 18th Bn PWO West Yorks Regt. Also to Brig J. M. Cubiss CBE MC, Regt Secretary of the PWO Regiment of Yorkshire, for permission to reproduce extracts from the war diaries of the 18th Bn and also for the photograph of the orderly room staff.

Mrs Margaret Mawby, Harold Scott's daughter, for her kind help with information about her father, and photographs.

Stephen Kerry of the Bradford Art Galleries and Museums, for his help with his recordings and photographs.

Neville Taylor and to John Cobb for their help with research.

Majs (Retd) L. C. Drouet and A. P. Joyce and to the *Guards Magazine* for reference to *Lest we forget*.

Dan James, Lt-Col L. M. Wilson MBE and Maj P. G. E. Hill, The Queen's Royal Surrey Regtl Association and Museum, for help with details and a photograph of Capt Charles Estall, and former RSM J. Ives.

Mrs Lilian Grimshaw for her kind consent to include extracts from former RSM Fred Grimshaw's recordings.

Peter Archer for allowing me to reproduce his paintings of *Ferozeshah* in chapter 4 and *The attack of 42 Commando on Mount Harriet*. Also to Maj J. H. Peters and Lt-Col D. A. S. Pennefather RMs.

To the Academy Sergeant Major RMAS for permission to reproduce the photographs of former RSMs of the RM College and Academy, from the Sergeants Mess.

GSM A. G. Mason and the *Guards Magazine* for kind permission to reproduce the photograph on 'rifles in use' and the article on the SA 80 rifle.

Dr T. A. Heathcote TD BA PhD, curator of the Sandhurst Collection, for permission to include the photographs of Eaton Hall and Mons OCS RSMs.

Lt-Col O. R. St J. Breakwell MBE, Commandant, Guards Depot, for his kind permission for the Standing Orders of the Depot RSM to be reproduced.

To the RSM of the Guards Depot for reproduction of the roll of former Depot RSMs.

Brig R. J. Lewendon (Retd) Historical Secretary, Royal Artillery Institute, for his kind assistance.

To *This England* for kind permission to reproduce extracts from *The Register of the Victoria Cross*.

P. E. Abbott, author of *Recipients of the Distinguished Conduct Medal 1855-1909* and to J. B. Hayward & Son.

P. W. Walker, author of *Recipients of the Distinguished Conduct Medal 1914-1920* and to Midland Medals.

Phil McDermott, for his kind permission to extract information relating to RSMs awarded the DCM.

AcSM Michael Nesbitt, RMAS, for his concluding message.

In thanking the publisher Ian Morley-Clarke for his help, I should mention that he also was greatly influenced by RSM J. C. Lord during service in The Parachute Regt.

Finally, I extend my thanks to David Charters who prepared a highly detailed contour relief map of the Waterloo battle area.

To my daughters Valerie Charters and Lindsay Alford for many hours of proof reading and to my son Jeremy for his photographic help. To my wife Eileen, without whose tremendous help and support, planning of detailed research trips and reading of the final draft, the project would not have been possible.

The Colour Party. Presentation of New Colours at Balmoral May 1955. Lt J. M. Barbour, 2/Lt J. C. C. Russell, C/Sgt McKay, Sgt Kermode, Sgt Lewis, followed by RSM R. Cooper.
Col A. A. Fairrie, Curator, Museum of Queen's Own Highlanders (Seaforth and Camerons)

Index

RSM Pat Chapman, 45 Commando Royal Marines, reads the lesson at a Memorial Service held at Royal Marines Condor Arbroath, Nov 1982. PR RMs, MOD, London

GSM A. G. 'Perry' Mason. Coldstream Guards, detailing the Marker Party at Horse Guards in May 1988.

Photo by the author